1994

EXPERTISE AND TECHNOLOGY

Cognition & Human-Computer Cooperation

EXPERTISE: RESEARCH AND APPLICATIONS

A Series Edited by:
Robert R. Hoffman, Michelene T. H. Chi, K. Anders Ericsson, and Gary A. Klein

Hoc/Cacciabue/Hollnagel • *Expertise and Technology: Cognition & Human-Computer Cooperation*

EXPERTISE AND TECHNOLOGY

Cognition & Human-Computer Cooperation

Edited by

Jean-Michel HOC
CNRS - University of Valenciennes

Pietro C. CACCIABUE
CEC Joint Research Centre, Ispra, Italy

Erik HOLLNAGEL
Human Reliability Associates

LEA LAWRENCE ERLBAUM ASSOCIATES, PUBLISHERS
1995 Hillsdale, New Jersey   Hove, UK

Lawrence Erlbaum Associates, Inc., Publishers
365 Broadway
Hillsdale, New Jersey 07642

Cover design by Kate Dusza

Library of Congress Cataloging-in-Publication Data

Expertise and technology: cognition & human-computer cooperation
/ Jean-Michel Hoc, Pietro C. Cacciabue, Erik Hollnagel, editors.
    p. cm. — (Expertise, research and applications)
  Includes bibliographical references and index.
  ISBN 0–8058–1511–2 (acid-free paper)
    1. Expert systems (Computer science) 2. Human-computer
interaction. I. Hoc, Jean-Michel. II. Cacciabue, Pietro C. III.
Hollnagel, Erik, 1941– . IV. Series.
QA76.76.E95E9467   1994
006.3'01'9—dc20   94–27068
                                                            CIP

Books published by Lawrence Erlbaum Associates are printed on acid-free paper, and their bindings are chosen for strength and durability.

Printed in the United States of America
10 9 8 7 6 5 4 3 2 1

CONTENTS

SECTION 1

COGNITION AND WORK WITH TECHNOLOGY

SECTION 2
DEVELOPMENT OF COMPETENCE AND EXPERTISE

SECTION 3
COOPERATION BETWEEN HUMANS AND COMPUTERS

SERIES FOREWORD

This volume launches the series *Expertise: Research and Applications.* This beginning is auspicious, for a number of reasons. First, the series will address a variety of topics and issues, all related to the central concept of *expertise.* The chapters in this volume cover man-machine interaction, human error and reasoning biases, ergonomic system design, cognitive simulation and theories of expert cognition, the issue of "trust" in complex systems, training issues and expert-novice differences, and social interaction among teams of workers, and so on.

Second, the series will touch base on expertise in a great variety of domains, domains such as medical diagnosis, industrial process control, air traffic control, and so on. It is fairly clear now in the research community that a great variety of domains will have to be investigated in detail for there to arise a good general understanding of expert knowledge and skill.

Third, titles in the series will present valuable reviews and summaries of background research and theory, methodological approaches, and philosophical points of view. The study of expertise, especially in the field of artificial intelligence, is filled with religious issues, issues that do not merely sidetrack us onto endless debate about what is meant by the phrase "artificial intelligence," but issues that stimulate healthy and productive debate about methods and methodology for the study of expertise and for the development of complex systems.

Fourth, it is our fervent wish that the series be both interdisciplinary and international in scope, and so we are especially honored to launch the series with a volume that reflects the efforts undertaken by the researchers participating in the programs sponsored by the French National Scientific Research Centre (CNRS). In 1986, an international working group was established with the support of the CNRS, in recognition of the necessity for interdisciplinary and international collaboration in the advancement of technology for the greater benefit of society. Although initiated in France, the CNRS programs quickly included researchers from many countries in Europe, such as Italy, Denmark, and the United Kingdom, and then broadened to include researchers from Canada and the United States. The CNRS programs have enabled computer scientists, cognitive scientists, ergonomists, engineers, and social scientists to work together. The present volume was edited by the coordinators of a number of biannual meetings at which researchers gathered to share their work in progress. The volume is intended to provide an overview of the CNRS efforts, present the most recent developments, and express the overall philosophy of the CNRS programs.

Fifth, the titles in the series, by virtue of focus on expertise in the "real world," will have a distinct pragmatic or applied science flavor to them — rich with the experiences of researchers and system developers who have been working "out in the trenches" to solve real and difficult problems and to create useful and usable technology. Perhaps no other aspect of research on expertise is as rewarding as the potential to make significant contributions to society and social policy. Make no mistake, there are serious outstanding challenges in the elicitation, representation, preservation, and dissemination of expert knowledge and skill; significant challenges in going from creativity to practical technological innovation. These challenges force one to deal with issues in economics and social policy as much as with the sorts of issues that are common fare in the extant literature on the psychology of expertise. The editors of this series hope that this theme of pragmatism is prominent in all of the titles to appear.

The contributions of prominent scientists, representative of various nationalities, representative of various disciplines and methodologies, the examination of various domains of expertise, the consideration of a variety of important issues and topics, the reviews of bodies of research — all these features make this inaugural title a useful and interesting addition to the library of any one who must be concerned, directly or indirectly, with the nature of expertise.

Robert R. Hoffman
Michelene T. H. Chi
K. Anders Ericsson
Gary A. Klein

EDITORS' FOREWORD

The technological development have changed the nature of industrial production so that it today no longer is a question of a human working with a machine, but rather that a joint human-machine system performs the task. This development, which started in the 1940's, has become even more pronounced with the proliferation of computers and the invasion of digital technology in all wakes of working life. The first area where radical changes took place was administration and clerical work - including such trades as typesetting and technical drawing. We are now seeing a similarly drastic change in the industrial process domain. Process automation has long been used to improve the efficiency and safety of industrial production, but the availability of cheap but powerful computers is at this time producing fundamental changes in the very nature of work. It may look as if the result is that the importance of human work has been reduced compared to what can be achieved by intelligent software systems. But in reality the opposite is the case: the more complex a system is, the more vital is the human operator's task. The conditions, however, have changed. Whereas people used to be in control of their own tasks, today they have become supervisors of tasks which are shared between humans and machines.

Engineers and technical specialists have often had as their goal the complete automation of the systems, i.e. making the human operator redundant. This goal has rarely been achieved. There are two main reasons for that. Firstly, it is not always technically possible to automate every function in a system. Secondly, and more importantly, it is impossible to anticipate the range of situations and conditions that can occur in the life of a system, except for very trivial cases. Human operators therefore still have an important role to play in providing the adaptation that is necessary when the systems go beyond their normal operating conditions. It follows that a proper understanding of the operator's cognition is at least as important as mastering the technical side of the systems. A thorough understanding and appreciation of human cognition is essential both to develop efficiently and safety functioning systems and to train the human operators to fulfill their assignments.

To attain these goals, multi-disciplinary interactions and collaboration are essential. A considerable amount of effort has been devoted to the domain of administrative and clerical work and has led to the establishment of an internationally based human-computer interaction (HCI) community, at the level of research as well as at the level of application. The HCI community, however, has paid more attention to static environments, where the human operator is in complete control of the situation, than to dynamic environments, where changes may occur independent of human intervention and actions. A typical case is that of industrial process control. However, many other situations share the same feature, for instance air traffic control, aircraft piloting, ship maneuvering, intensive care in hospitals, crisis management, electronic trading, etc.

In 1986 an international working group was established with the financial support of the French National Scientific Research Centre (CNRS). Two multi-disciplinary work programs on Work, and Cognitive Science enabled psychologists, ergonomists, computer scientists, and control engineers to work together. As a result, a series of bi-annual meetings has been organized since 1987 (CSAPC: Cognitive Science Approaches to Process Control). In addition, a more focused working group has held a number of meetings (CADES: Cognitive Approaches to Dynamic Environment Supervision), coordinated by J.M. Hoc, with the contribution of R. Amalberti, P.C. Cacciabue, J. Patrick, B. Pavard, and R. Samurçay; the aim of this working group was to produce an overview in the form of a book, which would take stock of recent research developments for the topic. The result is the present volume. Although the CADES group initially was created on a European basis, it has progressively been expanded to include also several colleagues from the US.

The basic philosophy of this book is the conviction that human operators remain the unchallenged experts even in the worst cases where their working conditions have been impoverished by senseless automation. They maintain this advantage due to their ability to learn and build up a high level of expertise, a foundation of operational knowledge, during their work. This expertise must be taken into account in the development of efficient human-machine systems, in the specification of training requirements, and in the identification of needs for specific computer support to human actions.

The book is divided into an introductory chapter (Ch. 1) organizing the common concepts used in the book, three main sections, and a conclusion (Ch. 17).

Section 1 deals with the main features of cognition in dynamic environments, combining issues coming from empirical approaches of human cognition and cognitive simulation. Ch. 2 integrates three key activities — diagnosis, decision-making, and time management — in a common framework, since they are always interacting in dynamic environment supervision. Ch. 3 reviews the main cognitive architectures which are used in cognitive modeling by the means of computers. Ch. 4 presents the four domains of application of cognitive simulation — system design, analysis and evaluation, human operator training and on-line support. Ch. 5 explores the ability of computer simulation to model the dynamics of Human-Machine Systems considered as joint cognitive systems.

Section 2 addresses the question of the development of competence and expertise. Ch. 6 analyzes errors in a medical context to catch novice/expert differences and suggest some ways to improve the development of expertise. Ch. 7 explores diverse conceptual models of technological processes for training process operators and examines the crucial question of the decomposition of complex systems into manageable knowledge units by beginners. Ch. 8 proposes a methodology to design training situations from real work situations, improving knowledge transfer. Ch. 9 stresses the need for developing expertise for cooperation in highly coupled systems.

Section 3 proposes some ways to take up the main challenge in this domain — the design of an actual cooperation between human experts and computers of the next century. Ch. 10 suggests that cooperative systems could be designed on the basis of human-human cooperation. Ch. 11 introduces key concepts in human-machine cooperation — the operators' trust in the efficacy of the automated systems and their self confidence in their abilities as manual controllers. Ch. 12 stresses that human-machine cooperation has to handle human error which is conceived as a product of conflict between the human and the physical or social artifacts. Ch. 13 combines the human engineering approach and the ergonomic approach to tackle the problem of cooperation between humans and intelligent support systems. Ch. 14 stresses the crucial role adaptation plays in the coupling between human and machine. Ch. 15 deals with the paradigm of "human-like" systems which could improve the human-machine cooperation. Ch. 16 presents a methodology to support human operator planning activities, taking the intentionality of industrial environments into consideration.

Jean-Michel Hoc
Pietro C. Cacciabue
Erik Hollnagel

LIST OF CONTRIBUTORS

René AMALBERTI
ISSMA-CERMA, B.P. 73,
91223 BRÉTIGNY-SUR-ORGE, FRANCE
Sebastiano BAGNARA
University of Siena, Department of Psychology, via Roma 47,
53100 SIENA, ITALY
Hakim BENCHEKROUN
CNAM, Department of Ergonomics, 41, rue Gay-Lussac,
75005 PARIS, FRANCE
Nicholas BOREHAM
University of Manchester, School of Education,
Oxford Road, MANCHESTER, M13 9PL, U.K.
Guy BOY
EURISCO, 10, avenue Édouard Belin,
31055 TOULOUSE CEDEX, FRANCE
Pietro C. CACCIABUE
CEC Joint Research Centre, SER Division, Ispra Establishment,
21020 ISPRA, ITALY
Donatella FERRANTE
University of Trieste, Department of Psychology,
TRIESTE, ITALY
Douglas HISKES
University of Illinois, Department of Mechanical and Electrical
Engineering, 1206, West Green Street, URBANA, IL 61801, USA
Jean-Michel HOC
CNRS-UVHC, LAMIH-PERCOTEC, B.P. 311,
59304 VALENCIENNES CEDEX, FRANCE
Erik HOLLNAGEL
Human Reliability Associates, 1, School Lane, DALTON,
WIGAN, WN8 7RP, U.K.
Johan KJAER-HANSEN
CEC Joint Research Centre, SER Division, Ispra Establishment,
21020 ISPRA, ITALY
Morten N. LARSEN
Technical Univerity of Denmark, IACS, DTH Building 326,
2800 LYNGBY, DENMARK
John LEE
Battle Human Affairs Research Centers,
SEATTLE, WA, USA
Morten LIND
Technical Univerity of Denmark, IACS, DTH Building 326,
2800 LYNGBY, DENMARK

René MANDIAU
CNRS-UVHC, LAMIH, B.P. 311,
59304 VALENCIENNES CEDEX, FRANCE
Patrick MILLOT
CNRS-UVHC, LAMIH, B.P. 311,
59304 VALENCIENNES CEDEX, FRANCE
Neville P. MORAY
University of Illinois, Department of Mechanical and Electrical
Engineering, 1206, West Green Street, URBANA, IL 61801, USA
Bonnie M. MUIR
University of Toronto, Department of Psychology,
TORONTO, CANADA
Leena NORROS
Technical Research Center of Finland, Electrical Engineering
Laboratory, Otakaari 7B, 02150 ESPOO, FINLAND
Bernard PAVARD
CNRS-MATRA, ARAMIIHS, 31, rue des Cosmonautes,
Z.I. du Palays, 31077 TOULOUSE CEDEX, FRANCE
Antonio RIZZO
University of Siena, Department of Psychology, via Roma 47,
53100 SIENA, ITALY
Janine ROGALSKI
CNRS-University of Paris 8, EPCE, 2, rue de la liberté,
93526 SAINT-DENIS CEDEX 2, FRANCE
Emilie ROTH
Westinghouse Science and Technology Center,
PITTSBURGH, PA 15235, USA
Pascal SALEMBIER
CNAM, Department of Ergonomics, 41, rue Gay-Lussac,
75005 PARIS, FRANCE
Renan SAMURÇAY
CNRS-University of Paris 8, EPCE, 2, rue de la liberté,
93526 SAINT-DENIS CEDEX 2, FRANCE
David D. WOODS
Ohio State University, Industrial and Systems Engineering,
1971, Neil Avenue, COLOMBUS, OH 43210-1271, USA

1

Work with Technology: Some Fundamental Issues

Erik HOLLNAGEL
Human Reliability Associates
Pietro Carlo CACCIABUE
CEC Joint Research Centre, Ispra, Italy
Jean-Michel HOC
CNRS - University of Valenciennes

COGNITION AND WORK WITH TECHNOLOGY

Working with technology is tantamount to working in a joint system where in every situation the most important thing is to understand what one is supposed to do. The *joint system* is the unique combination of people and machines that is needed to carry out a given task or to provide a specific function. In this book the focus is on a particular group of people that are called *operators*. An *operator* is the person who is in charge of controlling the system and who also has the responsibility for the system's performance. In the joint system, both operators and machines are necessary for function; it follows that operators need and depend on machines and that machines need and depend on their operators. The decision of how far to extend the notion of people and machines, that is, how much to include in the description of the system, is entirely pragmatic and should not worry us in this context. The important thing is to recognize that the joint system exists in an organizational and social context, and that it therefore should be studied *in vivo* and not *in vitro*. A particular consequence of this is that expertise should not be seen as the individual mastery of discrete tasks, but as a quality that exists in the social context of praxis (cf. Norros, chapter 9, this volume). Where the boundaries of the joint system are set may, for all practical purposes, be determined by the nature of the investigation and the level of the analysis. In some cases, the boundaries of the joint system coincide with the physical space of the control room. But it is frequently necessary to include elements that are distributed in space and time, such as management, training, safety policies, software design, and so forth.

It is quite common to refer simply to a man-machine system (MMS)[1], hence a joint system as the combination of a human and a machine needed to provide a specific function. The reason for using the singular "man and machine" rather than "people and machines" is partly tradition and partly the fact that we are very often considering the situation of the individual operator (although not necessarily an operator who is single or isolated). The term *machine* should not be understood as a single physical machine, for example, a lathe, a pump, or a bus, but rather as the technological part of the system, possibly including a large number of components, machines, computers, controlling devices, and so forth. An example is an airplane, a distillation column, a train, or even a computer network. Similarly, the term *man* should not be understood as a single person (and definitely not as a male person) but rather as the team of people necessary for the joint system to function. An example is the team of controllers in air traffic control.

The onus of understanding, of course, lies with the operator. Although it does make sense to say that the machine must, to a certain degree, understand the operator, the machine's understanding is quite limited and inflexible — even allowing for the wonders that artificial intelligence and knowledge-based systems may eventually bring. In comparison, the operator has a nearly unlimited capacity for understanding. The operator, who in all situations understands what to do, is a *de facto* expert and that expertise is slowly developed through use of the system. Given enough time, we all become experts of the systems we use daily. Some of us become experts in the practical sense that we are adept at using the system. Some of us become experts in the sense that we know all about the system, how it works, what the components are, how they are put together. Some of us become experts in the sense that we can explain to others how to use the system, or how the systems really should be working.

Understanding How A System Works

If we consider working with a system that is completely understood, the use of it will be highly efficient and error free. The system can be completely understood either because it is so simple that all possible states can be analyzed and anticipated, or because its performance is stable and remains within a limited number of possible states although the system itself may be complex. (The two cases are, of course, functionally equivalent.) An example of the former is writing with a pencil. There is practically no technology involved in using the pencil, save from making sure that the lead is exposed, and there are few things that can go wrong (the lead can break, the pencil can break, the paper can tear).[2]

---

[1]The term MMS will be used throughout this chapter to avoid clumsier expressions such as per-machine interaction. Similarly, the term MMI will be used to denote the interaction that takes place between the operator(s) and the machine(s).

[2]Among the things that can go wrong we must include the failure to write or draw what the intention was. There is a difference between using a pencil to write and using a pencil to write a brilliant essay or sketching a portrait. In the former case, the use of

Furthermore, everyone within a given culture, say, the Western civilization, knows what a pencil is for and how it should be used. (To illustrate that this is not an obvious assumption, consider for a moment how many Europeans would be able to write with ink and brush as effortlessly as the Japanese can.) Instructions are therefore not necessary and the person can use the pencil freely for whatever he wants (and problem-solving psychologists enjoy finding alternative uses). When it comes to pencils, we are all experts. We know how to use them and we can probably also explain how they should be used and why they work — at least on a practical level.[3]

This example is deliberately trivial, but things need only get slightly more complicated to see the problems that are characteristic of work with technology. Even a mechanical pencil or a ball-point pen may suffice, because the mechanism by which it is operated may not be obvious. Consider, for instance, how many different ways in which a mechanical pencil or a ball-point pen can be made. The mode of operation is not always obvious and getting the device into a state where it can be operated (e.g., where the lead is exposed so the pencil can write) can present a problem, although usually a small one. A second difference is that it is no longer possible to observe directly the state of the system (e.g., how much lead that is left). The same goes for ball-point pens and fountain pens; it may, for instance, be impossible to write with a ball-point pen because it is out of ink, because the ink has dried, because there is not enough friction on the surface, because the ball has gotten stuck. To find out what is the cause requires diagnosis. When it comes to mechanical pencils and ball-point pens we still all know how to write with them.[4] We can usually make them work, but it is less easy to explain how they work; for instance, what the internal mechanism of a ball-point pen is. Fortunately, we do not necessarily need to know the details of the mechanism in order to use the ball-point pen. Even for such a simple machine there are, however, several ways in which the device can malfunction, thereby introducing issues of diagnosis and repair.

An example of the latter, a complex system with a highly stable performance, can be found in many places. In daily life we need only think of cars and computers. In working contexts many processes spend most of the time in a highly stable region of normal performance, which may mislead the operator to think that he understands the system completely. In fact, it is the noble purpose of design and control engineering to ensure that the performance of the system is highly stable, whether it is a refinery, a blast furnace, a nuclear power plant, or an aircraft. If the presentation of the system states is mediated by a graphical user interface, the resulting "corrupted reality" may foster an impression of

---

the pencil *qua* pencil is the goal. In the latter case, the use of the pencil serves another goal; it is the means to achieve a goal. The work of the operator involves both uses, although training often only emphasises the former.

[3] A slightly more complicated example is the use of a VCR — to say nothing of programming it. Although ostensibly a very simple system with a very simple function, it befuddles a large proportion of the population — from the person on the street to the (former) President of the United States, and sometimes even specialists in MMI!

[4] However, these days not everyone can write with a fountain pen.

complete understanding. As long as the system performance remains stable, this does not present a problem. But the moment that something goes wrong, and in complex systems this seems to be inevitable (Perrow, 1984), the brittleness of the understanding becomes clear.

In order to work efficiently with technology we must have a reasonable degree of understanding of how we can get the technology or the machine to function. We need to be practical experts, but not theoretical ones. We can become practical experts if the machine is well designed and easy to use, that is, if the functions of the system are transparent (Hollnagel, 1988), if the information about its way of functioning and its actual state (feedback) is comprehensible, if it is sufficiently reliable to offer a period of undisturbed functioning where learning can take place, and if we are provided with the proper instructions and the proper help during this learning period. But we are not really experts if we only are able to use the system when everything works as it should, but unable to do so if something go wrong. All these are issues that are important for the use of technology, and are treated in this volume. And all are related to human cognition, and in particular to the ways in which we can describe and explain human cognition.

Working With Dynamic Systems

This book is about working with dynamic systems. It is characteristic of a dynamic system that it may evolve without operator intervention. Thus, even if the operator does not interact with the system, for instance, when he is trying to diagnose or plan, the state of the system may change.[5] The interaction may be paced or driven by what happens in the process, and the system does not patiently await the next input from the operator. Much of the work done in the field of human-computer interaction (HCI) refers to systems which are nondynamic, systems where there is little time pressure and where there are few, if any, consequences of delaying an action (Hollnagel, 1993a). The study of MMS and the study of HCI intersect in the design of interfaces for process control. The differences between dynamic and nondynamic systems, however, means that the transfer of concepts, methods, and results between the two disciplines should be done with caution.

Working with a dynamic system not only means that time may be limited, but also means that the mental representation of the system must be continuously updated. The choice of a specific action is based on the operator's understanding of the current state of the system and his expectations of what the action will accomplish.

---

[5]A more formal definition is: "a system in which the instantaneous value of a given state variable depends upon the values of the same and other state variables at previous instances" (Meetham & Hudson, 1969, p. 655).

If the understanding is incomplete or incorrect, the actions may fail to achieve their purpose. But dynamic systems have even more interesting characteristics as follows (Hoc, 1993):

- the system being supervised or controlled is usually only part of a larger system, for example, a section of a production line or a phase of a chemical process;
- the system being controlled is usually dynamically coupled with other parts of the system, either being affected by state changes in upstream components or itself causing changes in downstream components;
- effective process control often requires that the scope is enlarged in time or space; the operator must consider previous developments and possible future events, as well as parts of the system that are physically or geographically from the present position;
- crucial information may not always be easy to access, but require various degrees of inference;
- the effects of actions and interventions may be indirect or delayed, thus introducing constraints on steering and planning; this effect may be worsened by using the corrupted reality of advanced graphical interfaces (Malin & Schreckenghost, 1992);
- the development of the process may be so fast that operators are forced to take risks and resort to high-level but inaccurate resource management strategies;
- and finally process evolution may be either discontinuous, as in discrete manufacturing, or continuous, as in the traditionally studied processes.

In the context of dynamic systems, expertise refers to the availability of operational knowledge that has been acquired through a prolonged experience with the plant, rather than to academic or theoretical knowledge based on first principles. The operational knowledge is strongly linked to action goals and the available resources. It contains a large amount of practical knowledge that is often weakly formalized and partly unknown to engineers, because it has arisen from situations that were not foreseen by the plant designers. Operational knowledge is structured to facilitate rapid actions rather than a complete understanding. It is concerned with technical aspects of the process as well as the lore that goes with the process environment. The latter is crucial in the supervision of processes with small time constants where resource management is of key importance.

INTENTION AND WORK WITH TECHNOLOGY

When people work with technology they usually have an *intention,* a formulated purpose or goal that guides and directs how they act as well as how they perceive and interpret the reactions from the machine or the process. The intentions can be externally provided by instructions, by written procedures, or by unwritten rules, or, be a product of the operator's own reasoning — and, of course, a mixture of the two. In the former case, it is important that operator can accept and understand the goals that are stated in the instructions and that he knows enough about the machine to be able to comply with these goals. In the latter case, it is important that the operator has an adequate understanding or model of the machine, because otherwise he may reason incorrectly and reach the wrong conclusions, and follow goals that are not appropriate or correct.

When people work together, they are usually able to grasp the intentions of each other, either implicitly through inference or explicitly through communication. This mutual understanding of intentions is actually one of the foundations for efficient collaboration. Conversely, misunderstanding another operator's intentions may effectively block efficient collaboration and lead to unwanted consequences.

In work with technology, two problems are often encountered. The first is that operators may have problems in identifying or understanding a machine's intentions; clearly, a machine does not have intentions in the same way that a human has. Yet the machine has been designed with a specific purpose (or set of purposes) in mind, and the functionality of the machine is ideally an expression of these purposes. Therefore, if operators understand the purpose or the intention (the intended function) of the machine, as it is expressed through the design, they may be in a better position to use it efficiently and effortlessly. This understanding can be facilitated by an adequate design of the interface, in particular an adequate presentation of system states, system goals, and system functions. Much of this understanding is, however, achieved through practice. By working with the system, the operators gradually come to understand how it works and what the designers' intentions were. This can clearly only be achieved if the system has long periods of stable performance. Consequently, that operators have little possibility of understanding the system in abnormal situations where paradoxically the need for understanding may be largest. It is therefore very important that designers realize this problem, and increase the emphasis on proper interaction during contingencies.

The second problem is that the machine has no way of understanding the operator's purpose or intentions. (We here disregard the few attempts in artificial intelligence to apply intent recognition because they are of limited practical value.) This means that the machine is unable to react to what happens except by means of predefined response patterns (cf. Hollnagel, chapter 14, this volume). Many years ago, Norbert Wiener pointed out that the problem with computers (hence with technology and machines in general) is that they do what we ask them to do, rather than what we think we ask them to do. If machines could only recognize what the operator intended or wanted them to do and then did it, life would be so much easier.

The operator's intentions must somehow be translated into actions to achieve the goal. We must therefore be able to establish a correspondence between how we believe the machine works and how it actually works. This has also been expressed as the problem of mapping between psychological variables and physical variables. Norman (1986), in particular, has described what he called the *gulf of execution* and the *gulf of evaluation*. The gulf of execution denotes the situation that exists when the operator has a goal but does not know how to achieve it, when he does not know how to manipulate or control the machine. The gulf of evaluation characterizes the situation where the operator does not understand the measurements and indications given off by the system, when he cannot interpret or make sense of the current system state. Another way of expressing this is by saying that we must have a model of the system which enables us to come up with the appropriate sequence of actions as well as to understand the indications and measurements that the system provides. However, expressing it using the model metaphor hardly makes the problem any easier to solve! For the novice, the gulfs or execution and evaluation can be serious impediments for work while for the expert, the gulfs of execution and evaluation are fissures rather than chasms.

COOPERATION BETWEEN PEOPLE AND MACHINES

A main concern of this book is the cooperation between people and machines, today epitomized by the coveted cooperation between humans and computers. As defined above, this cooperation takes place in the context of a joint system where people and machines mutually depend on each other. Cooperation in itself requires that the two cognitive systems recognize that there is a coupling or dependence between the tasks they must carry out to attain their goals, and further that they both decide to modify their tasks to prevent possible conflicts and achieve a mutual advantage. (A highly relevant, but more formal, treatment of cooperation can be found in n-person game theory, cf. Poundstone, 1993; Rapoport, 1970.) The need for cooperation is obviously made easier if there is a representation of a common goal, but this is not strictly necessary. The common goal may simply be to avoid conflicts (for example, access to resources) or to increase efficiency and the need to cooperate may be realized as the actions are carried out. Cooperation between people can occur spontaneously because they can recognize the intentions of each other. Cooperation between people and machines must, in contrast, be planned and prepared by the system's designers. In both cases it becomes easier to establish the cooperation the greater the operator's experience and expertise is.

In order for the joint system to function efficiently, reliably, and safely it is essential that it is controlled. The essence of control is that unwanted deviations from the desired or prescribed course of development are reduced to a minimum or do not occur at all. Control can be accomplished if one part of the joint system completely controls the other, or if they jointly cooperate to achieve and maintain the needed equilibrium (e.g., the cybernetic description of the homeostat [Ashby, 1956]). As humans, we would like to think of the situation where we are in complete control of the machine. However, there are many cases where the opposite is actually the case, although they are not always recognized as such (for example, modern glass cockpits with displays driven by computer graphics systems). With complex systems, exemplified by most of the process environments that are described throughout this book, it is practically impossible for one part of the system to achieve complete control over the other. The couplings and interactions are simply too many and too complex to be exhaustively analyzed and described, hence to be covered by the design. It is furthermore unreasonable to expect that the operator of the system should be able to do what the designer could not, to understand adequately what goes on during the use of the system. A reasonable degree of control may be attained for the normal range of situations, which basically means those situations that occur frequently enough for learning to occur. This control is achieved because the operator becomes an expert, rather than because the machine is well designed. (If the system was well designed, then there really would not be any need for the operator to learn and become an expert!) But there will always be a much larger number of situations that deviate from the normal in one way or another, and where control therefore will be insufficient or lacking.

Returning to the gulfs of execution and evaluation, it seems appropriate to distinguish between the gulfs as they exist for normal conditions and for contingencies. When the system has been working for some time, it is reasonable to expect that the gulfs of execution and evaluation for the normal (or daily) range of situations have shrunk. This happens because the operator becomes an expert, either system or task tailoring (Cook, Woods, McColligan, & Howie, 1990). But in situations that deviate from the normal, the gulfs of execution and evaluation will clearly remain. Here the operator no longer is an expert and there may be little or no support in the machine's functionality because the designers have not anticipated these cases. There are two issues for the cooperation between men and machines: first, how to ensure that the gulfs of execution and evaluation narrow quickly for normal situations (by supporting and enhancing the building of expertise) and, second, how to ensure that the gulfs of execution and evaluation are not insurmountable in case of unexpected situations and events. To remain with the metaphor, if the gulfs are insurmountable or cannot be bridged, the operator cannot do anything to achieve his goals, nor can he understand or interpret the system correctly. The occurrence of these conditions should clearly be prevented at all cost. In practice most situations are neither absolutely safe nor absolute disasters. They rather occupy a middle ground, which provides a fertile field for research and development.

The chapters of this book describe in detail the many aspects of the cooperation between people and machines. Without preempting the conclusions, we can safely say that, on the whole, we do not completely understand the technology or the machines we work with. Understanding may be incomplete, both in terms of knowing how the technology can be made to work (the gulf of execution), and in terms of comprehending the basic principles of functioning (the preceding discussion of intention). Joint systems can function in many modes and respond in many different ways; this multiplicity creates a complexity that usually goes beyond what humans are able to grasp. In consequence of that, we do not always completely understand what we need to do to achieve a specific goal state or what the consequences of an action will be. In order to cope with the complexity, we usually rely on simplified descriptions or models of the system — both of the machines and of the people. Such descriptions are, however, only adequate for normal or frequently occurring situations where the conditions do not deviate too much from what was assumed or expected. In all other cases, the descriptions will be lacking in one way or the other and it is therefore difficult both to control the machine and to predict what the effects of specific actions will be, hence to form intentions and understand their consequences.[6]

The increasing amount of automation in industrial systems has progressively removed the operator from the actual control loop, associating the human role to supervisor of the process development. This does not imply that the operators are outside the plant management. On the contrary it means that the design of the control and management strategies of the plant must adopt a new perspective that includes the cooperation between humans and "intelligent" support systems — or joint cognitive systems. Here techniques such as Distributed Artificial Intelligence (DAI) and Multilevel Flow Modeling (MFM) are used to develop new approaches to design that can account for such cooperation.

Furthermore, the supervisory role of the humans in many cases implies the presence of a number of human supervisors. This raises to the problem of extending the joint system cooperation to include also the human-human interaction. In particular, strategies for training and the building of expertise requires a direct feedback from the observation of real work setting for the development of appropriate models of collaboration.

JOINT SYSTEMS AND ERRONEOUS ACTIONS

The term *human error* is commonly used to describe a certain class of human actions. As clearly demonstrated by Hollnagel (1993c), the term is seriously misleading because it can denote a cause as well as a class of actions. A better term is therefore *erroneous action,* which clearly refers to an event that was deemed to be incorrect.

Although erroneous actions are unavoidable, they are not necessarily only harmful. A so-called error is often the result of the operator's attempt to achieve a goal in an environment that is uncertain and incompletely known (cf. Rizzo, Ferrante, & Bagnara, chapter 12, this volume). Failure is necessary for adaptation to occur and adaptation is necessary because the system is incompletely specified and incompletely known. Even after long experience, operators will encounter situations where they do not know with certainty whether their actions will achieve the desired goal. If the system is sufficiently resilient and forgiving, imprecise actions may be beneficial because they create a potential for learning. Designer engineers should therefore not aim to eradicate human erroneous actions completely, but rather try to design systems that will be conducive to learning, while also protecting themselves against serious harmful effects of incorrect actions.

Many things can be said about human erroneous actions, and in relation to joint systems it is particularly important to consider the distinction between two categories of erroneous actions, those that are system induced and those that are not. The latter can be called residual erroneous actions or erroneous actions

---

[6]It may be added that this problem is not peculiar to technological systems, but exist for other systems as well. As an example, consider the problems in accounting for the economy of a nation, the behavior of the stock market, and so forth.

stemming from person related causes (cf. Figure 1). The distinction is to some extent arbitrary; any error or event analysis can always be taken one step further, and that step may lead to a complete revision of the identified cause (Woods, Johannesen, Cook, & Sarter, 1994). A person-related cause may, for instance, be due to an inadequate working environment which, however, only shows it effects through a person-related cause. However, in practice, there are large classes of actions that clearly and easily fall into one or the other category.

The importance of the two categories is that although it is possible to do something effectively about system related causes, it is usually either impossible or at least very difficult to do something about person-related causes. If, for instance, the cause of an erroneous action is found to be the fluctuation of attention, there are few things one can do about that because it is an inherent characteristic of human cognition. If, on the other hand, the cause turned out to be a mismatch between a procedure and the design of the controls, something can be done. The situation will usually be less clear cut, but the principle prevails. Erroneous actions are valuable indicators of the quality of the MMI and the physical and functional interface. They should always be carefully examined rather than hastily assigned to simplified categories — in particular the garbage can called human error. The indicators must be understood correctly and interpreted carefully in order to avoid inaccurate or superficial solutions. This requires a good appreciation of the complexity of MMI, and of the many aspects that are important in human work with technology.

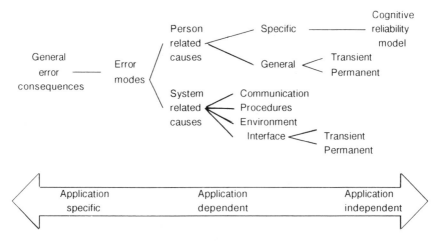

Figure 1 : A taxonomy of human error concepts.

MODELING OF HUMAN BEHAVIOR

The modeling human behavior is a complex and ambitious task that first of all demands a clear distinction between the concepts of *model* and the concept of *simulation*. Even though the terms frequently are used as synonyms, they are quite different. Modeling and simulation are two complementary ways of representing a process, which can be either physical or cognitive. In both cases the purpose is to explain past events as well as to predict time evolution within a certain margin of uncertainty and given boundary conditions. A *model* is essentially a theoretical description of a process or a system based on a number of hypotheses and simplifying principles, which can be formulated as analytic or lexicographic expressions (the model language). A *simulation* is a concrete expression or instantiation of the model in a form that is controllable or executable, for example, for a practical application or for computation. In the domain of thermohydraulics, for instance, the models of mass-flow and heat behaviors are governed by the well known Navier-Stokes equations, but the description of real situations can only be obtained by using a computerized simulation based on parametrization of the theoretical model. In the field of human performance, a similar distinction must be maintained, although it must be acknowledged that most of the models have been inspired by the information processing paradigm in one way or another, hence are relatively easy to turn into simulations, although they are more often proposed than actually done.

A crucial problem tackled by research on joint cognitive systems and cognitive ergonomics is the development of models of operators in control of complex dynamic systems (e.g., Hollnagel, Mancini & Woods, 1986). The models are useful expressions of our understanding of human cognition at work and also as a foundation for building symbolic simulations of operators. The need to model MMI in the control of joint systems can be deduced from the solutions to the control of mechanical system as described by, for example, cybernetics. Linear system theory, for example, has shown that the optimization of system performance can only be achieved if the dynamics of the system to be controlled are known and if a performance criterion is defined (Conant & Ashby, 1970; Francis & Wonham, 1975). This has also been expressed by the maxim that "every good regulator of a system must be a model of that system."

When an operator controls a complex system, several activities are necessary to keep the system in normal conditions, for instance, supervision, detection and diagnosis of perturbations, planning and execution of actions/procedures (Bainbridge, 1983; De Keyser, 1987; Edwards & Lees, 1974; Sheridan, 1985). These activities all put considerable demands to human cognition, hence present a challenge for system design. The facilitation of such activities can be achieved by including the simulation of human behavior among the techniques and methodologies for the design of procedures, interfaces, decision support systems.

There exists a number of theories and models of cognition, mostly derived from the domain of psychology, although with some help from the wider field of philosophy. The attempt to apply such theories through practical simulations for design or analysis purposes is a recent endeavor that has been accelerated by the availability of a highly suitable technology (cheap but powerful personal computers and high-level, object-oriented programming languages). The complexity of the models has increased to match the progressive evolution of operator roles in the context of their work environment, going from the purely manual control to the full supervisory control tasks of modern systems, as in the nuclear power and aviation domains. In the 1960s and 1970s, successful models of control engineering were developed to study and simulate manual control behavior. The then current theories of human cognition reflected the needs of that generation of control demands, based on information processing and supervision of remote and complex processes. Among the first generation of models, those based on control theory proved their value in the design of controls and displays (Kleinman, Baron, & Levison, 1971; McRuer & Jex; 1967); so did others based on signal detection theory and estimation theory (Sheridan & Ferrel, 1974). During the 1980s, the most applied models of cognition in the process control field were the step-ladder model of Rasmussen (1976, 1986; Rasmussen, Pejtersen, & Schmidt, 1990) and the underspecification theory of Reason (1990). A number of simulations were also developed using logic structures and mathematical approaches such as object oriented programming, blackboard architectures, fuzzy set theories and fuzzy logic, neural networks, and so forth. There are several reviews of the various approaches to modeling, made at different times and thus reflecting slightly different focuses, e.g., Pew, Baron, Feehrer, & Miller, (1977), Rouse (1980), Sheridan (1985), and the more recent review of Stassen, Johannsen, & Moray (1990).

A key issue related to models and simulation of human behavior is their applicability and usefulness. It is important to stress that a simulation of the operator's decision making or behavior gives the designer and analyst more flexibility and better means to evaluate potential solutions. In particular, the cognitive simulation can be used to encompass a wider range of situations and thereby obtain information in a cheap and rapid manner, which might otherwise require long and costly field analyses and questionnaires. Moreover, the use of a simple theory of cognition, that is, a theoretical model that adheres to the premises of simplicity, provides a viable alternative that both satisfies the need of a reference model for simulation purposes and acknowledges the impossibility to contain in the model the whole richness of human decision making and performance.

This view has been expressed by a Minimal Modeling Manifesto (Hollnagel, 1993b) which provides a basis for a consistent approach to the modeling of humans in interactive systems, and which can be formulated as follows: "A Minimal Model is a representation of the main principles of control and regulation that are established for a domain — as well as of the capabilities and limitations of the controlling system" (p. 379).

A minimal model is concerned with control and regulation, hence with cognition at work. The model is minimal because it tries to make as few assumptions as possible, but not because the phenomena it addresses are minimal or simplified. A minimal model may be specific for a given application or domain, such as a nuclear power plant, but is linked to other minimal models by the notion that there will be strong commonalties across a set of applications, and possibly even across a set of widely different applications. This may eventually enable the construction of a common minimal model, such as a model that represents the basic characteristics of humans as controllers. The advantages offered by the model/simulation approach must, however, not undermine the role and importance of actual observations and field analyses. These activities do, indeed, represent the fundamental and necessary basis for model and theory building in the first place. Empirical investigations are also necessary when a model has to be validated or substantiated — although from the minimal modeling point of view there is no strong need to validate the models. Observations and field analyses are further required as a basis for estimating the parameters of the simulation. The field experiments, if well planned and designed, usually produce a wealth of information that demands extensive analysis before its effects on the theoretical work are fully accomplished.

MODELING
AND DEVELOPMENT OF COMPETENCE

The operator's knowledge comes from basic education, training, and direct experience in working with the system. Through the basic education, the operator learns the physical laws underlying the process, the principles of functioning for the components, and the principles that govern the behavior of complex systems. It is, however, only through training and experience that the operator becomes acquainted with how the plant or the process conducts itself in normal and abnormal conditions. In training, individuals learn to operate on a system that is rarely working under normal operating conditions, whereas during everyday experience the opposite is the case. The experiences gained from training are thus only moderately representative of the system's actual behavior. This dichotomy may create a mental bias in the operator, who may overestimate the plant capabilities and thus not be prepared to react when anomalies occur. A first step in overcoming this bias may be to develop models for training and simulations of the three basic components of the working socio-technical systems: the operator(s), the machines, and the environment. This is treated more extensively by Samurçay, in chapter 7, this volume.

The lesson learned from the simulation approaches developed so far have been particularly illuminating with regard to some fundamental aspects of the modeling of cognitive activities, such as the possibility of extrapolating and creating a knowledge base starting from bounded experience. In the perspective of developing a safety culture, the interesting features of such cognitive simulation is the possibility of obtaining expertise artificially condensed, in relation to a specific dynamic socio-technical reality. The question is often put as how one can describe what the operator knows (this, for instance, is the central topic in knowledge acquisition). It might, however, be considered whether it is not more important to find out what the operator does not know or what he knows incorrectly, because these knowledge "deficiencies" often are the cause of unwanted consequences or events (erroneous actions). Although it is next to impossible to describe what the operator knows, because this evokes the issues of tacit knowledge and what AI calls the frame problem, it may be more manageable to describe what the operator does not know, that is, to identify the discrepancies between the expected and the actual knowledge. This discrepancy can be observed or deduced directly from experience, and it is this (lack of) knowledge, that is important — for performance studies and for design.

Another interesting possibility of simulating the interaction between cognitive and machine models is that this may strengthen the self-reflexive capabilities of the operator. Indeed, it can be envisaged that an operator could "look" through results of the cognitive model included in the simulator (have a look at himself while controlling the plant in situations which may not occur in reality). Such alternate (almost contra-factual) reality self-reflection simulates, in an artificial situation, second-level cognitive experience, that is, reflection on one's own perceptions (Piaget, 1964), which enables the construction of more appropriate mental structures for interpreting the experience of the world.

REFERENCES

Ashby, W. R. (1956). *An introduction to cybernetics.* London: Methuen & Co.

Bainbridge, L. (1983). The ironies of automation. *Automatica, 19,* 775-780.

Conant, R. & Ashby, W. R. (1970). Every good regulator of a system must be a model of that system. *International Journal of Systems Science, 1,* 89-97.

Cook, R. I., Woods, D. D., McColligan, E., & Howie, M. B. (1990, Sept.). *Cognitive consequences of 'clumsy' automation on high workload, high consequence human performance.* Paper presented at the *Fourth Annual Space Operations, Applications and Research Symposium.* Washington, DC.

De Keyser, V. (1987). Structuring of knowledge of operators in continuous processes: case study of a continuous casting plant start-up. In J. Rasmussen, K. Duncan, & J. Leplat (Eds.), *New technology and human error* (pp. 247-260). Chichester, UK: John Wiley.

Edwards, E. & Lees, F. (1974). *The human operator in process control.* London: Taylor & Francis.

Francis, B. A. & Wonham, W. M. (1975). The internal model principle of linear control theory. *Proceedings of 6th IFAC World Congress,* Boston, MA, Oxford: Pergamon Press [Paper 43.5].

Hoc, J.M. (1993). Some dimensions of a cognitive typology of process control situations. *Ergonomics, 36,* 1445-1455.

Hollnagel, E. (1988). Cognitive models, cognitive tasks, and information retrieval. In I. Wormell (Ed.), *Knowledge engineering* (pp. 34-52). London: Taylor Graham.

Hollnagel, E. (1993a, Sept.). *The design of reliable HCI: The hunt for hidden assumptions.* Invited keynote lecture, *HCI 93.* Loughborough, UK.

Hollnagel, E. (1993b). Requirements for dynamic modelling of man-machine interaction. *Nuclear Engineering and Design, 144,* 375-384.

Hollnagel, E. (1993c). *Human reliability analysis: context and control.* London: Academic Press.

Hollnagel E., Mancini, G., & Woods, D. D. (1986). *Intelligent Decision Support in Process Environments.* [Nato ASI Series, Vol. 21]. Berlin: Springer Verlag.

Kleinman, D. L., Baron, S., & Levison, W. H. (1971). A Control Theoretic Approach to Manned-vehicle Systems Analysis. *IEEE Transactions on Automatic Control, AC-16*, 824-832.

Malin, J. T., & Schreckenghost, D. L. (1992). *Making intelligent systems team players: Overview for designers* [Tech. Rep. No. NASA 104751]. Houston, Texas: Johnson Space Center.

McRuer, D. T. & Jex, H. R. (1967). A Review of Quasi-linear Pilot Models. *IEEE Transactions on Human Factors in Electronics, HFE-8*, 231-249.

Meetham, A. R., & Hudson, R. A. (Eds.) (1969). *Encyclopaedia of linguistics, information and control.* Oxford: Pergamon Press.

Norman, D.A. (1986). Cognitive engineering. In D.A. Norman & S.W. Draper (Eds.), *User centered system design: new perspectives on human computer interaction.* Hillsdale, NJ: Lawrence Erlbaum Associates.

Perrow, C. (1984). *Normal accidents: living with high-risk technologies.* New York: Basic Books.

Pew, R. W., Baron, S., Feehrer, C. E. & Miller, D. C. (1977). *Critical Review and Analysis of Performance Models Applicable to Man-Machine-Systems Evaluation* [Tech. Rep. No. 3446]. Cambridge, MA: Bolt, Beranek & Newman.

Piaget, J. (1964). *Logique et connaissance scientifique* [Logic and scientific knowledge]. Paris: Gallimard [Encyclopédie de la Pléiade].

Poundstone, W. (1993). *Prisoner's dilemma.* Oxford, UK: Oxford University Press.

Rapoport, A. (1970). *N-person game theory: Concepts and applications.* Ann Arbor: The University of Michigan Press.

Rasmussen, J. (1976). Outlines of a hybrid model of the process operator. In T. Sheridan, & G. Johannsen (Eds.), *Monitoring Behavior and Supervisory Control* (pp. 371-384). New York: Plenum Press.

Rasmussen, J. (1986) *Information processes and human-machine interaction. An approach to cognitive engineering.* Amsterdam: North Holland.

Rasmussen, J., Pejtersen, A. M., & Schmidt, K. (1990, May). *Taxonomy for cognitive work analysis.* Paper presented at the *First MOHAWC Esprit II-BR Workshop.* Liège, Belgium.

Reason, J., (1990). *Human error.* Cambridge, UK: Cambridge University Press.

Rouse, W. B. (1980). *Systems engineering models of human-machine interaction.* Amsterdam: North Holland.

Sheridan, T. B. (1985, Sept.). *Forty-five years of man-machine systems: history and trends.* Keynote Address at the *Second IFAC Conference on Analysis, Design and Evaluation of Man-Machine Systems.* Varese, Italy.

Sheridan T. B., & Ferrel W. R. (1974). *Man-machine systems: information, control and decision models of human performance.* Cambridge, MA: MIT Press.

Stassen H. G., Johannsen G., & Moray N. (1990). Internal representation, internal model, human performance model and mental workload. *Automatica, 26*, 811-820.

Woods, D. D., Johannesen, L. J., Cook, R. I., & Sarter, N. B. (1994). *Behind human error: Cognitive systems, computers and hindsight.* Columbus, OH: CSERIAC.

SECTION 1

COGNITION
AND
WORK WITH TECHNOLOGY

2

Human Operator Expertise in Diagnosis, Decision-Making, and Time Management

Jean-Michel HOC
CNRS - University of Valenciennes
René AMALBERTI
Centre d'Études et Recherches en Médecine Aérospatiale
Nicholas BOREHAM
University of Manchester

Although there are abundant theoretical frameworks for diagnosis in the laboratory or in the field, they present serious limitations in Dynamic Environment Supervision (DES). However, empirical data collected on expert operators can lead toward a more extended model which takes dynamic features of the environment into account. A functional analysis of the supervisory activity is delineated that stresses the link between diagnosis and overall operator activity (especially decision-making). The main theoretical contributions and limitations of current models of diagnosis are presented. Two aspects of diagnosis are examined: (a) the declarative basis — knowledge bases and representations on which it is established (in particular time knowledge); (b) the procedural basis — diagnostic strategies. This chapter ends with a proposal for an extended model of diagnosis and decision-making in DES.

Although everybody agrees that diagnosis is a central feature of Dynamic Environment Supervision (DES), the notion remains largely ill defined. One of the reasons is a positive aspect of research conducted in the field: It tries to study psychological activity as a whole, before attempting to decompose it into components between which interactions can be further investigated.

After Rasmussen's pioneering work (1986, for a recent overview) in the domain, it has become clear that studying diagnosis in process supervision, as well as troubleshooting, cannot be done without treating its relationships with action decision-making and implementation (Hoc & Amalberti, in press). Thus, experimental approaches that isolate diagnosis from other kinds of activities are no longer tenable while trying to model real situations. Here, the point is not so much to devise a task where what is termed diagnosis is well defined, but to make an attempt to identify a basic component within a complex activity which integrates diagnosing, monitoring, and acting.

Moreover, in DES, diagnosis more often than not is closely interwoven with prognosis. The situation is very different from the repair of electronic apparatus, which is generally taken out of service after a malfunction has occurred and is dealt with off-line. In the latter case, diagnosing a failed component and replacing it is generally sufficient to return the equipment to a satisfactory state. However, with continuous process supervision, the human operator is responsible for maintaining the system's safety while it is in operation, including reacting to transitions from normal to abnormal states which may occur only gradually. Thus, expertise should encompass early stages in the development of malfunctions, not just the final stage when the system breaks down. Moreover, because it is more important to avoid breakdowns than to recover from them, the support system should make this the prime objective. Automation, and especially computerized automation, sometimes results in providing operators with more and more means to anticipate future events, as well as to maintain systems within sharp bounds where systems are not only safer but also more productive and efficient. Prognosis thus becomes integrated with diagnosis. In the remainder of this paper, we shall use the term diagnosis as a generic expression which encompasses understanding the current state of the system, and at the same time its past and future evolution.

We will not be so reckless as to impose a definition without any discussion. But we will extract a workable conception from studies conducted in experimental settings as well as in a variety of field situations: troubleshooting, medical diagnosis, and process control, or more broadly DES, including for example crisis management (e.g., fire-fighting). This will lead us to consider diagnosis as a generic concept, while noting that this component of activity goes from skill-based identification of parameters immediately leading to action to harder knowledge-based productive activity combining hypothesis generation and test. Following the line of Bainbridge's (1984) reflections on *Diagnostic Skill in Process Operation,* we will consider action feedback as an intrinsic part of diagnosis, when action or the decision to "do-nothing-but-see-what-will-happen" is partly or mainly aimed at testing hypotheses.

If we consider DES as an activity which develops in an environment that also evolves without any operator intervention, as Bainbridge (1988) argued, two kinds of knowledge are necessary in supervision: (i) knowledge of the structure and operation of the environment under supervision; (ii) knowledge of operator goals and actions. The former clearly needs diagnosis to regularly update a mental representation of the state and evolution of the process, whereas the latter could be supported by predefined knowledge, at least at an expert level.

Section 1 is a proposal for an operational definition of diagnosis — operational in the sense of its link to action — within the framework of a functional analysis of supervisory activity. Then, we will briefly examine some theoretical frameworks available for understanding diagnosis, stressing both their values and limitations. In the three following and separate sections we will treat the dual nature of this psychological activity component. In Section 2, diagnosis will be seen as relying on a variety of knowledge representation formats which could be supported by suitable displays or information sources, not necessarily wholly computerized. In Section 3 we will separately address the question of time representation and management in DES, where this feature plays a crucial role. In particular, we will show that time management does not always depend on time representation. In Section 4, several kinds of well-known diagnosis strategies will be presented in relation to other activity components, and implications will be derived for the necessity of taking these links into account when designing support for diagnosis. Finally, in Section 5, we will propose a general framework to integrate knowledge, representations, and diagnosis strategies.

FUNCTIONAL ANALYSIS OF SUPERVISORY ACTIVITY

A functional perspective on diagnosis emphasizes its contribution to the overall performance of the system. This implies adopting criteria for designing and evaluating diagnostic systems which go far beyond the engineering requirements for physical operation. Instead, the appropriateness of diagnostic approaches must be measured in terms of their contribution to the commercial and/or social value of systems whose performance is being monitored.

Diagnosis must thus be viewed as a goal-directed activity, subordinate to the broader purposes of the system which is being diagnosed. A physician diagnoses not as an end in itself, but to assist in maintaining the patient's health. In some cases, the appropriate medical treatment may be selected without the need to undertake a formal diagnosis: for example, the choice of a broad spectrum antibiotic to cure an infection without identifying the exact organism which is responsible. In general, a diagnostic investigation will not usually be taken beyond the point when it ceases to refine the choice of treatment. This point may be reached before a complete scientific explanation of the cause of the problem has been attained. Similarly, a troubleshooter may not need to diagnose the precise component which has caused a domestic appliance to malfunction, if it can be restored to working order more efficiently by replacing a whole unit, such as the motor or control panel. Experts on inquiry boards after a disaster will be concerned to learn lessons for the future: The direction taken by their investigations will reflect this goal, which may lead into areas far removed from the technological failures which have occurred. The implication is that the diagnostic task cannot be defined solely in terms of finding the scientific explanation for a system malfunction, within purely technological parameters. If we are to specify a diagnostic procedure for training or decision support, we must do so in relation to the ultimate purpose of the system whose performance is being supervised.

Diagnosis will almost certainly incur costs. Collecting data takes an appreciable amount of time, and control actions may have to be postponed to permit observations to be made. While the consequent accretion of information will make a scientific explanation of the malfunction easier, in terms of contributing to overall system effectiveness, the costs may be too high. For instance, while the investigation is under way the system may move into a more dangerous state, or even sustain damage, and the costs of this may exceed the benefits of being able to make a scientifically accurate diagnosis. Another consideration is the financial cost of gathering the data, which has to be set against the financial benefit of maintaining the system in running order. Many diagnostic investigations involve operations which are very costly, yet in designing decision support these costs are not always taken into account. Finally, diagnosis is often invasive, reducing the system's performance, or even causing damage, in order to gain information. Under such conditions, a scientific diagnosis may do more harm than leaving the system undisturbed, albeit operating at a suboptimal level.

It is therefore necessary to move away from the traditional view of diagnosis as a cognitive problem-solving activity which establishes a complete scientific explanation of the cause of a malfunction before the operator chooses a course of action. Instead, a theory of diagnosis must be a theory of optimal behavior, in which some control actions may be performed prior to information gathering, and information gathering may be curtailed before a complete picture has been established in the interest of maximizing utility.

With these points in mind, there are several general characteristics of diagnosis in a complex, dynamic environment which need to be considered when designing the diagnostic activity required of a human operator. The first is the fact that the state of the system is evolving, which creates options for the human operator to intervene at alternative points in time. Of course, if the degradation of a system is catastrophic, this choice will not exist. However, the latencies in most continuous processes allow the operator to delay action while learning more about the state of the system. The significance of this for the design of diagnostic activities is that the intervention will have different goals at different stages in the evolution of a fault, ranging from prevention early in the process, through correction at an intermediate stage, to damage limitation if the intervention is made later. Table 1 demonstrates the different diagnostic goals of an operator at different times in the evolution of a malfunction — early, middle and late.

In general, then, understanding the system's problems early in the evolution of a malfunction implies identifying threat factors before they have progressed far enough to cause a malfunction. Understanding the problems at intermediate stages will focus on deciding how to get the destructive processes under control. Understanding problems when they have progressed to an advanced stage is a matter of identifying an intervention which will repair damage.

The second general characteristic of diagnosis in a complex, dynamic environment which needs to be considered when designing a diagnostic role for the human operator is the increase of information with time. Information about a system malfunction will accumulate, relatively little information being available early on, larger amounts later. The different diagnostic strategies adopted at different stages in the evolution of a malfunction will reflect these different amounts of information. In general, diagnosis attempted early in the development of a fault will use broader search strategies to compensate for the relative lack of pathognomic information at that stage. By considering the overall context, expectations can be formed which reduce uncertainty. This point is discussed at greater detail by Boreham, in Chapter 6 of the present volume.

TABLE 1
Different goals and sub-goals of diagnosis at different times in the evolution of a fault in a dynamic system

Time	Goals	Subgoals
EARLY	Prevent malfunction	Protect the system from external factors that cause malfunction
		Run the system in a manner that minimizes the chance of malfunction
		Contain specific agents which might cause malfunction
MIDDLE	Identify and control malfunction	Screen for asymptomatic faults
		Recognize a state of malfunction
		Predict the course of a malfunction
		Assess system response to control action designed to stabilize it
LATE	Minimize loss from malfunction	Repair damage
		Limit the spread of damage

LIMITATIONS OF CURRENT MODELS OF DIAGNOSIS AND DECISION-MAKING

Two main research trends may be considered as possible sources of theoretical frameworks in experimental psychology: (a) interpretative or understanding activities in problem-solving situations (Anderson, 1983; Richard et al., 1990); (b) structure induction (Klahr & Dunbar, 1988; Simon & Lea, 1974). The first trend drives our endeavor to avoid considering diagnosis as a specific psychological activity separate from other kinds of cognitive processes. The second trend provides us with a more precise framework which will be examined in a more detailed way.

The main contribution of the structure induction paradigm to the study of diagnosis is the definition of diagnosis within two dual spaces. This idea was first introduced by Simon and Lea (1974) in their well-known GRI (General Rule Inducer) and later refined by Klahr and Dunbar (1988) in their model SDDS (Scientific Discovery as Dual Search). The typical situation referred to by these models is concept identification (learning of the meaning of the command of a robot by doing, in the Klahr & Dunbar study). Search for a meaningful structure or rule is supposed to develop within two dual spaces — an example space from where facts are selected (examples of a concept or behavior of a robot responding to a particular command), and a rule or structure space where hypotheses on relevant properties of facts can be found.

Although this conception is of great value, it has to be modified to fit the diagnosis situation better. We therefore describe the two dual spaces as a fact space (FS) and a structure space (SS). However, there is a link between search in FS and SS since facts are not raw data and have to be interpreted by the means of meaningful structures (e.g., if a variable value is considered too low, such an identification relies on the context). In addition, hypotheses not only concern structures (e.g., syndromes) but also facts (e.g., application of a well-known syndrome to a patient may only be possible if some hypothesis is generated on the occurrence of a past fact such a trauma). Finally, following Klahr and Dunbar (1988) the SS has to be considered hierarchically organized, enabling the generation of hypotheses at diverse levels of schematization. Here, two dimensions have to be considered (Hoc, 1988; Rasmussen, 1986): (a) a refinement hierarchy which divides a structure into substructures; (b) an implementation hierarchy which bears on relationships between functions (or ends) and implementation (or means). These hierarchies can account for the common distinction between general and specific hypotheses (Elstein et al., 1978).

Seen at first as a model, and more and more as a generic cognitive architecture generating a class of models, Rasmussen's decision ladder partly picks up the link between diagnosis and decision-making (see Rasmussen, 1981, 1984, 1986). It is typical of the procedural and serial models elaborated in the work context (see also Rasmussen & Rouse, 1981). The route through the two entire portions of the ladder (Figure 1) corresponds to a fully developed and serial decision-making process. However, we have modified the original presentation of the model to overcome some of its main drawbacks (Figure 1):

(a) Situation analysis stage (left leg of the ladder):

Three successive modules lead to diagnosis (from bottom to top): detection of abnormal conditions, explicit search for information, and situation identification. Furthermore, interpretation and evaluation of consequences are interpolated between the two stages (top of the figure).

(b) Planning stage (right leg of the ladder):

Three other modules (from top to bottom) contribute to action: definition of a task, formulation of a procedure, and execution.

This architecture highlights the links between diagnosis and decision-making. Moreover, it supports possible shortcuts (from left to right) which correspond to different kinds of diagnosis, in regard to deepness (e.g., detection of abnormal — or normal, since identification of normal operation is also important — conditions can be sufficiently operational to trigger an appropriate action, for example in the case of emergency medicine). Nevertheless, the drawings in Figure 1 diverge from Rasmussen's original figure in three respects:

(i) Situation identification can result in an identification of the current system state (as in the original architecture), but now additionally in an anticipation of the system's future evolution (prognosis). Originally, this architecture was devised to account for elementary troubleshooting tasks, but we need this extension to introduce prognosis in DES (in blast furnace control, for example, about half of the verbal reports on representation concern evolutions rather than

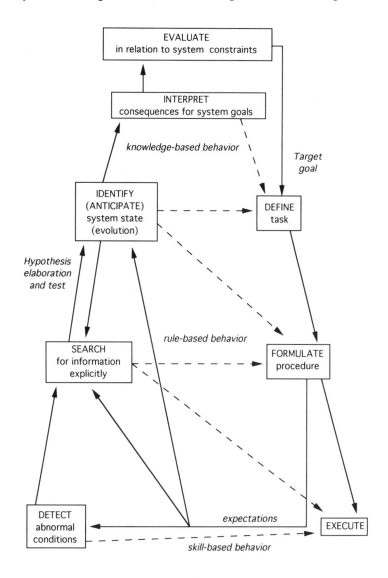

**FIGURE 1.   Rasmussen's step-ladder revisited
(after Hoc & Amalberti, in press)**
The left part of the ladder corresponds to diagnosis and prognosis, the upper part
goal setting, and the right part action planning. Rectangles represent processes,
lines information flow (dotted lines represent some possible shortcuts from
information to action).

states: Hoc, 1989b; in gas grid control, 28% of the verbal reports are devoted to
predictions of gas demand: Umbers, 1979; in modeling the supervision of a very

rapid process like fighter aircraft piloting, anticipation of diverse time span is put at the center (Amalberti & Deblon, 1992). Iosif (1968) showed that process operators paid more attention to parameters on which anticipation could be based (and also to frequently out-of-order parameters). This phenomenon was confirmed in blast furnace supervision (Hoc, 1989a). Anticipation also plays a crucial role in stepwise adjustment of doses of medicine to prevent epilepsy attacks (Boreham, 1992) and constitutes a central training topic in crisis management (Samurçay & Rogalski, 1988). The implication for diagnosis/prognosis support of these studies is clear: Designers must pay attention to parameters which have a high anticipation value.

(ii) Hypothesis generation and test strategies imply adding transfer of information from identification (or anticipation) to information search. This loop is crucial in problem-solving situations where the first hypothesis is not necessarily correct. However, the adequacy of the explanation of the system state is not the only criterion which determines how long the decision system stays in the loop. Because of the risks of delaying intervention while diagnosis is made, the operator may take provisional action before a full explanation is achieved. Moreover, it is difficult to represent on this kind of figure the dynamic features of the process to be supervised. Some hypothesis testing activities have to be postponed, waiting for the right time window when information is relevant to test hypotheses. Due to response latencies and spontaneous evolution of the process, timing does not rely on operator implementation of the architecture, but also on process timing (especially with long response latency processes like a blast furnace).

(iii) As Bainbridge (1984) put it, feedback loops are truly necessary to account for expectation effects: Operators are not passive devices simply waiting for information which they filter. When formulating a procedure (or a diagnosis) a number of expectations can be diffused through the network towards diverse control levels: detection (lower level processes), search for information, or diagnosis (upper level processes). Here again, time lags have to be taken into account when relevant information is waited for. In some cases expectations are preselected by a previous analysis before taking charge of the system in charge (e.g., shift change-over, mission planning in fighter aircraft piloting as shown by Amalberti & Deblon, 1992).

KNOWLEDGE BASES
AND KNOWLEDGE REPRESENTATIONS

As compared to static situations, where operators control the whole environment, dynamic situations need a wider variety of knowledge representation formats for diagnosis. Many empirical studies have been devoted to eliciting these formats from operators, by means of diverse techniques (interviews, questionnaires, observations in problem-solving situations, etc.), for example, polystyrene mill operators (Cuny, 1979), nuclear power plant operators (Alengry, 1987), and blast furnace operators (Hoc & Samurçay, 1992).

Although terminology differs from one theoretical contribution to another (Baudet & Denhière, 1991; Brajnik et al., 1989), mental models or Representation and Processing Systems (RPS: see Hoc, 1988) can be classified into five main categories: causal, functional, transformational, topographical, and life-cycle RPSs.

(a) Causal RPS

Probably due to the fact that, for the most part, knowledge elicitation techniques have been directed towards knowledge underlying procedures and strategies, empirical data are richest on causal RPSs. Usually, after Crossman (1965), such a RPS is represented by an "influence graph", which connects input variables (which operators can act upon) to intervening variables, and the latter to output variables, such as product quality, and the like. Examples can be found in Cuny (1979) or Hoc (1989a).

More often than not, this kind of network serves as a rationale for inductive inference (to causes) or deductive inference (to the consequences), the latter integrating temporal anticipation. Nevertheless, knowledge of this kind is not purely of a declarative kind, in the sense of a structure which would be very far from concrete implementation in action. For example, in blast furnace supervision, knowledge integrated into operator networks is mainly relevant to action (Hoc & Samurçay, 1992): (a) variables describing internal phenomena which operators can directly and plentifully act upon are more commonly reported and used than others; (b) each basic phenomenon is linked to available actions on it.

(b) Functional RPS

In situations where procedures play a major role, another representational format can be found for use by operators. Alengry (1987), for example, has elicited this kind of knowledge from NPP operators, who were asked to specify what they were doing while trying to implement some global goal, and why. He has collected causal representations as well as functional knowledge linking operator goals to operator actions, but also a causal rationale for the procedures. Systems are artifacts specifically designed to fulfill goals which are defined when structuring components and/or control loops in them. When a system is in nominal operation, these functional specifications play a major role in understanding and in diagnosing the system state or evolution. But, on the other hand, in abnormal conditions such a functional rationale can become invalid. Therefore, in this case, operators must rely upon more general knowledge of a causal kind.

(c) Transformational RPS

Representation of the system operation can also be in terms of transformations taking place in the system. But it is clearer in discontinuous processes, such as integrated manufacturing, than in continuous ones. In this case, diagnosis is largely determined by transformations, as shown by Guillermain (1988): operators pay less attention to the reasons behind a breakdown than to the specific transformation which has failed, trying to reset it before searching for causes (very often resetting is sufficient to recover from a breakdown diagnosed by probabilistic interference, for example, between a soldering robot operation and some dust).

(d) Topographical RPS

Another way of supporting diagnosis is using topographic references, when the system can be broken into distinct components. Much work has been done in the troubleshooting domain, trying to vary features of information displays (like mimic boards), especially giving hierarchical access to such decompositions to help locate deficient components (Brooke & Duncan, 1983; Morrison & Duncan, 1988; Patrick, 1993).

(e) Life cycle RPS

In dynamic contexts such as blast furnace supervision and the management of human illness, an important representational format is the life cycle, including the life cycle of the system and the subcycles of its constituent processes. Regularities can be observed indicating successive phases in the history of a plant, such as start-up, early maladaptations to the environment, trouble-free operation, occasional turbulences, cumulative multiple malfunctions, and obsolescence. Knowledge of the stage in the life cycle is crucial for making prognoses. It is also important for the interpretation of symptoms, as the same symptom may have different meanings at different stages in the life cycle.

It could be too simplistic to hope to be able to identify the operator's current strategy, and in real time, to decide what kind of support is needed. Diagnosis can have causal, functional, transformational, and topographical components. It is tempting to design mimic boards when the structure of the system is easy to break into well-identified components, but usually such decomposition provides operators with insufficient support. In certain cases, causal, functional, transformational, and topographical relationships cannot be integrated into the same kind of structure.

This is why Goodstein (Goodstein, 1983; Goodstein & Rasmussen, 1988) introduced the principle of multi-windowed displays that enable operators to quickly switch from one structure to another, making apparent the links between the diverse structures. Improvements have been further introduced in the implementation of this principle by Lind (Lind, 1991; Lind et al., 1989; Lind, in chapter 16 of the present volume), with his MFM (Multilevel Flow Models) interface.

To a great extent, knowledge embedded in the RPS described above is of a deep nature and can provide the operator with a basis for high level (knowledge-based) diagnosis. Expert operators are very often performing lower level (rule-based, skill-based) diagnosis, due to automatization of their activity. However empirical data (especially in medicine) show that deep knowledge (e.g., biomedical knowledge) is neither lost nor inert, but simply encapsulated in procedures (Boshuizen et al., 1992). Expert operators can access this knowledge, either in parallel when applying rules or triggering automatic procedures, or during interviews with the observer.

Thus the current representation of the situation, which diagnosis regularly updates, takes its inputs from diverse RPSs as well as from information gathering. This representation is hierarchically organized so that diverse levels of diagnosis can be performed concurrently. However, in the case of automatic processes (skill-based behavior) external information plays a major role and short cuts the symbolic representation level.

The diverse RPS refer to the operator's knowledge of the system *per se*. However, such a knowledge base is useless for diagnosis without a knowledge of specific failure modes. That this is a distinct body of knowledge is most clearly apparent in medicine, where "normal" physiology is one scientific specialism and pathology another. Typically, a failure mode will be designated in terms of four primitives: (a) the symptoms (e.g., abnormal display); (b) how the failed components generate these symptoms (i.e., causal links between the type of component failure and its external manifestations); (c) the way in which the components may fail (e.g., fissure, overheating, swelling, shrinking); and (d) the causes of the component failure (either extrinsic factors: corrosion, speed of operation, safety violations; or intrinsic factors: quality of materials, demagnetization). In general, operator knowledge of failure modes tends to emphasize knowledge of symptoms, and there has been considerable research into whether knowledge of the other factors is necessary at the immediate supervisory level of employment. However, decision support can represent failure modes in all four of the aspects listed above, and data can be collected about these in the absence of data about symptoms. In general, data on (c) and (d) are important for prognosis and preventive action.

TIME MANAGEMENT

Embedded in every RPS is knowledge of temporal changes in the process, especially when there are time lags along causal chains of events or between operator intervention and actual effects. This suggests that expertise is associated with improved time processing.

However time still remains one of the most difficult problems to understand. Different schools of thought approach the problem in specific contexts and have reached a range of solutions which are difficult to integrate into a coherent framework.

In Artificial Intelligence, several authors have proposed complex computer models for the processing of temporal information. But the main concern of these studies is text comprehension and production, which may be why linguistics was the main source of inspiration for AI systems. Three entities are brought into play (Bestougeff & Ligozat, 1989):
- abstract representational systems which model temporal features of entities;
- natural language which expresses temporal notions by temporal markers and grammatical tense;
- the real world, which is represented.

Hence, representational systems are models of previously expressed temporal contents. They deal with temporal functions relating properties of events to intervals (Allen, 1984), or to instants and intervals (McDermott, 1982). They mainly establish coherence testing and proposition validity checking. This formal approach is very different from the psychological approach, which does not presuppose that people explicitly process representations of time at this level. In addition, this approach makes no attempt to design models of psychological time processing. Nevertheless, it could be useful in approaching some aspects of psychological time.

Two recent books cover the state of the art in this domain (Block, 1990; Macar et al., 1992). Both volumes are striking for their reserve. The authors are cautious when discussing the range of applicability of their results as regards to specific situations (e.g., very short or long time psychophysics) and methodologies used (e.g., prospective evaluations where subjects are informed about their evaluation task beforehand or retrospective judgments without preparation). The major difficulty inherent to this issue is the tight relationship between the temporal and semantic (e.g., causality) aspects of events. Time is not easy to isolate.

However a consensus may be emerging from these studies, as shown by Michon (1990) — one of the best known researchers in this domain — who argues that there is adaptation to time which precedes the experience of time, although some circularity is possible. Temporal representation is thus a conscious product of an implicit tuning to the temporal dynamics of the environment. If temporal adaptation is successful, time need not be represented, in particular at a conceptual level. Awareness and symbolic representations only come into play when problem-solving or communication activities are involved, but processing can be solely based on verisimilitude — some kind of *a posteriori* reconstruction based on similarity with well-known situations — or metaphor (many linguistic expressions of time are metaphoric).

Hence, even in process control, operator behavior may appear to be very well adapted to temporal aspects of the process, without there being any conscious processing of time. Thus researchers must cope with the same methodological difficulties as those encountered in experimental approaches.

Major contributions to this have been made by the De Keyser research team (mainly accessible through a substantial report by Richelle & De Keyser, 1992). The originality of this approach lies in the assumption that operators can use a number of different "Temporal Reference Systems" (conventional, task-specific, or emerging from action regularities) which may be modeled by abstract representational systems. However, although the authors acknowledge implicit processing of time, there is no clear distinction between explicit and implicit processing in their formal approach. Data collected by their team, which are specific to time processing, are very scarce, as is the case in the process control literature, and restricted to system start-up (see also Decortis, 1988). Expertise appears to be related to knowledge enrichment of process variable evolutions, which enables operators to elaborate typical scripts and use them as reference frameworks. An extensive analysis of such scripts has been performed in a rapid process control situation (fighter aircraft piloting) by Amalberti and Deblon (1992).

Another study shows an effect of expertise in bus traffic regulation (Mariné et al., 1988). These authors report more frequent temporal markers in experts' verbal reports than in novices' (however, authors only report frequencies and not percentages). According to Michon's line of reasoning, this could have been caused by communication needs inherent to this kind of activity. As a matter of fact, the bus traffic controller needs to communicate time representations to drivers. Before generalizing this result to process control, more data are needed.

A recent study of time expressions in verbal protocols collected during blast furnace supervision does not show any difference between experts and beginners (Hoc, in press). These data are compatible with Michon's point of view on the automatization of expert behavior (implicit tuning to the temporal features of the process under supervision).

In DES situations, the temporal dimension can cover a variety of cognitive variables which call for specifications. Three main ones will be discussed here:

a) Time can be used as an *activity support,* freeing operators from processing complex representations of causal relationships among variables. For example, it may be sufficient to memorize a malfunction script, with temporal landmarks, to act at the skill- or rule-based level, without any need for a causal interpretation of the script or calculation of latencies. Date and period memory can replace causal reasoning and calculation. External synchronizers may have high utility.

b) In dynamic situations, operators need to deal with evolutions (changes in variables). In this case, time is not processed in isolation. Rather *temporal functions* are processed, that is relationships between variables and time. Response latencies are processed at this level, as well as forms of response.

c) The *speed of the (technical) process* can have an effect on the course of cognitive processes. Temporal pressure introduces what are now well-known effects on cognitive strategies, for example, the introduction of planning before task execution in fighter aircraft piloting (Amalberti & Deblon, 1992). In blast furnace supervision, this aspect of time is not relevant in most cases, since decision-making can take ten to thirty minutes without any risk of hazard.

DIAGNOSTIC STRATEGIES

Central to decision support is the reduction of uncertainty. Strategies of diagnosis can be represented as ways of resolving uncertainty about which control actions are most appropriate. Uncertainty can arise from the unreliability of data, resulting in failure to detect the true state and evolution of the system. Alternatively, it may be due to inadequacies of the representational tools which are instantiated by these data, resulting in failure to interpret system states and evolutions as significant (i.e., as justifying action or further investigation).

We owe the most extensive descriptions of diagnostic strategies to Jens Rasmussen (1981, 1984, 1986), who mainly based his theoretical work on observations collected in electronic troubleshooting (Rasmussen & Jensen, 1974). He proposed a distinction between two broad kinds of strategies: topographic and symptomatic search.

(a) Topographic search relies upon system decomposition based on the topography of physical components. Thus search is supported by topological RPSs, following diverse kinds of flow passing through the system, considered as a network of mass, energy, or information flow; the system outputs being identified as deficient, as regards to available knowledge on normal operation, and search consisting of attempting to identify the individual component that has to be changed on the same basis (comparison between normal output and actual output). At times, this kind of search can be supported by a functional search based on functional RPSs. In this case, knowledge of functions can orient operators to a function which is not properly performed, and knowledge of relationships between this function and components.

(b) Symptomatic search relies on knowledge of relationships between symptoms and causes or syndromes. It can take one of the three following forms.

(i) pattern matching

Pattern matching is abundantly described in the literature, recently conceived within a schema approach (Amalberti & Deblon, 1992; Govindaraj & Su, 1988; Hoc, 1989b). Environmental cues (the current situation) are matched to a well-known schema and, at the same time, produce a diagnosis and an action decision. This mechanism is considered as implying two basic cognitive components: similarity matching (which retains the best fitted schemata) and frequency gambling (which selects the more frequently encountered schema when there is competition, especially in the case of underspecification).

These two primitives have been introduced by Reason (1990), and some extension is necessary to apply them to DES. Selection among competitive schemata does not depend only on frequency. Other factors are influential, all the more in situations where breakdowns, faults or malfunctions are infrequent. Among them, representativeness and availability are perhaps the best known (Kahneman & Tversky, 1972), closely related to typicality (Rosch, 1975). The degree of belief that an exemplar belongs to a class is not only related to the frequency of the exemplar, but also to the richness of the matching between the specific properties of the exemplar and the general properties of the class. For instance, it is difficult to admit a bird that does not fly (such as an ostrich) in the class of birds.

(ii) search in a decision table linking symptoms to causes

It integrates probabilistic search that relies on knowledge of relationships between malfunctions and their temporal precursors. Bayes' theorem permits the representation of the conditional probabilities of various malfunctions, given certain prior system states. The calculation of these values is an important way in which the entire history of the system and others like it can aid the supervisory task through decision support. Much probabilistic search is a process of screening an asymptomatic system for signs of impending malfunction. In this kind of search, it is crucial to collect and interpret system data in a way which achieves reliable negative results, that is, which performs tests whose statistical properties include a high probability that there will not be a malfunction if the prior system state does not indicate one. Where a malfunction is indicated, decision support should continue to revise the prediction as the situation develops, but not necessarily on the basis of the same kinds of data. For once a specific malfunction is suspected, it is necessary to focus search on that particular eventuality. This requires a strategy which achieves reliable positive results, that is, which performs tests whose statistical properties include a high probability that there will be a malfunction if the system state indicates this.

However, there is a controversy on the Bayesian nature of expert strategies which are subject to the same bias as other kinds of probabilistic reasoning. Nevertheless, in the diagnostic context, Rigney (1969) showed that a Bayesian model could account for the data if applied to the actual problem space used by the operators, which is very often different from the frameworks used for theoretical analyses.

(iii) hypothesis generation and test strategies

Great attention has been paid to hypothesis generation and test strategies, in more novel situations. Research on medical diagnosis has provided us with rich empirical evidence about these strategies (Elstein et al., 1978; Groen & Patel, 1988; Johnson et al., 1981; Kuipers & Kassirer, 1984; Patel & Groen, 1986), likewise blast furnace supervision (Hoc, 1989b). Two findings have to be stressed here: (a) confirmation biases, orienting operators to positive information (confirming current hypotheses) rather than negative information (disconfirming them); (b) the use of hypotheses formulated at different levels (from general to specific). More controversial data have been collected on the use of hypothetico-deductive strategies. Some data support the hypothesis of a wider use of this strategy in beginners than in experts (Groen & Patel, 1988), whereas others do not show any difference (Elstein et al., 1978) or identify the implementation conditions of this strategy in situations necessitating the formulation of a hypothesis to guide the gathering of information (Hoc, 1991).

The terminology adopted by Rasmussen for these strategies (topographic and symptomatic) is influenced by the original data collected in troubleshooting. If we wish to extend this framework to other kinds of situations (DES, computer program debugging, or medical diagnosis) we need to import a more psychological interpretation of the phenomena. Clearly, the main feature of topographic search is its orientation by knowledge of normal operation of the system, while symptomatic search relies on knowledge of abnormal operation (failure modes). So the data bases are very different, but it is quite unreasonable to imagine expert operators relying only on one type of knowledge. Rasmussen and Jensen's original study, together with many studies conducted in training settings (especially Duncan, 1985, 1987a, 1987b), show that topographic search is a novice strategy that enables a fault to be diagnosed with minimal knowledge of the system.

Rasmussen's two strategies relate primarily to the task of fault localization. In the supervision of dynamic environments, where prognosis is as important as state diagnosis, it is necessary to consider other strategies. Topographic and symptomatic search both depend on the system having been degraded sufficiently to generate diagnosable symptoms. However, early in the development of a malfunction, the causal chain linking failed component with symptom will not yet have established itself. Any pre-emptive action must therefore be based on probabilistic search.

TOWARD AN EXTENDED MODEL
OF DIAGNOSIS AND DECISION-MAKING
IN DYNAMIC SITUATIONS

For many years, models of diagnosis were dominated by a strong serial (vs. parallel) and rigid (invariant succession of phases) assumption about human activity. In addition, the human operator has long been considered as reacting to unexpected events, rather than proactive — anticipating events. The contribution of information theory and the psychological models which were derived from it — in particular the metaphor of the brain as a computer and the idea of limited channel — permeated the information gathering/ analysis and diagnosis/ decision-making/ action chain.

In recent years cognitive psychology, although often critical of the simplistic models of the 1950s, has continued to adhere to the notion of serial work decomposable into goals and subgoals (Newell & Simon, 1972; Rumelhart, 1975; Schank & Abelson, 1977). On the level of diagnosis, this sequentiality is clearly illustrated in the Klahr and Dunbar (1988) model mentioned earlier: search for facts/hypothesis generation/hypothesis testing for diagnosis, which is clearly distinct from decision-making and action.

Two major changes have taken place in research over the last ten years, which have altered this sequential picture of activity.

First, there is a more molar vision of human activity, with a prevalence of performance models rather than skill models (Hollnagel, 1993; Woods & Roth, 1988), and dynamic rather than static models. This change, which can be attributed to the influence of ergonomic psychology, and which has been supported by a more ecological orientation of investigative methods (a shift from the laboratory to the field), has revealed numerous interactions between phases of activities which had previously been viewed as independent and successive. For example, the Rasmussen model presented above sparked debate about the effects of backward loops from decision-making to diagnostic activities. Interactions appear at many other levels: between the action repertory and the choice of hypotheses (blast furnaces, aircraft piloting, medicine), pre-selection of hypotheses (before an incident) and fact recovery, and hypothesis formulation (risky process control such as airplane piloting). In all cases, the dynamic nature of the process introduces specific constraints on activity and resource management.

The second change touches on a more polymorphous vision of diagnosis prompted by the range of applications of the concept of diagnosis. The variety of points in common between diagnosis in process control, breakdown diagnosis, medical expertise, inquiry board diagnosis, or a diagnostic model embedded in an AI machine have been reduced: Actors' social roles are not the same and the stakes are different. Some (process control operators) are oriented toward the future and toward explanations which lead to action, others (inquiry boards, medical expertise) are oriented towards the past — a causal diagnosis based on the identification of the historical causal chain. Breakdown diagnosis, and doubtless diagnostic models installed in machines, are midway between these two extremes.

It is beyond the scope of this chapter to describe these different domains, but it is obvious that diagnostic models differ radically as a function of activity. It is worth pointing out that this plurality (and perhaps ambiguity) of domains associated with the concept of diagnosis is a frequent cause of an erroneous overgeneralization in psychological studies from one particular type of diagnosis to another. This is the case, for example, when an operator is given the role of a superexpert evaluating a protocol produced by other operators (a change of role from actor to judge). This is also the case, for example, when an operator is restricted to diagnosis without action (paper and pencil work), which deprives the researcher of interaction effects and modifies the stakes of the task.

The diagnosis and decision-making model presented in the remainder of this chapter is restricted to cases where the operator executes work whose main objective is not the diagnosis of problems (for example process control, breakdown and repair, etc.). These activities contrast with situations where the actual nature of the work is causal diagnosis itself, as is the case in medical or technical superexpertise, inquiry boards, and so on.

The findings presented in earlier sections of this chapter show that diagnosis in these conditions reveals itself to be an activity which is: (i) neither independent and separable from other activities (the diagnosis is part of a goal-oriented activity and is not the prime goal of the activity itself), and (ii) neither strictly contemporaneous to the problem (diagnosis can start before the problem occurs or on the contrary be postponed for a variety of reasons such as different current priorities or expectations on upcoming supplementary information).

These evolutions in the concept of diagnosis in goal-oriented activities can be described by three additional dimensions:

(a) *The Parallelism/Seriality Dimension* of activity covers the simultaneous management of a diagnostic loop and a process control loop (in particular in dynamic situations where this system continues to evolve). These two loops are not necessarily synchronous, and process control actions may continue with some degree of cognitive autonomy, whereas a diagnosis activity with information search at the conceptual or symbolic level is taking place in parallel on features of the specific situation. This parallelism dimension is governed by the representation of available resources and cost/efficiency trade-offs at each point in time; regulation evolves constantly, but there is a priority for the control loop over the diagnosis loop. This dimension can lead to shortcuts in diagnostic activities. In all cases, priority of control results in evolutions in the situation and at times its return to normal without causal diagnosis. These dynamic evolutions interfere considerably with the set of givens and hypotheses.

(b) *The Autonomy/Dependence* on diagnosis outcome and in particular its implications in terms of actions. This dimension is the feedback of actions on the level of diagnosis and type of hypothesis entertained. On the one hand, diagnosis can take place with no consideration as to future actions (prospective diagnosis in the strict sense). The situation and the operator's knowhow can considerably reduce action possibilities (the link with action repertory). In this case, the fact space is filtered and viewed through the knowledge of these possible actions which exist prior to the knowledge of the incidents. Diagnosis thus consists of restricting the hypotheses to ones that are compatible with the available actions (operationalization of diagnosis). For example, in the final approach below 150 meters in a transport plane the only choices are between stepping on the gas or landing. If the pilot receives a warning, the target level of diagnosis, the fact search and the working hypotheses will be the possibilities for stepping on the gas. This dimension is governed by the representation of the (action) plan and its flexibility.

(c) *Diagnosis at the Time of the Event/Differed Diagnosis Dimension.* Diagnosis was long viewed as an activity that was reactive and contemporary to the onset of problems. Studies on rapid process control (Amalberti & Deblon, 1992) show that diagnosis can also be anticipatory by simulating types of events in advance, imagining diagnostic problems, and preparing response plans. In this case, the problem is shifted and the activity consists of maintaining the process on the basis of expectations in order to keep the preplanned diagnosis and responses valid. In contrast, diagnosis can be voluntarily postponed to give priority to control in risky phases or because the temporal evolution of the situation may itself provide the key to diagnosis and thus economize resources compared to the cost of an immediate diagnosis (for example, diagnosis of a breakdown in a plant: Decortis, 1992; diagnosis of bus traffic incidents: Cellier, 1987; diagnosis of pathological pregnancies: Sébillotte, 1982; or relationships between diagnosis and action in rapid subway system control: Sénach, 1982).

The dimensions listed above are compatible with a diagnostic model (Figure 2) based on a system of symbolic representations built up by the operator for the circumstances and containing three facets: (i) a representation of the process and its goals (which enables anticipation), (ii) a representation of possible actions (which serves to orient the diagnosis towards a level of understanding and a decision adapted to the available options, and avoids unnecessary loss of resources) and (iii) a representation of the available resources (which enables regulation of cognitive activities and a compromise on the desired level of understanding).

The core of this extended model of diagnostic activities is risk-management and the level of understanding of the situation.

Because their resources are limited, operators need to strike a balance between two conflicting risks: an objective risk resulting from context (risk of accident) and a cognitive risk resulting from personal resource management (risk of overload and deterioration of mental performance).

To keep resource management feasible, the solution consists of increasing outside risks, simplifying situations, dealing only with a few hypotheses, and schematizing the real. To keep the outside risk within acceptable limits, the solution is to adjust the real to fit as much as possible with the simplifications set up during job preparation. This fit between simplification and reality is the outcome of anticipation.

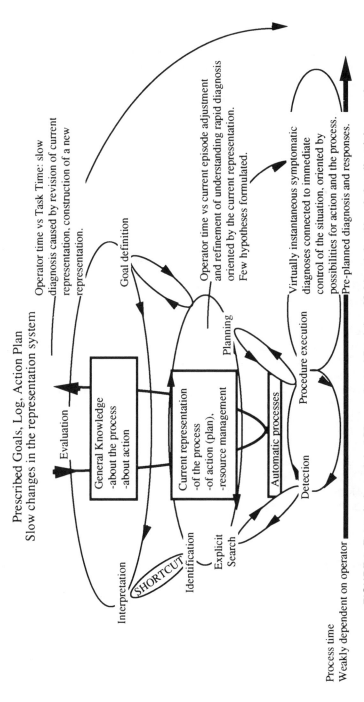

FIGURE 2. Extended model of Diagnosis and Decision-Making (after Hoc & Amalberti, in press)

Activity is organized and coordinated by a symbolic representation system of the current situation. Rasmussen's ladder has been incorporated (but reversed to symbolize the rising cost in resources when there is a need to revise the representation). The conception of a one-level diagnosis has been abandoned and replaced by several (possibly parallel) diagnosis loops characterized by different purposes and time perspectives as regards process evolution.

However, because of the mental cost of anticipation, the operator's final hurdle is to share resources between short-term behavior and long term anticipations. The tuning between these two activities is accomplished by heuristics which again rely upon another sort of personal risk-taking (Amalberti, 1992); as soon as the short-term situation is stabilized, operators invest resources in anticipations and leave the short term situation under the control of automatic behavior.

Any breakdown in this fragile and active equilibrium can result in unprepared situations, and turn to reactive behavior with a high demand on the level of understanding, a typical situation where operators are poor performers.

REFERENCES

Alengry, P. (1987). The analysis of knowledge representation of nuclear power plant control room operators. In H.J. Bullinger, & B. Shackel (Eds.), *Human-computer interaction: INTERACT'87* (pp. 209-214). Amsterdam: North-Holland.

Allen, J.F. (1984). Towards a general theory of action and time. *Artificial Intelligence, 23,* 123-154.

Amalberti, R. (1992). Safety in risky process-control: An operator centred point of view. *Reliability Engineering & System Safety, 38,* 99-108.

Amalberti, R., & Deblon, F. (1992). Cognitive modelling of fighter aircraft's process control: A step towards an intelligent onboard assistance system. *International Journal of Man-Machine Studies, 36,* 639-671.

Anderson, J.R. (1983). *The architecture of cognition.* Cambridge, MA: Harvard University Press.

Bainbridge, L. (1984). *Diagnostic skill in process operation.* Paper presented at the meeting of the *International Conference on Occupational Ergonomics.* Toronto, Canada.

Bainbridge, L. (1988). Types of representation. In L.P. Goodstein, H.B. Anderson, S.E. Olsen (Eds.), *Tasks, errors, and mental models* (pp. 70-91). London: Taylor & Francis.

Baudet, S., & Denhière, G. (1991). Mental models and acquisition of knowledge from text: Representation and acquisition of functional systems. In G. Denhière, & J.P. Rossi (Eds.), *Text and text processing* (pp. 55-75). Amsterdam, North-Holland.

Bestougeff, H., & Ligozat, G. (1989). *Outils logiques pour le traitement du temps* [Logical tools for time processing]. Paris: Masson.

Block, R.A. (Ed.). (1990). *Cognitive models of psychological time.* Hillsdale, NJ: Lawrence Erlbaum Associates.

Boreham, N., Foster, R.W., & Mawer, G.E. (1992). Strategies and knowledge in the control of the symptoms of a chronic illness. *Le Travail Humain, 55,* 15-34.

Boshuizen, H.P.A., & Schmidt, H.G. (1992). On the role of biomedical knowledge in clinical reasoning by experts, intermediates and novices. *Cognitive Science, 16,* 153-184.

Brajnik, G., Chittaro, L., Guida, G., Tasso, C., & Toppano, E. (1989, October). *The use of many diverse models of an artifact in the design of cognitive aids.*

Brajnik, G., Chittaro, L., Guida, G., Tasso, C., & Toppano, E. (1989, October). *The use of many diverse models of an artifact in the design of cognitive aids.* Paper presented at the *Second European Conference on Cognitive Science Approaches to Process Control,* Siena, Italy.

Brooke, J.B., & Duncan, K.D. (1983). A comparison of hierarchically paged and scrolling displays for fault finding. *Ergonomics, 26,* 465-477.

Cellier, J.M. (1987). Study of some determining elements of control orientation in a bus traffic regulation. *Ergonomics International* (pp. 766-768). London: Taylor & Francis.

Crossman, E.R.F.W. (1965). *The use of signal flow graphs for dynamics analysis of man-machine systems.* Oxford: Oxford University, Institute of Experimental Psychology.

Cuny, X. (1979). Different levels of analysing process control tasks. *Ergonomics, 22,* 415-425.

Decortis, F. (1988). Dimension temporelle de l'activité cognitive lors des démarrages de systèmes complexes [Temporal dimension of the cognitive activity during complex system start-up]. *Le Travail Humain, 51,* 125-138.

Decortis, F. (1992). *Processus cognitifs de résolution d'incidents spécifiés et peu spécifiés en relation avec un modèle théorique* [Cognitive processes solving specified and underspecified malfunctions in relation to a theoretical model]. Unpublished doctoral dissertation, University of Liège, Liège, Belgium .

Duncan, K.D. (1985). Representation of fault-finding problems and development of fault-finding strategies. *PLET, 22,* 125-131.

Duncan, K.D. (1987a). Fault diagnosis training for advanced continuous process installation. In J. Rasmussen, K.D. Duncan, & J. Leplat (Eds.), *New technology and human error* (pp. 209-221). Chichester: Wiley.

Duncan, K.D. (1987b). Reflections on fault diagnostic expertise. In J. Rasmussen, K.D. Duncan, & J. Leplat (Eds.), *New technology and human error* (pp. 261-269). Chichester: Wiley.

Elstein, A.S., Shulman, L.S., & Sprafka, S.A. (1978). *Medical problem-solving.* Cambridge, MA: Harvard University Press.

Goodstein, L.P. (1983). An integrated display set for process operators. In G. Johannsen, & J.E. Rijnsdorp (Eds.), *IFAC* (pp. 63-70). Oxford: Pergamon.

Goodstein, L.P., & Rasmussen, J. (1988). Representation of process state, structure and control. *Le Travail Humain, 51,* 19-37.

Govindaraj, T., & Su, Y.L. (1988). A model of fault diagnosis performance of expert marine engineers. *International Journal of Man-Machine Studies, 29,* 1-20.

Groen, G.J., & Patel, V.L. (1988). The relationship between comprehension and reasoning in medical expertise. In M.T.H. Chi, R. Glaser, & M.J. Farr (Eds.), *The nature of expertise* (pp. 287-310). Hillsdale, NJ: Lawrence Erlbaum Associates.

Guillermain, H. (1988, October). *Aide logicielle au diagnostic sur processus robotisé et évolution possible vers une extraction automatique des connaissances de base des experts* [Computer support to diagnosing an automated manufacturing process and possible evolution toward an automatic expert basic knowledge elicitation]. Paper presented at *ERGOIA'88,* Biarritz, France.

Hoc, J.M. (1988). *Cognitive psychology of planning.* London: Academic Press.

Hoc, J.M. (1989a). La conduite d'un processus à longs délais de réponse: Une activité de diagnostic [Controlling a continuous process with long response latencies: A diagnosis activity]. *Le Travail Humain, 52,* 289-316.

Hoc, J.M. (1989b). Strategies in controlling a continuous process with long response latencies: Needs for computer support to diagnosis. *International Journal of Man-Machine Studies, 30,* 47-67.

Hoc, J.M. (1991). Effet de l'expertise des opérateurs et de la complexité de la situation dans la conduite d'un processus continu à long délais de réponse: Le haut fourneau [Effects of operator expertise and task complexity upon the supercision of a continuous process with long time lags: A blast furnace]. *Le Travail Humain, 54,* 225-249.

Hoc, J.M. (in press). Operator expertise and verbal reports of temporal data: supervision of a long time lag process (blast furnace). *Ergonomics.*

Hoc, J.M., & Amalberti, R. (in press). Diagnosis: Some theoretical questions raised by applied research. *Current Psychology of Cognition.*

Hoc, J.M., & Samurçay, R. (1992). An ergonomic approach to knowledge representation. *Reliability Engineering and System Safety, 36,* 217-230.

Hollnagel, E. (1993). Models of cognition: Procedural prototypes and contextual control. *Le Travail Humain, 56,* 27-51.

Iosif, G.H. (1968). La stratégie dans la surveillance des tableaux de commande. I. Quelques facteurs déterminants de caractère objectif [The control panel monitoring strategy. I. Some objective determining factors]. *Revue Roumaine de Sciences Sociales, 12,* 147-163.

Johnson, P.E., Duran, A.S., Hassebrock, F., Moller, J., Prietula, M., Feltovich, P.J., & Swanson, D.B. (1981). Expertise and error in diagnostic reasoning. *Cognitive Science, 5,* 235-283.

Kahneman, D., & Tversky, A. (1972). Subjective probability: A judgment of representativeness. *Cognitive Psychology, 3,* 430-454.

Klahr, D., & Dunbar, K. (1988). Dual space space search during scientific reasoning. *Cognitive Science, 12,* 1-48.

Kuipers, B., & Kassirer, J.P. (1984) Causal reasoning in medecine: Analysis of a protocol. *Cognitive Science, 8,* 363-385.

Lind, M. (1991, September). *On the modelling of diagnostic tasks.* Paper presented at the *Third European Conference on Cognitive Science Approaches to Process Control,* Cardiff, U.K.

Lind, M., Osman, A., Agger, S., & Jensen, H. (1989, October). *Human-machine interface for diagnosis based on multilevel flow modelling.* Paper presented at the *Second European Conference on Cognitive Science Approaches to Process Control,* Siena, Italy.

Macar, F., Pouthas, V., & Friedman, W.J. (Eds.). (1992). *Time, action, and cognition.* Dordrecht: Kluwer.

Mariné, C., Cellier, J.M., & Valax, M.F. (1988). Dimensions de l'expertise dans une tâche de régulation de trafic: Règles de traitement et profondeur du champ spatio-temporel [Dimensions of expertise in a traffic control task: Processing rules and spatiotemporal field deepness]. *Psychologie Française, 33,* 151-160.

Michon, J.A. (1990). Implicit and explicit representation of time. In R.A. Block (Ed.), *Cognitive models of psychological time* (pp. 37-58). Hillsdale, NJ: Lawrence Erlbaum Associates.

Morrison, D.L., & Duncan, K.D. (1988). The effect of scrolling, hierarchically paged displays and ability on fault diagnosis performance. *Ergonomics, 31*, 889-904.

Newell, A., & Simon, H.A. (1972). *Human problem-solving.* Englewood Cliffs, NJ: Prentice-Hall.

Patel, V.L., & Groen, G.J. (1986). Knowledge-based solution strategies in medical reasoning. *Cognitive Science, 10,* 91-116.

Patrick, J. (1993). Cognitive aspects of fault-finding training and transfer. *Le Travail Humain, 56,* 187-209.

Rasmussen, J. (1981). Models of mental strategies in process plant diagnosis. In J. Rasmussen & W.B. Rouse (Eds.), *Human detection and diagnosis of system failures* (pp. 241-258). New York: Plenum.

Rasmussen, J. (1984). Strategies for state identification and diagnosis in supervisory control tasks, and design of computer-based support systems. *Advances in Man-Machine Systems Research, 1,* 139-193.

Rasmussen, J. (1986). *Information processing and human-machine interaction.* Amsterdam: North-Holland.

Rasmussen, J., & Jensen, A. (1974). Mental procedures in real life tasks: A case study of electronic troubleshooting. *Ergonomics, 17,* 293-307.

Rasmussen, J., & Rouse, W.B. (Eds.). (1981). *Human detection and diagnosis of system failures.* New York: Plenum.

Reason, J. (1990). *Human error.* Cambridge: Cambridge University Press.

Richard, J.F., Bonnet, C., & Ghiglione, R. (Eds.). (1990). *Traité de psychologie cognitive* [Handbook of cognitive psychology]. Paris: Dunod.

Richelle, M., & De Keyser, V. (1992). *The nature of human expertise* (report RFO/AI/18). University of Liège, Liège, Belgium.

Rigney, J.W. (1969). Simulation of corrective maintenance behavior. *Proceedings of the NATO Symposium "Simulation of human behavior"* (pp. 419-428). Paris: Dunod.

Rosch, E. (1975) Cognitive representation of semantic categories. *Journal of Experimental Psychology: General, 3,* 192-233.

Rumelhart, D. (1975). Notes on a schema for stories. In D. Bobrow & A. Collins (Eds.), *Language, thought and culture* (pp. 211-236). New York: Academic Press.

Samurçay, R., & Rogalski, J. (1988). Analysis of operator's cognitive activities in learning and using a method for decision making in public safety. In J. Patrick & K.D. Duncan (Eds.), *Human decision-making and control* (pp. 133-152). Amsterdam: North-Holland.

Schank, R.C., & Abelson, R. (1977). *Scripts, plans, goals, and understanding.* Hillsdale, NJ: Lawrence Erlbaum Associates.

Sébillotte, S. (1982). *Les processus de diagnostic au cours du déroulement de la grossesse* [The diagnosis process during pregnancy development]. Unpublished doctoral dissertation, University of Paris V, Paris, France.

Sénach, B. (1982). *Aide à la résolution de problèmes par la présentation graphique des données* [Supporting problem-solving by data graphical display] (Tech. Rep. No. CRER 8202R06). Rocquencourt, France: INRIA.

Simon, H.A., & Lea, G. (1974). Problem-solving and rule induction: a unified view. In L.W. Gregg (Ed.), *Knowledge and cognition* (pp. 105-128). Potomac, MD: Lawrence Erlbaum Associates.

Umbers, I.G. (1979). A study of the control skills of gas grid control engineers. *Ergonomics, 22,* 557-571.

Woods, D., & Roth, E. (1988). Aiding human performance (II): From cognitive analysis to support systems. *Le Travail Humain, 51,* 139-159.

3

Unitary Theories
of Cognitive Architectures

Johan KJAER-HANSEN
CEC Joint Research Centre, Ispra, Italy

Unitary theories of cognitive architectures have been suggested as "grand theories" of human cognition. Models of human cognition have been developed in order to predict human behavior through computer simulation. This chapter review three models, each based on unitary theories: Soar (Newell, 1990), ACT* (Anderson, 1983), and the Underspecification Theory (Reason, 1990). The notion of symbol systems is used as a guideline for specification of architectures, and specific attention is paid to the models as systems for information processing. Each of the models is briefly outlined, and the main components are discussed. Examples of research on regularities applied through the various architectures are characterized, especially in relation to complex domains and human expertise.

In the last couple of decades there has been an increasing interest within cognitive psychology and cognitive science to form global theories of human cognition. The aim has been to develop an understanding of the architecture and information processing, that is necessary but also sufficient to explain complex cognitive functions. The ambition of this investigation has been to explain cognitive functions in all their variety within a single architecture. As such it has been a way of formulating "grand theories" of human cognition, and as means for developing models for computer simulation of human behavior.

We may contrast *global theories* with *local theories* for human behavior, which are based on experimental investigations. Global theories have gained their content partially from such experimental investigations for local theories and partially from the notion of human cognition as being a result of information processing. The influence from the latter has found its root's in analogies of organizing and processing information in computers, and this bias has given it the name *information processing psychology*. By their very nature, global theories of human cognition just aim to be approximate, that is, to enable verification of findings on local phenomena with enough detail and evidence to justify their existence as coherent theories. As global theories provide a single framework for explanation of many aspects of human behavior, much effort has been devoted to the development of computer models for simulation studies.

Research on global theories of human cognition has paid its principal interest to the architecture of cognition. A cognitive architecture can be defined as the fixed[1] structure that provides the means (and constraints) for processing information. As such cognitive architectures provide the information processing framework within which cognitive functions can be defined.

The modeling of cognitive architecture can largely be separated into two opposing movements of conception. We shall refer to these conceptions as *the faculties of mind* and *unitary theories of cognition.*

The conception of the human mind as consisting of a set of "faculties" dates back into history and was promoted in the beginning of this century by researchers such as Gall, who introduced a "phrenological diagram" of the brain. Each cognitive function is assumed to be supported by a dedicated part of the cortex. Accordingly there exists specialized centers for achieving specialized cognitive functions, for example, language. The complex behavior of humans can be explained as the invocation of faculties. Many attempts have since been made to localize complex cognitive functions to specific spatial locations of the brain. A recent example is Chomsky's promotion of the concept of "mental organs" (Chomsky, 1980).

Luria (1973) suggests that one conceive the notion of cognitive functions as an expression of the invocation of the entire brain and not just specific tissue's of the brain. This suggestion proposes a new interpretation of cognitive functions as being *functional systems,* invoking not just a limited part of the cortex, but many parts at the same time. A functional system is characterized by the flexibility by which it can achieve tasks. The tasks and the result of achieving them are invariant, but the mechanisms supporting them can vary. The concept of functional systems introduces the notion of a layered model of complex cognitive functions, in which these higher level functions can be achieved by lower level mechanisms in a flexible way.

The notion of human cognition represented as a layered model has been the basic assumption for a set of unitary theories of cognition. This line of research conceives the complexes of the human mind as being the result of a limited set of intertwined structures and processes. The basic structure forms an architecture, characterized by a number of specialized information processes. The elements of such an architecture can be combined in a flexible way and thereby enable a large variety of responses of the cognitive system.

One might describe the differences between the unitary approach and the faculties approach, as whether a primitive set of structures and processes in combination can account for complex cognitive functions, or whether there is a one-to-one mapping, with a "mental organ" for each of the higher cognitive functions.

---

[1] Although fixed, we may envision an architecture to change gradually over time as a result of adaption.

The following sections present in more detail the characteristics of the unitary approach through a brief review of some of the most dominant unitary theories of human cognitive architecture.

SYMBOL SYSTEMS AND COGNITIVE ARCHITECTURE

When we talk about cognitive architectures, we address the properties of a system for handling symbols. Analogies with the way computers handle symbols at an appropriate level of description have provided us with the notion of *physical symbol systems* (Newell, 1990, 1980; Newell & Simon, 1972). The main source for this basic theory has been derived from computer science, in which the use of computers as symbol systems have a rich tradition.

Physical symbol systems (or symbol systems for short) can be characterized in a number of ways. At an abstract level, they can be described as systems, which take inputs based on patterns in outside structures (outside of the system) and provide for some *interpretation* (coding) into internal symbol structures. The result of internal processing provides for some response (again through interpretation) outside the system (decoding). Symbols are stored internally in *memory*, upon which *operations* are being performed. These are the basic components of symbol systems and these are the components that, in an abstract way, have provided a basic theory for the development of cognitive architectures.

Symbol systems take their definition within an *architecture*. The architecture provides the fixed structure within which functions for realizing the symbol system are achieved. We can view the distinction between symbol systems and architecture as one of content and structure.

The notion of symbol systems and architecture has been applied to provide theories of the cognitive architecture of the human mind. The architecture, which realizes the symbol system of human cognition, is not supposed to be equivalent to the physical structure of the human brain in the literal sense. It does however specify a functional system in which the basic symbol processing of the human mind can be described.

The relation between architecture and symbol systems provides us with a guidance for how higher level cognitive functions are brought about. The relation between the two carries the notion of two separate levels of description, one above the other. The architecture provides the means to achieve the symbol level. This conception, known within computer science as *virtual machines,* provides us with a theory for the way higher level cognitive functions can be achieved. In effect, the separation into levels of virtual machines defines distinct system levels, each characterized by different properties and each realized through the level beneath.

The notion of virtual machines on top of one another provides a way in which the approximation of rational and adaptive behavior of a cognitive system can be achieved. This orientation has been described by Rasmussen (1986) for representing system levels in an *abstraction hierarchy*.[2]

THREE THEORIES OF COGNITIVE ARCHITECTURES

As a way of illustrating some characteristics of cognitive architectures, the following sections briefly discuss three theories of cognitive architectures: *SOAR* (Newell, 1990), *ACT** (Anderson, 1983), and the *Underspecification Theory* (Reason, 1990).

All of the theories take as a basic assumption the unitary approach and all strive to describe the variety of cognitive functions in one framework. Each of them may be conceived as representing state of the art in modeling cognition and major contributions to the field. The theories of Soar and ACT* are closely linked to the synergy created in the area formed between cognitive psychology and computer science, and have mutually more in common than the Underspecification Theory.

Soar

Soar is a computer based embodiment of a *unified theory of cognition* set forth by Allen Newell (1990), defining an architecture capable of approximating rational and adaptive behavior. The notion of physical symbol systems has been formulated by Newell and is the underlying principle of Soar.

Historically Soar is the present result of research starting with the development of the Logic Theorist (Newell et al., 1957) and later the General Problem Solver (Ernst & Newell, 1969). Much of the theory forming the basis for the latter is collected in a general theory for human problem solving (Newell & Simon, 1972). The present architecture was initially developed in 1982 by Laird, Rosenbloom, & Newell (Laird et al., 1986) and collects much of the theory developed since the early days.

Soar is characterized by a uniform architecture. All tasks done by Soar are formulated by problem spaces; there is only one long-term memory consisting of productions; productions are matched with memory elements of working memory and all production that matches are applied. Subgoals are generated as a result of insufficient knowledge in the present problem space, and learning is achieved through chunking information as a result of subgoaling.

Soar specifies a basic organization of memory and primitive processing functions, called the symbol level (Figure 1). It does however go beyond this level of representation and build two abstraction levels above, called problem

---

[2] The application of distinct cognitive levels on a hierarchy of abstractions has been described in relation to The Underspecification Theory (Reason, 1990) in Kjær-Hansen et al. (1991).

space level, and knowledge level. Each of the three levels in Soar is organized as a virtual machine and each formulate a coherent *computational model*.

The *symbol level*, which is the lowest level, contains four major mechanisms: *recognition memory* (long-term memory), *working memory* (short-term memory), *decision procedure* (selector of next action), and *chunker* (providing the means for learning).

The decision procedure generates new elements in working memory by matching productions (from recognition memory) with the existing contents of working memory and asserting those that match into working memory (assertions may trigger other productions). On the basis of preferences a problem space, state, or an operator is selected.

During problem solving, situations may arise when Soar has incomplete or missing knowledge about which problem space, state, or operator to choose to solve a problem. In that case a new (sub)goal is defined and immediately processed. When the (sub)problem has been solved and the subgoal has been reached, Soar *chunks* the knowledge that was used to solve the problem of the subgoal (Laird et al., 1985; Rosenbloom, 1983). This knowledge is coded as productions and immediately added to the long-term recognition memory.

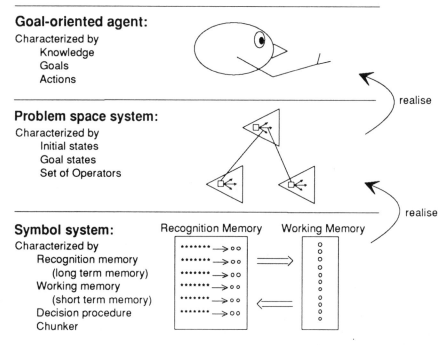

Goal-oriented agent:
Characterized by
   Knowledge
   Goals
   Actions

   realise

Problem space system:
Characterized by
   Initial states
   Goal states
   Set of Operators

   realise

Symbol system: Recognition Memory   Working Memory
Characterized by
   Recognition memory
      (long term memory)
   Working memory
      (short term memory)
   Decision procedure
   Chunker

FIGURE 1. The Soar architecture described at three levels of computational models (adapted from Newell, 1990).

The *problem space level* (the level above the symbol level) is based on the Problem Space Hypothesis (Newell, 1980), which argues for the existence of four model elements: *goals, problem spaces, states,* and *operators.* A task to solve is given through a goal. By choosing a problem space the environment for problem solving is selected, and a set of states can be explored by applying operators to these states. At any given time is has to be decided which problem space, state, or operator to use. When knowledge is unavailable for making this selection, Soar automatically sets up a new goal (a *subgoal*) of resolving this problem.

At the *knowledge level* (Newell, 1982) Soar can be described as a goal-oriented knowledgeable agent in an environment. It has *perceptions* of the environment and on the basis of a *body of knowledge* about the environment it can take *actions.* The body of knowledge is like a memory, but with no details of how it is encoded (this is implemented at the lower levels). Behavior at the knowledge level is based on the *principle of rationality:* If an agent has knowledge that one of its actions will lead to one of its goals, then the agent will select that action.

Soar has been applied to a large variety of tasks. The dominant search for psychological validity has been within problem solving, learning, and immediate-response tasks. It has been applied to syllogistic reasoning, natural language comprehension, algorithmic design, and so on. However, no major applications have been made with Soar to the modeling of human behavior in complex working environments.

ACT*

Although ACT* clearly belongs to the unitary approach, John Anderson has taken a critical stand concerning the simplicity that can be applied in the formulation of theories of cognitive architectures. The basic framework of ACT* can however be stated in simplified (although only approximate) terms, as done in the following.

The theory upon which ACT* (Anderson, 1983) is based is the most recent embodiment of a series of theories starting with ACTE (Anderson, 1976), and later ACTF (Anderson et al., 1977). As a computational framework ACT* specifies a set of invariant properties about its structure and some rules for ways in which to operate on the structure. One of the cornerstones in the theory of ACT* is the structure of memory.

The framework provided by ACT* is formed by three memories interconnected through a set of information processes (Figure 2). ACT* has a *working memory,* which contains the information that the system can utilize immediately. The information is provided by retrieval from the *declarative memory,* from temporal structures provided from the outside world by encoding processes, and by the application of productions from the *production memory.* The declarative long-term memory contains memory elements, each of which carry a degree of activation, in a semantic net. Productions in the production memory have a set of conditions in the working memory, that on activation create new memory elements in the working memory.

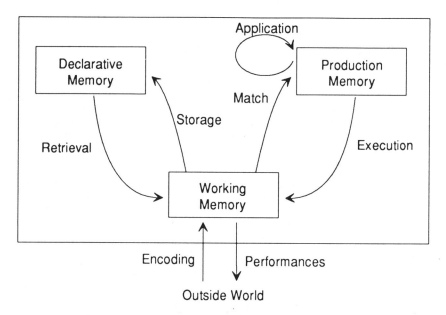

FIGURE 2. The ACT* cognitive architecture (adapted from Anderson, 1983).

The processes interconnecting the different kinds of memory form a unified set of primitives for processing information. The set of processes consists of some *encoding processes,* which provide the working memory with information about the outside world. Actions to the outside world are supported by *performance processes* based on commands in the working memory. The content of the declarative memory is formed and updated through *storage processes* on the basis of units of knowledge in the working memory: Likewise, the content of the working memory is provided by *retrieval processes,* based on units in the long-term declarative memory.

Memory elements in working memory are brought into contact with the productions of the production memory through *match processes,* and *execution processes* bring the actions of matched productions into working memory. The acquisition of new productions is done through *application processes.*

Anderson (1983) introduces a tri-code theory for representing knowledge. The theory assumes three different types of representation: temporal strings, spatial images, and abstract propositions. Temporal strings are created to record the sequential structure of events, spatial images preserve the configuration of elements of a spatial array, and abstract properties encode meaning.

As a theory, ACT* covers a large amount of regularities; at the immediate-response level it covers properties such as priming, fact retrieval, and memory effects. At higher levels of cognition, ACT* can account for elementary programming, geometry proofs, and language learning. Like Soar, ACT* has not been applied to model human behavior in complex environments.

The Underspecification Theory

Whereas the theories of Soar and ACT* have emerged in a scientific environment in which the analogy to the processing of information in computers has been a major source for the formulation of theories, the development of the Underspecification Theory (UT) has come in a different scientific environment, in which the purposes are slightly different.

To take the similarities between the different approaches first: Both traditions have urged for a theory for the basic cognitive architecture, and both have chosen the unitary approach as the basic standard. In the case of the UT, however, one main design criterion was the "design for a fallible machine". This emphasis was introduced due to interest in human error. To quote from James Reason's book about the UT (Reason, 1990, p. 125), the question raised was "... what kind of information-handling device could operate correctly for most of the time, but also produce the occasional wrong responses characteristic of human behavior?"

In the UT, the cognition architecture is presumed to possess two distinct structural components: a limited, serial, but computational powerful *working memory* (WM), and a virtually limitless *knowledge base* (KB).

The KB holds a vast set of structural knowledge encoded in frames or schema including both declarative and procedural knowledge. The knowledge of these structures captures the experience of an individual.

The WM represents a working area for the cognition processes, the management and the temporal storage of data. The role of the WM is: (1) to assess the external and internal cues of data from the environment to match with similarities in the KB; (2) to decide whether the hypothesis is appropriate, and if not (3) to reiterate the search with revised cues.

The cognitive architecture has two primitives for selecting stored knowledge units and bringing them into WM (Figure 3). These primitives, *similarity-matching* (SM) and *frequency gambling* (FG), operate in a parallel, distributed and automatic fashion within the KB. SM matches perceived cues coming from the work environment with corresponding diagnostic cues described in the KB. FG solves possible conflicts between partially matched hypotheses selected by SM, in favor of the more frequent, already encountered and well-known item of knowledge.

A third primitive, *direct inference* (DI), operates in WM when the SM and FG have not successfully identified an already compiled plan of actions contained in the knowledge base. DI is based on analogical and inductive/deductive reasoning.

Based on the UT, a cognitive model named COSIMO (COgnitive SImulation MOdel) has been developed to simulate human decision making and behavior in complex working environments (Cacciabue et al., 1989, 1992). The model is used to study human behavior in simulated accident situations and to identify suitable safety recommendations as well as reliability and effectiveness of procedures. The domain in which the model has been applied is supervision and control of nuclear installations.

In the COSIMO model it is assumed that, given the emergency situations in which it is to be applied, no sophisticated reasoning, such as direct inference, is performed and that the operator resorts to previous experience on similar cases. Consequently, COSIMO focuses on the KB of the dual architecture and on the cognitive primitives of SM and FG only. The combination of the capabilities of the KB component and the processing primitives of SM and FG supports a rapid selection of a frame for action.

As a computer model, the UT has been applied to the skill-based behavior in complex environments. Specifically the model has been applied to control a simulation of an auxiliary system of a nuclear-power plant (Cacciabue et al., 1992). Additionally the UT has been used to model the retrieval of incomplete knowledge (Marsden, 1987).

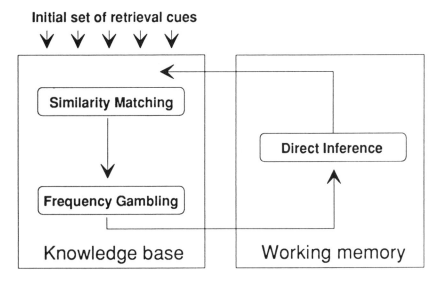

FIGURE 3. The architecture supporting the Underspecification Theory (Cacciabue et al., 1992).

DISCUSSION

Each of the theories of cognitive architectures discussed are based on the unitary approach, and as such represents the state of the art within research in this direction. The basic view held by the approaches discussed is that human cognition can be described as an information processing system. The models all call upon a basic arrangement of memory elements acted upon through a limited array of elementary information processes. The systems react upon stimulus from the environment according to rules guarding the cognitive architecture. They all focus on the elements of cognition and build complexes of cognitive functions from that. This characterization captures the strengths and weakness of the models.

An aspect of specific importance in this context, is how human expertise can be modeled and explained. Although the theories discussed do address the differences in strategy and behavior between experts and novices, they provide only little account of the structure of knowledge utilized by humans confronting complex systems. The models are rich on general control theory, but lack specifications on how human expertise in complex and rich domains develops and how it may be properly formalized.

The work on Soar and ACT* have dedicated little interest to the specific requirements of humans in complex domains, while the Underspecification Theory in its computer embodiment of COSIMO has been applied to model human supervisory control of nuclear power stations.

The information processing approach has been around for some time, and it has provided profound knowledge on cognitive behavior. Questions are however being raised as to whether theories of cognition should address the cognitive architecture as its basic principles. John Anderson has partially abandoned his approach taken in the work on ACT*, because "... it is just not possible to use behavioral data to develop a theory of the implementation level ..." (Anderson, 1990, p. 24).

Research on modeling of cognition has taken new directions, in which the notion of cognition as being the result of cognitive primitives has been partially abandoned. Instead the modeling of the overall behavior of human's and their activities is suggested (Hollnagel, 1993; Hollnagel & Woods, 1983). In this direction to model human behavior and expertise in complex domains, the main emphasis is on the structure of the tasks performed and the competencies to accomplish that.

REFERENCES

Anderson, J. R. (1976). *Language, memory, and thought.* Hillsdale, NJ: Lawrence Erlbaum Associates.
Anderson, J. R. (1983). *The architecture of cognition.* Cambridge, MA: Harvard University Press.

Anderson, J. R. (1990). *The adaptive character of thought.* Hillsdale, NJ: Lawrence Erlbaum Associates.

Anderson, J. R., Kline, P. J., & Beasley, C. M. (1977). A theory of the acquisition of problem-solving skill. In J.R. Anderson (Ed.), *Cognitive skills and their acquisition* (pp. 45-55). Hillsdale, N.J: Lawrence Erlbaum Associates.

Cacciabue, P. C., Decortis, F., Mancini, G., Masson, M., & Nordvik, J. P. (1989, September). *A cognitive model in a black board architecture: Synergism of AI and Psychology.* Paper presented at the *Second European Conference on Cognitive Science Approaches to Process Control.* Siena, Italy.

Cacciabue, P. C., Decortis, F., Drozdowicz, B., Masson, M., & Nordvik, J. P. (1992). COSIMO: A cognitive simulation model of human decision making and behaviour in accident management of complex plants. *IEEE Transactions on Systems, Man, and Cybernetics, 22,* 1058-1074.

Chomsky, N. (1980). Rules and representation. *Behavioral and Brain Sciences, 3,* 1-61.

Ernest, G. W., & Newell, A. (1969). *GPS: A case study in generality and problem solving.* New York: Academic Press.

Hollnagel, E. (1993). *Reliability of cognition: Foundations of human reliability analysis.* London: Academic Press.

Hollnagel, E., & Woods, D. D. (1983). Cognitive Systems Engineering: New wine in new bottles. *International Journal of Man-Machine Studies, 18,* 583-606.

Kjær-Hansen, J., Cacciabue, P. C., & Drozdowicz, B. (1991, June). *A framework for cognitive simulation.* Paper presented at the *CADES* meeting, Paris.

Laird, J. E., Rosenbloom, P. S., & Newell, A. (1985). *Towards chunking as a general learning mechanism.* Pittsburgh, PA: Carnegie-Mellon University, Department of Computer Science.

Laird, J. E., Rosenbloom, P. S., & Newell, A. (1986). *Universal Subgoaling and chunking: The automatic generation and learning of goal hierarchies.* Berlin: Kluwer Academic Publishers.

Luria, A. R. (1973). *The Working Brain: An introduction to neuropsychology.* Harmondsworth: Penguin Books.

Marsden, P. (1987). *The actual frequency of encounter of American Presidents.* Manchester: University of Manchester, Department of Psychology.

Newell, A., Shaw, J. C., & Simon, H. A. (1957, Sept.). Empirical explorations of the logic theory machine: A case study in heuristics. Paper presented at the *Western Joint Computer Conference.* Washington, DC.

Newell, A., & Simon, H. A. (1972). *Human problem solving.* Englewood Cliffs, NJ: Prentice-Hall.

Newell, A. (1980). Reasoning, problem-solving and decision processes: The problem space as a fundamental category. In N. Nickerson (Ed.), *Attention and performance VIII* (pp. 105-120). Hillsdale, NJ: Lawrence Erlbaum Associates.

Newell, A. (1982). The knowledge level. *Artificial Intelligence, 18,* 53-70.

Newell, A. (1990). *Unified theories of cognition.* Cambridge, MA: Harvard University Press.

Reason, J. (1990). *Human error.* Cambridge, UK: Cambridge University Press.

Rosenbloom, P. S. (1983). *The chunking of goal hierarchies: A model of practice and stimulus-response compatibility* (Tech. Rep. No. 83-148). Pittsburgh, PA: Carnegie-Mellon University, Computer Science Department.

4

Simulation of Cognition: Applications

Pietro Carlo CACCIABUE
CEC Joint Research Centre, Ispra, Italy
Erik HOLLNAGEL
Human Reliability Associates

This paper gives an overview of the current state of the art in man-machine systems interaction studies, focusing on the application of simulation of cognition dedicated to the highly automated working environments and the role of humans in the control loop. In particular, it is argued that the need for sound approaches to design and analysis of Man-Machine Systems (MMS) has given rise to two categories of modeling: macro-cognition and micro-cognition models. These architectures, theoretically, can cover all possible varieties of models of cognition. A number of existing model developments are described from the viewpoint of their domains of application, analyzing their validity and the scope of application.

The interest in and concern for human cognition has gathered momentum for a number of years and seems at the present time — the early 1990s — to have become a sweeping force. This is mainly due to the recognition from industrial applications that human cognition is an important constituent of system performance. The change started with the slow acknowledgment that man-machine systems (MMSs) were of a different nature than purely technical systems. Human factors engineering (ergonomics) had developed an approach to adjusting the interface between the human operator and the machine so that the worst violations of human performance integrity were avoided. But human factors engineering still considered a MMS as *a human + a machine,* hence as a simple aggregation of distinct elements, rather than as a joint system with properties that might differ from what was known for either part. The increasing concern for the prevention of unwanted consequences in complex systems slowly forced the focus of attention to turn from the overt manifestations of the interaction and the interface itself to the processes and functions that caused and shaped the interaction (Hollnagel, 1993). As a result, a new set of terms such as cognition, cognitive modeling, cognitive engineering, and so on, have practically become buzz-words in the general process control community.

Moreover, the need to account for all factors which play an important role in the control of a plant has led to modeling the man machine system using computer based simulations. This need is naturally explained, by analogy, with the evolution of analytical techniques for technological systems: In linear system theory, for example, it has been shown that the optimization of system performance can only be achieved if the dynamics of the system to be controlled are known and a performance criterion is defined; in optimal filter theory, one needs also to be informed about the statistics of the disturbances to be compensated. It is thus natural to conclude that, for the correct control of a plant, a model of the total man-machine system should become available (Mancini, 1986). There exist in the literature many reviews of the various approaches and methodologies dedicated to this modeling issue: Examples of well structured and complete analysis of the state of the art, made at different times and thus reflecting slightly different focuses, are the works of Pew, Baron, and colleagues (1977), of Rouse (1980), of Sheridan (1986) and the more recent survey of Stassen, Johannsen, and Moray (1990).

In this paper we will review the existing models of cognition from the viewpoint of the domains to which they have been applied, identifying also the scope and quality of the analysis that they can perform. We will concentrate firstly on the identification of two broad categories of models of cognition, that is macro-cognition and micro-cognition approaches, which can include all modeling developments. We will then discuss models of cognition in relation to four domains of application, namely Design, Analysis and Evaluation, Training, and On-line Support. Finally, some conclusions will be made identifying the major problems and possible ways of solution for the application of models of cognition.

THE SIMULATION OF COGNITION

Human cognition is not a single thing or a single phenomenon. It can be viewed from many aspects and in many contexts. There are many different motivations for being interested in human cognition and these will to a large extent determine where the focus is put and which techniques and methods are applied. One particular interest is the simulation of cognition in the service of a purpose — in order to solve a practical problem.

The simulation of cognition, as a scientific endeavor, is quite old. Many of the developments which have led to the present state-of-the-art have their roots in the simulation of cognition that took place in the late 1960s and early 1970s — primarily at the Carnegie-Mellon University (Newell & Simon, 1972). This type of simulation must be distinguished clearly from the type of simulation we are talking about here. One way of doing that is to make a distinction between micro-cognition and macro-cognition.

Micro-Cognition And Macro-Cognition

Micro-cognition is here used as a way of referring to the detailed theoretical accounts of how cognition takes place in the human mind. This distinguished it from the concern about cognition that takes place within Artificial Intelligence. Here the focus is on the "mechanisms of intelligence" *per se*, rather than the way the human mind works. Micro-cognition is concerned with the building of theories for specific phenomena and with correlating the details of the theories with available empirical and experimental evidence. Typical examples of micro-cognition are studies of human memory, of problem solving in confined environments (for example, the Towers of Hanoi), of learning and forgetting in specific tasks, of language understanding, and so on. Many of the problems that are investigated are "real," in the sense that they correspond to problems that one may find in real-life situations - at least by name. But when they are studied in terms of micro-cognition the emphasis is more on experimental control than on external validity, on predictability within a narrow paradigm rather than on regularity across conditions and on developing models or theories that go in depth rather than in breadth. Micro-cognition relinquishes the coupling between the phenomenon and the real context to the advantage of the coupling with the underlying theory or model.

Macro-cognition refers to the study of the role of cognition in realistic tasks, that is in interacting with the environment. Macro-cognition only rarely looks at phenomena that take place exclusively within the human mind or without overt interaction. It is thus more concerned with human performance under actual working conditions than with controlled experiments. Typical examples of macro-cognition are diagnosis, controlling an industrial process, landing an aircraft, writing a program, designing a house, planning a mission, and so forth. Some phenomena may, in principle, belong to both categories. Examples are problem solving, decision making, communication, information retrieval, and so on. But if they are treated as macro-cognition the interest is more on *how* they are performed and how well they serve to achieve their goals than on the details of *what* goes on in the mind while they are performed.

The simulation of micro-cognition is therefore radically different from the simulation of macro-cognition. The former is found in most of the early AI systems, such as EPAM and the General Problem Solver, and has more recently reached its high point in the theory of unified cognition — SOAR (Newell, 1990). The latter is found in — as yet — only a few cases such as COSIMO (Cacciabue et al., 1992), CES (Woods et al., 1987), and AIDE (Amalberti and Deblon, 1992).

Macro-Cognition And Simulation

The simulation of (macro-)cognition is always done with a specific practical purpose in mind. The concern is therefore basically one of maintaining a sufficient correspondence between the known or observed regularities of the target phenomenon and the outcome of the simulation. In technical terms, the simulation must be *isomorphic* to the phenomenon being modeled. There are many reasons why a simulation of cognition is used rather than, for example, a study of what happens in practice. It depends on the specific purpose (cf. later). Typical reasons are that access to a simulation may be easier than access to a workplace, that a simulation may cover a wider range of situations and events than can easily be observed, that a simulation may be controlled and restarted "at will" (for example, using snapshots and breakpoints or partial backtracking), and that a simulation provides a better record of what went on. (Many of these advantages are, of course, contingent upon how well the simulation has been made.)

The simulation of cognition should not be performed for the purpose of studying cognition in itself, but rather for the purpose of studying the kinds of performance where cognition plays a significant part. The relevant occurrences are those that manifest themselves in overt and observable performance, rather than those that only take place in the mind of the agent. It would therefore be more correct to talk of the simulation of cognition-based performance; but since this is rather cumbersome, we will continue to use the term "simulation of cognition." To emphasize that the focus is on macro-cognition rather than micro-cognition, the following definition is offered:

> The simulation of cognition can be defined as the replication, by means of computer programs, of the performance of a person (or a group of persons) in a selected set of situations. The simulation must stipulate, in a pre-defined mode of representation, the way in which the person (or persons) will respond to given events. The minimum requirement to the simulation is that it produces the response the person would give. In addition the simulation may also produce a trace of the changing internal mental states of the person.

When the simulation of cognition is contemplated as the possible solution to a problem, it is important to make clear whether the simulation is going to correspond to empirical or theoretical knowledge. The difference between the two views is captured in Figure 1. In the first case the simulation corresponds to the dominant relations that are found in the empirical knowledge — which in turn is based on the regularity of the work environment (cf. also the notion of requisite variety, Hollnagel & Cacciabue, 1991). In the second case the simulation corresponds to the required relations that are derived from the underlying theory — which in its turn is based on the ontology of cognition. There should, hopefully, be a substantial correspondence between the empirical knowledge and the theories of cognition, hence also between the dominant relations and the required relations. If this correspondence is insufficient, something is terribly wrong. In any case it is safer to base the simulation on the dominant relations; theories may come and go, but the regularities and constraints of the real world are less likely to change suddenly.

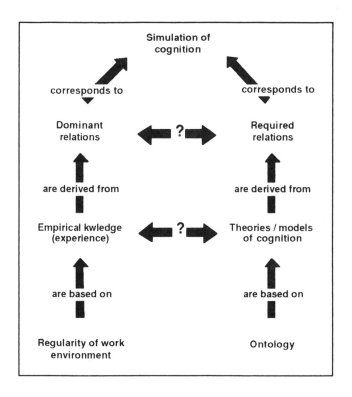

FIGURE 1: Role and scope of Simulation of Cognition

DOMAINS OF APPLICATIONS

In order to clarify better the scope of human behavior simulation and how it is used in many domains it is important to bear in mind that a model primarily is an efficient way to structure certain knowledge. The knowledge attempts to capture a part of the reality by means of a set of abstractions, such as mathematical relations, words, graphical symbols, and so on. A model is often used without an underlying theory, simply to describe some links between input and outputs. This is, however, an improper use since it provides no way of assessing the coherence of abstractions. When reviewing the domains of applications of human behavior simulation, it is therefore crucial to realize the limits and the terms of a model in relation to its goals.

In principle, there exist four domains of application, each of which has fostered several developments and simulations of human behavior modeling at various levels of complexity and generality. These are the domains of Design, Analysis and Evaluation, Training, and On-line Support.

Design

In the design of a process or a plant, the consideration of human cognition primarily affects the interfaces for the Supervision and Control (S&C) systems and the procedures for the plant management. Moreover, the evaluation and the optimization of the overall design of the plant requires the availability of a model to predict performance during both normal and contingency situations.

Design of Interfaces

The introduction of the human component for the design of display and information interfaces has been developing since the 1960's, with the application of models based on "information theory" (Senders, 1964) and "queuing theory" (Carbonell, 1966) for the evaluation of the cost of performing observation of information displays. The main weakness of these approaches was that they relied on environment properties or exogenous factors, such as uncertainty, system knowledge, degree of expertise, and strategic thinking, rather than on endogenous factors. The use of models based on Optimal Control Theory (OCT) and Optimal Estimation Theory (OET) (Kleinman & Curry, 1977; Stein & Wewerinke, 1983) already represented a step forward. These models implied the existence of an internal model, even if simple and related to the physical system, and of the estimation aspect that underlies the detection factor and orients the information acquisition.

The current techniques for the design of interfaces aim at formulating display systems which support the operator's perception and attention and enhance the understanding of physical processes and conceptual reasoning about plant behavior (Lind, 1991; Woods, 1984). The basic theme of these approaches is that the information content of the data depends on the state of the viewer person rather than on the properties of the display alone; the two important principles to analyze interface design are therefore (1) the study of the global properties of the stimulus and (2) a concept driven or top-down analysis starting from the person's internal model about the physical processes and the plant under control. The use of simulation of cognition in the design of user interfaces is nowadays a practice, based on a large amount of literature, work experience, and methods (Helander, 1988; Life, Narborough-Hall, & Hamilton, 1991; Weir & Alty, 1991).

Design of Procedures

The design of procedures in complex systems has for many years been a useful way to optimize plant production and safety and minimize operator workload (in order of priority!). The task analysis, which breaks down a task into sequences of "elementary" actions and control decisions, has progressively changed the focus from the analysis of the actual control procedure selected at the end of the reasoning process toward the aspects of human cognition related to the operator's decision making (Rasmussen, 1986), typically described as the performance of an internal information processing mechanism. This evolution of the design process of procedure closely follows the evolution in the role of the operator from a prime contributor in direct control of the physical process to a supervisor and decision maker of an automated system governed by computers. In this sense, the previously mentioned models, based on optimal control theory and queuing theory, which have been extensively used in design and analysis of procedures in domains like civil aviation (Baron et al, 1980 or Rouse, 1977), have to be updated by models based on Cognitive Task Analysis (CTA), which dedicate greater attention to the sequence of the information process involved in a control decision task.

Broadly speaking, there are two ways to tackle the issue of CTA for the design of procedures in complex plants control (Grant & Mayes, 1991; Hollnagel, 1989a; Kieras, 1988; Moray et al., 1992):

* The first way applies techniques for analyzing tasks which can be encoded in computer programs. In this way criteria other than modeling human cognition are considered, for example, logical structuring of rules, validation, maintenance, and so on. The first attempt to CTA modeling in this way was the GOMS (Goals, Operators, Methods, and Selection rules) type analyses (Card et al., 1983), which have been followed by models like ICS (Interactive Cognitive System) of Barnard (1985). These models try to account, in a "fully orchestrated way," for the processes of perception, memory, understanding, problem solving, and action during the performance of tasks in complex working environments.

* The second way represents an extension of the traditional task analysis, whereby the constituents processing resources for cognitive activity are studied and a general relationship between the properties of the human cognitive system and the characteristics of overt behavior are defined (Hollnagel & Woods, 1983).

Prototyping and Paradigms of Performance Predictions

Apart from the specific domains of interfaces and of procedures, the work in design of complex systems has also given rise to a variety of approaches oriented to the prediction of human performance during the management of the plant; models, paradigms, and frameworks have been developed at different levels of abstraction. In this category one of the most widely used frameworks for categorizing cognition developed in the 1980's is the Skill-, Rule-, and Knowledge-based (SRK) behavior model of Rasmussen (1986). The SRK framework, tightly coupled to the "step ladder" representation of the decision making, represents an often used model of human behavior adopted for simulating operator response in many fields and for many purposes: from design to safety and reliability, training and decision support development. Other approaches which have attempted to provide architectures describing human cognition in general are: Newell's SOAR model (1990), Anderson's ACT model (1983), Brunswik's lens model (Hammond et al., 1980), and the previously mentioned ICS model (Barnard, 1985).

Most of these simulation architectures are models of micro-cognition, as defined earlier. In order to be used as reasonable representations of human behavior in complex situations they may, for instance, be combined with a particular mathematical formalism and tailored to a specific working environment. In particular, the fuzzy set theory (Zadeh, 1965) has been one of the major methods adopted by many authors for the representation of imprecise and uncertain behavior of human beings. Examples of models using fuzzy sets theory are MESSAGE (Boy & Tessier, 1985) or KARL (Knaeuper & Rouse, 1985).

Analysis and Evaluation

Risk and Reliability Analysis.

The Probabilistic Safety Assessment (PSA) of plants is gradually becoming a common practice in domains other than the nuclear energy production, for example, as in chemical plants and avionics systems. A PSA consists of two main parts: the systems reliability assessment and the human reliability assessment (HRA). The latter, although tackled only in a second phase of the evolution of PSA, has become of primary importance due to the fundamental role of operators in recent accident and events which have produced catastrophic consequences. In HRA the consideration of the cognitive aspects of human behavior has developed in a similar way as in design. Indeed, the first systematic attempt to evaluate the probability of human erroneous actions, the method THERP (Swain & Guttman, 1980), does not include a consideration of the dynamic cognitive factors that affect operator behavior. The development of a second generation of approaches of HRA methods, following the THERP approach (Dougherty, 1990, 1991), has not succeeded to modify this fundamental drawback and even a model like HCR (Hannaman et al., 1984), which is based on the SRK model, fails to provide a proper treatment of human cognition.

The natural evolution of the human reliability approaches has led to attempts to solve the problem of HRA in terms of the "Reliability of Cognition" (Hollnagel, 1991). These solutions account for the dynamic effects of endogenous and exogenous factors on the inappropriate decision making and action (Cacciabue et al., 1993; Roth et al., 1991).

In parallel to the evolution of the HRA methods, the taxonomies dedicated to human erroneous behavior have also gradually modified their focus from the simple omission/commission alternative to more structured taxonomies of work environment based on cognitive analysis (Norman, 1981; Rasmussen et al., 1981; Reason, 1990). These new approaches to studying the reliability of cognition need to be coupled to appropriate taxonomies accounting for the socio-technical factors of the working environment (Bagnara et al., 1991) and for well structured definitions of causes, or "genotypes," and manifestations, or "phenotypes," and consequences of human erroneous actions (Hollnagel, 1993).

Evaluation of Decisions in Accident Analysis

In the domain of accident analysis and evaluation of decision, a number of models exist which aim to simulate human behavior in general terms, that is, to represent the human response during accidental conditions in terms of actions and decisions taken to control the plant.

The main characteristic of these models is that they focus on the simulation of accidents or very dynamic situations and consequently can create some assumptions which make the cognitive simulation more manageable. Many of the models described in the previous section, such as PROCRU or MESSAGE or even the simulations of micro-cognition, can describe the operator's behavior in accident cases. Due to their origin they are, however, less easily customized to the simulation of accident analysis than some recent developments carried out in the domain of nuclear reactor safety and avionics.

In this respect, there exists very little work in the literature from the 1960's and 1970's. The recent developments have thus immediately been focused on the simulation of cognition rather than on behavioral aspects of operator response to transients. In particular, the model AIDE (Amalberti & Deblon, 1992) has been developed for the simulation of meta-cognitive processes governing the decision making of fighter pilots during the planning and execution of military missions. The models CES (Woods et al., 1987) and COSIMO (Cacciabue et al, 1992) have been developed for the analysis of nuclear power plants operators during the management of accidents. Although these two models are based on different cognitive theories, they attempt, as does AIDE, to simulate operator behavior on the basis of the cognitive principles which govern the overall behavior and which are activated during and in consequence of the dynamic interaction of the operator with the plant. CES has already been adapted to the reliability analysis, and thus represents a step forward toward the inclusion of cognitive factors in reliability analysis. An even more recent approach is the SRG (Hollnagel & Cacciabue, in press), which is an ambitious attempt to provide a general simulation framework for man-machine interaction.

These latter model developments, even if based on some cognitive principles, and therefore related to a theory of cognition, have to be regarded as macro-cognition approaches. The reasons for such classification are that, contrary to the "hard" micro-cognition models, they are based and driven by a strict connection with the working environment in which they are being developed. This implies that the contribution of field observations as well as the demand of realism and practicality in simulation are considered key factors in the development of human behavior paradigms. These conditions are indeed accurately avoided, as contradictory to the general philosophy of the theory, when models of micro-cognition have been developed.

Training

The change in the nature of work not only has an effect on design practices and safety analysis approaches, as described above, but also demands operator training that focuses on problem solving and on the flexible use of multi-purpose Information Technology (IT). The use of IT depends on properly developed cognitive skills more than on perceptual-motor functions. In particular, at the level of responding to familiar situations the question is one of qualitative matching repertoires of pre-compiled control procedures with the perceived cues from the environment. For unfamiliar situations the problem solving and planning ability of specific persons are to be enhanced by increasing the ability to use qualitative models and combine relevant actions into appropriate tasks.

The need to consider training as a means to develop operators' ability to formulate mental strategies has been demonstrated several years ago focusing, for example, on diagnostic performance (Shepherd et al., 1977). However, the use of cognitive modeling of operator behaviors, similar to those adopted for system design and evaluation, has not been adopted until recently for training. One of the first attempts to use qualitative models for matching system requirements and human resources in training programs was developed in the early 1980s (Rouse, 1982).

Today the role and use of IT and cognitive science approaches to training practices is quite diffuse (Bainbridge & Ruiz-Quintanilla, 1989). The impact of psychological and socio-technical factors on operator performance and the importance of including cognitive processes analysis in training methods is widely accepted. It is used at all levels of training practices such as: the description of event sequences in the task, the development of new skills, the generation of new working methods or procedures, the support to learners, and the motivation for continued learning (Bainbridge, 1989). Even the use of simulators for training, which is a common practice in many complex technology-like avionics and nuclear power plants control, can be improved and optimized by considering the cognitive factor in the planning and by using the knowledge of operators while performing training sessions (Leplat, 1989).

While the introduction of IT in the control loop has enhanced the importance of cognition and thus has affected training practice, it has also generated an impact in the training tools themselves. Indeed, the idea of a Computer Assisted Interactive Instruction (CAII) (Crowder, 1959) system has been developing since the late 1950s — although initially within a behavioristic viewpoint. The current attitude towards computer based training systems is to develop an Intelligent Tutorial System (ITS) by which the learner is able to learn according to his prior knowledge, his ability and preferences, and his motivations (Ruiz-Quintanilla, 1989). In one word the ITS must be supported by a cognitive simulation of the student. The simulation should be as complete as possible, including state of knowledge, typical errors (bug catalogue), level of understanding, frequent misunderstandings, preferred learning method, and so on. This represents a very difficult and complex task which may not be fully achievable. However, the many existing models and paradigms allow the development of systems which, in specific and limited applications, can be rather useful. The technique of ITS represents the most advanced form of utilization of IT equipment for training purposes. This technique has found a much greater application in the domain of support to decision making, which is the last domain of application of simulation of cognition that we will consider here.

On-Line Support

The simulation of cognition plays a role in on-line support in two different ways. Firstly, as a way of tailoring the interaction to match the situational demands. Secondly, as a basis for the artificial intelligence that often is required of these applications.

Unlike the previous applications, on-line support has also a need for a timely response. In design and analysis, for example, there is no urge to respond rapidly. The simulation of cognition can, in principle, take its own time since it is not coupled to an external dynamic process. In training there may be a certain need to match the pace of the student in the actual training situation; however, the tempo of that process is usually rather unhurried and pauses or delays can be introduced without disrupting the training beyond repair. In on-line support such luxuries cannot be afforded.

The need for a rapid response has an impact on the simulation of cognition: It needs to be similarly rapid. As a consequence, the search is more for methods and solutions that work fast and efficiently, rather than for solutions that give complete answers. This moves the goal for simulation of cognition even further away from the micro-cognition discussed above. The first priority is to get something that works.

We may summarize the use of simulation of cognition in on-line support as follows:

• **Expert Systems (ES).** ESs are used in on-line support for a limited number of tasks, although the variations are many. The tasks typically have to do with procedure generation (in contrast to procedure design), with diagnosis, and with planning. In some cases the simulation of cognition is included explicitly to improve the functionality of the system for example, in providing explanations, in formulating advice, and so on.

• **Intelligent Decision Support Systems (IDSS).** The changing role of the operator from an active participant in the loop to a more passive monitor of safety and control systems has produced an emphasis on decision making as the pivotal cognitive function. Decision making was seen as crucial not only for actually making decisions on the spot, but also for diagnosis, problem solving, planning, and scheduling. During the 1980's there had been a series of activities, sponsored by the NATO Scientific Affairs Division, which had looked at various aspects of human performance in process supervision and control. This led to two conferences that specifically focused on the design and use of intelligent decision support (Hollnagel et al., 1986; Hollnagel et al., 1988).

Earlier studies of decision making and decision support had very much been influenced by the existing normative and descriptive theories of decision making (Lee, 1972) and several computer-based systems had been built. None of these had employed simulation of cognition as an option. They had tried to provide decisions support according to acknowledged decision rules or principles of choice, but had not included adaptation in any notable sense. The developments of Artificial Intelligence in the late 1970's and the early 1980's (which to some measure had continued and extended the earlier trend of cognitive simulation from the Carnegie-Mellon school) did, by the mid 1980's, provide a set of methods which could conceivably improve the solutions. Out of this grew the notion of joint cognitive systems (Woods, 1986) which provided a new paradigm for the design of Intelligent Decision Support Systems.

Since the late 1980's there has been a considerable number of IDSSs built and installed. This tendency has been most visible in the nuclear field, but a similar development has taken place in a number of other cases, for example, the Pilot's Associate project or various space related projects. The extent to which simulation of cognition actually takes place varies, but in general the emphasis has been on very well-defined modeling — perhaps as a way of complying with the demand for rapid response. Some of the best examples are found in Japanese systems (e.g., Monta et al., 1985).

• **Action Monitoring.** This differs from the previous categories by having the clear goal of mapping or modeling the operator's intentions. The result of that can then be used in various ways, for example, for error detection, formatting of advice, display control, procedure following, and so on. Action monitoring, or intent recognition, is a growing field which usually is based on well-known techniques such as plan recognition. A few systems have been built for demonstration purposes (Hollnagel, 1989b; Masson & De Keyser, 1992) but none have been used in practice. Action monitoring represents a different side of the simulation of cognition. It is not the main stream of cognition (the primary process) that is in focus, but rather the way in which it is controlled (the secondary process). The interest is not in modeling what the operator does but why he does it. It is therefore, in a certain sense, the simulation of meta-cognition (Valot & Amalberti, 1992).

- **Enhancement of Man Machine Interaction (MMI).** The scope of this type of application is to increase the robustness of the MMI by enabling the system to detect and recover from minor errors made during the interaction. It differs from action monitoring in having a very short time span, that is, limited to the duration of the current action rather than extended to the duration of the current plan or strategy. The problem is a very real one: Everyone makes mistakes in using the interactive devices that are part and parcel of computers, process control, communication equipment, navigation systems, and so on. In most cases the mistakes can be recovered because the person detects it almost immediately and/or because the system is sufficiently forgiving. But there are a number of cases where these conditions are not true; a notable one is Air Traffic Control (ATC). In these cases it is important if the system itself can include the feature of error tolerance.

In this field the simulation of cognition is concentrated on the need to detect inconsistent actions (e.g., typing mistakes, incorrectly used control keys) and to interpret ambiguous commands or queries. The emphasis is on the typical or frequent modes of error rather than on the long-term intentions. The simulation of cognition can therefore benefit from extensive studies of, for example, the performance of temporarily or permanently disabled people, of known distributions of incorrect actions in various categories, and so on.

DIMENSIONS OF SIMULATION

The simulation of cognition can be characterized on a number of dimensions, which serve as a basis for comparing different approaches to simulation and to choose the one that is best suited to a given purpose. The main dimensions are the following:

- **Static versus dynamic simulation.** This dimension denotes whether the simulation is of a static or dynamic nature. All simulations do, by definition, contain a dynamic aspect in the sense that they reproduce how the person's response corresponds to how the event unfolds. The difference between dynamic and static is therefore whether the simulation would develop or change in the absence of an external event, or whether it will only change in response to an external event.

- **Normative versus descriptive simulation.** We have already discussed this in the beginning under the issue of micro-cognition and macro-cognition. It was concluded there that a simulation of cognition should be descriptive rather than normative. It is nevertheless impossible to ensure a clean separation between the two, and it is consequently relevant to try to describe the balance that the simulation achieves between them.

- **Level of granularity of the simulation.** A simulation can be either very detailed in the way in which it accounts for cognition, or remain on a relatively high level with few details. This is typically referred to as the level of granularity. The constituent granules or grains correspond to the elementary cognitive functions and/or structures (e.g., knowledge elements). These can obviously be described and simulated on different levels, for instance as a decision making processor as the steps in decision making.

- **Degree of specificity of the simulation.** This could also be called the degree of generality. The dimension is used to describe how specific (or conversely, how general) the simulation is. This is of importance when the transfer of the results is considered, that is, whether the results are valid for only that situation or set of events that were simulated, or whether it is possible to draw conclusions for other, related types of situations.

These dimensions can be used to describe different types of simulations, but also to establish requirements for a simulation based on an analysis of user needs.

CONCLUSIONS

In this chapter we have attempted to place into perspective the concept of simulation of cognition, which has been defined as the way to describe the cognitive and behavioral processes occurring during human activities. In particular we have identified two main categories, namely macro- and micro-cognition, in which the models can be classified according to their explicit attempt either to give a detailed theoretical account of how cognition takes place in the human mind (micro-cognition) or to refer to the study of the role of cognition in realistic tasks (macro-cognition).

The application of models of cognition has been analyzed in four domains of application, namely Design, Analysis and Evaluation, Training and On-line support.

For each of these four domains a number of problems and specific needs have been analyzed. The major issue identified in almost all domains has been the adaptability of the model to the real working domain of interest. In this respect it can be observed that the macro-cognition models are more suitable to the designers and ergonomists of man-machine systems, even if a considerable effort is still required for including in the models the feedback of the experience from field analysis and the ability to simulate complex reasoning processes. Indeed, in general these are still correlated to a more immediate (and easier to simulate) behavior or reaction to cues of the environment.

On the other hand, the micro-cognition approaches, even if less relevant as far as practical applications are concerned, are also important and necessary in the realm of simulation because they maintain open, as well as continuously active, the attempt to represent, by a general architecture of cognition, the basic processes and the primitives of cognition which are the basis of all decision making processes and action performance.

Ideally, the optimal model of cognition should be defined and characterized by means of the correlations of the micro-cognition approaches but should be able to tackle and solve the practical problems typically represented by the macro-cognition approaches. In other words, the two categories of models are in a converging mode of development, which will require some more advances in the philosophical thinking on cognition as well as in the methods and computerized means of simulation.

REFERENCES

Amalberti, R., & Deblon, F. (1992). Cognitive modeling of fighter aircraft process control: A step towards an intelligent onboard assistance system. *International Journal of Man-Machine Studies, 36* , 639-671.

Anderson, J.R. (1983). *The architecture of cognition.* Cambridge, MA: Harvard University Press.

Bagnara, S., Di Martino, C., Lisanti, B., Mancini, G. & Rizzo, A. (1991). A human error taxonomy based on cognitive engineering and social occupational psychology. In G.E. Apostolakis (Ed.), *Proceedings of the International Conference on Probabilistic Safety Assessment and Management (PSAM)* (pp. 513-518). New York, NY: Elsevier.

Bainbridge, L. (1989). Development of skill, reduction of workload. In L. Bainbridge & S.A. Ruiz Quintanilla (Eds.), *Developing skill with Information Technology* (pp. 87-116). Chichester, UK: Wiley.

Bainbridge, L., & Ruiz Quintanilla, S.A. (Eds.). (1989). *Developing skill with Information Technology.* Chichester, UK: Wiley.

Barnard, P.J. (1985). Interacting cognitive subsystems: a psycholinguistic approach to short-term memory. In A. Ellis (Ed.), *Progress in the psychology of language* (pp. 25-53) Hillsdale, NJ: Lawrence Erlbaum Associates.

Baron, S., Muralidharan, R., Lancraft, R., Zacharias, G. (1980). PROCRU: A model for analysing crew procedures in approach to landing. (Tec. Rep. NAS No. 2-10035). Ames, CA: NASA

Boy, G.A., & Tessier, C. (1985). Cockpit analysis and assessment by the MESSAGE methodology. *Proceedings of the second IFAC Conference on Analysis, Design and Evaluation of Man-Machine Systems* (pp. 73-79). Oxford: Pergamon Press.

Cacciabue, P.C., Decortis, F., Drozdowicz, B., Masson, M. & Nordvik, J.P. (1992). COSIMO: A cognitive simulation model of human decision making and behavior in accident management of complex plants. *IEEE Transation System Man & Cybernetics, 22,* 1058-1074.

Cacciabue, P.C., CarpignaNo. A., and Vivalda C. (1993). A Dynamic Reliability Technique for Error Assessment in Man-Machine Systems. *International Journal of Man Machine Studies, 38* , 403-428.

Card, S.K., Moran, T. P., & Newell A. (1983). *The psychology of Human Computer Interaction.* Hillsdale, NJ: Lawrence Erlbaum Associates.

Carbonell, J. R., (1966). A queuing model of many-instrument visual sampling. *IEEE Trans. Human Factors Electron., 4,* 57-164.

Crowder, N.A. (1959). Automatic tutoring by means of intrinsic programming. In E. Galanter (Ed.), *Automatic teaching: The state of the art,* (pp. 127-155). New York: Wiley.

Dougherty, E.M. (1990). Human reliability analysis. Where shouldst thou turn? *Reliability Engineering & System Safety, 29* , 283-299.

Dougherty, E.M. (1991). Issues of human reliability in risk analysis. In G.E. Apostolakis (Ed.), *Proceedings of the International Conference on Probabilistic Safety Assessment and Management (PSAM)* (pp.699-704). New York, NY: Elsevier.

Grant, S., & Mayes, T. (1991). Cognitive task analysis? In G. R. S. Weir & J. Alty, (Eds.) *HCI and complex systems,* (pp. 145-164). London, UK: Academic Press.

Hammond, K.R., McClelland, G.H., & Mumpower J. (1980). *Human judgment and decision making.* New York: Hemisphere Publishing, Fredrick A. Praeger.

Hannaman, G.W., Spurgin, A.J., & Lukic, Y.D. (1984). Human cognitive reliability model for PRA analysis. (NUS-4531). San Diego, CA: NUS Corporation.

Helander, M., (Ed.). (1988). *Handbook of human computer interaction.* Amsterdam, The Netherlands: Elsevier Science Publishers.

Hollnagel, E. (1989a, November). *Performance improvement through cognitive task analysis.* Paper presented at the *Workshop on Task-Oriented Approach to Human Factors Engineering,* Noorwijk, The Netherlands.

Hollnagel, E. (1989b). *Action monitoring and plan recognition: The response evaluation system (RESQ).* (Tech. Rep. No. P857-WP6-Axion-099). Birkeroed, Denmark: Computer Resources International.

Hollnagel, E. (1991). Cognitive ergonomics and the reliability of cognition. *Le Travail Humain, 54,* 305-321.

Hollnagel, E. (1993). *Human Reliability Analysis: Context and Control.* London: Academic Press.

Hollnagel, E., & Cacciabue, P.C. (1991, September). *Cognitive modelling in system simulation.* Paper presented at the *Third European Conference on Cognitive Science Approaches to Process Control,* Cardiff, UK.

Hollnagel, E., & Cacciabue, P.C. (in press). Modelling cognition and erroneous actions in system simulation contexts. *International Journal of Human Computer Studies*

Hollnagel, E., Mancini, G & Woods, D.D. (Eds.) (1986). *Intelligent decision support in process environments,* NATO ASI Series. Berlin: Springer-Verlag.

Hollnagel, E., Mancini, G, & Woods, D.D. (Eds.). (1988). *Cognitive engineering in complex dynamic worlds.* London: Academic Press.

Hollnagel, E., & Woods, D. D. (1983). Cognitive systems engineering: New wine in new bottles. *International Journal of Man-Machine Studies, 18*, 583-600.

Kieras, D.E. (1988). Towards a practical GOMS model methodology for user interface design. In M. Helander (Ed.), *Handbook of human computer interaction,* (pp. 322-367). Amsterdam, The Netherlands: Elsevier Science Publishers.

Kleinman, D. L., & Curry, R. E. (1977). Some new control theoretic models for human operator display modelling. *IEEE Transation System Man & Cybernetics, 7,* 1074-1103.

Knaeuper, A., & Rouse, W.B. (1985). A model of human problem solving in dynamic environments. *IEEE Transation System Man & Cybernetics, 15*, 708-719.

Lee, S.M. (1972). *Goal programming for decision analysis.* Berlin: Auerbach.

Leplat, J. (1989). Relations between task and activity in training. In L. Bainbridge & S.A. Ruiz Quintanilla (Eds.), *Developing skill with Information Technology* (pp. 125-130). Chichester, UK: Wiley.

Life, A., Narborough-Hall, C., & Hamilton I. (Eds.), (1991). *Simulation and the user interface.* London: Taylor & Francis.

Lind, M. (1991). Representation and abstractions for interface design using multilevel flow modelling. In G.R.S. Weir & J. Alty (Eds.), *HCI and complex systems* (pp. 221-239). London: Academic Press.

Mancini, G. (1986). Modelling humans and machines. In E. Hollnagel, G. Mancini & D. D. Woods (Eds.), *Intelligent decision support in process environments* (pp. 307-323). NATO ASI Series. Berlin: Springer-Verlag.

Masson, M., & De Keyser, V. (1992, June). *Human error: Lesson learned from a field study for the specification of an intelligent error prevention system.* Paper presented at the *Annual International Ergonomics and Safety Conference.* Denver, CO.

Monta, K., Fukutomi, S., Itoh, M., & Tai I. (1985, September). *Development of a computerized operator support system for boiling water reactor power plants.* Paper presented at the *International topical meeting on computer applications for nuclear power plant operation and control.* Pasco, WA.

Moray, N., Sanderson, P.M., & Vicente, K.J. (1992). Cognitive task analysis of complex work domain: a case study. *Reliability Engineering and System Safety, 36,* 207-216.

Newell, A. (1990). *Unified theories of cognition.* Cambridge, MA: Harvard University Press.

Newell, A., & Simon, H. A. (1972). *Human problem solving.* Englewood Cliffs, NJ: Prentice-Hall

Norman, D.A. (1981). Categorization of action slips. *Psychological Review, 88,* 1-15.

Pew, R.W., Baron, S., Feehrer, C.E., & Miller D.C. (1977). *Critical review and analysis of performance models applicable to man-machine-systems evaluation* (Tech. Rep. No. 3446). Cambridge, MA: Bolt, Beranek & Newman.

Rasmussen, J. (1986). *Information processes and human-machine interaction: An approach to cognitive engineering.* Amsterdam: North Holland.

Rasmussen, J., Pedersen, O.M., Mancini, G., Carnino, A., Griffon, M., & Gangolet, P. (1981). *Classification system for reporting events involving human malfunctions* (Tech. Rep. No. RISOE - M - 2240, EUR-7444 EN). Luxembourg: Commission of the European Communities.

Reason, J. (1990). *Human error*. Cambridge, UK: Cambridge University Press.

Roth, E.M., People, H.E., Jr., & Woods, D.D. (1991). Cognitive environment simulation: a tools for modelling operator cognitive performance during emergencies. In G.E. Apostolakis (Ed.), *Proceedings of the International Conference on Probabilistic Safety Assessment and Management (PSAM)* (pp.959-964). New York, NY: Elsevier.

Rouse, W. B. (1977). Human-computer interaction in multi-task situations. *IEEE Transactions System Man & Cybernetics 7*, 384-392.

Rouse, W. B. (1980). *Systems engineering models of human-machine Interaction*. Amsterdam: North Holland.

Rouse, W. B. (1982). A mixed-fidelity approach to technical training. *Journal of Educational Technology Systems, 11*, 346-385.

Ruiz Quintanilla, S.A. (1989). Intelligent tutorial systems (ITS) in training. In L. Bainbridge & S.A. Ruiz Quintanilla (Eds.), *Developing skill with information technology* (pp. 329-338). Chichester, UK: Wiley.

Senders, J. W. (1964). The human operator as a monitor and controller of multi-degree of freedom systems. *ERE Transactions in Human Factors in Electronics, 7*, 103-106.

Shepherd, A., Marshall, E. C., Turner, A., & Duncan, K.D (1977). Control panel diagnosis: A comparison of three training methods. *Ergonomics, 20*, 347-361.

Sheridan, T.B. (1986). Forty-five years of man-machine systems: history and trends. Keynote Address. *Proceedings of the Second IFAC Conference on Analysis, Design, and Evaluation of Man-Machine Systems* (pp. 6-14) Oxford, UK: Pergamon Press.

Stassen, H.G., Johannsen G., & Moray, N. (1990). Internal representation, internal model, human performance model and mental workload. *Automatica, 26*, 811-820.

Stein, W., & Wewerinke, P. (1983). Human display monitoring and failure detection: control theoretic models and experiments. *Automatica, 19*, 189-211.

Swain, A. D., & Guttman, H.E. (1983). *Handbook on human reliability analysis with emphasis on nuclear power plant application* (Tech. Rep. No. NUREG/CR-1278. SAND 80-0200 RX, AN). Albuquerque, NM: Sandia National Laboratories.

Valot, C., & Amalberti, R. (1992). Metaknowledge for time and reliability. *Reliability Engineering and System Safety, 36*, 199-206.

Weir, G. R. S., & Alty, J. (Eds.). (1991). *HCI and complex systems*, London, UK: Academic Press.

Woods, D.D. (1984). Visual momentum: A concept to improve the cognitive coupling of person and computer. *International Journal of Man-Machine Studies, 21*, 229-244.

Woods, D.D. (1986). Paradigms for intelligent decision support. In E. Hollnagel, G. Mancini & D. D. Woods (Eds.), *Intelligent decision support in process environments*, (pp. 230-254) NATO ASI Series. Berlin: Springer-Verlag.

Woods, D.D., Roth, E. M., & Pople, H., Jr. (1987). *Cognitive environment simulation: An artificial intelligence system for human performance assessment. Volumes 1 - 2* (Tech. Rep. No. Nureg-CR-4862). Washington D.C: US-NRC.

Zadeh, L.A. (1965). Fuzzy sets. *Information & Control, 8*, 338-353.

5

Symbolic AI Computer Simulations as Tools for Investigating the Dynamics of Joint Cognitive Systems

David D. WOODS
The Ohio State University
Emilie M. ROTH
Westinghouse Science and Technology Center

Based on our experience in developing a symbolic AI computer simulation, we explore how such simulations can be used as a tool in the study of joint human-machine cognitive systems in field settings. We contend that cognitive simulation is best seen as a tool to aid a cycle of empirically based model development and model-based empirical investigations of joint cognitive systems. The chapter is organized around a series of principles or claims about simulations of cognition as related to complex human-machine systems.

The thesis of this chapter is that cognitive simulation is best seen as one of a set of complementary tools for the study of joint cognitive systems in field settings. Cognitive simulation is a technique invented by Newell and Simon (Newell & Simon, 1963; Newell & Simon, 1972; Simon, 1969,) where information processing concepts about human cognitive activities are expressed as a runnable computer program, usually through symbolic processing techniques (cf. Corker et al., 1986; Johnson, Moen, & Thompson, 1988; Kieras and Polson, 1985; Woods et al., 1987 for examples using symbolic processing techniques; cf. also Axelrod, 1984; Kirlik et al., 1989; Payne, Johnson, Bettman & Coupey, 1990 for examples using conventional programming techniques). The cognitive simulation can be stimulated by inputs from a domain scenario to generate computer system behavior which can be compared to observed human behavior for the same scenario. These computer simulations are more accurately referred to as simulations of cognition (cf. Cacciabue & Hollnagel, in chapter 4, this volume). But since Newell and Simon originally used the label 'cognitive simulation' we will sometimes retain their terminology.

The advantages of simulations of cognition revolve around the fact that building a runnable computer program (cf. Simon, 1969) forces the modeler to describe mechanisms in great detail. In particular, expressing a model as a runnable program forces the developer to make explicit the knowledge and processing that are implicit in the practitioner's field of activity. Running the simulation through a scenario produces specific behavior that can be analyzed and compared to other data. As a result, it is possible to uncover a variety of consequences of the basic information processing mechanisms that are instantiated in the program. Furthermore, the resulting simulation can be run on a variety of scenarios, including scenarios that were not part of the original design set. Thus, the implications of assumptions or concepts about human cognitive activities captured by the simulation can be explored in a wide range of domain specific circumstances. As a result, one can see cognitive simulation as a method for linking more directly theory building and empirical investigations of human problem-solving activities in semantically rich domains.

One connotation often associated with cognitive simulation is that the information processing mechanisms bestowed on the computer are intended to be a model or theory about the information processing mechanisms of the human mind, for example, the physical symbol system hypothesis (Newell, 1980; Newell, 1990). In this sense of "cognitive simulation", the computer program is seen as a formal theory about human cognitive processes. However, this is not the only sense in which computer simulations have been or can be used in cognitive science or in various scientific and engineering specialties (cf. Pylyshyn, 1991)

Several years ago, we faced the problem of developing an analytic strategy that would be useful to identify places/circumstances where erroneous situation assessments could develop and propagate during dynamic fault management as in nuclear power plant emergency operations (Woods & Roth, 1986). We discarded the notion that symbolic processing mechanisms must be a direct model of human cognition. Instead, we focused on other properties of a computer simulation approach in a project that later came to be called the Cognitive Environment Simulation (CES).

In this paper we will use our experience in that project and experience from related efforts to develop cognitive simulations to describe how AI based computer simulations can be used as a tool in the study of joint cognitive systems in field settings. We contend that cognitive simulation is best seen as a tool in a cycle of empirically based model development and model-based empirical investigations of joint cognitive systems. As such, the computer program in itself has no special status as a specification of *the* cognitive process employed by people to accomplish the task at some level of description.[1] We

---

[1] Note that the relationship between concepts and formalization as a computer program is different here as compared to the relationship between concepts and formalization in other areas of study where the formal expression of the model (e.g., in mathematical terms) is intended to be the theory and other types of descriptions

will attempt to explore the role of simulations of cognition by posing a series of principles or claims about cognitive simulation as related to complex human-machine systems.

THE ROLE OF COGNITIVE SIMULATION

Cognitive simulations are tools for investigation of cognition.

In the CES project, in collaboration with H. Pople, we tried to use symbolic processing computer programming techniques, as other computer programs have been used (e.g., Axelrod, 1984), as tools to explore the ramifications of some concepts about the cognitive activities that underlie human performance in different kinds of circumstances. The AI was not to be seen as the model of human cognition, but rather as a language for expressing concepts about some of the cognitive factors at work in dynamic fault management. This is the sense in which we used the term cognitive simulation.

In other words, strip away from symbolic AI its claims to be a model of mind and what you have left is a set of powerful techniques using symbolic programming for building computer programs that perform cognitive work. Examples of symbolic processing mechanisms used in Pople's artificial intelligence performance system EAGOL[2] that were found to be useful in the CES project include (a) distributed software agents with local information processing tasks, with local knowledge resources that are activated by particular triggering events, and who share working results through message passing (in effect, working in parallel on pieces of the problem); (b) ways to represent knowledge about physical processes, fault categories, disturbance propagation, operational goals, corrective responses; (c) qualitative reasoning techniques about how measured data on the state of the monitored process change given different patterns of control and fault-related influences acting on the process.

One can use these various symbolic processing mechanisms to build computer systems that perform cognitive work. When stimulated with input from a scenario (a temporal stream of the data about the state of the monitored process that is or could be available during an unfolding incident), the computer simulation can be made so that it carries out cognitive functions such as monitoring for changes in process state or diagnosis of underlying faults. For example, CES performs some of the cognitive functions involved in dynamic fault management (Woods, in press-b): it monitors and tracks changes in process state, identifies abnormal and unexpected process behaviors, builds and revises a situation assessment (what influences are currently acting on the monitored

---

(e.g., verbal specifications; models or analogies) are considered to be mere approximations intended to foster comprehension or application.

[2] EAGOL is a proprietary product of SEER Systems.

process), formulates hypotheses to account for unexplained process behavior, and formulates intentions to act based on its situation assessment. While a cognitive simulation provides a compelling demonstration of the cognitive work entailed by the environment, the specific software mechanisms employed in the simulation do not constitute a theory of human cognition in that environment. For us, cognitive simulations specify theories, but are not theories. The simulation is a representation or realization of a set of concepts; a way to formalize the concepts so that one can explore and investigate the explanatory power of the concepts in a wide range of circumstances. Thus, cognitive simulations embody theories of human cognition at the level of cognitive competencies, not in the details of implementation. While the computer simulation can bring out in bold relief the cognitive functions required to operate successfully in the environment, the specific symbolic processing mechanisms employed to achieve those cognitive functions in the computer program do not in any sense constitute a theory of how people perform the same cognitive functions. The theory embodied in the computer simulation is intended to apply at the level of cognitive competencies (similar to Newell's 1982 concept of the knowledge level) rather than at the symbol manipulation level (what Newell has referred to as the program level). The role of the cognitive simulation is to help get greater leverage from a set of concepts -- what do these concepts explain about the cognitive system in question (Elkind et al., 1990). Hence, the CES project began with and continues to evolve with reference to a model of the cognitive activities and demands of dynamic fault management tasks based on empirical studies and explanatory concepts (Roth, Woods & Pople, 1992; Woods, 1992; Woods, in press-b; Woods & Roth, 1986).

As Heil (1981) has pointed out in reference to computer programs as models of cognition, "... we must take care to avoid the error of supposing that descriptions of things done are really *indirect* descriptions of the mechanisms which get them done" (italics in original). It is the investigator's intelligence in setting up a correspondence between the cognitive functions performed by the program and the hypothesized cognitive demands and activities in the field of practice that determines the usefulness of the simulation as a tool. Symbolic processing techniques are resources that can be used to build programs that carry out the cognitive functions which the investigator thinks are important in this setting or scenario. The modeling concepts exist separate from their instantiations within the simulation tool. Wielding the simulation in relationship to other sources of data provides the potential for learning about the dynamics of human performance in complex environments. This leads us to one criterion that determines if a computer program is to count as a cognitive simulation -- one must explicitly specify the concepts about cognitive activities and demands in the target situations that govern the development and evolution of the simulation.

When one sees cognitive simulations as tools for investigation, the implementation details of the simulation as computer program are of secondary interest. What are important are the competencies of the program in relation to a model of the cognitive activities and demands of the tasks in question. For example, CES builds and revises a situation assessment by keeping track of what influences it believes are currently acting on the monitored process. This includes both influences produced by control activities and those produced by hypothesized faults. The set of influences is used to compute expected and unexpected process behaviors. There is no claim that how the computer program fulfills this competency corresponds directly to mechanisms of human cognition. The modeling claim is that forming expectancies based on consideration of multiple influences is a cognitive function that goes on in dynamic fault management and that this cognitive function can account for the behavior observed in empirical studies. This example raises another criterion that must be fulfilled if a computer program is to count as a cognitive simulation -- one should specify the competencies of the program and explicitly map them onto concepts about the cognitive activities and demands of the field of activity in question (Roth & Woods, 1988).

Computer simulations of complex human-machine systems address distributed cognitive systems.

In actual fields of practice, the focus is rarely on the activities of a single cognitive agent. Cognitive work goes on in the context of multiple people, machines that perform aspects of cognitive work, and a variety of tools and external representations of systems, devices, or processes. In the CES project, we tried to shift the focus from modeling and simulating human cognitions to modeling and simulating cognitive systems that are distributed across multiple people, machines (e.g., AI advisors), and external representations or cognitive tools that are shaped by the cognitive demands of the specific task domain (Hutchins, 1991; Woods & Roth, 1988). There are three parts to a cognitive systems view of a human-technical system: (1) the set of agents who perform cognitive work (this includes multiple people and algorithmic and heuristic machine information processors in supervisory control applications, e.g., Hutchins, 1990; Roth & Woods, 1988); (2) the external representation of the monitored process and the cognitive tools available which shape the cognitive strategies of the practitioners in the system (e.g., Hutchins, 1991; Woods, in press-a); (3) the demands of the task domain in terms of the challenges or constraints they pose for any cognitive agent or set of agents to function in that setting (Woods, 1988).

To be relevant, cognitive simulations must address how cognitive activities are distributed across multiple people and machines, how cognitive activities are shaped by characteristics of the available external representations and cognitive tools, and how cognitive activities are locally rational responses to the cognitive demands and constraints (e.g., competing goals) of the specific task domain (Hutchins, 1991; Woods, Johannesen, Cook, & Sarter, in press; Woods & Roth, 1988). Note that these are not three independent aspects. Modeling a joint cognitive system is about understanding how the interactions among these factors -- demands, external representation and tools as resources, individual strategies and the distribution of activities across agents -- mutually shape each other (cf. Hutchins, 1991; Roth & Woods, 1988 for two examples of studies that investigate the mutual shaping across these factors).

Computer simulations of complex human-machine systems can be used to explore how the demands of the specific task domain constrain or shape the behavior of cognitive systems.

Research on human error today often assumes that erroneous actions and assessments result from rational but limited or bounded cognitive processes (Woods, Johannesen, Cook, & Sarter, in press). People behave consistent with Newell's principle of rationality -- that is, they use knowledge to pursue their goals (Newell, 1982). But, there are bounds to the data that they pay attention to, to the knowledge that they possess, to the knowledge that they activate in a particular context, and there may be multiple goals which conflict (e.g., bounded or limited rationality; Reason, 1987; Simon, 1969). Thus, one approach to modeling a cognitive system in a particular task context is to trace the problem-solving process to identify points where limited knowledge and processing resources can lead to breakdowns given the demands of the problem (Woods, 1990). A cognitive simulation can be an excellent tool for exploring different concepts about limits on cognitive processing (e.g., attentional bottlenecks; limited knowledge activation) in relation to the demands imposed by different kinds of problems that can occur in the field of practice. The cognitive simulation can be constructed then to allow the investigator to vary the knowledge resources and processing characteristics of a limited resource computer problem-solver and observe the behavior of the computer problem-solver in different simulated domain scenarios. This strategy depends on mapping the cognitive demands imposed by the domain in question that any intelligent but *limited resource* problem-solving agent or set of agents would have to deal with. The demands include the nature of domain incidents, how they are manifested through observable data to the operational staff, and how they evolve over time. Then, one can embody this model of the problem-solving environment as a limited resource symbolic processing problem-solving system.

In effect, with this technique one is measuring the difficulty or complexity posed by a domain incident, given some set of resources, by running the incident through the cognitive simulation (Kieras & Polson, 1985; Woods et al., 1990). In other words, the cognitive simulation supports a translation from the language of the individual field of practice to the language of cognitive activities -- what data needs to be gathered and integrated, what knowledge is required to be used and how is it activated and brought to bear in the cognitive activities involved in solving dynamic problems. In effect, the cognitive simulation yields a description of the information flow and knowledge activation required to handle domain incidents. One can investigate how changes in the incident (e.g., obscuring evidence, introducing another failure) affect the difficulty of the problem for a given set of knowledge resources. Conversely, one can investigate how changes in the knowledge resources (e.g., improved mental models of device function) or information available (e.g., integrated information displays) can affect performance.

While this approach has clear limitations, it does allow an overall assessment of the range and complexity of cognitive activities demanded by the situation. In the CES project we were able to deal with only a subset of the factors that make up a joint or distributed cognitive system. Workload management and the role of cognitive tools were two of the many requirements that we originally set but are not captured within the current version of the computer simulation. Nevertheless, in several instances we were able to elucidate information about the information flow and knowledge activation required to handle domain incidents with specific implications for the field in question. For example, we analyzed variations within one fault category to determine which are likely to be difficult diagnostically (Woods, Pople & Roth, 1990). We explored how different types of fault management situations where problem solution goes beyond rote following of procedures (Roth, Woods, & Pople, 1992). In using the cognitive simulation in a variety of incidents we learned about the role of practitioner expectations and violations of those expectations in guiding and simplifying diagnostic search (Woods, in press-b).

In their current stage of development, models of cognitive systems in natural settings are probably much more about developing a cognitive language for describing the task environment than about modeling specific internal psychological mechanisms. As Hogarth (1986) has commented, "Good models of decision behavior gain much of their explanatory power by elucidating the structure of the task being investigated" (p. 445). Even in traditional cognitive psychology and cognitive science there is a growing appreciation that the demands of the environment play a significant role in defining human performance and that significant insights can be gained by exploring the nature of the problem being solved using minimal information processing assumptions (cf. Anderson, 1990; Marr, 1982). "An algorithm is likely to be understood more readily by understanding the nature of the problem being solved than by examining the mechanism (and the hardware) in which it is solved" (Marr, 1982, p. 27). Given the range of cognitive activities that come into play in complex fields of practice, a model of task properties may be the critical bottleneck to progress (e.g., Hammond, 1988). Of course, models of the cognitive demands of fields of practice cannot be pursued independent from understanding the psychological processes that occur in those tasks; the two are mutually constrained (Simon, 1991; Woods, 1988). Cognitive simulation can be a powerful tool, in part because it links cognitive demands and cognitive activities together so that the dynamics of their interaction and interdependence can be explored.

Cognitive simulations are needed to explore the temporal dynamics of cognitive systems in relation to the temporal characteristics of incidents.

In dynamic environments, data comes in over time, changes, and occurs in the presence of other events. Faults propagate chains of disturbances that evolve and spread through the system (Woods, in press-b). Counteracting influences are injected by automated systems and by practitioners to preserve system integrity, to generate diagnostic information, and to correct faults. Information is based on change, events (behavior over time), and the response to interventions. Static models are incapable of expressing the complexity of cognitive functioning in dynamic environments -- the interaction of data-driven and knowledge-driven reasoning, the role of interrupts in the control of attentional focus, the scheduling of cognitive activities as workload bottlenecks emerge, the interaction of intervention and feedback on process response.

One can appreciate the complexities of the situation faced by practitioners only through developing runnable computer systems that must deal with the dynamics of problems. In the CES project it became clear that to follow and control dynamic events it was necessary to use a computer program with elaborate mechanisms adapted to problems that evolve and change over time. For example, CES contains mechanisms (a) for tracking over time interactions among multiple influences acting on the monitored process (e.g., qualitative reasoning); (b) for tracking when automation should activate or inactivate various control systems and how goal priorities change through an incident; (c) for projecting the impact of a state change on future process behavior to create temporal expectations such as reminders to check whether the expected behavior is observed, or, more importantly, not observed. Interestingly, in one study that used CES as a tool (Roth et al., 1992), the factors that made the class of incidents difficult could be found only through an analysis of the dynamics of the incident in relation to the dynamics of the joint cognitive system.

Cognitive simulation provides the potential to explore the dynamic interplay of problem evolution and cognitive processing. This may be critical to be able to make progress on the problem of how does control of attention work (Woods, 1992). Many demanding tasks such as dynamic fault management are practiced in a cognitively noisy world, where very many stimuli are present which could be relevant to the problem-solver (Woods, in press-b). There are both a large number of data channels and the signals on these channels, usually are changing (i.e., the raw values are rarely constant even when the system is stable and normal). Given the nature of human attentional processes and the large amounts of raw data, human monitors focus selectively on a portion of the field of data. These types of task worlds demand facility with reorienting attention rapidly to new potentially relevant stimuli. Given the large field of changing data, one challenge in building a cognitive simulation is getting the program to ignore "uninteresting" changes and to focus only on "interesting" ones. The problem is that what is interesting depends on a set of factors that include domain specific knowledge, the state of the problem-solving process, the relevant goals, and tradeoffs about how to respond to trouble under conditions of irreducible uncertainty, time pressure, and the possibility of very negative outcomes.

For example, in the CES project, we found that diagnostic engines developed for static situations, when applied to dynamic processes, bog down in pursuing too many irrelevant data variations. What is needed is some front end capability to recognize which out of a set of changes (or when the absence of a change) should initiate diagnostic search. In CES this is accomplished by forming a situation assessment that consists of the 'known' influences acting on the monitored process. This influence set is used to evaluate process changes to determine if the change was expected given the influence set or unexpected. Unexpected findings act as a trigger for diagnostic search mechanisms whose charter is to determine an explanation for the unexpected finding. This kind of process greatly reduces the amount of diagnostic work required to track changes in the monitored process. Thus, an important area for future work is how to build cognitive simulations that can exercise control of attention in principled ways.

Investigations using cognitive simulations must be part of a larger cycle of empirically based model development and model-based empirical investigations of joint cognitive systems.

CES was part of a process of trying to expand and deepen our understanding of the cognitive activities and demands of fault management tasks, especially what makes fault management difficult and vulnerable to breakdown. Several activities contributed to this learning process. We learned from the struggles to get a research AI software system to behave reasonably in a supervisory role when stimulated by data about a developing incident in a specific domain (nuclear power emergency operations). We learned from the differences between the behavior of the simulation and empirical data available from previous studies of nuclear power emergency operations (Woods, Pople, & Roth, 1990). We learned from new data collected on human performance in this setting, motivated in part to better understand how the simulation should function (Roth, Woods, & Pople, 1992).

The value of a cognitive simulation is in wielding it to learn about the dynamics within a particular cognitive system or the dynamics of cognitive systems in general. In wielding a cognitive simulation one designs and carries out a kind of experimental investigation. One collects data about the behavior of the simulation across a range of problems/domain scenarios that represent a sample of the space of problems or scenarios that could occur (Simon, 1969). Setting up this type of investigation requires thoughtful consideration of which set of scenarios to use, what empirical data can serve as contrasting cases, and what comparisons to make that will lead to new learning (again, see Axelrod, 1984, for a classic example of the use of a computer simulation as a tool for investigation in association with empirical data and the evolution of modeling concepts). One designs a cognitive simulation study. When does a computer program function as a cognitive simulation? When you can describe the study that you did with it, and when you can specify what you learned from that effort.

Wielding a cognitive simulation is the equivalent of an empirical study. What is of primary interest is the methodology, results, and implications of an investigation using cognitive simulation as a part of the study. This implies that there is a need to observe the behavior of the computer program across a range of problems. As a result, development of a map of the problem space is needed so as to know what kinds of problems should be posed to the cognitive simulation. As in any study, there are uncertainties and limits; the skill in study design is how to balance uncertainties and limits so as to tentatively learn about joint cognitive systems.

It is important to emphasize that wielding a cognitive simulation as part of an empirical study does not depend on achieving a correspondence between computer and human protocols. Information lies in the differences between practitioner behavior and the behavior of the cognitive simulation relative to the concepts instantiated (and those not instantiated) in the simulation.

A cognitive simulation is always a partial incomplete realization of the modeling concepts.

A cognitive simulation captures some aspects of the cognitive factors at work; it addresses only some part of the task environment.

The scope of cognitive activities that occur in complex fields of practice is daunting. These diverse cognitive activities are not modular either, whether considered from the point of view of developing AI software or from a psychological point of view. Often the target domain itself is very complex — nuclear power plants and emergency operations; flightdecks in commercial aviation; anesthetic management under surgery. This means that the scope of knowledge and strategy development is very great. The breadth of human cognitive activities that come into play in just a single scenario or subtask can be extremely wide. Even a relatively simple subtask may involve several components that are normally studied or modeled in isolation in the laboratory (Woods & Roth, 1988).

Furthermore, our state of understanding of cognition is not static. The evolution of knowledge in the field of cognitive science can be expected to overturn working assumptions, approximate models, or specific concepts that were used to guide the development of the cognitive simulation. All of these factors point out that it is very difficult to see a cognitive simulation as a finished static system.

A cognitive simulation, as a complex software system, is subject to all of the difficulties that can plague software development.

Some of the classic advantages of cognitive simulation — detailed specification of processes, openness to inspection, runable across many scenarios, comparability to data from people (Simon, 1969; Newell & Simon, 1972) — depend in part on the assumption that the underlying computer program exists as an objective entity. But when is a cognitive simulation program finished enough to count? As a large software development project, one can be subject to software stability problems and difficulties in iterative refinement across specific scenarios, among other problems. AI software can be tailored relatively easily to run well for a particular scenario or set of human data, but generate inadequate or nonsensical behavior when confronted with a substantially different scenario.

Constraints on software development interact with the breadth and diversity of cognitive activities to be captured (claim 6.1). The next scenario is likely to invoke new types of knowledge about the domain and to bump into cognitive competencies that were not evident in the cases addressed up to that point in the development process. Sometimes, these new elements may be addressed through modular additions, but the likelihood of success depends on how well the architecture is designed relative to the desired cognitive competencies. And then, in wielding the simulation, one is likely to discover new things about cognitive systems which may very well demand changes in the simulation program. Given these and other pragmatic factors in software engineering, it is very difficult to see a cognitive simulation as a finished system. Rather, cognitive simulations are always in a state of evolution.[3]

In principle, an advantage of a cognitive simulation is that the processes used by the computer program in response to input about the evolution of the monitored process are open to inspection by the investigators. But what aspects of the program need to be seen? It is important to remember that a protocol of the behavior of a cognitive simulation in response to an incident is but one kind of many possible reports on the behavior of the computer program (Dennett, 1968). Similarly, a protocol on the behavior of a person or a team during a particular incident is but one kind of report on the behavior of those individuals. The specific constraints on access differ between human and machine cognition, but a protocol of a machine's cognitive activities has the status of a report about its activities.

Theoretically, there can be many kinds of descriptions of the behavior of a computer program (Newell, 1982). Pragmatically, the software system designer develops mechanisms that give the program observable behavior and provides tools for inspecting the changes in the internal states of the program. What constrains these software capabilities or tools? The developer's judgment about the factors that are important in the program's behavior? The developer's judgment about the appropriate grain of description? The debugging mechanisms and programmer's interface provided by the development environment? The project resources or the level of effort that remains to be devoted to building an investigator's interface? The developer's notions of what is a good human-computer interface for monitoring the performance of a cognitive simulation?

---

[3] Though small by many yardsticks, the CES project ran into many of the troubles that can arise in software engineering, especially symbolic processing software development, including software stability problems and difficulties in iterative refinement across specific scenarios. The MIDAS project to develop an integrated suite of computer simulations for the design of human-machine systems at NASA was a much larger software engineering effort (e.g., Corker, 1993). For a counter-example where the software development was kept simple and small but still resulted in successful simulation-based investigations of the dynamics of a joint cognitive system see Benchekroun and Pavard (this volume).

Again, it is theoretical concepts that stand outside of the cognitive simulation itself, theoretical concepts about the cognitive demands and strategies within a cognitive system, that provide a means to decide in a principled manner the kinds of reports of simulation behavior that should be available (examples of where this has been done include Newell's SOAR system as an instantiation of his theoretical concepts about human cognition; Newell, 1990). This defines another criterion for when a computer program counts as a cognitive simulation -- the developers/investigators must provide theoretically motivated or methodologically motivated capabilities for accessing the behavior of the software system.

A cognitive simulation, as a computer program, may contain a variety of ancillary mechanisms that are needed simply to make the software run, but are not related to the concepts under investigation. However, these auxiliary assumptions can affect or drive the behavior of the computer program (Newell, 1990; Simon, 1991). This creates a problem: How does one know when the behavior of the simulation is due to the concepts instantiated in the program and when is it due to auxiliary aspects required to have a runnable computer program (Newell, 1982)?

Newell (1982) makes this point by distinguishing different levels of realization for a computer program. His point reminds us that cognitive simulations can be used to specify theories, but are not theories (i.e., Newell's distinction between the knowledge level and the program level of description of a cognitive system). For computer simulations, the program is not and cannot be the model; it is only one realization of the concepts. Newell's work on a unified theory of cognition as embodied in the SOAR software system illustrates that, to combat the knowledge level "problem", the mapping between concepts and program mechanisms must be as explicit as possible. The mapping between concepts and program mechanisms becomes a bridge that creates a productive link between the particular and the universal in cognition: General concepts need to be articulated into a system that could meet the cognitive demands of a field of practice, but a system only can do such cognitive work in the particular as a response to a particular scenario sampled from a larger space of problems.

Approximate and incomplete cognitive simulations, if wielded intelligently, can contribute useful results both in general and in particular for an application area.

Validation of a cognitive simulation is probably a fruitless question. Rather than ask validation questions (is this the correct model?), we contend that questions of usefulness and fruitfulness are the measure of the value of a cognitive simulation (what did it help you discover or learn or test?). The value is not as an entity in itself, but rather the power of discovery that it can provide as part of a kind of difference equation in the hands of intelligent investigators. The information lies in the differences between empirical results and simulation results (Roth et al., 1992), in comparisons across different scenarios and conditions.

A cognitive simulation, at some stage of evolution and in the context of a designed study, represents hypotheses about the dynamic interplay across the parts of a cognitive system. The value lies in enhancing our ability to engage in an empirical confrontation when the target of interest is cognition embedded within some complex, multifaceted field of practice.

Similarly, Don Norman and others (Barnard, Wilson, & MacLean, 1988) have pointed out that for many complex settings what is needed are approximate models of cognition and human-computer cooperation. As Barnard et al. (1988) expressed it, such models must capture empirical phenomenon of interest at *molecular* rather than atomic levels of description. Such models are tentative and subject to revision as knowledge and results in cognitive science evolve. The use of such models should contribute to the evolution of knowledge in cognitive science. Such models are explicit in regard to the elements of analysis and the principles on which it is based. The process of creating and using a cognitive simulation contributes to making concepts and their interaction explicit, if done in the ways outlined above. Achieving these criteria requires linking modeling and empirical techniques in a reinforcing and interactive cycle. In the end, the yield from cognitive simulation techniques depends more on the intelligence of the investigator than on the sophistication of the tool per se.

CONCLUSIONS

The value of a computer simulation of cognition is not to simply have it, but rather to use it. Running the simulation through a scenario produces specific behavior that can be analyzed and compared to other data. As a result, it is possible to uncover a variety of consequences of the information processing mechanisms that are instantiated in the program.

Since cognitive simulations are a tool for investigation, the architectural aspects of the simulation as a computer program are of secondary interest. It is relatively easy to build an AI system that does some parts of the cognitive work involved in various fields of practice. What is important is the competencies of the program in relation to a model of the cognitive activities and demands of the tasks in question. If a computer program is to count as a cognitive simulation, these competencies must be specified. What parts of the cognitive work involved in a complex task like dynamic fault management should be simulated? What are the cognitive activities involved in the area of dynamic fault management? How should one use an imperfect simulation of cognition (remember it is utopian to quest after the perfect cognitive simulation) to learn more about the dynamics of joint cognitive systems in general or about a particular joint cognitive system?

Cognitive simulation is one potentially powerful tool in a cycle of empirically based model development and model-based empirical investigations of joint cognitive systems. But it is not a panacea; nor is it without pitfalls. Has the technique been useful? Yes, there are outposts of investigations that involved cognitive simulations and that seem to have added to the research base on joint cognitive systems. However, it is not clear whether the insights gained depended on the role of the cognitive simulation so much as on the insight of the investigators (e.g., the cognitive simulation may play the role of a demonstration vehicle for insights worked out through careful observation and analysis by the investigators).

Areas where cognitive simulation studies can contribute to advancing our understanding of joint cognitive systems in context include: (a) how do temporally evolving situations, as compared with static one shot decision situations, create different cognitive demands and provide opportunities for different cognitive strategies?; (b) how is attentional focus managed in fields of activity that are data rich and involve multiple interleaved tasks?; (c) how do possibilities for action constrain cognitive systems?; (d) what is the contribution of perceptual or recognition driven or pattern processing to cognition (rather than modeling cognition as decoupled from perception)?; (e) how does effort or cognitive cost play a role in cognition systems given finite resources available to human or machine agents within a cognitive system?

While cognitive simulation is a powerful technique and while there are many computer systems being developed that claim to be cognitive simulations, the burden lies with the developers/investigators to use them in a fashion that adds to and stimulates a process of critical, cumulative growth of knowledge about the dynamics of joint cognitive systems in the field.

REFERENCES

Anderson, J.R. (1990). *The adaptive character of thought.* Hillsdale, NJ: Lawrence Erlbaum Associates.

Axelrod, R. (1984). *The evolution of cooperation.* New York: Basic Books.

Barnard, P., Wilson, M. & MacLean, A. (1988). Approximate modelling of cognitive activity with an expert system: A theory-based strategy for developing an interactive design tool. *The Computer Journal, 31,* 445-456.

Corker, K., Davis, L., Papazian, B., & Pew, R. (1986). *Development of an advanced task analysis methodology and demonstration for Army aircrew/aircraft Integration* (Tech. Rep. No. BBN 6124). Cambridge, MA: Bolt Beranek and Newman.

Dennett, D. (1968). Computers in behavioral science: Machine traces and protocol statements. *Behavioral Science, 13,* 155-161.

Elkind, J., Card, S., Hochberg, J., & Huey B. (Eds.). (1990). *Human performance models for computer aided engineering.* New York: Academic Press.

Hammond, K.R. (1988). Judgment and decision making in dynamic tasks. *Information and Decision Technologies, 14,* 3-14.

Heil, J. (1981). Does cognitive psychology rest on a mistake? *Mind, 90,* 321-342.

Hogarth, R.M. (1986). Generalization in decision research: The role of formal models. *IEEE Systems, Man, and Cybernetics, 16,* 445.

Hutchins, E. (1990). The technology of team navigation. In J. Galegher, J. R. Kraut, & C. Egido, (Eds.), *Intellectual teamwork: Social and technological foundations of cooperative work* (pp. 191-220). Hillsdale, NJ: Lawrence Erlbaum Associates.

Hutchins, E. (1991). *How a cockpit remembers its speed* (Tech. Rep.). University of California at San Diego, Distributed Cognition Laboratory.

Johnson, P.E., Moen, J.B., & Thompson, W.B. (1988). Garden path errors in diagnostic reasoning. In L. Bolec & M. J. Coombs (Eds.), *Expert system Applications* (pp. 395-428). New York: Springer-Verlag.

Kieras, D.E., & Polson, P.G. (1985). An approach to the formal analysis of user complexity. *International Journal of Man-Machine Studies, 22*, 365-394.

Kirlik, A., Miller, R.A., & Jagacinski, R. (1989). A process model of skilled human performance in a dynamic uncertain environment. In *Proceedings of IEEE Conference on Systems, Man, and Cybernetics, 1*, 1-23.

Marr, D. (1982).*Vision.* San Francisco: Freeman.

Newell, A. (1980). Physical symbol systems. *Cognitive Science, 4*, 135-183.

Newell, A. (1982). The knowledge level. *Artificial Intelligence, 18*, 87-127.

Newell, A. (1990). *Unified theories of cognition.* Cambridge, MA: Harvard University Press.

Newell, A., & Simon, H.A. (1963). GPS, a program that simulates human thought. In E. A. Feigenbaum & J. Feldman (Eds.), *Computers and thought* (pp. 279-293). New York: McGraw Hill.

Newell, A., & Simon, H.A. (1972). *Human problem solving.* Englewood Cliffs, NJ: Prentice-Hall.

Payne, J. W., Johnson, E. J., Bettman, J.R., & Coupey, E. (1990). Understanding contingent choice: A computer simulation approach. *IEEE Systems, Man, and Cybernetics, 20*, 296-309.

Pylyshyn, Z.W. (1991). The role of cognitive architectures in theories of cognition. In K. VanLehn (Ed.), *Architectures for intelligence: The 22nd Carnegie Mellon Symposium on Cognition* (pp. 189-223). Hillsdale, NJ: Lawrence Erlbaum Associates.

Reason, J. (1987). A preliminary classification of mistakes. In J. Rasmussen, K. Duncan, & J. Leplat (Eds.), *New technology and human error* (pp. 15-22). Chichester, UK: Wiley.

Roth, E.M., & Woods, D.D., (1988). Aiding human performance: I. Cognitive analysis. *Le Travail Humain, 51*, 39-64.

Roth, E.M., Woods, D.D., & Pople, H.E. (1992). Cognitive simulation as a tool for cognitive task analysis. *Ergonomics, 35*, 1163-1198.

Simon, H.A. (1969). *The sciences of the Artificial.* Cambridge, MA: MIT Press.

Simon, H.A. (1991). Cognitive architecture and rational analysis: Comment. In K. VanLehn (Ed.), *Architectures for intelligence: The 22nd Carnegie Mellon Symposium on Cognition* (pp. 25-39). Hillsdale, NJ: Lawrence Erlbaum Associates.

Woods, D.D. (1988). Coping with complexity: The psychology of human behavior in complex systems. In L. P. Goodstein, H. B. Andersen, & S. E. Olsen (Eds.), *Mental models, tasks and errors* (pp. 128-148). London: Taylor & Francis.

Woods, D.D. (1990). Modeling and predicting human error. In J. Elkind, S. Card, J. Hochberg, & B. Huey (Eds.), *Human performance models for computer-aided engineering* (pp. 248-274). New York: Academic Press.

Woods, D.D. (1992). *The alarm problem and directed attention* (Tech. Rep.) Columbus, OH: The Ohio State University, Cognitive Systems Engineering Laboratory.

Woods, D.D. (in press). Towards a theoretical base for representation design in the computer medium: Ecological perception and aiding human cognition. In J. Flach, P. Hancock, J. Caird, & K. Vicente (Eds.), *The ecology of human-machine systems*. Hillsdale, NJ: Lawrence Erlbaum Associates.

Woods, D.D. (1994). Cognitive demands and activities in dynamic fault management: Abductive reasoning and disturbance management. In N. Stanton (Ed.), *The human factors of alarm design*. (pp. 63-92). London: Taylor & Francis.

Woods, D.D., Johannesen, L., Cook, R.I., & Sarter, N. (in press) *Behind human error: cognitive systems, computers and hindsight*. Wright-Patterson AFB, OH: Crew Systems Ergonomic Information and Analysis Center.

Woods, D.D., & Roth, E.M. (1986). *Models of cognitive behavior in nuclear power plant personnel, Vol. 2* (Tech. Rep. No. NUREG-CR-4532). Washington DC: U.S. Nuclear Regulatory Commission.

Woods, D.D., & Roth, E.M. (1988). Cognitive systems engineering. In M. Helander (Ed.), *Handbook of human-computer interaction* (pp. 3-43). New York: North-Holland.

Woods, D.D., Roth, E.M., & Pople, H.E. (1987). *Cognitive environment simulation: An artificial intelligence system for human performance assessment, Vol. 2* (Tech. Rep. No. NUREG-CR-4862). Washington DC: U.S. Nuclear Regulatory Commission.

Woods, D.D., Pople, H.E., & Roth, E.M. (1990). *The cognitive environment simulation as a tool for modeling human performance and reliability, Vol. 2* (Tech. Rep. No. NUREG-CR-5213). Washington DC: U. S. Nuclear Regulatory Commission .

ACKNOWLEDGMENTS

Our ideas about the role of cognitive simulation evolved throughout the Cognitive Environment Simulation project especially through collaboration with Harry Pople, Jr. We would also like to thank Bernard Pavard for many wonderful discussions of the potential of cognitive simulation techniques. Kevin Corker and the computational human factors team at NASA Ames Research Center have also influenced our ideas on the role of cognitive simulation. The preparation of this paper was supported, in part, by the Aerospace Human Factors Research Division of the NASA Ames Research Center.

SECTION 2

DEVELOPMENT OF COMPETENCE AND EXPERTISE

6

Error Analysis and Expert-Novice Differences in Medical Diagnosis

Nicholas BOREHAM
University of Manchester

Training and support for diagnosis are often based on a narrow definition of the cognitive skills involved in this critical task. The present chapter examines the complexity of medical diagnosis by analyzing errors and comparing expert and novice diagnostic strategies. The results suggest that diagnosis may involve as many as five interacting lines of reasoning. Training and decision support in complex, dynamic environments should take account of all the cognitive operations these imply.

What is diagnosis? The word entered the English language in the seventeenth century, introduced from the ancient Greek writings of Galen and Hippocrates. Its meaning was derived from the original Greek words dia (differentiation) and gnosis (knowledge) "to know the situation that confronts you well enough to differentiate it from other situations with which it might be confused." This has remained the everyday meaning of the word up to the present time. It implies the ability to understand a problem as the basis for taking action, an essential requirement for the supervisor of any continuous process.

In many technical contexts, however, the word has acquired a much narrower meaning. In fault-finding, diagnosis usually means the localization of a specific defect which is causing the system to malfunction. In medicine, it usually means the identification of the precise pathophysiology which is causing a patient's illness. The argument of the present chapter is that this concept of diagnosis is too narrow to serve as a basis for designing training and support in complex, dynamic environments. Diagnosing dynamic systems under conditions of uncertainty involves a much wider range of cognitive operations than the convergent search process implied by localizing a fault or naming a disease. This argument is developed by examining the case of medical diagnosis.

EXPERTISE IN MEDICAL DIAGNOSIS

We begin with a brief review of research in the psychology of medical diagnosis. Early work in this field assumed that expertise depended on skill at hypothesis testing. Many different versions of a hypothetico-deductive model of diagnostic reasoning were proposed. The following is typical, diagnosis being represented as a sequence of stages.

1. hypothesis generation (i.e., listing the diseases which are consistent with the patient's complaint);

2. information search (i.e., gathering further data relevant to each disease hypothesis);

3. data interpretation (i.e., classifying abnormal findings as confirming (occurring in both disease and patient), non-confirming (occurring in disease but not patient), and non-contributory (occurring in patient but not disease);

4. hypothesis evaluation (i.e., accepting or rejecting disease hypotheses, or ranking them in order of probability).

The advantage of this strategy was believed to be its capacity for converting an open problem (What's wrong with the patient?) into a set of closed problems (Has he got disease X? Has he got disease Y?) (Elstein, Shulman, & Sprafka, 1978). The hypothetico-deductive model does indeed converge rapidly on the subjectively most probable disease hypothesis. However, later in this chapter, it will be argued that this convergence can result in error.

The main building blocks of the model, disease hypotheses, were viewed as a framework for organizing the information the doctor acquired as he/she proceeded with the diagnostic investigation (Barrows & Bennett, 1972). This was regarded as crucial to expertise, because diagnostic problems generate huge quantities of information which may result in error unless the doctor finds a way of structuring and chunking it (British Medical Journal, 1977). Some studies found that doctors generated multiple hypotheses simultaneously, and some that they generated hypotheses sequentially. However, there was general agreement that the number of working hypotheses was small, generally not more than about five.

Various forms of simulation were used to explore the hypothetico-deductive model. Two major projects used high-fidelity simulation, employing actors and actresses to play sick patients who were interviewed by medical students, interns and experienced doctors as if in real-life consultations (Elstein et al., 1978; Barrows & Tamblyn, 1980). Videotaping was used to capture all aspects of these diagnostic encounters, including body language. However, most of the research employed low fidelity simulation. A frequently-used instrument of this kind was the patient-management problem, in which a patient's medical history and presenting complaint is described and the subject is required to gather information by asking questions from a list (McGuire & Babbott, 1967). The high fidelity approach enabled qualitative data to be gathered about the way hypotheses were tested — such as their content, or how they related to the history taking or physical examination (Barrows & Tamblyn, 1980). In contrast, much of the low-fidelity research focused on information-theoretic aspects of data gathering, expertise being defined in terms of efficient search strategies which avoided irrelevant and redundant questioning.

The view that expertise in diagnosis could be equated with the hypothetico-deductive method failed to find support. Four findings were particularly significant for this conclusion. First, many studies found that diagnostic expertise was case-dependent: That is, a doctor would diagnose successfully if knowledgeable about the pathology in question; unsuccessfully if not knowledgeable (McGuire, 1976; Elstein et al., 1978). Moreover, the between-case variation in the performance of individual doctors was so great that Leaper, Gill, Staniland, Horrocks, & de Dombal (1973) concluded "the diagnostic process does not exist" (p. 569).

Second, although a difference was found in questioning strategy — experts tending to ask fewer questions, each of which produced greater payoff in terms of reduction of uncertainty (Leaper et al., 1973) — doctors with different levels of diagnostic skill did not show many other differences in the extent to which they followed the hypothetico-deductive method. Thus in Elstein et al.'s (1978) study, when a comparison was made between superior and non-superior diagnosticians (as judged by their peers), no differences were found in the point of generation of the first hypothesis, the total number of hypotheses generated, nor the number of cues acquired.

Third, the hypothetico-deductive method itself can be a source of error. For example, Elstein et al. (1978) found that hypothesis formation led to premature closure and restricted information gathering, which reduced the accuracy of the diagnosis if the initial hypothesis was not correct.

Fourth, what distinguished the best diagnosticians was the content of their hypotheses — the experts were more likely to include the correct diagnosis in the initial hypothesis set (Elstein et al., 1978; Neufeld, Norman, Feightner, & Barrows, 1981).

When it emerged that knowledge of the problem domain was a better indicator of diagnostic expertise than adherence to the hypothetico-deductive method, the attention of researchers shifted to eliciting and modeling medical knowledge. Undoubtedly, experts know more than novices — the basis of expertise was sought rather in the way that expert knowledge is organized. An early study by Wortman (1966) had failed to confirm the discrimination net as an explanatory model of the structure of doctors' knowledge of neurological diseases, albeit in a small sample. In the search for the structure of expert medical knowledge that followed, one line of research applied the recall techniques developed by Chase and Simon (1973) for studying expertise in chess. When asked to recall the details of a patient case history, experts did so in a smaller number of "runs", each of which contained a larger number of items, than was the case with novices. This suggests that expert medical knowledge is organized into coherent large-scale units, whereas novice knowledge comprises more isolated elements (Muzzin et al., 1982). This may explain how experts are able to extract more meaning from a set of data, for example, by recognizing syndromes. A further contribution to understanding the knowledge base in medicine is Feltovich's (1981) suggestion that experts re-organize their knowledge of diseases into disease competitor sets (groups of similar and therefore confusable diseases).

To model the representation of disease hypotheses in memory, the idea of disease frames was developed. A disease frame is a schematic knowledge structure which depicts and organizes the pattern of patient data expected in a given disease (Pople, 1977). Through experience and exposure to the different manifestations of a disease in many patients, an expert differentiates a single disease frame into numerous variants. Diagnostic reasoning proceeds by matching patient data with the disease frames stored in memory (Johnson, Duran, Hassebrock, Moller, Priutela, Feltovich, & Swanson, 1981).

Another popular concept is the mental model. An early study by Kleinmuntz (1968) proposed that experts in neurology diagnose by reference to a stored model of the nervous system. Both Kuipers and Kassirer (1984) and Patel and Groen (1986) have since proposed that expert diagnosis depends on possession of a causal model of the problem domain.

However, knowledge is not sufficient to explain diagnosis. We also need to explain how the individual operates on this base. Patel and Groen (1986) used discourse analysis of think-aloud protocols to model expert diagnosis as a process of forward reasoning through a network of rules. Forward reasoning is data-driven, the antithesis of the hypothetico-deductive method which reasons backwards from disease hypotheses to data in an attempt to confirm or falsify the hypotheses. In the Patel and Groen study, backward reasoning was associated with less success in diagnosis than forward reasoning. Other recent work has focused on comprehension, that is the interpretation of patient data in terms of an existing knowledge base. Using techniques of conceptual analysis, many researchers — notably Feltovich, Spiro, & Coulson (1989) — have identified differences between expert and novice understanding of key disease entities, such as heart failure. They have demonstrated medical students' misconceptions of pathology which can misdirect their diagnostic thinking. It has even proved possible to trace a direct influence for such misconceptions and errors to the primary instructional materials used by medical students (Feltovich, Johnson, Moller, & Swanson, 1984).

Thus in the space of forty years, research into the psychology of medical diagnosis has made significant progress. It has developed a hypothetico-deductive model of expertise, and has replaced it by a knowledge-based model which guides most contemporary research. Hypothetico-deductive reasoning has not been discarded completely; it accounts for some of the data found in protocols. However, today it is regarded as a "weak" problem-solving method used most frequently by novices.

The starting point for the present chapter is the concept of disease. This has been the main building block in the psychological theorizing reviewed above. Although, as we have described, the disease hypothesis (conceived as a verbal proposition to be tested against data) was replaced by the idea of a cluster of pathophysiological concepts and their relationships, the assumption that diagnostic expertise depends on the ability to operate on representations of disease entities has remained unchanged. The present chapter questions this. The argument is that the identification of a disease entity may be the *end-point* of diagnosis, but the *process* by which experts reach it involves a far wider variety of reasoning processes, among which thinking about disease entities is only one. Like the hypothetico-deductive method itself, diagnostic thinking that restricts itself to a consideration of disease entities alone is characteristic of novices, and may lead to error. The first step in the argument is to distinguish between the diagnosis of diseases and the diagnosis of patients.

DIAGNOSIS OF DISEASES
AND DIAGNOSIS OF PATIENTS

Diagnosis of Diseases

Feinstein (1973) defines the diagnosis of diseases as the process of: "converting observed evidence into the names of diseases. The evidence consists of data obtained from examining a patient and substances derived from the patient; the diseases are conceptual medical entities that identify or explain abnormalities in the observed evidence" (p. 212).

Originally, the concept of "disease" simply meant dis-ease, that is feeling unwell. However, with the advent of scientific medicine, physicians began to identify different disease entities underlying different complaints of "dis-ease." Each was viewed as the cause of a distinct set of clinical signs and symptoms. In the 19th century, anatomists succeeded in correlating patterns of clinical findings with specific anatomical disorders found in cadavers at post-mortem examination. In the view of many, it became the task of the clinical diagnostician to infer from outward appearances what inner disease entity was causing the patient's illness.

Thus conceptualized, a disease is a causal chain: Manifestations (e.g., symptoms) are caused by disorders (gross abnormalities in the structure or function of an organ or system of the body, e.g., an increase in size), which in turn are caused by pathological processes (morphological or biochemical events such as inflammation), which are caused by etiological factors (genetic or environmental states which set the whole chain in motion). The diseases — causal chains — are ordered within taxonomies such as the International Classification of Diseases, and diagnosis becomes a process of placing a case within one (or more) of these categories. The process of causal diagnosis usually begins with an investigation of the patient's symptoms, tracing them back down the chain until the source of the problem is confirmed

To classify a problem in this way adds information to the clinical findings by suggesting the etiology, pathogenesis, prognosis, and many other characteristics of the illness. On another level, the use of diagnostic labels in place of a diverse collection of findings facilitates the chunking of information, necessary for communication, record-keeping, and research.

This concept of disease is similar to the fault-finding model of system malfunction, where causal chains link the symptoms of a breakdown to the failure of one or more components. In both models, diagnosis tends to be regarded as the localization of the failed component on the basis of the symptoms. However, if disease is conceived on a broader basis — for instance, as a system-level problem — then an alternative approach to diagnosis becomes necessary.

Diagnosis of Patients

Before the correlation of internal lesions with external symptoms, physicians were unable to diagnose in the way outlined above. Nevertheless, they often made intelligent assessments of their patients' problems, and selected treatments that were effective within the limits of what was available. A study of these ancient methods can be revealing. The Hippocratic school is said to have diagnosed the patient rather than the disease. That is, they diagnosed by differentiating between individuals, not between pathophysiological conditions. This involved generating a holistic picture of the patient by gathering a prodigious range of details, including the minutes details of his or her complaint, environment, appearance, and lifestyle. On the basis of this idiographic representation, the physician would predict the likely course of the particular illness and choose a treatment to divert it from its trajectory. Insofar as there existed concepts of different diseases, these were little more than names for groups of patients who tended to fall ill in much the same way. The fact that common etiological factors were subsequently discovered for many of these empirical groupings, and that causal definitions of disease names replaced symptomatic ones, does not destroy the distinction between these two ways of diagnosing. They are based on different sets of data and involve different patterns of information search. What now needs to be considered is whether, in the age of scientific medicine, the broader perspective offered by the diagnosis of patients has entirely lost its place in expert reasoning.

DIAGNOSIS IN GENERAL PRACTICE

The general practitioner is usually the first to be consulted by a patient who has experienced a symptom and who seeks medical advice. The consultation is a complex event with a high level of uncertainty — many patients report symptoms which are normal reactions to the stress of everyday living, rather than the result of organic disease. Even when organic disease is present, it may be in an early stage, before the symptoms by which it can be diagnosed have appeared. This uncertainty reduces the extent to which the doctor's task can be represented solely as the diagnosis of diseases.

Michael Balint, an influential figure in the education of British general practitioners, was one of the first to question the adequacy of traditional concepts of diagnosis and disease for general practice. He distinguished between the "conventional diagnosis" taught in medical school, and what he called the "overall diagnosis," defined as the understanding of people in a professional capacity. Overall diagnosis is patient-centered and holistic. It encompasses "the external pressures on the patient, his internal world, his relationship with significant people around him, and the way in which the doctor-patient relationship has developed" (Norell, 1973, p. xv).

A similarly holistic perspective on heart disease has been suggested by Nixon, who regards much of this kind of illness as a system-level failure attributable to the pursuit of a lifestyle incompatible with one's physiological reserves. He argues the insufficiency of conventional diagnostic approaches in the following terms: "People push themselves or allow themselves to be driven beyond their physiological territory into boundary-testing. Some live with sick or inadequate systems for years on end without having the energy, the information, or the opportunity for recovery. The label 'ME' or 'post-viral syndrome' does not point out the remedy" (Nixon, 1990, pp. 460-461).

These ways of understanding patients' problems are quite different from the localization of specific organic defects. They are more in line with the ancient method of diagnosing patients. To explore this dimension of expert thinking further, we will consider some examples of diagnostic error in general practice.

DIAGNOSTIC ERRORS IN GENERAL PRACTICE

Three illustrative cases are described here, all of which have been taken from a study of diagnostic errors made by trainees in general practice. In each case, the trainee's diagnostic thinking is compared with that of an expert general practitioner who was providing supervision.

Case One

A trainee was called to a patient who complained of a stiff neck and muscle spasms. The trainee inquired about recent accidents and the patient reported that she had scratched herself on a rose tree when gardening — a plant which is often fertilized in England with horse dung. When the trainee examined her, he found facial stiffness. He diagnosed tetanus and telephoned the covering general practitioner for advice.

As he listened over the telephone, the more experienced doctor immediately doubted the diagnosis. He inquired whether the trainee had asked the patient what drugs she was taking. This, however, he had omitted to do. The experienced doctor went to the patient's house, but the patient did not seem to him like a case of tetanus. In his own words, she was "not ill enough." He went into the kitchen, found the cupboard in which she kept her personal hoard of medicines, and opened it up. In this way, he discovered that she had been dosing herself with a drug whose side effects include facial stiffness, and the diagnosis of tetanus was disconfirmed.

In comparing how the trainee and the more experienced doctor approached this problem, the most obvious difference is the breadth of their information search. The trainee focused narrowly on the abnormal physical finding of facial stiffness and the etiologically significant history of a rose-scratch. Such a convergent search is typical of the diagnosis of a disease. In contrast, the more experienced doctor set the abnormal findings within the context of the patient as a person — how ill she was in herself, and her hypochondriacal lifestyle. The broader search brought disconfirming evidence into the picture, enabling the doctor to fit the data to an alternative pattern — the anxious patient who is causing her own symptoms by self-medication. This way of reasoning was based on knowledge of human nature, and has much in common with the ancient diagnosis of patients. However, the expert doctor was doing much more than this: He also made use of his knowledge of disease entities. Having seen cases of tetanus before, he realized instantly that the patient was not ill enough for it to be tetanus. Thus in the expert, diagnosing the disease was performed in tandem with diagnosing the patient.

Case Two

A trainee just two months into his post was called out at midnight to a 29-year-old female patient who complained of a central right abdominal pain of four hours' standing. He suspected appendicitis, although there had been no vomiting (which would have increased the probability of this diagnosis). When the patient refused further physical examination, the trainee proposed emergency admission to hospital for suspected appendicitis. When the patient refused this too, he called the covering general practitioner.

The experienced doctor arrived and immediately recognized the patient as an attention-seeking individual well known in the practice. He doubted the trainee's diagnosis and suggested that the patient attend the morning surgery in a few hours' time for further investigation. In the event, the trainee's diagnosis turned out to be a false alarm.

In comparing how the trainee and the more experienced doctor approached this problem, once again a difference in the breadth of information search is apparent. The trainee focused on pathognomic symptoms and diagnosed a disease, while the experienced physician diagnosed the patient on the basis of his knowledge of her as a person. However, the expert followed this line of reasoning in parallel with diagnostic thinking of the conventional, disease-centered kind. Since the pain was only of four hours' standing and there had been no vomiting, he reasoned that if it really was appendicitis, this was only the early stage. It would therefore be safe to wait until morning to observe further developments — for example, whether the classic pattern of signs and symptoms appeared. The trainee did not think of using time as a diagnostic tool in this way.

Case Three

A 62-year-old construction worker, who was a rare attender at the surgery, reported a sudden attack of central chest pain radiating to the neck. The trainee took the patient's blood pressure, and on finding that it was high, diagnosed hypertension. In fact, the patient had suffered a heart attack, the symptoms being classic. The misdiagnosis was primarily due to the trainee not knowing that blood pressure can be transiently high in ischaemic attacks, that is ignorance of the relevant disease entity.

However, this was not the only source of the error. In comparing the trainee's approach with that of the experienced general practitioner who was supervising him, it emerged that in such circumstances the latter would have asked himself why the patient had come to the surgery, and would have taken the patient's occupation into account. This is to diagnose the patient: When it is asked why a heavy manual worker who rarely attends the surgery has come to report a chest pain, that particular symptom acquires more significance than it was given by the trainee.

EXPERTISE

The point illustrated by these cases is that diagnostic error in uncertain environments can be due to adopting a narrow perception of the problem. Such narrowness is encouraged by the traditional concept of disease entities, which tends to focus attention on pathognomic signs and symptoms to the exclusion of the patient as a whole. In contrast, the experienced doctors viewed the cases in broader terms. Their perceptual field was the patient, conceived as an individual whom they expected to behave in particular ways, with the physical signs and symptoms only part of this larger picture.

To understand the advantage of the expert diagnostic strategy, it is necessary to appreciate the high level of uncertainty in this particular task environment. A very wide range of problems can walk through a general practitioner's door, but the resources for investigating them by the methods of hospital medicine are limited. The broad purview of experienced general practitioners can be interpreted as a way of solving the problem of lack of fidelity in the signal by increasing the bandwidth of their search. In other words, construing ambiguous signs and symptoms in the context of expectations about the patient's behavior can clarify their meaning.

This strategy has much in common with the diagnosis of patients in prescientific days, and with Balint's concept of overall diagnosis. However, it differs in important ways. It differs from the ancient diagnosis of patients because it is not a substitute for reasoning about pathophysiological entities, but an overarching strategy which includes the latter as a subroutine. It differs from the Balint approach by including in its scope illnesses that are organic in origin, whereas Balint was primarily concerned with the minor psychiatric illnesses that produce physical symptoms.

If diagnosis is represented as identifying specific disease entities, then the reasoning process is relatively simple. The knowledge base consists of specific pathophysiological conditions and how they manifest themselves. However, when problems are more complex, expert diagnostic reasoning is based on a more complex set of reasoning processes and on a broader knowledge base. Current research focuses on disease knowledge, but the cases discussed above suggest that the expert knowledge base also includes an understanding of patients as people. The remainder of this chapter describes five lines of reasoning which may be interwoven in this kind of thinking.

FIVE LINES OF DIAGNOSTIC REASONING

Understanding Normal Variability

The diagnostician must differentiate normal system states from abnormal ones. Abnormality is an ambiguous concept, that has both causal and stochastic meanings: It may be construed either as a malfunction or as a deviation from average behavior. A source of uncertainty in many diagnostic tasks is that particular systems, whether human beings, blast furnaces, computer installations or flexible manufacturing plants, have idiosyncratic ways of behaving. Consequently, knowledge of the range of behavior manifested by a particular system in a healthy state can assist in understanding whether or not its abnormal behavior indicates a defect. This line of reasoning is illustrated by the expert doctor in Case One. An important part of the knowledge base is familiarity with the specific environment in which the problem has occurred — in general medical practice, this may include personal knowledge of individual patients.

Attributing Abnormal Signs and Symptoms to the System's Normal Response to Adverse Operating Conditions

Whereas the first line of reasoning sets the boundaries of normal and abnormal behavior for a particular system, this one draws causal links between the behavior of a system and the conditions under which it is operating. It enables the diagnostician to interpret supposed abnormalities as the normal responses to the way an intrinsically healthy system reacts to adverse operating conditions. The knowledge base comprises how the system functions in a healthy state, and which environmental factors may disrupt it. However, when training is based on the narrow view that diagnosis is the localization of a specific defect, it tends to neglect the latter.

Assessing the Response of the System to an Intervention Designed to Remove the Symptoms

Diagnosis is sometimes represented as a discrete event which precedes treatment, the latter being selected in the light of the former. In complex, dynamic environments, however, attempts to understand the problem may alternate with attempts to solve it. Symptomatic treatment is a powerful diagnostic tool in uncertain environments: Whether or not the symptom disappears may generate crucial information. So we may define a third line of reasoning — assessing how the system is responding to attempts to control its abnormal behavior by purely symptomatic treatment, before any physical defect has been identified. Assessment of this kind probably takes up more of the general practitioner's time than efforts to diagnose diseases in the conventional way.

These three lines of reasoning support the broader diagnostic strategy demonstrated by the experts whose decision making was discussed earlier. However, they operate in parallel with the traditional disease-oriented approach to diagnosis, so for completeness we must include the two other lines of reasoning which relate to that way of thinking.

Identifying a Specific Defect That is Causing Symptoms

This is the identification of a causal link between symptom and etiological entity, which (we have argued) is often wrongly assumed to be the sole line of reasoning in diagnosis. The dangers of this assumption have already been emphasized — increased chances of error in uncertain environments, and the delay of intervention until the fault has caused sufficient damage to generate the data by which it can be diagnosed.

Predicting How a Defective System Will Continue to Malfunction

After a disease has been diagnosed, a prognosis of its future course may be made. This is distinct from the prediction of normal system functioning defined above. It may be a crucial line of reasoning where a specific fault has been found and the main concern is damage limitation.

KNOWLEDGE FOR TRAINING AND SUPPORTING DIAGNOSIS

The practical purpose of defining these five lines of diagnostic reasoning is to identify the knowledge which should underpin training and decision support. The technical knowledge required for the last two lines of reasoning has been extensively discussed elsewhere. The main point to be made about the first three is that they require a broadening of the conventional knowledge base. One direction this broadening must take is towards the representation of whole systems interacting with their environments. Another is the incorporation of idiographic knowledge of the peculiarities of individual systems. Unfortunately, the training of diagnosticians, insofar as it is based on "fault localization" models, gives insufficient emphasis to holistic, contextualized, and idiographic knowledge. Similar concerns must be expressed about many conventional approaches to decision support.

REFERENCES

Barrows, H.S., & Bennett, K. (1972). The diagnostic (problem-solving) skill of the neurologist: Experimental studies and their implication for neurological training. *Archives of Neurology, 26,* 273-277.

Barrows, H.S. & Tamblyn, R.M. (1980). *Problem based learning. An approach to medical education.* New York: Springer.

British Medical Journal (1977). Reducing doctors' errors (editorial). *British Medical Journal, 1977, 1,* 1178-1179.

Chase, W.G., & Simon, H.A. (1973). Perception in chess. *Cognitive Psychology, 1,* 55-81.

Elstein, A.S., Shulman, L.S., & Sprafka, S.A. (1978). *Medical problem solving: An analysis of clinical reasoning.* Cambridge, MA: Harvard University Press.

Feinstein, A. R. (1973). An analysis of diagnostic reasoning. I. The domains and disorders of clinical macrobiology. *Yale Journal of Biology and Medicine, 46,* 212-232.

Feltovich, P.J. (1981). *Knowledge based components of expertise in medical diagnosis* (Tech. Rep. No. PDS 2). Pittsburgh: University of Pittsburgh, Learning Research and Development Center.

Feltovich, P.J., Johnson, P.E., Moller, J.H., & Swanson, D.B. (1984). DCS: The role and development of medical knowledge in diagnostic expertise. In W.J. Clancy & E.H. Shortcliffe (Eds.), *Readings in medical artificial intelligence: The first decade* (pp. 55-65). Reading, MA: Addison-Wesley.

Feltovich, P.J., Spiro, R.J., & Coulson, R.L. (1989). The nature of conceptual understanding in biomedicine: The deep structure of complex ideas and the development of misconceptions. In D.A. Evans & V.L. Patel (Eds.), *Cognitive science in medicine* (pp. 102-120). Cambridge, MA: The MIT Press.

Johnson, P.E., Duran, A.S., Hassebrock, F., Moller, J., Prietula, M., Feltovich, P.J., & Swanson D.B. (1981). Expertise and error in diagnostic reasoning. *Cognitive Science, 5,* 235-283.

Kuipers, B., & Kassirer, J. (1984). Causal reasoning in medicine: Analysis of a protocol. *Cognitive Science, 8,* 363-385.

Leaper, D.J., Gill, P.W., Staniland, J.R., Horrocks, J.C., & de Dombal, F.T. (1973). Clinical diagnostic process: An analysis. *British Medical Journal, 3,* 569-574.

McGuire, C.H. (1976). Simulation technique in the teaching and testing of problem-solving skills. *Journal of Research in Science Teaching, 13,* 89-100.

McGuire, C.H., & Babbott, D. (1967). Simulation technique in the measurement of problem-solving skills. *Journal of Educational Measurement, 4,* 1-10.

Muzzin, L.J., Norman, G.R., Jacoby, L.L., Feightner, J.W., Tugwell, P., & Guyatt, G.H. (1982, September). *Manifestations of expertise in recall of clinical protocols.* Paper presented at the *21st Annual Conference on Research in Medical Education,* Washington DC.

Neufeld, V.R., Norman, G.R., Feightner, J.W., & Barrows, H.S. (1981). Clinical problem-solving by medical students: a longitudinal and cross-sectional analysis. *Medical Education, 15,* 315-327.

Nixon, P. (1990). Contribution to discussion. *Philosophical Transactions of the Royal Society of London, B327,* 449-462.

Norell, J. S. (1973). Introduction. In E. Balint & J. S. Norrell (Eds.), *Six minutes for the patient* (pp. ix-xxi). London: Tavistock/Routledge.

Patel, V.L., & Groen, G. (1986). Knowledge based solution strategies in medical reasoning. *Cognitive Science, 10,* 91-116.

Pople, H.E. (1977, August). *The formation of composite hypotheses in diagnostic problem-solving: An exercise in synthetic reasoning.* Paper presented at the *Fifth International Joint Conference on Artificial Intelligence.* Pittsburgh, PA.

Wortman, P.M. (1966). Representation and strategy in diagnostic problem-solving. *Human Factors, 8,* 48-53.

7

Conceptual Models for Training

Renan SAMURÇAY
CNRS - University of Paris 8

There is a general consensus that operators of complex systems use and control these production tools by forming mental models of the system which can differ from those used by system design engineers. The aim of this chapter is to develop the idea that a conceptual model is a kind of system model that combines the properties and functionalities of both the operator's mental model and real operating models. The present discussion centers on the relevance of these conceptual models for operator training, particularly in the domain of dynamic environment management tasks.

In current technical environments, human operators are used to working with artificial systems that have been designed to fulfill functions corresponding to designers' intentions. These artificial systems cover devices used by practically everyone such as computers, calculators, and so on, but also complex systems which are used in the field of production and which require more professional users such as NPP, industrial processes, and so forth. These systems are designed on the basis of existing engineering models which are more or less calculable and carry out expected goals and functions. As a general rule, these models describe the theoretical normal operations of the systems.

In real operations the role of human operators is either to use these devices as tools to accomplish various tasks (such as e-mail or word processor users), or to intervene in the process of production by adjusting deviations of system functioning from the theoretical model (such as NPP operators or aircraft pilots). In this latter case operators are not mere users but are on a par with the system as regards the functions to be fulfilled for task achievement.

It is often argued that users and operators interacting with such systems use and control them by forming mental models of the system which differ from those used to design the systems. Although the concept of mental models has gained a broad audience since the seventies, there is no one definition or formalism to represent such models, as shown by different overviews on this topic (Gentner & Stevens, 1983, Goodstein et al., 1988; and Rogers et al.,

1992). The aim of this chapter is not to give a complete explanation of a mental model, but to introduce the idea of "conceptual model" as a sort of device or system model which combines the properties and functionalities of both the operator's mental model and real operating models. The second aim is to discuss the relevance of these conceptual models for the training of operators, particularly in the domain of dynamic environment management tasks.

This chapter aims to discuss various models developed to describe complex system functioning . A theoretical frame is proposed to categorize these models and discuss their relevance for training purposes.

TASKS, ACTIVITIES, AND MODELS

The main function of models is to enable us to make predictions about external events before carrying out an action. They also help us understand and explain the reality we observe and act on. These models can be more or less calculable, formalized, predictive or descriptive depending both on the state of knowledge about the phenomena to be modeled and the language of description used. As stressed by Hollnagel (1988), the nature of these models depends to a great extent on the characteristics of the object system and the purpose of modeling.

Models in complex tasks

To characterize the complexity of a given task domain such as a dynamic environment supervision task, the four dimensions emphasized by Woods (1988) can be used:

- dynamism of the system (the changes occurring in the system are not all introduced by the operator's actions, the system has its own dynamics, the nature of the problem to be solved can change over time; multiple on-going tasks can have different time spans);

- the number of parts and the extensiveness of interconnections between the parts of variables (a given problem can be due to multiple potential causes and can have multiple potential consequences);

- uncertainty (the available data about system functioning can be erroneous, incomplete, and ambiguous; future states may not be completely predictable);

- risk (the consequences of operators' decisions may be catastrophic or costly as regards the expected task goals).

It is now well known that to manage such complex and dynamic systems, operators need to build and use mental models of the system that provide them with an appropriate level of abstraction to deal with these highly demanding cognitive activities; in this task they are usually assisted by different operative tools which take over part of the cognitive load. The adequacy between the operative tools and the activity supported by them will be discussed below. Mental models form the basis for the operational knowledge which itself constitutes the core of professional competence, as discussed by Rogalski in this volume (see chapter 8). They are constructed either by explicit training or by the activity itself. Their mode of construction may also impact on their properties.

Types of models

Figure 1 presents four main distinctions between the different types of models to be discussed from the point of view of their adequacy and relevancy for operator training.

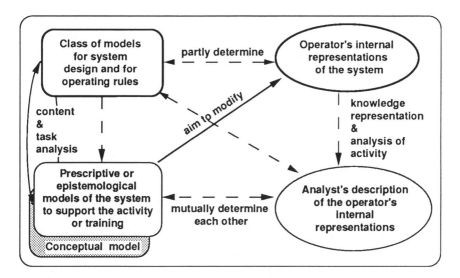

FIGURE 1.   Different   types   of   models   in   terms   of   the structure   and   the   function   of   the   representation   and processing system taken into account in modeling.

The first class covers models that engineers use to design systems and those dealing with automatic regulations: These models are mainly computational and obey physical, chemical, or biological laws and are supported by the existing scientific and engineering knowledge of the domain. The second type of models (operator's models) is concerned with operators' internal representations about the system they are controlling: They are not directly observable but are inferred from observable behaviors. The third model corresponds to the description by the analyst of these internal representations, which can be defined at different levels of abstraction and different levels of granularity. Finally, the fourth type of model (conceptual models) covers the description of plant functioning which aim at supporting activity or training. In this case we will distinguish models based solely on an epistemological analysis of task (prescriptive models) and those which integrate data from the analysis of activity (operative models). Similar distinctions can also be found in Hollnagel (1988).

There are tight connections among these four types of models. The operator model is partly determined by the models used by engineers for plant design and the external representation implemented in cognitive operative tools. The distance between the two types of models can vary as a function of the nature of the plant or device. For example, in some cases such as robotics, operators may need to know how the model of the automatism functions. Norros stresses in this volume (see chapter 9) the critical role of design models in the development of expertise via the construction of theoretical thinking.

The analyst's description of the operator model is highly dependent on the task model that analysts are referring to. Conversely, the elaboration of conceptual models is based on the analysis of operators' activity. Although this chapter focuses on the representational aspects of operators' knowledge, operational knowledge is nevertheless defined as a knowledge structure that incorporates both declarative (system model), procedural knowledge (procedures for determining how to operate on the system), control knowledge (knowledge which determines how to use declarative and procedural knowledge in problem solving) and meta knowledge (knowledge about self competence and self preferences).

PROCESS ENGINEERING MODELS

The main aim of the models used in process engineering is to design, calculate, and operate industrial plants which carry out desired transformations of matter. Process engineering is a very young science, but it has already a number of invariant concepts. Thus, each process, regardless of what it produces can be analyzed in terms of unitary operations (matter and energy transfer between different solid, fluid, and gas phases with respect to the energy required) and reactors (technological tools leading to a given transformation). Moreover, these design models integrate automatic control and regulation models which ensure optimal functioning of the system in real conditions. In the literature, this kind of model is also known as a designer's conceptual model (Wilson & Rutherford, 1989).

It is well known that these types of models cannot be used directly to infer the knowledge basis that operators should acquire to be able to control plants efficiently. Nevertheless, the issue of how and at what level the elements elaborated by process engineering models must be taken into account in the development of conceptual models for training design remains open.

OPERATORS' INTERNAL REPRESENTATIONS AND THEIR DESCRIPTION

The internal representations that operators construct about the plant on which they are acting are not directly observable, but can be inferred from observable behavior. In the past twenty years a great deal of research has been done on operators' internal representations of plants and generally about different kinds of devices (programmable devices, computers, software, etc.). The descriptions used for modeling operators' knowledge depends on both the purpose of modeling, the framework considered for task analysis, and the methods used to collect data. Nevertheless, research in this area can yield some generic properties and the functionalities of these representations and their descriptions.

(1) The first dimension concerns the characteristics of operators' knowledge models. In fact, operators' knowledge about system functioning can involve concepts, rules, procedures and general physical or chemical laws, and the way to implement them in an operative way in specific situations. These two poles, which should in fact be seen as a continuum, are designated by various authors as "declarative versus procedural," "static versus dynamic," "general versus operative," and mainly express the idea that operators' mental models are highly structured by the activity, and that declarative knowledge about the process is not necessarily the operational one. This distinction is also used to characterize operators' expertise: Level of experience is correlated with the degree of operativity of knowledge.

(2) The second dimension concerns the notion of operativity. Operators' internal representations are not simple mappings of engineering or prescriptive models: They are simpler or more schematic. This simplification can be explained by Ochanine (1978, concept of "operative image") who considered that operators' representations of systems are both laconic and functionally deformed by action requirements. The notion of operative image should not only be considered in its figurative aspects, since its form may be propositional as well as schema — or frame — like. Today the terms of "operative representation" or "operative knowledge" are used to designate this kind of knowledge specific to a task or activity.

Ochanine contrasts operative image to cognitive image, which is defined as theoretical and exhaustive knowledge about the system. In some cases the cognitive image has been confused with engineers' knowledge and not believed to be necessarily operational to control the system. Currently there is not enough data to confirm this hypothesis, but there is sufficient information to believe that operators' operational representations are not always sufficient or adequate to solve all classes of problems and some aspects of engineers' knowledge are useful in treating complex problems.

(3) The representations that operators construct about the process are specific to the activity: The control operator's model of a given plant is different from the ones used by maintenance operators although they work in the same plant. This knowledge can be described by taking two components into account (Bainbridge, 1988):

- knowledge about the functioning of the process
- knowledge about goals and actions on the process

Even though these two components can be described separately for purposes of analysis, in the operator's mind they should be tightly connected. In static environments such as the use of a text editor or calculator, users' representations are generally structured in terms of action goals. The transition from this representation to knowledge about the functioning of devices occurs most often when action fails. In dynamic environments knowledge about goals and actions on the process is not sufficient to maintain the system at the desired equilibrium. Moreover, the action-feedback relationship can not be constructed by observing the results of actions, when these integrate both the operator's own transformations and process transformations themselves.

These representations are constructed both by training and by action and experience, and they do not cover the functioning of the process as a whole. Rather they are restricted to that part of the process on which the operator can act directly and to a class of situations for which the operating rules are well known.

(4) Process characteristics partly determine the nature of the representations which need to be constructed by operators. Hoc (1989) defined certain dimensions affecting operators' representations of a process:

-proximity of control: Operators cannot act directly on some variables they have to control; they have to identify those on which they can act to obtain an indirect effect on these control variables.

-information accessibility: Information about some process variables cannot be obtained directly; they should be inferred from directly observable information.

-feedback delay: Effects of some actions may be very long (several hours).

-continuity of variables and process transformations: These are not easy to decompose into a succession of discrete states.

These properties have major effects on the content and the form of operators' mental representations. For instance, it has been shown for a processes such as the blast furnace that operators' knowledge represents observable process variables and some conceptual entities (descriptors of phenomena) which correspond to schematic representations that are operational for control activity (Hoc & Samurçay, 1992). These conceptual constructs enable the operator to understand the current state of the system, to generate possible further evaluations, and to decide on appropriate actions.

The presence in operator's representations of this kind of constructed variable (in contrast to observable variables which are measurable) has been shown to exist also in other process control tasks (Pastré, 1992) and in fire fighting (Rogalski & Samurçay, 1993). These variables, which are also termed "pragmatic concepts," play an important role both in the reduction of complexity and structuration of operative knowledge.

(5) For a given system, different representations with different levels of abstraction and natures can coexist in the operator's mind. According to Rasmussen's (1986) definition of abstraction levels, operators' knowledge about the process is organized in terms of a two-fold hierarchy: part-whole and mean-ends. This description serves to link decision making strategies to the knowledge type (structural, functional) and to the abstraction level (for instance, general functions or physical form) required for the implementation of these strategies.

At the lowest level there is very detailed knowledge about the physical form of a system. Moving upwards the system can be represented as subsystems formed by collections of physical components. The generic function level serves to view the subsystems in terms of their functionnalities. The next level is the level of abstract function such as energy flows. Finally the system can be represented at the level of its overall goal and purpose. Here the main idea is the relationship between the abstraction level and the nature of the task: The system should be viewed at different appropriate levels when performing different tasks.

(6) The form and the content of operators' mental models can be marked by the properties of external representations, such as displays, graphics, tables, language, and so forth. Even though there are very few studies on this point, the form in which system information is presented (for instance, table of values vs. curves) is likely to have an effect (positive or negative) on the way this information is encoded in memory and used in problem solving. Payne (1992) argues for the development of research which examines the sensitivity of content and use of mental models to variations in the representational properties of cognitive artifacts.

PRESCRIPTIVE MODELS

Prescriptive models aim at describing the functioning of a processes in a way that make its comprehension easier for the operator. These descriptions are used mainly for the design of control support systems and for operator training. They are primarily based on epistemological process analysis and assumptions about general human reasoning mechanisms.

In the past fifteen years, one of the challenges to the AI community has been to build models based on "human reasoning" about physical systems. This approach, called "qualitative physics," is aimed at developing systems which can reason about the physical world as well as engineers or scientists can. As stressed by Weld and de Kleer (1990) some important tasks that could drive qualitative physics are diagnosing, designing, operating, and explaining (for instruction) physical systems. According to Forbus (1990) the goal of qualitative physics (QP) is to capture both the common-sense knowledge of the person on the street and the tacit knowledge underlying the quantitative knowledge used by engineers and scientists.

The key idea to qualitative simulation is to find a way to represent the continuous properties of the world by a discrete set of symbols. This is based on the evidence that human operators hardly ever use numerical values of the variables in their reasoning processes: They mainly use qualitative values such as "too high," "too low," and so on. In other words, their decision rules are not only based on the specific values of parameters but also on the classes of values which are interpreted by the operators in a more general context. In this frame the qualitative values are represented by bounded intervals, and their temporal evolution by logical expressions which can take on three values: increase, decrease, stable. Algorithms serve to calculate the possible states of the system by transition rules as a function of the knowledge of the current states.

Some of the potential applications are intelligent tutoring systems and engineering design. Envisionment as an explicit representation of all different possible behaviors of the system is used as a technique to simulate process behavior. Causality plays a major role in qualitative physics; it is the bridge that links reasoning about structure and function. A cause-effect diagram is one of the possible ways to make the device behavior explicit .

Qualitative physics approaches have generated numerous studies describing the functioning of simple physical devices (Weld & de Kleer, 1990) based on some assumptions about human reasoning such as structural abstraction, simplifying assumptions, and operating assumption (for the normal mode alone).

The qualitative simulation approach has been criticized for several reasons:

-it is generally poor at dealing with large complex systems such as real plants and in particular with systems containing feedback: The existing examples only deal with parts of simple physical processes;

-the difficulty involved in dealing with order of magnitude of variables and taking temporal reasoning into account;

-difficulties in distinguishing structure and function: In fact qualitative simulation does not account for the different points of view and levels that can be used to view the system and thus neglects the functional relationships between control task and action;

-the human reasoning models underlying the device models are weak: They only include successful human reasoning and well known human errors and do not consider the variability of available human strategies.

Points of view on the system

Human ability to reason about physical systems or devices depends on the types of knowledge used and on the way this knowledge is organized. There are three main assumptions:

-knowledge about the process has multiple sources and corresponds to the different types of models

-each piece of knowledge can support one or more specific reasoning paradigms

-depending on the situation, human operators can shift from one type of model to another.

Brajnik et al. (1989) suggest analyzing knowledge relevant to a physical system along three dimensions: epistemological type, aggregation level, and physical view. These dimensions can be found under different terms in other authors' classifications for different kinds of tasks such as electronic troubleshooting (White & Frederiksen, 1990) and process control task (Goodstein & Rasmussen, 1988).

The first dimension concerns the type of objects and relations included in the descriptions of the system (such structural, behavioral, functional, teleological, empirical descriptions, and so on). Descriptions are assumed to exhibit partial overlap and each epistemological model may be more or less appropriate for some specific task. The *structural* representation describes what components constitute the system and how they are connected to each other. The *behavioral* representation describes how components work and interact, in particular the time evolution of crucial system variables according to physical laws. The *functional* representation is devoted to describing the specific functions associated with the components of the system; it may depart in varying degrees from behavioral and functional description. The *teleological* representation describes the purpose of the device, its subcomponents, and the operational conditions that enable the achievement of these goals through a correct use of the system. The *empirical* representation covers the associations between system properties that humans usually acquire through direct operation on the system. This knowledge can express empirical laws which to date have no explanatory scientific theories or laws.

The aggregation level represents the degree of granularity of knowledge. The concept of granularity has also been used by Goodstein and Rasmussen (1988) in their concept of abstraction levels and is defined as the level of decomposition of the problem space. Depending on the nature of the task, the various components of the system should not only be considered at different levels of abstraction, but these different levels should also be coordinated to guarantee an appropriate action. For instance, to achieve a particular task the system should be conceived of at the level of generic function (heating or temperature control) and simultaneously at the level of physical form (temperature switches) by passing through the level of physical function (heating circuits). Moray (1990) proposed the lattice formalism to represent the organization of the operator of a complex system in terms of these levels of abstraction. In this formalism a lattice can be defined for each level of abstraction and description. Operator errors are interpreted as arising when nodes of the mental lattices are not connected in the same way as the physical system lattice.

The physical view expresses the idea of the existence of different points of view when considering plant functioning. Views are ways of looking at the plant from a given perspective using an appropriate filter. For instance, in a complex production system such as a blast furnace, a given phenomenon may be analyzed from both thermodynamic and chemical points of view, and this point of view can change both the description of transformations and system decomposition. Of course these views do not always exist for a given device. For instance, the comprehension of a simple electrical circuit does not require multiple physical views, as has been shown in White and Frederiksen (1990).

CONCEPTUAL MODELS

Conceptual models, as stressed before, attempt to integrate both the specificities of process and the organization of operator knowledge about this particular process in prescriptive model design. The notion of conceptual model is related to the notion of "operational knowledge" developed by Rogalski in this volume (see chapter 8). The notion of "operational" refers to invariants in efficient strategies. Thus, analyzing operational knowledge consists in describing efficient operator knowledge implemented in professional practice: It amounts to identifying what categories of objects and procedures are common to efficient practices, even when these practices are specific to the specific situations. This analysis is equivalent to epistemological analysis in the domain of the didactics of sciences, which aims at identifying classes of problems for which a given concept constitutes an appropriate answer.

This approach has been used to describe operational knowledge in different domains such as air traffic control (Bisseret & Enard, 1970), fire fighting (Rogalski & Samurçay, 1993), blast furnace supervision (Hoc & Samurçay, 1992), and automated plastic production control (Pastré, 1992). These different analyses have shown that all the entities manipulated by operators mentally do not entirely match the ones identified in the prescriptive models; the representation and processing systems used by efficient operators involve some operational entities. What was designated above by constructed variables are typical examples of this kind. For instance in a blast furnace supervision task, it has been shown that operators use such variables (descriptors) to designate and evaluate observable process phenomena indirectly. Air traffic controllers' mental maps contain elements which are different from those appearing on a geographic map. For fire fighting commanders the most relevant variables are "tactical variables" which are not the roads on the geographical map, but rather the access roads, defined by their relative positions in space with respect to fire evolution. Pastré (1992) has shown also that the constructed variables are useful in defining incidents such as feed jamming that operators of a plastic injection machine use to diagnose the operation mode of the system.

The second point is related to the adequacy of epistemological types and the part-whole decomposition for all types of processes. For instance, a blast furnace is a process which is not easily decomposable in terms of well identified sub components with corresponding functions (the physico-chemical transformations all occur in a single large tank). Thus, operators use a phenomenological decomposition which promotes to define the equilibrium states to maintain. Decomposition, instead of being given by the structural and functional properties of the system, is governed by the properties of transformations applying to actions.

The third point relates to ways in which actions drive relationships. In operator representations, system variables vary in degree of importance, and do not necessarily introduce causal relations, as can be defined in a process model. Prescriptive models are ill equipped to represent the delay and magnitude of transformations (operators' actions and process transformations) or the way operators represent continuous variables. This is probably due to the extreme difficulties researchers have in accessing this kind of information that operators can not easily make explicit.

Operational models can be classified into two categories with respect to the nature of knowledge they model: *representation* oriented and *strategy* oriented. The first type of model mainly describes operational entities and relations (causal, functional, transformational, etc.) among these entities. The second type mainly describes the organization of information processing which should be implemented when searching for a solution in a particular task domain. The problem solving methods belong to this latter category: They guide and organize subjects' problem solving strategies. This distinction is not really an opposition, but rather highlights the main characteristics of the models. For example, the phenomenological model designed by Hoc & Samurçay (1992) for blast furnace supervision task is more representation oriented in that it describes the entire process functioning around the phenomena which are related to each other mainly by causal relationships and for which four types of entities (causes, consequences, indicators, and possible actions) were defined. Conversely, the goal-oriented model developed by Patrick (1989; 1993) for fault finding in an automated hot strip mill is mostly strategy oriented: It defines three stepwise goals (initial symptom identification, global fault set reduction, and searching within a subsystem) to guide operators' search by prescribing more tractable goals and sub goals. Similarly, the method for tactical reasoning designed for emergency management tasks is a strategy oriented model (Samurçay & Rogalski, 1991): it describes the invariant strategies implemented by efficient operators in the form of a control loop composed of different phases of the decision task (information gathering management, planning, decision and control).

The purpose here is not to contrast prescriptive models to conceptual models, but to argue that the functional deformations of the operators' model should be taken into account in the design of conceptual models for training. In this case, engineers' knowledge can be used to improve and complete operative representations. In this way it is possible to establish a dialectic relationship between different approaches.

CONCEPTUAL MODELS AND TRAINING

Needs for operator training

Why do operators need to acquire operational models of the processes they control? To reach optimal productivity within safety and reliability norms not only requires technical solutions but stable and efficient operator performance as well. Most technological changes require operators to develop new systems of representation. In well known, familiar situations operators handle problems by working with skill based and/or rule based knowledge by using a set of mental actions and shortcuts which enable them to handle the problem without needing to work at the knowledge base level. The problems encountered by operators when dealing with new and unforeseen problematic situations are not completely defined, particularly in the most complex dynamic environment management situations.

On the other hand, there is numerous evidence that internal representations spontaneously built up by people about the process or the device in action situations are not always the optimal ones although they are sufficient to solve a limited class of problems. For instance, one of the main dimensions of expertise in blast furnace supervision tasks was found to be the richness of the operational knowledge activated during diagnosis activity (Hoc, 1990). In fact, more expert operators were found to use a wider frame for analysis of the situation by considering more constructed variables and by elaborating more operational hypotheses on these variables. This justified the elaboration of a conceptual model for the training of less expert operators (Hoc & Samurçay, 1992).

The main problem today in training is to design operational models for experienced operators who already have strongly constructed rule-based knowledge. There is a need to link system knowledge to decision making strategies and the class of situations. Conceptual model based training can be seen as a transition from previously internalized models to more generative, where each handles a given class of problems.

Can operators be trained to use conceptual models?

The HCI literature is replete with information on the training of novices in the use of mental models for running a computer or, more generally, a device. The major conclusion which can be drawn from this literature is that users develop useful knowledge about the device's behavior from instructions. However, as stressed by Bibby and Payne (1992), the form and content of representation structures that people internalize are closely related to the instructional materials that users are given, and the process of internalization of external representations depends highly on the informational and computational nature of these external representations, that is, the capacity of the model to make relational computations possible.

A considerable amount of work has also been done on the area of fault-finding training (for a recent overview of training approaches, see Patrick, 1993). The main outcome of these studies is that training with a qualitative model of plant functioning improves diagnosis of both familiar and novel faults. The results obtained by Patrick (1993) on the training of hot strip steel mill operators are promising. Both apprentice and experienced operators who participated in model based training improved speed and demonstrated better identification and interpretation of the symptoms as a result of training. However, even though there is some evidence that model based training improves task performance in different domains, this does not imply that all model based training material and situations are useful. The content and the form of the knowledge represented in the model has to be both valid and capable of being translated into operational knowledge.

In contrast to the processing of static situations, in dynamic environment management, simulation of physical systems (in order to make behavior explicit through envisionment techniques) is considered to be the best way to train people to understand them. This approach however has two shortcomings. First, with the exception of simple or highly deterministic systems, the behavior of most systems such as a blast furnace or fire propagation is not completely modeled, making it impossible to simulate the functioning of the entire system. Second, adaptation to the simulator does not necessarily produce transferable knowledge to unforeseen problem situations and does not allow the operators to modify their points of view on their practice. Shifting from actions to conceptualization is not an easy task and calls for a change in perspective on the situation. Even in very simple dynamic systems such as the paradigms used by Broadbent, the initial training of novice subjects, on the simulator, to system controlling shows that the knowledge acquired by the subjects remained very specific to the situations encountered during the interaction (contextualized), had local validity, and did not generalize to control of the whole system (Marescaux & Luc, 1991). However the authors conclude that debriefing after simulation could contribute to the construction of more generalizable knowledge.

Which training methods and material should be used?

Moving from the simple things to the complex ones is a very common idea in training design. Because of its complexity most training designs in dynamic environment management tasks are based on knowledge decomposition. In many training programs, plant knowledge is divided into smaller sub-parts which are supposed to be easier to understand.

Bainbridge (1990) suggests that there are at least three principles of dividing a complex process into smaller sub-parts:

-dividing the process into unit operations, sub-parts of the plant where cross-flows are relatively simple;

-grouping parts of the plant devolved to the same function;

-making divisions based on the task rather than on the plant.

Even if this kind of decomposition can in some cases be useful for the initial stages of training, its efficiency for professional training is debatable for two reasons. First, this cumulative approach to knowledge construction does not lead to the necessary coordination of the parts in real task settings. Second, the use of some concepts and strategies are only warranted in a certain level of complexity.

An alternative method consists of viewing the training and learning process as a restructuring process. In this perspective the organization of the learning is seen in a different way: Instead of learning each component separately, the learners encounter all the components at an initial level of complexity before encountering the same components in a more complex context. The interactions among elements are always present, but in progressively more complex contexts. This method was used by Bisseret and Enard (1970) to design training for air-traffic controllers. In each conceptual model task unit a system of representation and processing was defined (e.g., categorize planes with respect to their estimated landing time and location). In the training situation, controllers worked on complex real work situations in which their task was to deal with the restricted problem. The interactions of these subtasks with the other aspects of the general task were simulated by the instructors.

An analogous approach was used by White and Frederiksen (1990) to teach how simple electrical circuits work to college students. Again, instead of constructing a training method based on system decomposition, the authors devised an instructional system based on a progression of the conceptual models of electrical circuit behavior. The model progression was used to create relatively complex problem sets in each stage of learning, so as to introduce successive refinements in students' mental models. The progression of the model was based on changes in perspective (as described previously) of the circuit representation (e.g., functional, behavioral, reductionistic) combined with orders of the model: zero order (when reasoning deals with the binary states of the device) or first-order model (when reasoning must deal with evolutions).

An important issue in the literature is whether theoretical understanding of system functioning can support effective diagnosis or supervision activities in a complex industrial context. The idea of "theoretical" training has been criticized by various authors along two lines:

(i) Knowledge acquired in this way is hard to proceduralize immediately (in fact many experimental results comparing declarative versus procedural training have drawn this conclusion). Duff (1992) compared theoretical versus operative knowledge based training and concluded that even though the second type of learning produces more accurate and rapid performance during initial learning, the accuracy drops in novel problem situations: Performance is enhanced by theoretical learning although it is slow during initial learning.

(ii) After this type of training, declarative knowledge declines while skills increase with field experience. Conflicting data however have been published and alternative interpretations of the same evidence can be developed by raising the issue of the meaning of "theoretical": Efficient theoretical knowledge is knowledge which turns into efficient operational knowledge that enables the operator to anticipate and control actions in situations even when the formal form is forgotten. Theoretical knowledge can also be seen as a type of external representation of operational knowledge. Its content and form is tightly related to the nature and characteristics of the task.

Role of the external representations in the acquisition of the operational models

The acquisition of new knowledge or the reorganization of old knowledge and in fact most of our mental and work activities are mediated by the use of external representations. The object of mediatization is also known as "cognitive artifacts" (Payne, 1992), "operative cognitive tools" (Rogalski, see this volume chapter 8) or "instruments" (Rabardel, 1991). The main function of an external representation is to support cognitive activities as is the case for most aid systems such as displays, diagrams, graphics, automatisms, and so on.

The main hypothesis is that there is a strong interaction between the representation that develops during the learning process and the internal representations manipulated when performing a task. When external representations can support activity and their use is integrated in the activity, they can produce new knowledge about the activity itself. A study by Bibby and Payne (1993) on the internalization of device knowledge is based on this assumption. Their learning study clearly shows that different external representations (picture, connection diagram, procedures, list of conditions) of device knowledge support different kinds of inference to a greater or lesser extent and thus enable a range of various forms of performance in different tasks (fault-finding, switch setting, operating, etc.). Subjects conserve and continue to use some features of their initial instructional device description even after extended practice in solving problems on the device.

On the other hand, in many cases the appropriation of external representations such as instruments may require specific knowledge acquisition. Rogalski and Samurçay (1993) have shown that in two dynamic environment management tasks such as fire fighting and blast furnace supervision, non specific training and a lack of the specific knowledge such as basic operations (adding, comparing, transforming of curves) on the graphic representation of the linear functions is an obstacle to using them as tools in the main activity. In contrast, learning something about the tool itself can facilitate the construction of new knowledge about the activity.

The conceptual model we built up for blast furnace supervision aims at a dialectic construction of these two kinds of knowledge (Hoc & Samurçay, 1992). This model decomposes system operations as a whole into elementary phenomena and serves to analyze a given process situation from any one standpoint such as thermodynamics, chemical equilibrium, and so on. The model is hybrid from two points of view: It is based on the operators' representation of the process, and on engineers' "scientific" knowledge. It refers simultaneously to causal, topological, functional, empirical, and operational knowledge (repertory of actions on the process). The conceptual model has been tested through analysis of existing data: It is sufficiently viable in terms of hypothesis generation in supervision activity. It takes into account the hybrid nature of knowledge representation of the process and enables links with actions. Descriptors of phenomena are promising tools for displaying information, particularly when the aim is to improve the reliability and exhaustiveness of hypothesis management. General operator consensus on their semantics could provide an operational language for communicating with computer support, as well as with operators on the next shift. A prototype of a support system based on this model has been constructed: The implemented model is not a dynamic simulation of the process (which is impossible given current scientific and engineering knowledge for process modeling) but rather an interface which mainly structures information gathering and management activities (Samurçay & Hoc, 1991). The preliminary findings show that training (solving simulated diagnosis problems) at least improved anticipation of possible evolutions of the process.

TRAINING IN WORK SITUATIONS

What is the optimal way to integrate conceptual models as tools into the development of competences by research and analysis in work situations themselves? In many cases the artificial construction of new problem situations or complex situations which justifies the use of model based knowledge is difficult or impossible.

Baerentsen (1991) has pointed to the importance of extensive use of episodic memory and narrative accounts of incidents in system control. He argues that episodic memory serves as a basis for analogical problem solving in the case of the occurrence of similar events, and as a medium for creating a foundation for shared knowledge among operators as well as general system knowledge. Norros (see this volume chapter 9) argues along similar lines by describing reflexive and cooperative activities such as mechanisms for development of expertise in everyday work situations. In these cases, conceptual models could be used to build specific tools to share and construct a common knowledge base among engineers and operator and among operators themselves.

These tools should support at least three types of activities which are usually implemented after major incidents:
-anticipate possible problem situations,
-analyze previous problem situations,
-analyze previously used knowledge and action rules to handle these situations and construct a posteriori possible knowledge and actions which could be used. These kinds of analyses are usually carried out by technical services alone without any feedback to operators.

Many of the mechanisms involved the development of competence in work situations remain to be discovered.

REFERENCES

Baerentsen, K.B. (1991, September). *Knowledge and shared experience.* Paper presented at the *Third European Conference on Cognitive Science Approaches to Process Control.* Cardiff, UK.

Bainbridge, L. (1988). Types of representation. In L.P. Goodstein, H.B. Andersen, & S. Olsen (Eds.), *Tasks, errors and mental models* (pp. 70-91). London: Taylor & Francis.

Bainbridge, L. (1990). Development of skill, reduction of workload. In L. Bainbridge, & S.A. Ruiz Quintanilla (Eds.), *Developing skills with information technology* (pp. 87-116). Chichester, UK: Wiley.

Bibby, P.A., & Payne, S.J. (1992). Mental models, instruction and internalization. In Y. Rogers, A. Rutherford, & P.A. Bibby (Eds.), *Models in the mind: Theory, perspective & application* (pp. 153-172). London: Academic Press.

Bibby, P.A., & Payne, S.J. (1993). Internalization and the use specificity of device knowledge. *Human-Computer Interaction, 8,* 25-56.

Bisseret, A., & Enard, C. (1970). Le problème de structuration de l'apprentissage d'un travail complexe [Structuring training for complex work. A training method based on continual interaction between programmed units: MICUP]. *Bulletin de Psychologie, 284*, 11-12, 632-648.

Brajnik, G., Chittaro, L., Guida, G., Tasso, C., & Toppano, E. (1989, September). *The use of many diverse models of an artifact in the design of cognitive aids.* Paper presented at the *Second European Meeting on Cognitive Science Approaches to Process Control.* Siena, Italy.

Duff, S.C. (1992). Mental models and multi-record representations. In Y. Rogers, A. Rutherford, & P.A. Bibby (Eds.), *Models in the mind: Theory, perspective & application* (pp. 173-186). London: Academic Press.

Forbus, K.D. (1990). Qualitative process engine. In D.S. Weld, & J. de Kleer (Eds.), *Readings in qualitative reasoning about physical systems* (pp. 220-235). San Diego, CA: Morgan Kaufmann Publishers.

Gentner, D., & Stevens, A.L. (Eds.). (1983). *Mental models.* Hillsdale, NJ: Lawrence Erlbaum Associates.

Goodstein, L.P., Andersen, H.B., & Olsen, S.E. (Eds.). (1988). *Tasks, errors and mental models.* London: Taylor & Francis.

Goodstein, L.P., & Rasmussen, J. (1988). Representation of process state, structure and control. *Le Travail Humain, 51*, 19-37.

Hoc, J.M. (1989). Cognitive approaches to process control. In G. Tiberghien (Ed.), *Advances in cognitive science, Vol 2: Theory and applications* (pp. 178-202). Chichester, UK: Horwood.

Hoc, J.M. (1990, September). *Operator expertise and task complexity in diagnosing a process with long time lags: blast furnace supervision.* Paper presented at the *Third European Conference on Cognitive Science Approaches to Process Control.* Cardiff, UK.

Hoc, J.M., & Samurçay, R. (1992). An ergonomic approach to knowledge representation. *Reliability Engineering and System Safety, 36*, 217-230.

Hollnagel, E. (1988). Mental models and model mentality. In L.P. Goodstein, H.B. Andersen, & S. Olsen (Eds.), *Tasks, errors and mental models* (pp. 261-268). London: Taylor & Francis.

Marescaux, P.J., & Luc, F. (1991). An evaluation of the knowledge acquired at the control of a dynamic simulated situation through a static situation questionnaire and a "teaching back" debriefing. In F. Daniellou, & Y. Quéinnec (Eds.), *Designing for everyone* (pp. 1673-1675). London: Taylor & Francis.

Moray, N. (1990). A lattice theory approach to the structure of mental models. In D.E. Broadbent, A. Baddley, & J.T. Reason (Eds.), *Human factors in hazardous situations* (pp. 129-135). Oxford, UK: Clarendon Press.

Ochanine, D. (1978). Le rôle des images opératives dans la régulation des activités de travail [The role of operative images in the regulation of work activities]. *Psychologie et Education, 2*, 63-72.

Pastré, P. (1992). Requalification des ouvriers spécialisés et didactique professionnelle [Professional qualification of control operators and occupational education]. *Education Permanente, 111*, 33-54.

Patrick, J. (1989, September). *Representation and training of fault-finding*. Paper presented at the *Second Conference on Cognitive Science Approaches to Process Control* . Siena, Italy.

Patrick, J. (1993, September). *Training fault-finding skills in complex industrial contexts*. Paper presented at the *Fourth European Conferences on Cognitive Science Approaches to Process Control* . Hilerød, Denmark.

Payne, S.J. (1992). On the mental models and cognitive artifacts. In Y. Rogers, A. Rutherford, & P.A. Bibby (Eds.), *Models in the mind: Theory, perspective & application* (pp. 103-118). London: Academic Press.

Rabardel, P. (1991). Activity with a training robot and the formation of knowledge. *Journal of artificial intelligence in education*, 3-14.

Rasmussen, J. (1986). *Information processing and human-machine interaction*. Amsterdam: North-Holland.

Rogalski J., & Samurçay R. (1993). Représentations: Outils cognitifs pour le contrôle d'environnements dynamiques [Representations: Cognitive tools for dynamic environment management]. In A. Weill-Fassina, P. Rabardel, & D. Dubois (Eds.), *Représentations pour l'action* [Representations for acting] (pp. 183-207). Toulouse: Octarès.

Rogers, Y., Rutherford, A., & Bibby, P.A. (Eds.). (1992). *Models in the mind: Theory, perspective & application*. London: Academic Press.

Samurçay, R. & Hoc, J.M. (1991). Modelling operator knowledge and strategies for the design of computer support to process control. In F. Daniellou, & Y. Quéinnec (Eds.), *Designing for everyone* (pp. 823-826). London: Taylor & Francis.

Samurçay, R., & Rogalski, J. (1991). A method for tactical reasoning (MTR) in emergency management: Analysis of individual acquisition and collective implementation. In J. Rasmussen, B. Brehmer, & J. Leplat (Eds.), *Distributed decision making: Cognitive models for cooperative work* (pp. 291-301). Chichester, UK: Wiley.

Weld D.S., & de Kleer, J. (Eds.). (1990). *Readings in qualitative reasoning about physical systems*. San Diego, CA: Morgan Kaufmann Publishers.

White, B.Y., & Frederiksen, J.R. (1990). Causal model progression as a foundation for intelligent learning environments. *Artificial Intelligence, 42*, 99-157.

Wilson, J.R., & Rutherford, A. (1989). Mental models: theory and application in human factors, *Human Factors, 31*, 617-634.

Woods, D.D. (1988). Coping with complexity: The psychology of human behavior in complex systems. In L.P. Goodstein, H.B. Andersen & S. Olsen (Eds.), *Tasks, errors and mental models* (pp. 128-148). London: Taylor & Francis.

8

From Real Situations
to Training Situations:
Conservation of Functionalities

Janine ROGALSKI
CNRS - University of Paris 8

Simulation is often presented as the core of training and competences assessment in Dynamic Environment Management. The question of why and how to modify or conserve real task functionalities is a crucial one. Organizational settings, human-human interactions, resources and constraints are task components which may be affected in the transposition of real situations into simulation situations. The key components of professional expertise are presented in a model of operational knowledge as a framework for analyzing competences and training. The central point is then developed: How intractable new situations may become manageable by trainees. Confronting task analysis and operator's model of operational knowledge serves to identify crucial variables for managing task functionalities for training goals and draw implications for training situations.

Simulation is often presented as the core of training in Dynamic Environment Management or at least as the main training tool, although evaluation of training on performance in real situations is less frequent: This raises the issue of the ecological validity of simulated situations for training. Moreover, numerous studies have been run using simulators to analyze operators' competences and strategies, for instance on Nuclear Power Plant Control. One main and obvious reason is the scarcity of real problem solving situations being not pure routine operations which can be observed in research settings (the exception of traffic control with buses or planes and crisis management is due to the role of operative communication). Although simulation is virtually the only way to analyze and improve competence in Dynamic Environment Management, the question of why and how to modify or to conserve[1] real task functionalities is a crucial one, if

---

[1]Vocabulary choices require some comments. The term "conservation" is chosen in

one wants to avoid circular reasoning about training efficiency.

After an era where tasks were defined mainly at the level of one man-machine interaction, the existence and effects of several tasks components led to the main conclusion that simulated situations could not be not reduced to technical simulators (Leplat, 1989). In vitro (simulation and/or experimental settings) and in vivo (on real DEM) observations and data show the effects of the environment in which a goal is defined for a task: namely human-human interactions, organizational settings, resources and constraints. The need to conserve functionalities in training situations touches on all these tasks components and are discussed in part one.

A theory of operational knowledge acquisition is also required. A model is briefly outlined in part two, in which professional competence is attested by but not reduced to the tasks an individual is able to tackle and solve efficiently, and includes symbolic representation (mental models) as well as experience. This model was developed to reflect components of expertise in academic or occupational domains, and to suggest some mechanisms for the development of competence. It aims at expressing training needs in terms of skills, knowledge, and abilities in task performing. Another dimension is the articulation of perceptual-motor, representational (cognitive) and psycho-sociological levels in the carrying out of real and simulated tasks: Needs for training "beyond technical knowledge" have to be stressed.

Last, but not the least, the key point is developed: How should intractable new situations become manageable by trainees? By modifying task complexity components, making all external conditions perfect, or decomposing complex tasks? Designing training tasks with real tasks functionalities in order to ensure efficiency on these real tasks is not the only goal: Designing unusual tasks to train operators to manage unforeseen situations and/or develop knowledge on crucial points is also needed. However, even if task functionalities are all, and clearly, identified, is it really possible to avoid all simulation biases?

In conclusion, some implications for training design in dynamic environment management are underlined, based on the notion of "generativeness" of competences and on the role collective reflexivity should play in individual and collective learning and in competence development.

TASK-ORIENTED TRAINING AND SIMULATION

Task oriented training requires cognitive task analysis in order to identify what is cognitively required for performing the task in an efficient and reliable way, and the consequences of conserving or modifying task functionalities in the design of

reference to the Piagetian notion of invariants, conserved through transformations. "Competences" is used for its wide range of meaning including knowledge as well as skills. "Didactical" is preferred to "didactic" because the term "didactics" is frequently used in the international community of researchers on mathematics education (for the scientific discipline itself). "Mediatization" is a neologism, as in French, used to translate the german word "Indirekheit." The term "operational device" is used not only in its concrete meaning but also in a more abstract meaning.

training situations. These involve components of task complexity and dimensions of the organizational setting.

Conserving and modifying task functionalities

The term "task functionalities" refers, on the one hand, to properties of the deep structure of the task, involving cognitive requirements and, on the other hand, to properties of what is often seen as "context," which are in fact closely tied to the task and have strong effects on operators' behavior when performing a task. Designing training situations results in a trade-off between conserving and modifying task functionalities in order to manage efficiency in current situations as well as behavior accuracy when faced with the unforeseen (routine vs. crisis, see Norros, chapter 9, this volume) and to ensure or at least facilitate transfer of competences to future professional situations such as using new systems or facing new tasks due to change in organizational setting.

The discrepancy between operators' efficiency after training in simulated situations and observations made "in vivo" on errors in performing real tasks has been clearly demonstrated in situations such as flight studies (Amalberti, 1993; Green, 1990). This led to the decision to conserve task components such as human-human interaction (pilots are trained on collective Cockpit Resources Management), and integration of specific tasks in a larger one (Line Oriented Flight Training). Our own studies on training in Emergency Management (Samurçay & Rogalski, 1993) show that competences acquired individually on a method taught as a support for decision-making in crises were insufficient to explain differences in collective use of this method as in real settings. There were major interactions between efficiency, task distribution, and effective use of the acquired method. Moreover, the organizational setting dimension was of main importance in the implement of the task (Rogalski, 1989). Regardless of domain, all these studies highlight the need to include human-interactions as specific task functionalities to be conserved in training tasks

However, modifying task components for training purposes is sometimes needed in order to control the level of task difficulty in training, to cover a wider range of tasks than the current ones, or to train subjects on specific difficulties. Controlling the level of difficulty does not always involve maintaining a constant level of difficulty for "adaptive learning," or staying in the subject's "zone of proximal development" (Vygotsky). For instance, teaching methods for a strategic approach to dynamic environment control may require dealing with the entire cognitive task complexity, to make the method meaningful, and long-term temporal organization of training is then used to handle complexity. Because the task changes with growing expertise, as it was shown for medical diagnosis (Boreham, Chapter 6, this volume) and through learning, changes are required, in and during training, to confront learners with different task demands.

Whatever the goal, conserving or modifying task components, there is a need for deep analysis of what can be transposed form real to simulated tasks, that is what the so-called "didactical variables" are in the cognitive, organizational, intentional and emotional dimensions of the task. Leplat's definition of a task, "a goal to achieve in specific conditions: technical conditions of the controlled system, physical and organizational conditions and the operator" (Leplat, 1989), needs to be somewhat more detailed in order to specify possible variables between real and simulated tasks.

On the one hand, a task links a system of prescribers and a system of operators, with some explicit and/or implicit contract, which is an occupational contract in real situations, a didactical one in training. The "prescribed task" (Leplat) is seen from the point of view of the prescribers, the "effective task" from the actors' perspective. On the other hand, a task may be defined by a set of three components. First, a task has a specific goal (a target state for the dynamic environment to be managed); this goal is embedded in an organized system of general purposes, goals and sub-goals, and may interact with the goals of other tasks (tasks interdependence). Second, criteria are used for evaluating if and how the target-state of the dynamic environment has been reached; these criteria may be hierarchized and are embedded in a system of more general values (personal and cultural values). Finally, a task has to be performed through a system of resources and constraints (time allotted, predefined rules or procedures, operative tools such as displays, support systems, etc.).

Realistic situations: Components of task complexity

Conserving or modifying tasks functionalities in training situations touches on the **components of task complexity**. We refer to a typology of process control complexity developed in chapter 1, this volume, and an analysis of components of complexity in open dynamic environment management such as emergency and crisis management, aircraft piloting; (Baron et al., 1989). Some of the variables which can be conserved or modified when transposing a real situation into a training one are examined below.

Temporal variables are probably the most crucial ones. De Keyser and her colleagues have stressed the cognitive difficulty in dealing with time (de Keyser; 1990; van Daele & de Keyser, 1991). In fact, several temporal variables are involved in an interactive way. "Tempo" may be defined by the relevant time unit to evaluate situation evolution (very high for flight, low in blast-furnace control): It introduces task constraints per se, such as time pressure in decision-making or stress. Continuity and duration of events in dynamic environments also affect task complexity (they are involved in time evaluation, memorization and planning). Latencies are also time parameters: Delays in information gathering affect subjects' performance (Brehmer & Allard, 1991), system response latencies to operators' actions may modify strategies, while delayed feedback about actions makes control and learning more difficult. Coordination of moments and durations for collective synchronization, that is succession and simultaneity, are parameters of tasks interdependence, and factors of complexity.

Control and command proximity are also key points as components of task complexity. They involve several dimensions: causality, "intermediate entities," and mediatization through an automatized device or through human actors. The parameters are, respectively: the length of causal chains between "physical" measured variables, the existence of "intermediate entities" (expressing global properties of the process to be controlled at a symbolic level), which are "constructs" between physically measured and/or controlled variables (Samurçay, chapter 7, this volume), the "cognitive transparency/opacity" of the automatisms, and the "deepness" of human mediatization (complexity of the communicative chain in command implementation of action or in information gathering). Most often control and command proximity is intrinsic to the task: modifying them induces substantial change in the task itself. However external representations can be played with to manipulate cognitive transparency as a variable in training tasks.

Controlling the **system of evaluation criteria and values** is another important point in ecological validity of training: There are instances where trainees set an "operational approach", in which a decision was evaluated by raw results, against a methodical approach evaluated in terms of its conformity to a "handbook" method: They did so although this method was designed to be and had the properties of an aid for operational decision-making. Moreover, it is not always possible to transpose the embedding of goals and values in training situations; rather the possible impact of the resulting modifications although difficult, needs to be analyzed.

The other task component, **resources and constraints**, is more flexible. The key is that procedures and operative rules are both resources, which enable rule-based instead of knowledge based activity, and constraints, which exclude other solutions which could be best adapted to the actual situation, due to circumstances. In her analysis of responsibility and risk control as elements of process operators' professional expertise, Norros underlines that "facing and solving the basic conflict of doing wrong in order to do right... constitutes the essential learning process and results in the increase of expertise through which a stepwise integration of the traditional user orientation to the designer orientation is taking place" (Norros, 1989). Interaction of individual cognitive activity (and more general behavior) with properties of organizational settings is in fact the crucial factor.

Organizational settings

Organizational settings have effects which impinge on the transformations introduced in designing training situations in this multidimensional space. Defining dynamic environment management at the most general level (the abstract functional level in Rasmussen's terms, Rasmussen; 1986) leads to the notion of virtual operational device, which involves modeling task organization in a "vertical" (hierarchical) dimension and a "horizontal" dimension of cooperative work (Rogalski, 1991). In real organizational settings, when a given control task is performed, operators cooperate in a real operational device, with rules for task sharing, information, and command flows. They are involved in complex prescribers/actors relationships (from the Management to the roundsmen in a plant for instance, or between a chief and his/her on-line staff).

Comparison of the communication flow in a real and in a simulated open dynamic environment management (large forest fire) reveals differences which can be explained by the transposition of the structure of the operational device (artifactual devices and human settings) to a training situation, whereas some other differences were due to a lower level of trainees' competences (Rogalski, 1989). Training goals concerned with a complete achievement of cooperative tasks requires conserving operators' organizational place and role in the "operational device," whereas making the "rules of game" clear can be sufficient when aiming at a more specific technical purpose.

Studies in the military field have shown the need to take into account the entire context, as is the case in leaders' training for battle as well as for garrison command (Hunt & Phillips, 1991). Taking into account the operational device embedding a given set of tasks implies overcoming the dominant and overly narrow meaning of team (as a permanent unit at a given hierarchical level) to incorporate the "vertical" dimension in collective activities and training. A recent book on team performance and training (Swezey & Salas, 1992) underlines the unresolved problems in this field.

Designing training situations for cooperative work requires taking the "secondary task" due to interaction into account. On the one hand, operators' tasks are inserted in a network, from a logical and organizational point of view. Operators have to learn how to deal with this task interdependence and to manage the required communication. On the other hand, real tasks involve individual (and collective) representations of goals with potential conflicts, individual criteria, and systems of values which may differ; they also involve various knowledge and mental models about the situation itself. These two perspectives can result in different training situation properties. The first perspective centers on conservation of task functionalities (in terms of organizational settings), as observed in comparing situations for training officers in operational command posts for emergency management. The second may be achieved via meta-cognitive activities, as indicated by a study on collective operators training (nuclear power plant) for the management of unforeseen events where the main training goal was "to construct a common mental model and/or models of others cognitive functioning" (Jansens et al., 1989). A survey of this specific issue of collective training is presented elsewhere (Rogalski, in press).

MODELING ACQUISITION OF OPERATIONAL KNOWLEDGE

In operational knowledge, knowledge (K), experience (E), operative cognitive tools (O) and problem solving (PS) are dynamically linked in a model — KEOPS — developed for analyzing professional competence. Beyond technical operational knowledge, metaknowledge and psycho-social representations intervene in individual and collective activities in professional settings. All of these are affected by training.

Developing all the components of operational knowledge

Modifying or conserving real task functionalities in training situations depends on training purposes. The first main distinction differentiates training mainly concerned with increasing the automaticity of behavior and training concerned with developing the knowledge for devising a new working method (Bainbridge; 1989). Looking at professional competence for actors at various hierarchical levels in dynamic environment management should also involve consideration of the set of tasks actors are able to tackle and their capability to use cognitive aids, from making use of an abacus to calling for human expert specialists.

A diagramatic model of integrated operational knowledge is in figure 1 below. The four components (knowledge, problem solving, experience, operative cognitive tools) on which general cognitive "functions" operate, such as hypothesizing, inferring and deducing, planning, and controlling, are embedded in metaknowledge about tasks and about our own knowledge and know-how. In KEOPS terms, knowledge-based, rule-based, and skill-based behaviors are respectively connecting a given situation to knowledge structure, problem solving, or in an automatized, direct way to experience.

Training can be oriented toward all these components. New open situations develop Experience, structure Problem–Solving, and may require new Knowledge to be taught. They can also be used for structuring previous Knowledge in a new way: introducing "intermediate entities," constructing new levels in the knowledge architecture. Developing Experience may form units from pieces of knowledge giving rise to "encapsulated notions" or from a set of isolated procedures to "precompiled strategies." Available as units, these new entities in Knowledge structure contribute to decreasing the cognitive work load in Problem solving. This process also develops a form of automatization (in cognitive activity) which is constructed from explicit knowledge, from a skill-based behavior. It enables individuals to retrieve rule-based or knowledge-based behavior if required by incidents. A comparison of training methods for diagnosis of plant failures, based on one of three facets: a) knowledge ranging from faults to consequences; b) rules (after presentation of the plant), which in our model are defined as operative modes for the subclass of diagnosis PS in plant control; or c) only training on specific cases (experience) shows similar efficiency for trained faults, but better results for new faults for the method (b) based on rules for PS (Shepherd et al., 1977). Note however that the trainees performed less well on the post test as compared to the pretest on new faults, which could indicate that the individuals did not assimilate the knowledge on plant presented at the beginning of training.

Depending on the process to be controlled, training may have to cope with a transition in both directions from the physical level (in the real situation) to symbolic representations (involved in KEOPS): Controlling the properties of experience acquired through training situations with respect to what is needed in real situations may appear less complex in highly automatized processes where interaction with a process is nevertheless accomplished through symbolic representations. In fact, collective work on complex cases requires controlled interactions across various processing levels and raises the issue of developing or maintaining ability in relating symbolic representations (structured Knowledge and Problem–Solving) to perceptual-motor level (Experience). Collective reflexive activities on previous situations may also develop shared Experience (Baerentsen, 1991) and thus enable learning through others' Problem solving.

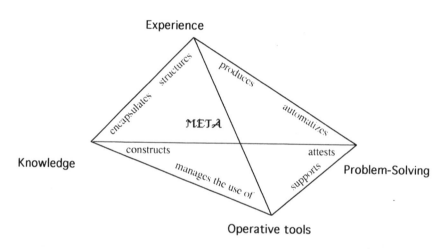

FIGURE 1.   KEOPS, a model for operational knowledge.
Knowledge, Experience, Operative cognitive tools and Problem solving are dynamically linked in KEOPS: In a given occupational domain, Knowledge structures Experience, and manages the use of Operative cognitive tools; Experience encapsulates Knowledge and automatizes Problem solving; Operative cognitive tools support Problem solving; Problem solving constructs and attests Knowledge, and produces and structures Experience; Metaknowledge and metacognition regulate cognitive activities.

Let us turn to the fourth component: "Operative cognitive tools" (OCT). Operative cognitive tools are external aids for problem solving. They take charge of some part of the cognitive load because knowledge is implemented in their design; they may be numerical aids such as tables of values on several parameters, graphical tools such as an abacus representing functions (depending on parameters), artifacts such as a pocket calculator or professional software. Integrating OCTs in the personal problem solving process is a component of professional competence. As underlined by Hutchins as regards technology in team navigation, they do not amplify the cognitive activities of the team members, but instead transform what are normally difficult tasks into easy ones. They need training to be used and "assimilated" in the Piagetian sense. In fact, operative cognitive tools may also play a role in modifying operators tasks and (internal) representations of the situation and hence the Knowledge component itself (Rogalski, 1993; Rogalski & Samurçay, 1993; Samurçay, chapter 7, this volume).

Learning how to manage task complexity is a part of methodological training which deals with Problem solving structuration (classification, identification of common operative modes, change of representative frames, strategy and tactics adapted to a class of problems). Managing task complexity is an important point in competence in handling new, unforeseen situations. From this point of view, Operative cognitive tools, which can be seen as interfaces between the individual and the task, are often an underestimated component in operational competence. Conserving or modifying the place of OCTs in task achievement may have striking consequences on what is really acquired during training.

Analyzsing operational knowledge into interacting components indicates that different training goals may be defined, leading to various constraints on appropriate training situations, and simulation situations are not the only ones dealing with problem solving and experience. Moreover the "target object" in dynamic environment management is a physical one (a chemical process, an aircraft in physical space, etc.) whereas simulations mainly deal with interfaces, at a more functional and symbolic level: They do not conserve a main task functionality.

Beyond "technical" knowledge

KEOPS schematizes relationships between the four main components of "technical" knowledge related to the content of the dynamic environment (what process has to be managed). Three other points are worth stressing. The first is metaknowledge, which is related to individual activity; one dimension of metaknowledge is reflexivity, linked to expertise (Olsen & Rasmussen, 1989). The two others involve psycho-social representations and abilities to manage social implementation of action (giving/receiving missions or orders); both deal with collective activities and organizational setting effects.

The role of metaknowlege in learning as well as in performing a task must be stressed: It intervenes in evaluating knowledge complexity, the "distance" between one's knowledge and knowledge required for given problem solving; studies on pilots have shown that the choice of a strategy in mission execution depends on pilots' representations of their operational abilities. This is indirectly related to individual emotional and motivational properties involved in decision-making, as well as in social interactions. This metaknowledge--self-knowledge-- plays a functional role in regulating individual activities and managing internal resources and constraints, in particular under high external temporal constraints (Valot & Amalberti, 1992)

The role of psycho-social representations is developed by Norros in chapter 9, this volume. Her paper presents existing interactions between metaknowledge (awareness and language for making knowledge and strategies explicit) and collective competence. Her analysis converges with Hutchins' study on team navigation, which underlines the fact that supporting the continuity of team over time through career cycles of team members (reproduction function vs. production function) involves knowledge overlapping. Overlapping of knowledge is facilitated by "openness" of operative tools and by the ability of more expert team members to make knowledge and strategies explicit. In turn, it "allows the system to respond robustly to failure of individual team members and to avoid breakdowns" (p. 218) (Hutchins, 1990).

This leads to the fact that beyond the *production function* of tasks which guarantees a set level of production, two other functions are present, and more or less fulfilled: a *reproduction function* of the system which performs the production tasks and a *training function* to improve operators' competences. Training situations are mainly oriented towards the first and main function: production. More attention should be paid to possible interactions with the two others.

MAKING COMPLEX TASKS
IN DYNAMIC ENVIRONMENT MANAGEMENT
TRACTABLE IN TRAINING SITUATIONS

Managing task complexity

Decomposing complex tasks into unitary ones, and dividing long term work into more restricted time units provides solutions to some of the problems of managing task complexity, particularly when the training purpose is focused on skills automatization. However knowledge tends to be acquired at the lowest level, with local structuration; experience only deals with well-defined situations, while problem solving is concerned with "pocket problems." Articulating such local fields of operational knowledge or automatized procedures is not a simple process and requires specific training actions. For instance, "Line Oriented Flight Training" was integrated in the pilot training as a response to the problem of articulating previously acquired skills on sub-tasks (Amalberti, 1993; Green, 1990).

Managing complexity due to task dependence ("parallel tasks" for an operator or interdependent tasks for a team) can be done in two ways: choosing tasks parameters in order to simplify all tasks other than the target-task, and increasing complexity in a controlled manner (Bisseret & Enard, 1972), or focusing on the target-task by delegating other tasks to trained subjects or instructors. Observations of high level firemen officers indicated that it is more efficient than training on separate sub-tasks, because it preserves the "logic of the global task," which is the key-point to be acquired and is easily lost in task decomposition.

In a similar way, integration of technical knowledge (using operative tools, or acquiring specific notions related to the process) into training about organization and planning of operations involved in DEM requires a dialectical solution: Technical knowledge acquires meaning and operational "virtue" through real problem solving, while problem solving requires previous technical knowledge. In-service training observations show that a solution could be found in taking the long-term effects in the didactical processes and the constructive role of reflective thinking (metaknowledge) into account.

Another dimension of task complexity needs to be managed in training situations, which involves the problems encountered in *information gathering or action implementation* when operators have to mediatize their activity through devices or human beings. Simplifying real tasks can be done in training situations where "all external conditions are fulfilled": no errors in communication flow; correct implementation when using "complex" operative devices or human mediation; no interaction with "external factors" (such as cabin problems in flight simulation or pressure of media on decision-makers in emergency management training).

Time management raises many open problems. Such constraints as constructing a correct mental representation of process tempo (as for instance flight simulation in Computer Assisted Learning) are unavoidable. However, as artifacts simulators can suspend time: It is a way to "discretize" a continuous environment, as well as modify time units for slowing an overly fast tempo. Metaknowledge may be used in managing action control: Suspending time enables proximal debriefing based on immediate feedback. As we know more about existence than about nature of complexity introduced by interaction between time parameters, managing task complexity through these parameters must be explored with caution.

Control and command proximity can be modified by "envisionment," introducing a symbolic and fictive "situation visibility", as in Brehmer's or Dörner's fire simulators. This evisionment could possibly play the role of an operative dynamic image with respect to real situations (see discussion in Samurçay's paper, Chapter 7, this volume): Validation of such a hypothesis requires studies on professional operators. Introducing feedback (retroaction) and/or anticipation of consequences of actions (proactive feedback) may be a productive means of shortening the control-command loop. As simulated situations do not have productivity constraints, which are concerned with general values above specific task evaluation criteria, and they allow for systematic exploitation of the principle of "knowledge of results" and "action shaping" (Leplat, 1989).

Training can also avoid or limit "over-complexity" of a task produced by the trainees' actions which could make the situation worse, or create new problems to be solved in interaction with previous ones. This may be seen as a "positive one-way" for interaction between trainees' actions and process evolution, but requires tight simulation-trainer interaction.

Design of unusual tasks and biases in tasks transposition

Transposition of functionalities of real situations to simulated ones is not always necessary or possible. On the one hand, training purposes may lead to design tasks which do not have any equivalent in real situations; on the other hand, there are avoidable biases due to the training situation itself.

In fact, training may require designing unusual tasks: modifying real task functionalities or defining highly unrealistic tasks with respect to work situations, or confront trainees with more complex tasks than are in real, common situations. Training purposes may consist of enabling trainees to tackle unforeseen or rare events; to confront them with specific points of operational knowledge in an appropriate problem solving situation, or to disentangle specific questions from "technical" problem solving, for instance by introducing "role plays" to initiate cooperative work.

Elsewhere, biases are due to the training situation itself: For instance in flight simulation, trainees expect troubles while in real situations incidents are perhaps expected (decreasingly with progress in automation), but accidents tend to be unexpected. It changes the orientation phase of the control task drastically in a general case, except for emergency management where accidents are initial conditions of action in real professional situations. Another unavoidable bias is related to risk transposition: No physical risk is involved in training situations; there are only cognitive and narcissistic issues in decision-making. Nature and possible effects of stress can not be managed in a simple way.

Conflicts between the didactical and professional "contract" may also arise in simulated situations. What the goals really are, the systems of values, who is the task prescriber, who evaluates trainees' activities, the trainer or the professional prescriber? In high level firemen officers training, trainee's evaluation of simulated situations showed that two approaches were possible: an "operational approach," which was expressed through comments on situation ecological validity and representativity, and a "didactical approach," with comments centered on the adequacy of the situation for implementing a previously taught method for dynamic environment management. Even in "full size" simulations, this conflict has had to be managed as a significant variable.

CONCLUSION

We defined a task as a node in a network, with partial order linking prescribers and executive operators; a task involves three components: goals to be achieved, evaluation criteria, resources and constraints. This definition allowed us to analyze task functionalities which should be conserved, and define those which can be modified for individual or collective training in dynamic management environment.

Beyond the well-known issues concerning simulation fidelity, a number of features have been emphasized. The first point is the need to recognize that the target task, as well as its goals and the actors involved in performing it, is "embedded" in a socio-technical system. Local functionalities of the "current task" have to be related to more global funtionalities of the embedding tasks. Organizational impact has to be evaluated in designing training situations where trainees may have to cope with conflicts about evaluation criteria or even goals, negotiate resources and constraints, and handle the ways in which their own decisions can propagate effects on lower and higher processing levels. Adequate mental representations on the part of actors about their own work position may in fact be crucial in unexpected situations, overriding their technical skills and their level of responsibility.

Another point is the issue of managing temporal task dimensions: Preserving the tempo of the dynamic environment is an unavoidable constraint and acts to alleviate conflicts on the skill-based control level in task performance. Conserving the temporal context also involves integration of (simulated) tasks into the flow of long term activities. Actually, several temporal horizons have to be considered in complex dynamic situations; they tie actors at various levels, from management to executive operators. In any case, the preparation phase (briefing in collective activities) and the phase of action evaluation (debriefing) should be included systematically in training settings using simulation.

Modifying task functionalities in order to make difficult situations tractable requires a cautious analysis of possible negative side effects, such as oversimplifying interactions between tasks, communication constraints, or complexity due to human limitations and possibilities for error. One solution could be to design simulations with "parametrizable" cognitive models of interacting actors (a solution which requires much research for cognitive modeling), and/or in designing training situations involving actors (trainees) at various levels in the operative setting, and various levels in previous training and competence.

The advantages of simulated settings, such as action recording, clock stopping, experimenting, etc., could also be used to develop self-knowledge at an individual and a collective level, that is metaknowledge about own knowledge, personal ways of thinking and reacting, possible biases. Methodological training about task and activity self-analysis could reinforce the purpose of developing reflexivity, aiming not only at increasing reliability in task performing but also engaging in a dynamics of training through the work situations themselves. From this point of view, initial or in-service training situations should provide opportunities to "anchor" in all actors the use of collective discussions for transforming individual experiences into shared knowledge, that can surpass knowledge and experience limitations due to the rareness of severe incidents, a consequence of the improvements in systems safety.

REFERENCES

Amalberti, R. (1993). Safety in flight operations. In B. Wilpert & T. Qvale (Eds.), *Reliability and safety in hazardous work situations. Approaches to analysis and design* (pp.171-193). New York: Lawrence Erlbaum Associates.

Bærentsen, K. B. (1991, September). *Knowledge and shared experience.* Paper presented at the *Third European Conference Cognitive Approaches to Process Control.* Cardiff, UK.

Bainbridge, L. (1989). Cognitive processes and training methods. In L. Bainbridge & R. Quintanilla (Eds.), *Developing skills with information technology* (pp. 177-192). Chichester, UK: Wiley.

Baron, M., Rogalski, J., & Samurçay, R. (1989). Un système de traitement de situations dynamiques complexes: Analyse de la décision avec une méthode de raisonnement tactique (MRT); conséquences pour l'élaboration d'aides informatiques et la formation [A system for managing complex dynamic situations: decision analysis through a method for tactical reasoning, MTR; consequences for designing support systems and training]. *First European Congress on System Science* (pp. 697-709). Paris: AFCET.

Bisseret, A., & Enard, C. (1969). Le problème de la structuration de l'apprentissage d'un travail complexe: Une méthode de formation par interaction constante des unités programmées (MICUP) [Structuring training for complex work. A training method based on continual interaction between programmed units: MCIPU]. *Bulletin de Psychologie, 284*, 632-648.

Brehmer, B., & Allard, R. (1991). Dynamic decision making: The effects of task complexity and feedback delays. In J. Rasmussen, B. Brehmer & J. Leplat (Eds.), *Distributed decision making: Cognitive models for cooperative work* (pp. 317-334). London: Wiley.

De Keyser, V. (1990). Fiabilité humaine et la gestion du temps dans les systèmes complexes [Human reliability and time management in complex systems]. In J. Leplat & G. de Terssac (Eds.), *Les facteurs humains de la fiabilité dans les systèmes complexes* (pp. 85-108). Marseille: Octarès.

Green, R. (1990). Human errors on the flight deck. In D.E. Broadbent, J. Reason, & A. Baddeley (Eds.), *Human factors in hazardous situations* (pp. 503-512). *Philosophical Transactions of the Royal Society of London, B 327.*

Hoc, J.-M. (1989). Cognitive approaches to process control. In G.Tiberghien (Ed.), *Advances in cognitive science, vol 2: Theory and applications* (pp. 178-202). Chichester, UK: Horwood.

Hunt, J.G., & Phillips R.L. (1991). Leadership in battle and garrison: A framework for understanding the differences and preparing for both. In R. Gal & A.D. Mangelsdorff (Eds.), *Handbook of military psychology* (pp. 411-429). Chichester, UK: Wiley & Sons.

Hutchins, E. (1990). The technology of team navigation. In J.Galegher and C.Kraut (Eds.), *Intellectual team work* (pp. 191-220). Hillsdale, NJ: Lawrence Erlbaum Associates.

Jansens, L., Grotenhuis, H., Michiels, H., & Verhaegen, P. (1989). Social organizational determinants in nuclear power plants: Operators training in the management of unforeseen events. *Journal of Occupational Accidents, 1*, 121-129.

Leplat, J. (1989). Simulation and simulators in training: some comments. In L. Bainbridge & R. Quintanilla (Eds.), *Developing skills with information technology* (pp. 277-291). Chichester, UK: Wiley.

Norros, L. (1989, September). *Responsibility and risk control as elements of process operators professional expertise.* Paper presented at the *Second European Meeting on Cognitive Sciences Approaches to Process Control.* Siena, Italy.

Olsen, S.E., & Rasmussen, J. (1989). The reflective expert and the prenovice. In L. Bainbridge and R. Quintanilla (Eds.), *Developing skills with information technology* (pp. 9-33). Chichester, UK: Wiley.

Rasmussen, J. (1986). *Information processing and human-machine interaction.* Amsterdam: North-Holland.

Rogalski, J. (1989, September). *Cooperative work in emergency management: Analysis of verbal communications in distributed decision making.* Paper presented at the *Second European Meeting on Cognitive Science Approaches to Process Control.* Siena, Italy.

Rogalski, J., & Samurçay R. (1991, September). *Effects of expertise on knowledge representation in dynamic environment management.* Paper presented at the *Third European Conference Cognitive Approaches to Process Control.* Cardiff, UK.

Rogalski, J., & Samurçay, R. (1993). Représentations: Outils cognitifs pour le contrôle d'environnements dynamiques [Representations: Cognitive tools for dynamic environments management]. In A. Weill-Fassina, P. Rabardel & D. Dubois (Eds.), *Représentations pour l'action* (pp. 183-207). Toulouse: Octarès.

Rogalski, J. (1991). Distributed decision making in emergency management: using a method as a framework for analyzing cooperative work and as a decision aid. In J. Rasmussen, B. Brehmer & J. Leplat (Eds.), *Distributed decision making: Cognitive models for cooperative work* (pp. 291-301). Chichester, UK: Wiley.

Rogalski, J. (1993, September). *Designing operative cognitive tools for open dynamic environment management.* Paper presented at the *Fourth European Conference Cognitive Science Approaches to Process Control.* Hilerød, Denmark.

Rogalski, J. (in press). Formation aux activités collectives [Training for collective activities]. *Le Travail Humain.*

Samurçay, R., & Rogalski, J. (1993). Cooperative work and decision making in emergency management. *Le Travail Humain., 56, 1,* 53-77.

Sheperd, A., Marshall, E.C., Turner, A., & Duncan, K. (1977). Diagnosis of plant failures from a control panel: A comparison of three training methods. *Ergonomics, 20,* 347-361.

Swezey, S.R, & Salas, E. (Eds.). (1992). *Teams: Their training and performance.* Norwood, NJ: Ablex.

Valot, C., Amalberti, R. (1992). Metaknowledge for time and reliability: Luxury or necessity? *Reliability Engineering and System Safety, 36,* 199-206.

Van Daele, A., & De Keyser, V. (1991). Distributed decision making and time in the control of continuous processes. In J. Rasmussen, B. Brehmer & J. Leplat (Eds.), *Distributed decision making: Cognitive models for cooperative work* (pp. 261-273). Chichester, UK: Wiley.

9

An Orientation-Based Approach to Expertise

Leena NORROS
Technical Research Center of Finland

The expertise of operators of complex dynamic processes expresses itself in the operators' ability to interpret the process situation on the basis of mediated and often uncertain information of the process. An orientation-based approach was developed to study mastery of this demand from the point of view of operators' diagnostic and prognostic decision making. According to this approach, in problem solving situations, operators adopt qualitatively different orientations towards the target process. It is, further, supposed that differences in orientations correlate with differences in action strategies and efficiency of actual process control performance and, perhaps, even with differences in the acquisition of the mastery of the target process in the long run. The results of the studies reported in the paper give tentative partial support to these assumptions. As relatively stable regulatory structures orientations would effect operators' decisions both in regard with normal and disturbance situations. Thus, this framework opens up a coherent way to investigate activities under these, seemingly polarized conditions, promoting understanding of the development of operators' expertise in daily work.

INTRODUCTION

There are two mutually related tendencies in the development of work associated with the increasing utilization of information technology. These are automation and "informatization" of work (Zuboff, 1988; PAQ, 1987). Automation refers to the materialization of human cognitive skills in machines, which increases the subject's physical distance from the object of work. One of the most important aspects of this distancing is that knowledge of the process events is not immediate. On the contrary, it is mediated through measurements and transformed into information that appears in symbolic form. In this sense, information technology not only automates, but also simultaneously informates work. Utilization of this information prerequires its conceptual interpretation. As a result, representations of the process events may be deepened as unperceivable events become conceivable and as relationships and dependencies between events are established. The realization of the informing potential of information technology is thus dependent on the acquisition of the relevant conceptual skills among the personnel and on the creation of organizational requirements for learning and utilization of such skills (Zuboff, 1988).

Increasing reliability in the implementation of automation seems to imply the existence of two discrete operating states in production, the normal operation and the rare disturbance or accident situation. This fact has commonly been considered to create a polarized cognitive demand structure in the process control activity, characterized by the daily routines and the highly demanding novel problem solving, sometimes in an actual crisis. The question of how operators in the daily routine are able to learn those skills which are necessary in an accident situation, challenges the idea of polarized demands and calls for an elaboration of the connections between them.

In our research, we have attempted to define the general common demands of expertise that must underlie the specific demands in routine and crisis situations. We see that interpretation of information in a complex situation is the key problem through which expertise in process control activities could be studied.

In order to investigate the work demands as a unity we need to focus on the processes that control actions in different situations. Because the object of activity, its motive, is the controlling instance of actions, we become interested in how the persons define the object of their activity (Leontyev, 1981). This process is called *orientation* which becomes manifest in a person's way of framing a problem situation (Galperin, 1979). In our study, the concept of *orientation* is used to define the operators' way of coping with the problems of interpreting information.

In the following sections, an orientation-based approach to expertise is described. The presentation consists of three major parts. First, the role of disturbances in work as a challenge for the personnel's expertise is discussed. Second, the personnel's optional approaches to disturbances in work are identified, and two ways to utilize orientations as indications of expertise are explained. Third, the development of expertise is discussed from the point of view of the orientation approach. This approach has been developed through the analysis of the mastery of different kinds of industrial work, both from the point of view of daily work, and from the point of view of control of difficult disturbance situations. Some results of these studies are brought up in order to elaborate the steps in the development of the approach, and references to publications that contain more detailed results are indicated.

DISTURBANCES IN THE SYSTEM AS A CHALLENGE TO EXPERTISE

Due to the principal difficulty, even impossibility, of precisely anticipating the functional and economical constraints of the system in its future operation, the system deviates in design from the system in operation. Future operational demands of a complex system, and direct faults in design create uncertainty in the process. This becomes apparent in different kinds of everyday problems, deviations and disturbances in the normal planned operation. It is the operators who directly face these problems, and, as a result of their handling of them identify the features that complete the design. The more complex the system is, the more difficult it is to anticipate such problems. At the same time, due to safety and economical reasons, the more important it becomes to identify them. Thus, the operators who handle difficulties are not restricted to identifying problems that are predictable, but they are also required to define the world of the possible. The users' interventions can be interpreted as an opportunity for them to complete the design and continue the construction of the system. Through the handling of problems, a potential for learning is opened up for the user.

The intersection of the top-down design activities and the bottom-up user interventions are the *disturbances* caused by the unanticipated behavior of the system. Disturbances have a double nature. On the one hand, they are *threats* to the proper functioning of the system, and on the other hand, they include the *possibility of developing* the system.

It is a typical theoretical system idea to study a system's functions from the point of view of its deviations. Thus, the approach is well known in the field of industrial safety where it is applied to controlling occupational accidents (Kjellen, 1987). In their book *Individual Behaviour in the Control of Danger*, Hale and Glendon (1987) referred to a number of accident sequence models based on this concept. These models define different sequential states that a system may take when a disturbance is imminent. Not only the functions of the technical system but also the system operators' activity has been analyzed from this point of view. There is a wide range of models of human error mechanisms from which taxonomies of errors are derived (Rasmussen, 1982; Reason, 1987).

These "orthodox disturbance models" refer to the first aspect of disturbance, that is . disturbance as a threat to the functionality of the system. The deviation is typically interpreted as a state that falls out of the set norm which can be, for example, the planned functioning of the system. When analyzing disturbances, interest is concentrated on the deviation process itself, for example, failure causes and mechanisms are studied and disturbance classifications constructed with the aim to prevent the threat caused by the deviation. Corrections of the system are carried out by design engineers. As a consequence of the assumptions of the orthodox disturbance models, a high disturbance rate during implementation, a steady low rate at normal operation due to the feedback control of disturbances, and an acceleration of disturbances due to normal wear during later years of the system's operation can be predicted. Possible design failures as signs of "teething problems" are supposed to be identified and eliminated during the implementation.

In a research project on the implementation of a new flexible manufacturing system (FMS), different research interventions and a follow-up after 1 1/2 years of normal operation were carried out. The disturbances in the system were investigated in this study (Toikka, Norros, Hyötyläinen, & Kuivanen, 1991). The results of the follow-up indicate that, against predictions of the orthodox disturbance model, the failure rate at normal operation was very high, the disturbance time accounting for 25% of the total time. An analysis of the causes of the failures further indicated that the proportion of design failures and failures of undefined cause were higher than could be expected on the basis of the disturbance model.

Thus, the results indicate that neither the rate of the disturbances nor the distribution of the disturbance types supports the prediction based on the aforementioned orthodox disturbance model. The results became more comprehensible when the unpredictability of complex systems was taken into account. When analyzing the design-based failures in detail, it was found that only one part of the cases could be considered design failures in the strict sense; that it could have been possible to make a better design decision. Instead, some of these disturbances were caused not by deficient, but rather by limited design. In other words, unpredictability of some functional requirements and unanticipated interactions of the complex system had made complete design unattainable. The high rate of design-based disturbances during the normal operating period would thus indicate that new questions and knowledge of the system had been created during the operating period.

Given that the data supports the assumption of the unpredictability of a complex system, and the existence of disturbances as the more or less "normal" state of the system, it would further imply that there exists pressure on the users, as well as opportunities for them to develop the system during the operation. Thus, disturbances should also be taken into account as a basis for innovation and change. Support for this implication can be found in the studies made by Hutchins (1988), who identified such innovations in his study of a disturbance situation on the bridge of a large ship. Hutchins conceived the construction of practices in an unexpected situation as an evolutionary transformation of the socio-technical system and discussed it as a complement to direct design. Also, Friedrich (1992) studied the operators' role in the implementation of modern production systems in several case studies and came to similar conclusions. Of course, this hypothesis contradicts the orthodox disturbance model and typical assumptions derived from the psychology of work, that after implementation (learning phase), the developmental demands of a new system decrease, and the operators' activity becomes routine.

It is an obvious conclusion from the above that the actual handling of disturbances by operators should become the focus of investigation. It might also be concluded that the afore mentioned data afford a simple extension of the orthodox model of system disturbances. However, we claim that such an extension is inadequate. We argue that it is necessary to reconceptualize system disturbances as an *essential feature* rather than merely an *eliminable feature* of system functioning. This and other studies described in this chapter aim to do this.

As was mentioned, the rate of disturbances in normal operation of the FMS studied was high. In our analysis, we found that during the 24-hour observation period, each operator in the shift used on average 1.5 hours (i.e., 21% of his working time) for disturbance handling. However, considerable differences among individual operators were found. The proportion varied from 0% to 47% of the total working time, depending on each shift's interpretation of the official division of labor.

These facts demonstrate, of course, that disturbances threaten the functionality of the system. They also suggest individual differences in reacting to them. It is now claimed that, depending on the users' choices in reacting to the disturbances, the developmental challenges of the present system can be exploited to a greater or lesser extent. In a disturbance situation, the system is, in a sense, restored back to its design phase. The problem situation tells the users that design is not yet completed and that something can and must still be done. To catch the decision space and the learning potentials of the users' problem-solving activities, we have defined optional problem orientations (Norros, 1989a) which can act as a heuristic for exploiting the developmental potential of system disturbances. Orientation is discussed in detail in the next section.

Considering disturbances as an essential feature of system functioning not only means an extension of the orthodox disturbance model but it also affects the conception of expertise. Disturbances are faced by the operators, whose reactions to them indicate the expertise that is available (or that operators are willing to make available in the situation). This indication is based on the afore mentioned double nature of disturbances; that is., disturbances as threats to the functionality of the system, and as possibilities to develop the system. It is the expertise of the operators that defines the extent to which the possibilities for development are exploited. At the same time, the utilization of these possibilities, that is, developing the system, is also an opportunity for the users to construct their expertise.

The way of defining expertise just described has two major advantages. First, through relating expertise with disturbances, the human skills that make up expertise are described in connection with the functional demands of the system. This means that a *contextual* definition of expertise can be achieved. Second, essential in the conception of expertise is the idea that the operators *construct* their own expertise through identification of development needs of the system and through participation in the implementation of changes to the system. In this point, we can agree with Engeström (1989), who emphasized that the development of expertise means the ability to reconceptualize the skills of existing experts, and the ability to create new forms of practice. Thus, instead of concentrating on the processes of assimilation and application of expertise, attention should be directed to an analysis of the construction of expertise.

ORIENTATION AS INDICATION OF EXPERTISE

The concept of *orientation* was originally used by Galperin (1979) to refer to a subject's cognitive, motivational and volitive reactions to the task he or she is supposed to solve, or to a situation to be mastered. "Most important in life is to orientate adequately in a situation that demands activity, and to direct one's actions properly" (Galperin, 1979, p. 93). We have adopted this concept to indicate the subject's way of framing the problem in a situation that requires activity. Orientations are, on the one hand, thought to control the subject's actions and efforts in the utilization of the development potentials. On the other hand, problems in actions may require reorientations. It is assumed that, through analysis of different orientations, it is possible to make inferences of operators' expertise because the orientations are some kind of construction principles of expertise.

Orientations represent different ways of framing the problems. Thus, they also define qualitative differences in expertise. Engeström (1989) pointed out the existence of qualitatively different types of expertise. He noted that this fact questions the common tradition of conceiving expertise in universal terms, which, further, has led to a more or less quantitative handling of expertise in research. This is expressed, for example, in the prevailing novice-expert continuum and in its wide adoption as a research paradigm in studies on expertise. There are, however, examples of studies that challenge the implicit notion of universality. Thus, Lawrence (1988), in her analysis of judicial decision making introduced the concept of frames of reference to point out the qualitative differences in judges' definitions of their problem spaces. Schön (1988) also draw attention to differences in people's framing of problems, and he considered them as important determinants of expertise.

The development of our orientation approach to expertise has, until to now, comprised three temporally partly parallel and conceptually interrelated research phases. In the first phase, a typology for problem orientations was created in a research on implementation of flexible manufacturing systems (FMS). In the second phase, a method for description of everyday work orientations was developed in a study within the maintenance organization of a nuclear power plant (NPP). The third phase comprised the analysis of the role of orientation in the control of problem solving in an acute disturbance situation. This study was carried out during the NPP operators' simulator training.

Development of Problem Orientation Typology

In our attempt to conceptualize the optional orientations that operators might adopt when handling a problem or disturbance, two aspects were found to be important. First, it should be asked *what* is conceived as the *object* of disturbance handling activity. The decisive distinction is whether the disturbance is conceived and handled locally as a temporary deviation from normal situation, or in relation to the system's global functions, including diagnosis of the problem and feed back to the system in a normal situation. Second, it can be asked who actually handles the disturbance and how widely distributed the activity in disturbance handling is; that is, *who* is the *subject* of the disturbance handling activity. The typology that includes five basic options was originally based on these two criteria (Norros, 1989a). A schematic representation of the model is depicted in Figure 1.

The typology was developed during the analysis of the data of the aforementioned follow-up study of the implementation of FMS (Norros et al., 1988; Norros 1991; Toikka et al., 1991). A description of the options, including the major functional restrictions of each orientation from the point of view of the management (top-down), and from the operators (bottom-up), are presented in the following.

Withdrawal From Disturbance Handling.

This option refers to the possibility that an operator does not handle the disturbance when it occurs. The basis of this orientation is thought to lie in the acquisition of a deterministic representation of the system through direct tacit learning of normal operation routines. Restricting activity to mere normal execution of routines is a rather extreme orientation. It might express workers' attempts to achieve short term efficiency in work, or it might also be an indication of workers' active resistance. Besides being a possible individual choice, this orientation can also be due to Tayloristic organizational principles.

The top-down limits of the withdrawal orientation are met when the restricted capability and motivation of the operators get economic weight that is big enough. The bottom-up need to overcome the withdrawal orientation is a result of the meaninglessness of this orientation from the users' standpoint. This is the case when the personal costs of this type of activity (monotony and frustration from underutilization, stress caused by the contradiction of responsibility for expensive technology, or the feeling of inability to adequately respond to unexpected situations) exceed the benefits.

In our FMS case study, this type of problem orientation was principally ruled out by the management through its choice for a flexible organizational strategy that emphasizes homogeneous and high expertise. However, we did observe withdrawal during the implementation period.

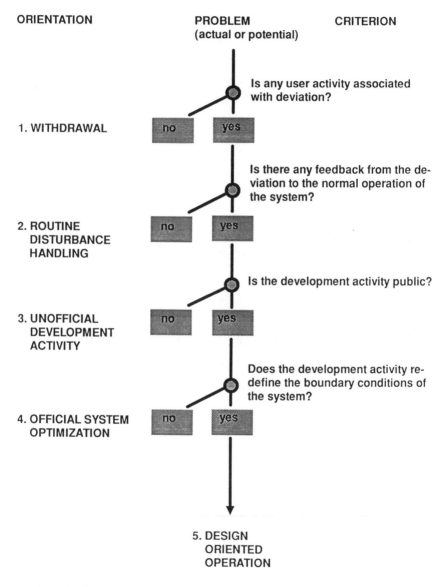

FIGURE 1. Typology of problem orientations.

Routine Disturbance Handling.

The normal work of the user is interpreted as carrying out prescribed tasks. Handling disturbances in a routine way without making an attempt to analyze the causes of the disturbance or change the system or situation is a part of this.

The user is identifying problems and troubleshooting, reacting to some familiar disturbances one by one, according to known procedures, and locally, without searching for any general reason or systematic connection behind them. Restrictions and inadequacies of the operators' representation of the system prevent them from anticipating more complex and latent interactions and possible failures of the system.

Our data from intensive observation of the FMS operation include examples that demonstrate routine problem orientation. This orientation first prevailed in the handling of a disturbance that occurred during the observation. However, repetition of the problem increased the pressure to change the orientation. The attempt to diagnose the problem, an indicator of a more advanced orientation, was facilitated by the interaction with the fellow operator.

Private Development Activity.

The transition to more developed management of disturbances takes place when this reactive disturbance orientation loses its meaning for the user, and anticipation of disturbances, and activities to change the system, replace it. This is the case when the routine becomes too arduous or challenges his or her safety, and the user invents a better way to solve the problem by making improvements to the system. The users privately take the authority to define their tasks or make a change to the system aimed at making their jobs smoother. Such an activity prerequires relational models of the system for the systematic collection of experiences in order to consider the competing functional goals of the system. The activity is still, in most cases, triggered by repeated problems, or in some cases, acute demands of the situation.

In transition from the routine disturbance handling to this level of orientation, the operator is making a diagnosis of the disturbance. This involves reflection and redefining the constraints, and possibly the goals of activity in a problem situation. In a way, the user unofficially adopts the authority of the supervisor, and even that of the designer. Paradoxically, this unofficial developmental work maintains the traditional division of labor between operation and design by preventing the revelation of the design deficiencies. This also means that the operator takes personal responsibility for the improvements, which in many cases includes the risk of making errors. This is why, in complex risk processes, the users are advised to rely on known practices, rather than very eagerly invent their own improvements. This conflict creates pressure for public and cooperative development activity.

Public System Optimization.

As unofficial development efforts do not lead to sufficient improvements in the system, and, at the same time as it is clear the user's knowledge is not efficiently exploited, a tendency to establish the user participation might officially appear. At this stage, the design efforts are directed to optimizing the system functions within the given boundary conditions.

From the operators' point of view, this orientation requires maintenance of the disturbance as a problem and object of development activity, and explicit knowledge of the system as the condition of its optimization. Learning can remain mainly experiential and on-the-job learning, but some conceptual elements might be needed (e.g., adoption of common planning and working routines, independent use of process-oriented quality control systems, or use of documentation systems for collecting operation experiences)

Explicit rules are made for group work and for the relationship between work groups and the rest of the organization. The critical decision is the transition from the traditional resistance of mass production or craft work culture into participation in official development activities of the organization and cooperation with management.

Expansive System Development.

In this problem orientation, development activity is not limited to optimizing system functions within the given constraints but, instead, directed to redefining the boundary conditions of the system. Operative experiences are systematically collected and fed back to the development of the structure, functional principles and organization of system. Thus, for the first time, the users adopt systematic conceptual design methods. The design tasks include the socioeconomic and technical basis of production, and new work methods are created to organize the cooperation between designers and users.

As the continuous development of the system through its lifetime becomes an economical and functional necessity (product quality, safety, ecological effects, etc.), the sporadic cooperation between design engineers and users becomes insufficient. The integration of the expertise of these two acting groups has to become institutionalized through top-down decisions to form new organizations, and a common system of conceptual tools and working methods must be created. This development includes coping with conflicts of power and social relations as Zuboff (1988) demonstrated in her case studies.

Evaluation of the FMS operators' disturbance orientation was carried out in normal operation with the help of a check list including the characteristic features of disturbance orientation from the cognitive and cooperative point of view in different sequential phases of disturbance handling. We evaluated those activities that were carried out as a reaction to 36 different disturbances during 24 hours of intensive observation. Further information of the operators' disturbance orientation was obtained in interviews held 2 weeks after the intensive observation. The results indicate that 67% of the disturbances were handled in a routine way, whereas in 33% of the cases, a more advanced orientation was typical. It was also found that, if a disturbance was a repetitive one, it was more likely to be handled in a nonroutine way.

On the basis of the operators' and system leaders' interviews, we were also able to collect information on developmental measures that had been initiated by the operators during the 1 1/2 years of normal operation. According to the operators' description, it was estimated that 69% of the developmental measures were optimizing activities without direct connection to disturbances. The rest of the cases were immediate reactions to the disturbances.

According to common expectations, it was shown that users participate in system development during implementation. But the data further indicates that the acquired developmental orientation was also maintained during normal operation. Moreover, not only disturbances but also increasingly anticipated problems trigger these activities. This tendency is related to the bottom-up pressure to reach the type 5 disturbance orientation, *expansive system development.*

Among the developmental measures we were able to register, there were two that indicated the operators had approached the fifth orientation option as they clearly challenged the frames of the given system. These included measures to overcome bottlenecks in the production and developments of the control system, which were not achievable within the present frames, but still close enough to be within reach if new design decisions were considered. However, our interview data also elaborates power issues related to the users' increased abilities to develop the system. The impression of the users was that their proposals and ideas for the future development of the manufacturing were not especially welcomed by the management. This management attitude became even more apparent through direct omission of engineering resources that were needed to carry out the development suggestions.

The significance of the FMS study from the point of view of the development of the orientation-based approach to expertise was the formulation of types of orientation, which could be considered relevant basic options that system operators would choose when facing a problem situation in their work. In the next phase, an attempt was made to utilize the orientation typology to describe work orientation in daily work on the basis of interviews with personnel.

Orientation in Everyday Work

During the FMS study, it became more and more evident that it would be inadequate to consider orientations merely determined as straightforward individual choices. Instead, the fact that optional orientations to the system disturbances are socially constructed became evident through the study. Thus, adopting an orientation option is a contradictory situation of problem-solving and decision-making. The contradictions to be coped with are already structured top-down by techno-organizational design, but there are also social contradictions within the management, between management and the shop-floor, and within the shop-floor organization itself, as well as psychological contradictions of the organization's individual members. Setting the orientations of different personnel groups in relation with each other (i.e., operators to maintenance personnel, operative personnel to management or to design), a diagnosis for the development potential of the organization can be achieved. This would signify the viability of the organization.

Further study focused on the organizational assessment of a maintenance department at a nuclear power plant, in which the problem orientation typology was utilized (Reiman & Norros, 1994; Wahlström, Norros, & Reiman, 1992). For this kind of "high-hazard-low-risk" plant, it is particularly significant to evaluate the personnel's expertise from the point of view of the control of safety and quality in their daily work activities. The everyday judgments made by the maintenance personnel in the control of safety and quality are affected by problems in interpreting information of a complex phenomenon in which different sources of uncertainty are present. These judgments affect the prediction of future maintenance tasks. Control of safety and quality have gained increasing attention within the nuclear community, as the recent discussion on the "Safety Culture" indicates (International Atomic Energy Agency, 1991).

This study attempts to diagnose the personnel's conceptions of the problems of maintenance activity, and the conceptions of their own tasks. It was assumed that these conceptualizations of their daily work would reveal the personnel's general work orientation, which could be interpreted as a contextual indication of expertise. Thus, comprehensive interviews were carried out with three different personnel groups — plant management, maintenance foremen, and maintenance technicians. The interviews focused on the main functions of the subject's activity, and particular interest was devoted to the means and constraints of the achievement of high quality and safety in maintenance. The questions were aimed at bringing forward practical cases, where problems in the execution of managerial activities and maintenance work had existed.

The problem orientation typology was utilized in the description of orientations. A new adaptation of the basic orientation types was created for the analysis of managerial orientations, whereas the typology just described was utilized for maintenance foremen and technicians. The typology was operationalized by using particular dimensions of work activity. Thus, an attempt was made to predict expressions of the different orientation options with regard to four dimensions, object of work, work motivation, cooperation, and work culture. Each of these four activity dimensions comprised several subcategories. Descriptive matrices, including the orientation types and dimensions, were constructed for the personnel groups to serve as reference tables in the assessment of orientations. The cells of the matrixes included descriptions of work practices that are thought to manifest different orientation types. On the basis, orientation profiles for each person and average profiles for each personnel group could be achieved .

As a result of the analysis of the interviews, a diagnosis of the major problems of maintenance activity as a whole could be achieved. These problems found specific expressions in the work of each group. Further, it turned out that expertise and development potential, as assessed with the help of orientations, only partially met with the demands expressed in the problems of work. The inadequacy to tackle major demands of work became particularly clear with regard to the utilization of information technology and conceptual tools of activity. This applied to all personnel groups. Underestimation of the role of new tools can essentially weaken the efficiency of the personnel in their attempts to predict future demands and formulate adaptive maintenance strategies. Management was efficient in the control of technical development activities, but less adequate in the identification of the role of communication and of personnel's participation in goal-setting as resources of management functions. Foremen and technicians seemed to make use of cooperation in task performance, but they did not consider cooperation as a resource to be developed consciously. The quality and safety conceptions of the latter groups were adequate, the functional demands of the whole production process being their reference. In summary, the evaluation indicated that the present expertise within the personnel was internally contradictory, and partly inadequate to tackle the development demands of the maintenance.

Some important conclusions concerning the orientation approach as a contextual assessment method of expertise can be made. The methodical lessons learned through this study concern the criteria for defining the optional orientation types. As was mentioned earlier, there were two aspects of significance in defining orientation: The conceptions of the object of the disturbance-handling activity and the cooperation in disturbance handling.

The use of the typology in the evaluation of everyday work orientations supported the assumption that the way of conceptualizing the object of activity is a significant aspect of orientation. This aspect can be called *conceptual orientation.*

The basic question is how the persons conceptualize the functional principles of the object they control, which is reflected in the persons' conceptions of the disturbances of the system. This can be inferred on the basis of how persons handle actual problems or potential disturbances that they identify in the system. In the aforementioned study, this was diagnosed through the personnel's safety and quality conceptions, through their anticipation of disturbances or problems, and their definitions of their responsibilities in the control of problems. The general distinction that can be used to define the options is between the conception of disturbances as discrete events, and the conception of them in their relation to the global functioning of the whole system. The more functionally a disturbance is conceived, the more general the concept of disturbance is. This also means that disturbance and normal situations are not discretely separated but rather interpreted through a common reference and represented as a continuum. This promotes anticipation of disturbances and their detection on the basis of early signs; this is the central task in daily work.

The conceptual aspect of orientation has been in the foreground of those studies in the literature that identify different frames of reference as determinants of expertise, and also in those works in which the concept of orientation has been used deliberately (e.g., Engeström, 1989).

· The second aspect for making a distinction in orientations turned out to be more problematic in the analysis of the data. As we have discussed so far, the crucial problem of expertise is the construction of meaning for the available information. Many authors have pointed out that, due to the complexity of the process, different views of the process coexist. Thus, the construction of meaning has to be carried out cooperatively. For the same reason, Brehmer (1991) emphasized the necessity of communication and distributed decision-making in the control of systems. Thus, cooperation should be taken into account when describing activity but, as such, it is not an aspect of orientation.

What makes cooperation and communication interesting with regard to orientation, is a further aspect that is demonstrated in a study by Abercrombie (1989). She studied difficulties in perception and construction of meaning in complex objects during medical training. In her teaching, she noticed, e.g., that students had difficulties in constructing the meaning of the object seen in the microscope, and the tendency of the students to see the expected object described in the textbook. She carried out an experimental training series with medical students, during which she could point out the advantages of multivoiced dialog in the context of making diagnostic judgments. It was shown that dialogue contributed to awareness of the factors that affect judgments, and, thus, it enhanced judgments.

The connection between communication and self-monitoring, or critical evaluation, is important for our reasoning. Communication was, in this Abercrombie's experimental training, deliberately used as a resource for enhancing task performance. Focusing on communication as a resource resulted in critical evaluation of one's own activity. Through such changes in the focusing, which can be called *reflective relation to problem situation,* a distancing effect is achieved, and a redefinition of the activity and the means of activity may result. This seems to promote task performance. This effect has been identified in the studies on expertise. One of the main results of the research on expert skills is that experts typically have strong self-monitoring skills (Glaser and Chi, 1988). Olssen and Rasmussen (1989) also emphasized reflectivity as a characteristic of expert activities.

Thus, we conclude that the critical relation to the problem situation, just described should be considered the second aspect of orientation, *reflective orientation.* Both aspects of orientation, conceptual orientation and reflective orientation serve as criteria for distinguishing orientation types. This conclusion was affected by the methodological results achieved in the study on process operators' disturbance-handling activity, which will be discussed in the next section. The redefinition of originally the second aspect may cause a need to refine the typology. Instead of utilizing cooperation as criterion, we should see how the subjects conceive resources of activity, for example., communication and cooperation, as a means and as an object of development within the whole activity.

Orientation in the Control of Actual Disturbance-Handling Activity

In the study just described, the inferences on orientations and respective evaluations of expertise were based on the subjects' verbal reactions to diagnostic questions. In this case, the subjects were "talking about practice" (Lave & Wenger, 1991), but equally important is to study practice itself. When doing so, orientation can be inferred from the persons' utilization of available information. We now turn to this question.

Process operators of large automated systems ultimately control the system in real time. The demands faced by the operators represent the requirements of informated work, in which the interpretation of actual process information on the basis of previous experiences and conceptual knowledge of the process are essential. Interpretation of the situation becomes critical when the process reaches an unstable or disturbed state. Operating experience and research results indicate that in such a situation the operators do not always adequately succeed in their interpretations. Typical problems are either nonoptimal utilization of process information or inability to operationalize former knowledge of the system. These problems also could be identified earlier in our own study on nuclear power plant operators' errors in simulated disturbance situations (Norros & Sammatti,1986).

In order to understand the origin of these problems, the question of the role of orientation in the control of the crew's diagnostic and prognostic interpretations of the problem situation was raised in the new study (Hukki & Norros, 1993a, 1993b).

Before starting the new study, the methodology of the earlier one (Norros & Sammatti , 1986) seemed to require consideration and a critical evaluation. In the latter study, the operators' task was described as an ideal sequence of actions in the predefined disturbance situation. This ideal sequence was then used to define errors and evaluate the adequacy of the operators' performance. This implies a traditional interpretation of expertise as an ability to reproduce actions that have been defined to represent excellency. This definition of expertise is not explicit but is embedded in the experimental technique used and the model of human cognition behind it. As has been pointed out by Collins (1990), this widely accepted model implicitly assumes that human actions are governed by plans because, retrospectively ,they can be described as following plans. This planning metaphor of action was criticized by Suchman (1987) who saw action as situated. "The fact that we can always perform a post hoc analysis of situated action that will make it appear to have followed a rational plan says more about the nature of our analyses than it does about the situated actions" (Suchman 198, p.53).

The notion of situated action draws attention to the constructive aspect of activity, which we had found essential to our conception of expertise, as noted in the third section. Instead of analyzing the fulfillment of the predefined sequence of acts, it is necessary to scrutinize, from moment to moment, how the operating crew navigates in the genuinely uncertain situation and gradually succeeds in structuring the situation.

Based on the critique of the earlier study and the research on the concept of orientation just described, the model of the interpretation of a disturbance situation was created. The focus in the model was the role of orientation in the control of actual disturbance handling, and the purpose of it was to guide the analysis of complicated data of the plant events and the crew's performance. The model that represents the assumed basic relationships is depicted in figure 2. It was constructed during the evaluation of six process operator crews' activity during a simulated difficult disturbance situation (Hukki & Norros, 1993a, 1993b).

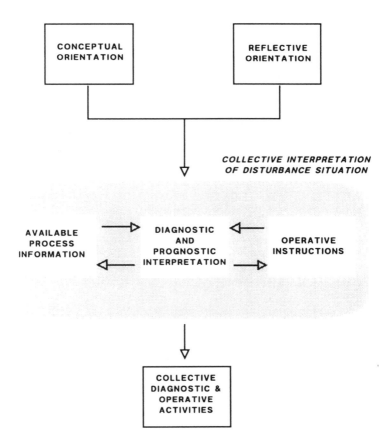

FIGURE 2. Model of interpretation of a disturbance situation.

As indicated in the model (Figure 2), task performance is supposed to consist of intertwined diagnostic activities (i.e., selection of information and definition of the problem situation) and prognostic activities (anticipation of the development of the situation in relation to possible action alternatives) leading to operations. Carrying out these activities requires an interpretation of the meaning of the whole situation, both from the diagnostic and prognostic point of view. The interpretation is thought to be based on the utilization of available information (dynamic process information and operating instructions, especially emergency procedures). These interactions between interpretations and information (indicated by the horizontal arrows in figure 2) are directed by the crew's orientation to task performance.

Orientation is naturally dependent on the operators' knowledge of process dynamics. The coherence of the representation manifests the *conceptual aspect* of orientation. The other aspect of orientation, the actors' *reflective* attitude towards their activity, i.e. their critical evaluation of their own activity, is also important for the interpretation of the situation. These two aspects of orientation contribute to the construction of interpretation of the meaning of the situation.

Because of the collaborative nature of the process control activity, the operators' activity has to be considered as group activity, as collective decision-making. The construction of the interpretation is collective, and therefore the operators' orientation to the task performance affects their interpretation of the disturbance situation through collaboration.

By using this model, the construction of the interpretation of the disturbance situation and, inferred from the basis of it, the orientation of the crews can be evaluated by analyzing the way the operators use available information. The possibility of making inferences from conceptual orientation is based on the idea that the informating power, that is the *informativeness* of information available, may differ. The better information reflects the dynamically essential functions of the process, the better it can be used as evidence of the functional state of the process on a global level, and the higher its informativeness is. The orientation is supposed to be reflected in the degree of utilization of this informativeness. The functionality of conceptual orientation can be evaluated on this basis.

The results of the analysis indicated that there were differences between the crews' utilization of informativeness of available process information. Those crews whose conceptual orientation was evaluated to be functional seemed to be more efficient in their diagnostic and operative activities. This was interpreted as resulting from a more functional orientation by these crews, which had created a coherent reference for diagnostic and prognostic interpretation of the situation. The results concerning the reflective orientation were not equally confirmative, but clear indications of lack of reflectiveness by the less functionally oriented crews could be found. This was associated with signs of subjective uncertainty, which could be seen as a reflection of incoherence between diagnostic and operative interpretations of the situation among these less functionally oriented crews.

The results of the application of information interpretation model were interpreted as indicating the efficiency of the model in the analysis of the crews' performance in a dynamic situation. With this model it seemed to be possible to conceive the crews' activity as it was constructed in the situation. In relation to that, instead of primarily emphasizing the situatedness of activity (Suchman, 1987), we would, on the basis of this analysis, stress the *contextuality* of activity. Orientation can be seen to serve this contextualization both through conceptual and reflective control processes.

DEVELOPMENT OF EXPERTISE

Two different ways of analyzing orientations as indications of expertise have been constructed in our studies. In the first, orientation was inferred on the basis of verbal descriptions of work practices, whereas, in the second, specific features of the utilization of information was the basis of our inferences. The basic aspects of orientation, the conceptual and reflective orientation are utilized both for constructing the typology of problem approaches and for explaining the control processes that affect interpretation of information in an actual situation. Coherency of the two analytical approaches is important for the possible combination of the two approaches in a study.

A further question that can be raised is whether a functional and reflective orientation in a problem situation would predict effectivity of learning from actual problem experiences and, thus, the development of expertise.

One of the most influential theories about the development of expertise is the one proposed by Hubert and Stuart Dreyfus (1985). In their model of development of skills or expertise, Dreyfus and Dreyfus make the distinction between analytical and intuitive thinking. According to them, it is the level of expertise that defines the prevalence of one or the other type of thinking. Expertise is gradually developed from an initial novice stage through a less committed use of simple and context independent rules. As a result of repeated confrontation with practical situations, the cognitive skills are supposed to transform into expert thinking. This is characterized as contextually adequate, comprehensive and intuitively "seen" decisions that show high intellectually mediated commitment to the object of activity.

Although we find this description of an expert intelligible, we would like to understand better how such a novice could develop into such an expert. Thus, there are a number of questions we would like to have clarified. The first questions are related to the formation principle of intuitive thinking. In the description of the stages of expertise, it seems that the basic mechanism is repetition and identification of similarities on the basis of experience of the repetitive but variable practical situations. This leads to the conclusion that, in a novel situation, an expert acts analytically and becomes a novice again. This seems to be a contradiction to the everyday notion of expertise, and also to, for example, Hammond's cognitive continuum theory, which assumes that, in a novel situation, an expert acts intuitively (Hammond, 1981). In addition, if intuition is exclusively thought to rely on nonsymbolic forms of representation, it becomes difficult to explain the ability of an expert simultaneously to be a good teacher, which many experts are known to be.

A further question is: Would it be necessary to assume something that is common to or similar between a novice and an expert for explaining the development from a novice to expert, and to understand why every novice does not become an expert?

Could there be an alternative formation principle for intuitive thinking other than repetition that would allow intuition also to be usable in novel situations, and also by inexperienced persons? The Russian author Dawydow (1977) would offer his conception of *theoretical thinking* as a candidate to that. Dawydow makes a distinction between empirical and theoretical thinking derived from the Hegelian dialectics and principles of dialectical logic (see, e.g., Ilyenkov, 1977). He claims that empirical, or formal, thinking is directed to visible overt features of the object and comparison between them. Consequently, it produces a descriptive and classificatory concept, the operativity of which is questionable. Theoretical or substantial thinking, to his mind, could be characterized as an attempt to reveal internal relations and contradictions of the object that could explain its development and essential nature. A theoretical concept is operative because it includes the construction principle of the object, and, thus, it can also be useful in novel situations. To speculate even further, we have found interesting the notion of intuitive thinking that Spinoza used (1677/1975) in his Ethics to signify the highest form of thinking. Instead of stressing repetition or similarities, he focused on conceiving the essential structure of the object, which can principally be possible straight away.

A further question regarding the theory of Hubert and Stuart Dreyfus relates to the assumption of the theory that learning starts with procedural rules. This implies the notion that the context of expertise is given principally — it exists but it is not yet known by the novice. The development of expertise could thus primarily be conceived as internalizing given expertise through a large amount of practice. This strikes a contrast to some of the results in literature to which we referred earlier in this chapter and also to our own results. On the basis of this, essential to expertise is its constructive character.

Our ongoing work is to study the development of expertise on the basis of the orientation approach. Research work has to be directed to operationalization of the conceptual and reflective aspects of orientation from the point of view of development of expertise. The previously mentioned theoretical thinking, typical to which is the conception of internal dynamical principles of the object, seems to be closely related with what we have called *functionality of conceptual orientation*. Our results support the conclusion that the functionality of orientation explains the expert's capability to interpret a concrete situation in a coherent way, in its relations. This capability to contextualize the particular situation seems to be very much the same as what is often meant by intuitive problem solving, typical to which is operative efficiency based on immediate insight of the problem situation. Emphasis on the contextuality rather than intuitiveness of problem solving would have the benefit that the former not only needs to be restricted to characterize experts' thinking, but could as well appear at least in some novices. Our further assumption is that these novices would learn more effectively, due to the fact that the coherent frame, which allows an effective interpretation of a particular situation, could also serve as a frame for the accumulation of experiences. A bridge between disturbance situation and routine could also be created, as the functional conception of disturbance of the system would offer a frame to anticipate the evolution of disturbances, and to interpret the role of small changes in the system from this point of view. Likewise, a basis for development activities could be found.

The aforementioned hypothesis, that functional orientation would promote learning and development activities, is incomplete without additional assumptions of the role of reflective orientation. Larkin, McDermot, Simon, and

Simon (1980) pointed out an important paradox when concluding that teaching physics problems to students does not result in good performance in practice, because teaching is too practical, it is oriented directly to learning operations.

This conclusion demonstrates the potentials of theoretical instruction that for some reasons are often not realizable. Needs to reconsider one's own tools or to invent new ones are, however, actually present themselves in any real-life work process. In our Nuclear Power Plant maintenance study for example, it was evident that lack of conscious development of the tools of one's own activity becomes an obstacle to overcome the restrictions of one's own expertise. Munley and Patrick (1990) demonstrated that, in simulated fault diagnosis, those persons who were reminded of the possibility of further types of failures than that included in a typology of faults, could act more adequately in a novel situation. When the operators were made conscious of the possible restrictions of their disturbance model, they became able to complete the model and act more effectively.

Thus, it can be hypothesized that promoting the reflectiveness of orientation is an important condition for the development of expertise. Deliberate learning of conceptual tools that enhance the functionality of orientation is one way toward this aim. However, reconsideration and refinement of other resources of activity is as important. Multivoiced dialogue and participation in common activity are resources of learning too often neglected (Lave & Wenger, 1991).

CONCLUSIONS

The way expertise is conceived has practical relevance because this conception influences the way expertise is developed through training. The concept adopted influences at least three activity areas. First, one would expect that it effects *research on expertise*. This chapter has brought up a number of conceptual distinctions that can be considered as suggestions to revise prevailing conceptions of expertise. Thus, our approach has brought up the issue that expertise should not be considered as individual mastery of tasks but should be defined in the social context of activity. The formation of orientations as a contradictory process within the social organization of labor is an indication of this.

Through the adoption of the idea that disturbances reveal both the developmental needs of the system and the possibilities to develop the system, we have adopted a view of expertise that emphasizes its constructive nature. In our approach, expertise manifests in the ability to utilize the potentials for development that are overt in the disturbance. Thus, this view demonstrates that expertise is constructed through the actual problem-solving or development activity.

Further, it follows that expertise is analyzed concretely in connection with the object of control. In this sense, our conception of expertise is context-dependent or contextual. Furthermore, contextuality also refers to relating the particular situation with the functions of the system and with the constraints of activity on a more global level. Contextuality in this sense was seen to relate with the functionality and reflectivity of orientation. This point of view was seen to open possibilities of tackling important theoretical questions of the relationships between the intuitiveness of thinking and theoretical thinking, which are central issues in the development of expertise.

On the basis of the redefinitions concerning the nature of expertise, transformation in research paradigms may be expected. This question was not deliberately discussed here but was brought up as our own reorientation in choosing the research methodology in our studies on Nuclear Power Plant operators' activity in disturbance situations.

The concept of expertise adopted should have implications on the deliberate *development of expertise*. It seems that the approach to expertise presented here could lead to changes in the learning of expertise and, thus, new training methods should be derived. Essential reorientation would be needed towards the theoretical elements in training. Instead of understanding theory as a set of declarative knowledge, knowledge as activity should be emphasized. One way to develop substantial knowledge of the process could be a training process that uses extensive modeling activities (Norros, 1989b). Tools for the analysis of the basis of the operators' decision-making in problem situations would also promote the critical evaluation of their own activity and enhance learning from experience. But, even more profound reorientation would be needed in conceiving the relationship between the development of expertise and development of production technology and tools. There is increasing evidence of incremental technological innovations that are made by operating personnel. Simultaneously, this demonstrates that the expertise of the operators exceeds the level expected. The need to utilize this eventual potential is reflected in the growing interest in the participatory design. Much more emphasis should, however, be put on the conceptual tools of the participating personnel.

Third, the concept of expertise should affect our conceptions of *operators' daily activities*. Expertise in automated work includes conceptual comprehension of the uncertainty inherent in the process. Insight into these facts might cause a revision of the attitude toward daily routines. If work is conceived as mere routine, being prepared for problems and learning are hindered. As a result, overconfidence of control and regression of actual expertise may appear simultaneously. This is a combination that gives little possibility to master a novel situation. On the other hand, an understanding of the complexity of the system and its inherent uncertainty could create an attitude of respect and curiosity toward routine and small problems. A consciousness of the need of change embedded in the routine, together with a comprehension of oneself as a subject of this change, adds to the routine the possibility of learning and development of expertise. Our concept of expertise would suggest qualification measures and restructuring of daily routines in such a way that the polarization of demands between routine and crisis would tend to decrease.

REFERENCES

Abercrombie, M.L.J. (1989). *The Anatomy of Judgement.* An investigation into the processes of perception and reasoning. London : Free Association Press.

Brehmer, B. (1991). Distributed decision making: Some notes on the literature. In J. Rasmussen, B. Brehmer, & J. Leplat (Eds.), *Distributed decision making. Cognitive models for cooperative work* (pp. 3-18). Chichester, UK: Wiley.

Collins, H.M. (1990). *Artificial Experts.* Social Knowledge and Intelligent Machines. Cambridge, MA: The MIT Press.

Dawydow, W.W. (1977). *Arten der Verallgemeinerung im Unterricht* [Types of generalization in teaching]. Berlin: Volk & Wissen.

Dreyfus, H.L., & Dreyfus, S.E. (1985). *Mind over machine.* New York: Macmillan/The Free Press.

Engeström, Y. (1989). *Developing thinking at the changing work place: Toward a redefinition of expertise.* San Diego, CA: University of California, Laboratory of Comparative Human Cognition.

Friedrich, P. (1992). *Kompetensutveckling vid lokal teknikförändring: Operatörsarbete och datorstödd automatisering i verkstadsindustrin* [Development of expertise on incremental changes of technology: Operator's work and computerization in manufacturing industry]. Unpublished doctoral dissertation, The Royal Institute of Technology, Stockholm.

Galperin, P.J. (1979). *Introduction to psychology* (in Finnish). Helsinki: Kansankulttuuri..

Glaser, R., & Chi, M.T.H. (1988). Overview. In M.T.H. Chi, R. Glaser, & M.J. Farr (Eds.), *The Nature of Expertise* (pp xi-xxvi). Hillsdale, NJ: Lawrence Erlbaum Associates .

Hale, A.R., & Glendon, A. I. (1987). *Individual behaviour in the control of danger.* Amsterdam: Elsevier.

Hammond, K.R. (1981). *Principles of organization in intuitive and analytical cognition* (Tech. Rep. No. 231). Boulder: University of Colorado, Center for Research on Judgment and Policy.

Hukki, K., & Norros, L. (1993a, September). *An orientation based approach to evaluation of process operators' diagnostic activity.* Paper presented at the *Fourth European Meeting on Cognitive Science Approaches to Process Control.* Hillerød, Denmark.

Hukki, K., & Norros, L. (1993b). Diagnostic orientation in control of disturbance situations. *Ergonomics, 36,* 1317-1328.

Hutchins, E. (1988, July). *Organizing Work by Evolution.* Paper presented at the conference *Work and Communication.* La Jolla, CA.

IAEA Safety Culture. (Safety Series No 75-INSAG-4). (1991). Vienna: IAEA.

Ilyenkov, E. (1977). *Dialectical logic: Essays on its history and theory.* Moscow: Progress.

Kjellen, U. (1987). Deviations and the feedback control of accidents. In J. Rasmussen, K. Duncan, & J. Leplat (Eds.), *New technology and human error* (pp. 143 - 156). Chichester, UK: Wiley.

Larkin, J., McDermot, J., Simon, D.P., & Simon, H.A. (1980). Expert and novice performance in solving physics problems. *Science, 208*, 1335-1342.

Lave, J., & Wenger, E. (1991). *Situated learning. Legitimate peripheral participation.* Cambridge: Cambridge University Press.

Lawrence, J.A. (1988). Expertise on the bench: Modelling magistrates' judicial decision-making. In M.T.H. Chi, R., Glaser & M.J., Farr (Eds.), *The nature of expertise* (pp. 229-260). Hillsdale, NJ: Lawrence Erlbaum Associates.

Leontyev, A.N. (1981). *Problems of the development of the mind.* Moscow: Progress.

Munley, G.A., & Patrick, J. (1990, September). *A strategy based approach to training transferable fault-finding skill. Operator training and aqcuisition of cognitive skills.* Paper presented at the first meeting of the international network on *Cognitive Approaches to Dynamic Environment Supervision.* Cardiff, UK.

Norros, L. (1989a, October). *Responsibility for system development as an element of process operators' professional expertise.* Paper presented at the *Second European Meeting on Cognitive Science Approaches to Process Control.* Siena, Italy.

Norros, L. (1989b). Simulation in industrial work training. In L. Bainbridge & A. Ruitz-Quintanilla (Eds.), *Developing skills with information technology* (pp. 315-328). Chichester, UK: Wiley.

Norros, L. (1991, July). *Development of operators' expertise in implementing new technologies. Work and Welfare.* Paper presented at the *Second Karlstad Symposium on Work.* Karlstad, Sweden.

Norros, L., & Sammatti, P. (1986). *Nuclear power plant operator errors during simulator training* (Tech. Rep. No. 446). Espoo, Finland: Technical Research Centre of Finland.

Norros, L., Toikka, K., & Hyötyläinen, R. (1988). Implementation of a FMS — Results of a case study. In J. Ranta & P. Huuhtanen (Eds.), *Information technology and work environment part III.* The Finish Work Environment Fund Publications A3 (pp. 139-189). Espoo, Finland: Technical Research Centre of Finland.

Olssen, S.E., & Rasmussen, J. (1989). The reflective expert and the prenovice: Notes on skill, rule and knowledge-based performance in the setting of instruction and training. In L. Bainbridge & A. Ruitz-Quintanilla (Eds.), *Developing skills with information technology* (pp. 9-34). Chichester, UK: Wiley.

Projektgruppe Automation und Qualifikation (PAQ) [Project group automation and expertise] (1987). *Wiederspruche der Automationsarbeit.* (Contradiction of automation work). Berlin: Argument Verlag.

Rasmussen, J. (1982). Human errors. A taxonomy for describing human malfunctions in industrial installations. *Journal of Occupational Accidents, 4,* 311-333.

Reason, J. (1987). A framework for classifying errors. In: Duncan, K., Leplat, J., and Rasmussen, J. (Eds), *New technology and human error* (pp. 5-14). Chichester, UK: Wiley.

Reiman, L., & Norros, L. (1994, March). *Organizational assessment of a maintenance department at a nuclear power plant.* Paper presented at *PSAM-*

II:An international Conference Devoted to the Achievement of System-based methods for the Design and Operation of Technological Systems and Processes. San Diego, CA.

Schön, D. A. (1988). *Educating the reflective practitioner.* San Fransisco: Jossey Bass Publishers.

Spinoza, B. (1975) *Ethik* (J. Stern, Trans.). Leipzig: Verlag Philipp Reclam jun. (original work published 1677).

Suchman, L. (1987). *Plans and situated action. The problem of human-machine communication.* Cambridge: Cambridge University Press.

Toikka, K., Norros, L., Hyötyläinen, R., & Kuivanen, R. (1991). *Control of disturbances in Flexible Manufacturing* (Tech. Rep. No. A14) (in Finnish). Tampere: Work Environment Fund Publications.

Wahlström, B., Norros, L., & Reiman, L. (1992, August). *Human Factors Research in the Nuclear Power Field in Finland.* Paper presented at the *Fifth IEEE Conference on Human Factors in Power Plants.* Monterrey, CA .

Zuboff, S. (1988). *In the age of the smart machine.* New York: Basic Books.

ACKNOWLEDGMENTS

Development of this approach has taken place at the Technical Research Centre of Finland in diverse research projects carried out in collaboration with Kristiina Hukki, Raimo Hyötyläinen and Kari Toikka. Also Lasse Reiman from The Finnish Centre for Radiation and Nuclear Safety, and Ari Kautto from Imatran Voima Power Company have contributed to the development of the approach.

SECTION 3

COOPERATION BETWEEN HUMANS AND COMPUTERS

10

Design of Cooperative Systems in Complex Dynamic Environments

Hakim BENCHEKROUN
Conservatoire National des Arts et Métiers
Bernard PAVARD
CNRS
Pascal SALEMBIER
Conservatoire National des Arts et Métiers

We describe a general method we use to design cooperative environments in real situations. We develop the notion of environmental resources and show how cognitive simulation can be used to design and test the new working environments. This general approach is centered around two work situations (air traffic control and emergency center) where cooperation can be viewed as the key point for task accomplishment.

INTRODUCTION

Understanding cooperative activity and developing methodologies to design and test cooperative environments (groupware, cooperative expert systems, team behavior) is crucial today in the field of cognitive engineering. There are numerous obstacles to an understanding of cooperative activity: Cognitive processes underlying cooperation are difficult to directly investigate (i.e., mechanisms of intent recognition, mutual knowledge, recursivity of mutual representations, modal knowledge, multimodality in speech acts, difficulty in formalizing collaboration procedure, and so on). From a designer or human factor point of view, the difficulties are even greater because it is not enough to understand cognitive processes, it is also necessary to be able to predict new behaviors in relation to the "to be designed" environment.

The design process must also include analysis of "borderline situations" where operators are in exceptional situations such as high workload, incidental or stressful contexts. We know that in such situations, operators not only change their cognitive strategies (through cognitive regulations) but they also may not use the same resources from their working environment.

To be really operational, the cognitive modeling of working activities must incorporate some of these factors. The models we are working with must explain how, why, and when behavior changes when operators are dealing with degraded situations or when the designer changes some aspects of functional resources. The current trend in cognitive modeling is to favor "internal" models where representations and control structures are independent of external factors (i.e., GOMS model, CLG, TAG, ACT, SOAR.). Although the advantage is clear cut (gain in generality), the approach is detrimental from the designer's point of view because it is extremely difficult to take into account real environmental constraints and hence predict realistic behavior. This difficulty may not only depend on the soundness of cognitive models but also on theoretical frames : in real work situations the cognitive representations used by operators are often associated with the external devices that constitute the whole environment. For example, Hutchins (1991) showed how memory processes in a cockpit are dynamically distributed among human agents and external representational devices. The difficulty of making a clear distinction between representations that are internal to the operator and those that are deeply rooted in the environment has been shown in other domains such as word processing (Pavard, 1987; Scavetta & Pavard, 1989), music composition (Marmaras, Pavard, & Xanthoudakis, 1987) and aircraft radar control (Bressolle, 1992).

Our approach will start with this premise and will address the issue of how to articulate these "internal" models of cognition with external constraints (work environment). In other words, are we able to handle the vicariance of human behavior at the level of the internal models (the current tendency) alone or do we have to work out a "pragmatic layer" (by analogy with the linguistic domain) whose purpose is to explain how external functional resources are incorporated and operationalized in the operator's mental representation? We will show how cognitive simulation appears to be an efficient paradigm to 1) combine in a unified formalism internal and external representations and 2) model situations where complexity (representational and operational) cannot be localized at the individual level but rather is distributed over several interacting entities (agents or devices). A case study where complex interactions arise between operators and an environment and where human behavior is highly dependent on environmental resources is illustrative of this issue and will be developed.

COOPERATION AS A COGNITIVE REGULATION MECHANISM

Cooperation is a special feature of collective activity oriented towards a specific goal. It can take on many forms (Zachary & Robertson, 1990). For example:
- agents can share goals and accomplish them without any cooperative activity,

- agents can negotiate their contributions to cooperative activity,
- agents can have different goals and still cooperate,
- agents may have coordinated activity without any cooperative goals and so on.

These different forms of cooperation are not mutually exclusive but they may alternate during the course of a dialogue.

From the modeling (internal) point of view, communication can be seen as a resource allocation problem. The basic mechanisms can be stated as follows:

- agents are resource limited,
- having limited resources and goals to fulfill, they must allocate cognitive resources to what they estimate to the most efficient activity (perception, problem solving, hypothesis evaluation, situation assessment).
- cooperation between agents can be seen as an answer to the resource limitation problem but cooperative actions are also resource consuming and must be evaluated before being initiated.

This approach, if well formalized, can yield a dynamic view of human cognition and is a classical frame to analyze specific problems such as relationship between cognition and workload or modeling of human errors (Cacciabue & Kjaer-Hansen, 1992; Woods, Pople, & Roth, 1990).

In order to be more predictive in a realistic context, models need to include more information about the trade-off between the "advantages" and "cost" of cooperation such as :

- cooperation (by sharing goals) implies mutual knowledge but mutual knowledge is resource consuming (for example it requires intention perception),
- cooperation calls for availability from colleagues but availability depends on workload.

As we will see from the work analysis, these regulations are highly dependent on the characteristics of the work environment, and the theoretical issue is where, in the general architecture of models, do we implement these kinds of "interactions" between external constraints and cognitive regulations which are decisive to the final operationality of human environment interaction.

In the next section, we describe the notion of environmental resources in two examples.

ENVIRONMENTAL RESOURCES

Environmental resources are defined as all the potential resources (information, informational supports, etc.) that are available in the operator's environment that can be used to fulfill a task. Different environmental resources may be used at different times during the work process.

In the domain of air traffic control, for example, environmental resources are very dense and at times hard to identify exhaustively. The basic tools an air traffic controller uses are the radar screen, where he can visualize the position and speed of flights and flight strips (small pieces of paper on which aircraft characteristics and destinations are written). These strips in fact are used to code much more information than the basic information printed on the paper (Shapiro, Hughes, Randall, & Harper, 1991). For example, controllers can actively organize these strips on the flight progress board to spatially code dynamic information such as vertical speed, position, abnormal flight, as well as the state of problem solving (what has been done and what remains to be done) (Figure 1).

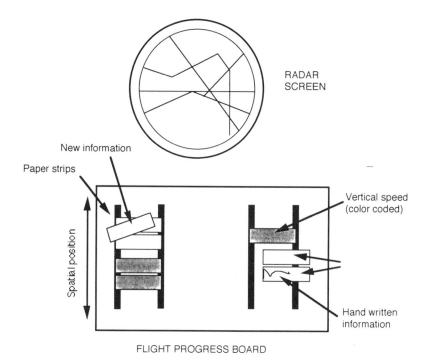

FLIGHT PROGRESS BOARD

FIGURE 1.   Example of environmental resources provided by air traffic control environment: the flight progress board for air traffic controllers
The positioning of paper strips on the board is a prime means of memorizing the dynamic state of the world.   The progress board is also extensively used by controllers to update their mutual knowledge.

The resources specifically associated with the flight progress board can be defined as the mobility, writability of strips, visual accessibility of this information by agents, and gestual modality in strip transmission between controllers (new information or abnormal information can be expressed by controllers through gesture).
     The following example illustrates the role of active organization of the strips on the flight progress board (Figure 2). In what is called a terminal sector (in the vicinity of an airport area) two different kind of spatial organization of strips can be found. The first orders the strips as a function of category of flight (towards

the airport area or leaving the airport area - even if the flight did not take off from this airport). Alternatively, strips can be ordered in terms of the location of the flights in the critical sector, with the airport as a reference point.

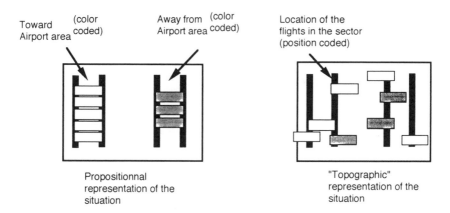

FIGURE 2. Two different external representations used by air traffic controllers

As a function of traffic complexity and environmental constraints, the controller can use a propositional style of external representation (left) or a more analogical, topographical oriented organization of the progress board (right).

In some situations the inherent complexity of the flights configuration in the sector makes one type of representation predominate. However the selection of a specific external representation is highly dependent on contextual features of the situation. For example, even though traffic complexity is not solely determined by the number of flights at hand, this factor may constrain the choice of representation because of space on the flight board: Too many strips at one time may make the use of a topographic representation unfeasible. In other words the controller uses the flight board as an external memory and can choose the most relevant organization and information format at a time, but contextual feature elements may highly restrain the span of this choice (Figure 3).

Furthermore, all this strip information is also used to update mutual knowledge (Bressole, 1992) which is a prerequisite for an efficient cooperation.

As a second example, take the cooperation between agents situated close together in a task of cooperation in an emergency room (Pavard, Benchekroun, & Salembier, 1990). A detailed work analysis showed that in this situation, cooperation is extremely dependent on the notion of agent mutual knowledge and mutual knowledge is made possible in this case by environmental resources such as "proximity of agents," and "possibility of direct visual contact." Proximity of agents makes passive and active information acquisition possible. Information acquired in this case can be used later for cooperation. Possibility of direct visual contact is also one of the most important factors in conversation regulation: Agents can listen to all communication (when they are not themselves busy) and they can adjust the strength (illocutionary force) of their request in relation to the estimated (by visual perception) urgency of the request.

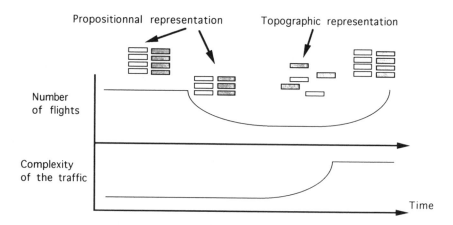

FIGURE 3. Effect of traffic complexity and number of flights to control at a given time on the selection of relevant external representation by air traffic controllers.
The controller's choice of representation may vary as a function of changes in context.

ENVIRONMENTAL RESOURCES AND THE DESIGN OF A NEW WORKING ENVIRONMENT

Changing the working environment requires being extremely aware of the consequences of the new environmental resources on the organization of work, problem solving strategies, management of risks, and so on. For example, as shown below, introducing an electronic mail system in a group of cooperating people (even if this new tool is merely added to the previous situation) can radically alter communication regulation strategies and how the work is really done. Similarly in air traffic control, going from paper strip to electronic display cannot be without extensive investigation of how it will affect the resources implemented in the traditional system.

Another type of difficulty arises from the fact that working conditions usually evolve over time. Workload may increase for a short period of time (burst of external calls in an emergency center) or may start to evolve in an unexpected way (abnormal air-flight trajectory). To handle such situations operators change their cognitive strategies (or regulate their activities). These regulations have been extensively studied in domains such as air traffic control (Sperandio, 1972) or aircraft piloting (Hutchins, 1992). The main point is that in these situations, operators or cooperating agents may use different environmental resources to fulfill their tasks.

At this point, it is important to realize that without specific work analysis on critical situations such as high workload or unexpected event scenarios, it is very difficult to assess all the resources an environment provides[1] and, furthermore, it would be difficult to anticipate how a new working environment could provide the required functionalities. The methodology we propose has been elaborated through different complex interface design projects that attempt to overcome the difficulties described earlier. It is mainly based on the identification of environmental resources, the understanding of how operators use these resources both in nominal and exceptional situations, and finally, the modification of the environment and a simulation of cognitive regulation mechanisms.

Methodology

From a practical point of view, our methodology is based on the following steps:

Work analysis

Identification of the cognitive regulation mechanisms in the situation. Cognitive regulation mechanisms arise because operators have limited cognitive resources (memorization, attention, etc.). Therefore, they must adapt (regulate) their cognitive mechanisms to allocate their resources in an optimal way, which depends on many factors such as previous experience, knowledge of interface functionalities, environmental factors, and so on.

Cognitive regulation modeling on a rule-based system

From previous work analyses, a collection of typical scenarios are identified and stored (typical scenarios are segments of activities, usually a few seconds or a few minutes, that characterize how operators behave in response to particular tasks or outside disturbances). Strategies observed on the previous step are formalized taking into account the role of environmental factors. The model is based on speech act theory (to handle the pragmatic components of communication in relation to environment resources) and on information processing theories (to handle cognitive resource limitation constraints).

---

[1] Hutchins uses the concept of "opportunistic use of the structure of the environment" in a way similar to ours (Hutchins, 1992).

Confrontation with video scenarios

We test the model with previously monitored scenarios. The model must be able to describe the evolution of cognitive strategies in relation to the different environmental constraints (workload, stress, etc.).

Simulation of what the scenario would become in the new situation.

Rules are modified in order to take into account the new working environment and, with the same input (external events, communication intentions, etc.), we visualize what the initial scenarios would become.

A CASE STUDY OF COOPERATIVE ACTIVITY: COMMUNICATION REGULATION IN AN EMERGENCY CENTER

The emergency center (SAMU 91) is in charge of all medical emergency calls in the Southern Paris area (one million people). Currently the emergency team is made up of two operators (nurses) and two physicians. The task, referred to as "phone call regulation" consists in assessing the level of emergency of phone calls, diagnosis, and decision making about sending the right medical help (counseling, ambulance, etc.). This task is a complex one because it implies decision making under uncertainty and time constraints, management of ambulance resources, up-date of log books, management of patient stress, and so on. The object of the study was the design of a cooperative computer tool (groupware) that would improve communication efficiency between the members of the emergency team, both in normal and overload situations (peaks of emergency calls either due to statistical phenomena or accidents involving many patients).

Work analysis and identification of regulation mechanisms through cooperation

During an emergency call, more than one agent may have to cooperate, either due to simple information requests or a process of distributed diagnosis between operators and physicians. This collaboration process is usually facilitated by collaboration awareness within the group: Each agent tries to be aware of all ongoing events, even if these are managed by colleagues.
This organization makes cooperation at a high cognitive level possible (shared cognition) where any agent can handle a phone conversation, even if it is not

initiated by him/her. Several other regulation mechanisms have been identified (Pavard, Benchekroun, & Salembier, 1990) and we focus on two because of their stability over many situations.

Communication regulation through less constrained agents (operators or physicians)

The task requires that any phone call must be answered as soon as possible. Three configurations are possible :
a) the operator is available: He/she will take the phone call.
b) the operator is not available but one of his/her colleagues is available and will take the phone call.
c) no operator is available: In this degraded mode, operators use a regulation mechanism based on an evaluation of the level of emergency of all their phone calls. Less urgent calls are put on a waiting list.

Communication regulation through turn-taking protocols.

Conversational analysis has clearly pointed to the importance of turn-taking in ordinary conversation. The key notion is that conversation between people is structured by alternating dialogues which are controlled by social and organizational rules (Procter, 1991). Turn-taking not only reflects the structure of group communication but also helps sustain it. In our situation, turn-taking plays an important role because it is the process by which cognition is distributed through agents. The particularity of this mode of communication is that responsibility for organizing shared cognition is distributed across participants and not controlled by any external structure.

Communication Modeling

The theoretical framework for interpreting communication is inspired by the theory of speech acts (Searle, 1969), the theory of intentionality (Searle, 1985) and the formal model of illocutionary acts of Allen, Cohen, and Perrault (Cohen & Perrault, 1979). In this approach, the action of talking corresponds not only to the desire to transmit information but also to modify the universe of thought of the interlocutor (non-explicit). Communication can be categorized into three parts:
- the preparation of the request (illocutionary act): A needs a certain piece of information, and he believes that B has it. A will then prepare his request according to what he knows about B (i.e., B knows it, now, not busy, and so on),
- the formulation of the request (locutionary act): The request itself, that is the words employed to convey the message,

- the impact of the request on the interlocutor (perlocutionary act): B hears the A's request, interprets it, and eventually responds. For personal reasons B may decide not to satisfy A's request. In this case, the communicative act intended by A is either an explicit failure (i.e., B disregards the information completely) or will have an impact in the future (i.e., the locutionary act affects B's universe of thought).

This theoretical framework is nevertheless not sufficient to formalize communication in real situations because, as we pointed out for work analysis, speech acts are preceded by a turn-taking process where the listener's availability is assessed. Availability is evaluated through many non verbal channels such as gesture, posture, facial expressions, and so on. These channels are supported by what we call "environment resources" and constitute what is called elsewhere "collective space" (Procter, 1991) and are responsible for the "social presence" by which members of the group signal their intentions, monitor, detect, and resolve ambiguities and conflicts. As a function of this evaluation, the speech act will be either canceled or reinforced.

Three situations can then occur:
- B is perceived as available, then A will perform the speech act.
- B is not perceived as available, then A can delay his request or eventually increase his illocutionary strength in order to interrupt B's conversation.
- A's judgment of B's availability is erroneous and the communication process is canceled.

As an example, we take the situation where operator A wants to make a request to operator B about proposal P:

P : *"Which physician is working next Sunday ?"*

To formalize the communication process, we use the following rules :

illoc_rule :
        want (A, request (A,B,P,Level_i)),
        believe (A,availability (B,Level_j)),
        Level_i>Level_j,
        retract (want (A,request (A,B,P,Level_i))),
        assserta (request(A,B,P,Level_i))).

This illocutionnary rule states that if A wants to make a request to operator B about the proposal P (A supposes that B has the information), and if the degree of B's availability is greater than the emergency of the request, then A will transform his intention to communicate into a speech act.

Another rule is necessary to make a distinction between illocutionary act and its perlocutary effects, as in the Searle model.

perloc_rule_1 :-
        request (A,B,P,Level_i))),
        availability (B,Level_j)),
        Level_i>Level_j,
        assserta(believe (B,A,request (A,B,P,Level_i))).

The perlocutary effect is bound by a time constraint: Listener B must allocate time to receive the verbal message from A (not shown in this example for reasons of simplicity). This duration is picked up from real scenarios monitored during work analysis. The recognition by B of A's intention is not enough to complete the communication process: B must also assess the request in the context of his own activity. If the request is taken into account, listener B will answer. For this purpose, he will again allocate time to answer and interrupt the current task in order to pursue it later:

perloc_rule_2 :-
    believe (B,A,request(A,B,P,Level_i)),

    availability (B,Level_j)),
    Level_i>Level_j,
    interrupt_current_task (B),
    want (B,inform (B,A,Answer,Level_i)).

Communication rules are written in a formal language (Prolog in this case) from the results of work analysis and tested in relation to the typical scenarios we identified from the work analysis. The second step in the modeling process consists in the specification of the new rules related to the electronic mail environment. It is then possible to "replay" the original scenarios in relationship to the new communication rules (Benchekroun et al., 1990).

Comparison with video scenarios

Real communication scenarios are interpreted in terms of the model described above. In the following example (Figure 4), many communication intentions are not followed by speech acts (see broken arrows in Figure 5).
For example, Ph gets an outside phone call at time 1 that should be handled by operator P15 (personal call).
P15 already has an interlocutor.
Ph tries to inform him unsuccessfully.
Ph must then allocate cognitive resources to pick up the end of P15's conversation if he wants to transfer this personal phone call to him.
Two other cases of unsuccessful communication arise in this example:
- P15 tries to interrupt R15 at time 3' and must wait till the end of R15's communication (time 5).(who speaks to whom) is distributed over the different
- Between Ph and R15 at time 7.
In this case, Ph decides to transfer the phone call to P15 instead of R15.
operators and rule
    All these communication regulations are handled well by our model provided that there is a good description of phone call priorities (depending on their degree of emergency) and provided that operators clearly manifest their availability in relation to the degree of emergency of the calls they are handling (Grice's sincerity axiom). As mentioned before, in these situations, the control of communication governed. Communication patterns and the global efficiency of communication

in the group is very sensitive to environmental resources such as the possibility to visually assess interlocutor availability, the possibility of "staying in the loop" by listening to other conversations, and so on.

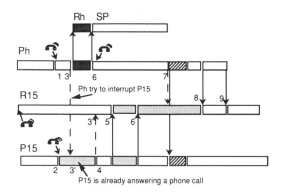

FIGURE 4. Real communication between three agents (R15 and RH are physicians, P15 and PH are operators, SP is an external call).
Verbal communications are represented by full arrows, while intentions of communication (i.e., which are not followed by a verbalization) by broken arrows. External calls are shown as telephone icons. Shaded areas indicate temporal discontinuity in communications.

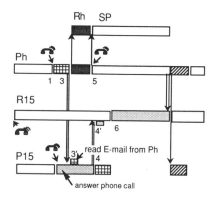

FIGURE 5. The simulation of the communication scenario shown in Figure 4 in the new environment (hand written graphic E-mail).
Groupware communications are represented by double arrows. Intentions of communication is always completed; in this case the interlocutor is busy; a message is left in the listener's E-mail box .

In the next section, we will show how a computational model of communication can be used to predict how a given communication pattern can be improved by introducing new groupware.

Simulation of communication in the new working environment

The rational principles behind the groupware we designed are based on the fact that the communication rules for turn-taking used in normal situations stay unchanged during a peak of activity (when many phone calls arrive during a short period of time): Operators try to interrupt each other, looking for cooperation, but, as everybody struggles to handle their own phone calls, they are no longer ready to cooperate (Salembier, Pavard, Benchekroun, de Medeiros, & Denier, 1992). The simulation of this process is shown in Figure 5.
Due to a burst of phone calls, operators cannot transfer them immediately to the right agent.

A phone waiting list then occurs at all workstations. In order to overcome this situation, we introduced a new communication medium: a hand writing graphic network. Operators can write information manually (on a digitizing tablet) and send it to any other operator in the group. Turn-taking rules can then be based on the new information seen on the computer screen of the agent who receives the message. By this process, communication can be improved without changing the organizational principles of the team. The simulation of the impact of this new environment leads to a modification of communication rules. For example, it is necessary to add rules to modelize the situation where operator A wants to interrupt operator B who is already answering a phone call. Operator A will then decide to send operator B a message on the network :

com_rule :-
        want (A,inform (A,B,P,Level_n)),
        activity (B,phone,_),
        send_E_mail (A,B,P).

This rule states that if the goal of operator A is to inform B of a proposal P (emergency level n) and if B is already answering a phone call, then A will send B an E-mail, whose content is P. The predicted consequences of introducing this new groupware can be seen in Figures 5 and 6 C.

Figure 5 (a real scenario), shows that P15 reads on his screen the information sent by Ph (time 3') concerning a personal phone call that will be handled at time 4. The overall impact of the groupware can be evaluated in Figure 6 C. This last step allows for exploration of different kinds of environmental resources. For example, multimodal information interfaces can be tested virtually. In the above case, it is also possible to compare the functional operationality of audio and visual alarms when electronic messages are sent to other agents: auditory and visual cues can be hierarchized in relation to their attentional effects. Interaction between perceptual modalities can also be modeled easily (visual information can be read on the screen at the same time as a phone call is handled, but two conversations cannot take place at the same time).

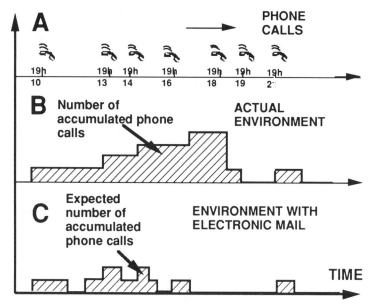

FIGURE 6. Modeling of a cooperative activity in a group of agents (two in this case) answering phone calls in an emergency center.
A: A burst of phone calls rings on the same telephone line
B: In the present environment (without electronic tools), there is an accumulation of calls because the operator cannot transmit phone calls to the other agents (they are supposedly busy themselves).
C: Simulation of the previous scenario within the new environment (with voice, visual, and electronic communication media).

CONCLUSION

This chapter addresses the issue of using cognitive simulation as a tool to anticipate human-environment interactions when we design new working situations. In the context of cooperative activities, cognitive information processing is tightly connected to functional environmental resources.
Thus, the first priority is to have a model of how internal processes are "tuned" in relationship to functional properties of the environment and the task at hand (what could be called the ecological dimension of the cognitive simulation).
Too much emphasis on the "internal cognitive processes" may lead to difficulties in generalizing observations to a new situation. Cognitive simulation emerges as a good paradigm to handle operator knowledge not only at the individual level

but also for interactions between operators or between operators and the environment.

REFERENCES

Benchekroun, T.H., Pavard, B., Salembier, P. & de Medeiros, E. (1990, October). *Analyse et modélisation des interactions dans un centre de régulation des appels d'urgence*. Paper presented at the *XXVIème congrès de la SELF*. Montréal.

Bressole, M.C. (1992). *Intention perception and cooperation in the process of air traffic regulation*. Unpublished master's thesis, University of Toulouse le Mirail.

Cacciabue, P.C., & Kjaer-Hansen, J. (1992). Cognitive modelling and human machine interactions in dynamic environments. *Le Travail Humain.*, *56*, 1-26.

Cohen, P.R., & Perrault, C.R. (1979). Elements of a plan based theory of speech acts. *Cognitive Science*, *3*, 3-20.

Hutchins, E. (1992) *How a cockpit remembers its speed* (Tech. Rep.). San Diego: University of California, Distributed Cognition Laboratory.

Marmaras, N., Pavard, B., & Xanthoudakis, H. (1987). Les changements de représentation induits par les systèmes informatiques: Le cas de la synthèse musicale [Representational changes induced by computer systems]. *Revue of Academy of Sciences of URSS*, *8*, 120-133.

Pavard, B. (1987). La conception des systèmes de traitement de texte [Text editors design]. *Intellectica*, *1*, 37-68.

Pavard, B., Benchekroun, T.H., & Salembier, P. (1990, October). *Simulation des mécanismes de régulation collective dans un environnement complexe* [Simulation of collective regulation mechanisms in a complex environment]. Paper presented at *Ergo-IA'90*. Biarritz, France.

Procter, R. (in preparation). *Supporting Distributed Cognition in Groupware*.

Salembier, P., Pavard, B., Benchekroun, T.H., de Medeiros, E. & Denier, J.P. (1992). Cognitive engineering as a tool to design human-computer interfaces in complex environments. *Proceedings of the International World Space Congress* (pp. 75-80). Washington, DC: International Astronomical Foundation.

Scavetta, D. & Pavard, B. (1989, March) Le traitement de texte professionnel: vers un modèle cognitif intégrant les caractéristiques de l'outil de travail [Professional text processing: toward a cognitive model including working tool features]. Paper presented at *Colloque sur l'Interactivité*. Paris.

Searle, J.R. (1969). *Speech acts*. Cambridge, UK: Cambridge University Press.

Searle, J.R. (1983). *Intentionality: An essay in the philosophy of mind*. Cambridge: Cambridge University Press.

Shapiro, D.Z., Hughes, J.A., Randall, D., & Harper, R. (1991). *Visual representation of database information: The flight data strip in air traffic control*. University of Lancaster.

Spérandio, J.C. (1972). La régulation des modes opératoires en fonction de la charge de travail chez les contrôleurs de trafic aérien [Strategy regulation in relation to air traffic controllers' workload]. *Le Travail Humain, 40,* 249-256.

Woods, D.D., Pople, H., & Roth, E.M. (1990). *The cognitive environment simulation as a tool for modeling human performance and reliablity* (Tech. Rep. No. NUREG/CR-5213). Washington, DC: U.S. Nuclear Regulatory Commission.

Zachary, W.W., & Robertson, S.P. (1990). Introduction to cognition, computation, and cooperation. In S.P. Robertson, W. Zachary, & J.B. Black (Eds.), *Cognition, computing, and cooperation* (pp.1-19). Norwood, NJ.: Ablex.

11
Trust and Human Intervention
in Automated Systems

Neville MORAY
University of Illinois
Douglas HISKES
University of Illinois
John LEE
Battle Human Resources Center
Bonnie M. MUIR
University of Toronto

As automation becomes increasingly common in industrial systems, the role of the operator becomes increasingly that of a supervisor. Nonetheless, operators are required to intervene in the control of automated systems, either to cope with emergencies or to improve the productivity of discrete manufacturing processes. Although there are many claims in the literature that the combination of human and computer is more effective than either alone, there is little quantitative modeling of what makes humans intervene, and hence little support for a scientific approach to the design of the role of operators in automated or hybrid systems. In this paper we describe a series of experiments which show that intervention is governed to a large extent by the operators' trust in the efficacy of the automated systems, and their self confidence in their abilities as manual controllers. A quantitative model for the operator in continuous process control is described, and some preliminary data are introduced in the field of discrete manufacturing.

INTRODUCTION

Ever since the introduction of the idea of supervisory control by Sheridan (1976, 1987) there has been speculation about the role that trust plays in the relation of humans to automated systems. Despite this, very little has been done to develop quantitative theories of human-machine relations which could help a designer to allocate functions between human and machines in modern automated systems.

It is important to note that the notion of "Fitts' Lists" is no longer adequate, if indeed it ever was. It makes no sense to draw up lists describing which activities are best performed by humans and which best performed by machines. Today almost any function can be automated if one is prepared to pay the price. One should not approach function allocation as a once-and-for-all activity which is performed when the system is designed and implemented. Rather, one should see it as a dynamic process in which, from moment to moment, the human decides whether to intervene or to leave the system running under automation. Function allocation should be seen as part of adaptive behavior in the face of system and environmental dynamics (Rasmussen, 1993, personal communication).

Although one can find examples of design engineers who have expressed their intention to remove humans completely from automated systems and develop "lights out" factories, there is now a growing realization that it is important to include the abilities of humans as part of industrial processes (see Sanderson, 1989, for a review in the context of discrete manufacturing). The problem is that complex systems, whether for continuous process control or discrete manufacturing, are generally optimized for automatic control. Hence one does not want humans to intervene unless it is necessary. On the other hand, one certainly does want them to intervene if the plant develops faults, or if there is a window of opportunity which long term optimization misses but which humans, with their excellent pattern perception, can notice.

What then is it that makes operators decide to intervene manually, and then to return control to automatic controllers? What kind of model can account for such nonlinear control by operators? We believe that one way to approach this problem is through the concept of the psychological relationships between humans and their machines, in particular through the concept of trust between human and machine. Zuboff (1988) has drawn attention to the importance of trust in the successful introduction of automation in various settings, and Sheridan (e.g., 1987) has frequently mentioned its importance in supervisory control.

In this paper we will describe the current status of trust and self confidence as intervening variables in human operator decisions to intervene in the control of automated systems. We begin by reviewing the concept of trust as applied to the relation between humans and machines, and then describe some experiments in which operators had to decide when to intervene to compensate for faults in the automated controllers of a simulated process control plant. We show that a quantitative time series model can be developed to predict such intervention, and that such a model must include the operators' trust of the machine and their self-confidence in their ability to control it manually. Finally we briefly describe recent work which shows that the results apply also to discrete manufacturing, suggesting that the model of the roles of trust and self-confidence can be generalized to many complex human-machine systems.

THE PSYCHOLOGY OF TRUST BETWEEN HUMANS AND MACHINES

A search through the literature of engineering psychology by Muir (1987, 1989) revealed almost no research on trust between humans and machines. She was able to show that models which had been proposed for the development of trust between humans could be applied to humans' attitudes to machines (Muir, 1987, 1989, and in press). In particular she found that the suggestions of Remple, Holmes, & Zanner (1985) and of Barber (1983) can provide a framework to describe the development of trust between humans and machines. She suggested that Barber's dimensions of Persistence of Natural Laws, Technical Competence, and Fiduciary Responsibility, which Barber claimed underlie why one person trusts another, could be identified respectively with the reliability of machines, the predictability of machines' behavior, and with the degree to which the behavior of machines is in accordance with their designer's stated intentions for their properties. She likewise suggested that the dimensions of trust suggested by Remple et al. (1985), namely predictability, dependability of disposition, and faith in the other's motives could be interpreted readily in the framework of machine performance. She suggested that inappropriate levels of trust in machines may lead to inappropriate strategies of control and function allocation. The development of trust and faith by an operator in a machine revealed the importance of predictability, reliability and extrapolation to faith in future performance of the Other which Remple et al. applied to humans. In particular she found a very strong relation between an operator's judgment of the "Competence" of a machine, defined as the extent to which it does its job properly, and the amount of trust placed in the machine.

We believe that there is good reason to think that the social psychology of trust can be applied to relations between humans and machines in general, mutatis mutandis, and that this is an area which deserves more research. To support this claim we will summarize work by Lee (1992) and Lee & Moray (1994) have developed her ideas further.

Experiments On Trust And Intervention In Continuous Process Control

Muir's work suggested that one should be able to understand the relation of humans and automated machines by asking for ratings of trust in the machines with which they work. In our laboratory first at Toronto and then in Illinois Muir, Lee, and Hiskes have pursued these ideas. We have used a combination of objective measures of system state and operator behavior together with subjective ratings by operators of their attitude towards the components of the plant over which they are exercising supervisory control. In addition we have measured their subjective ratings of self confidence in their manual control ability, the impact of faulty plant components, and productivity. The main testbed for the research has been a simulated pasteurizing plant (Figure 1).

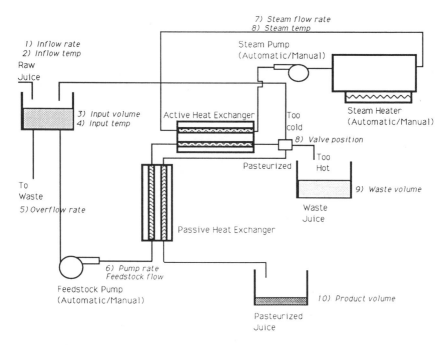

FIGURE 1. **The simulated pasteurizer and the state and control variables of each subsystem.** **(From Lee, 1992)**

The task of the operators is to maximize production of pasteurized juice. A slightly variable input arrives through the pipe in the top left corner of the screen, and is held in the vat below. From here it is pumped by the feedstock pump through a passive and then an active heat exchanger. In the active heat exchanger it is heated by superheated steam.

The feedstock pump, the steam pump and the heater can be either manually or automatically controlled. Operators can change from manual to automatic control and back by typing appropriate commands on the keyboard, and when in manual mode can type in the required settings for the pumps or heater. The heat transfer equations are realistic, and changes in pump rates take several seconds to reach their target values. Heat is derived from a boiler ("heater") by means of a steam pump. These three subsystems are the controllers, and can be run either automatically or under manual control. If they are adjusted appropriately the temperature of the feedstock leaving the active heat exchanger is between 75 and 85 degrees Celsius, and the pasteurized juice is passed through the pipe leading back to the passive heat exchanger where it gives up its energy to preheat the incoming feedstock, and is then collected in the output vat. If the temperature rises above 85 degrees Celsius the juice is spoiled and is passed to the waste vat. If it is below 75 degrees Celsius it must be reheated and it is recirculated to the input vat where it alters the temperature of the feedstock.

Muir trained her operators for many hours on a normal plant until they were very skilled at controlling it. She then exposed them to a variety of faults in the plant. Faults affected both trust and behavior. There was a strong tendency for operators to change to the manual mode of control when the plant became unreliable, a strong tendency for trust to decline progressively as the plant became more unreliable, and a strong tendency to monitor more frequently those subsystems which were identified by the operators as being the source of the unreliability. Reliable subsystems tended to be ignored, which may be a case of rational cognitive tunnel vision (Moray, 1981). Her work provides a strong basis for empirical work on trust between humans and machines.

The same pasteurizer, slightly modified and with improved controllers, was next used by Huey (1989) to study operator workload, but this work will not be reviewed in this paper. Finally Lee performed a series of experiments with an improved automated system, starting from the lead given by Muir, with the intention of developing a quantitative model of supervisory control (Lee, 1992; Lee & Moray, 1994).

Whereas Muir trained her operators to a high level of skill, Lee was interested in the acquisition of process control skills, in the effects of transient faults, and in developing a model which would predict the proportion of time spent in manual versus automatic control. His experiments consisted of giving each operator some 60 relatively short trials, (each approximately 6 minutes long,) and asking for a rating of trust after each. The first ten trials alternated between fully manual and fully automatic control, so that operators were certain to understand the dynamics of each. They then continued to operate the plant until on Trial 26 a transient fault occurred. This fault, as in Muir's work, consisted of the feedstock pump suffering random disturbances so that when either the automatic controllers or the manual controllers called for a particular setting, the actual obtained speed might be randomly too high or too low. In the next trial the fault disappeared, and on Trial 40 it reappeared and remained for the rest of the experiment. In later experiments Lee used an experimental design in which faults occurred either only in manual mode or only in automatic mode. In all cases, operators were asked to rate their trust in the quality of the plant at the end of each run, and in later experiments also to rate their self confidence in their ability to run the plant in manual control mode.

Several striking results appeared which have been reported elsewhere (Lee, 1992; Lee & Moray, 1994). Even when the fault was chronically present performance showed only a small decline of about 10% below the level it had attained prior to the occurrence of the fault. Operators adopted a wide variety of strategies to cope with the faults, and managed to maintain productivity at the cost of a very great increase in workload, which would probably be intolerable over a sustained period. Trust also declined (as would be expected from Muir's earlier work) and then recovered slowly and to a much lesser degree than did performance, still being some 50% lower on the final trial than just before the chronic fault appeared. Furthermore, the fall and rise in trust did not appear to be instantaneous, but took several trials to recover after the transient fault and to reach its minimum after the chronic fault began. Lee (1992) identified the causal factors in trust using a multiple regression model, and found that trust varied as a function of the occurrence of a fault and the system performance level measured as

% productivity. He then went on to develop a time series ARMAV model for the dynamics of trust, and found that trust could be predicted by the equation shown in Figure 2, which describes not just the causal factors but the dynamics of trust over trials (see Figure 2).

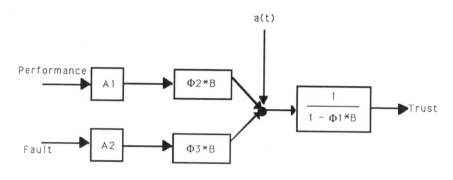

$$Trust(t) = \Phi_1(Trust)(t-1) + A_1 Performance(t) + \Phi_2 A_1 Performance(t-1)$$
$$+ A_2 Fault(t) + \Phi_3 A_2 Fault(t-1) + a(t)$$

FIGURE 2.   A time series model for the dynamics of trust, and the related times series transfer function.
Subscripts t, t-1, refer to the current and immediately prior trials. Φ's are backshift operators in the ARMAV model.   A's are weighting coefficients.   a is a random noise element.

The model accounted for up to 80% of the variance in the ratings of trust, a highly satisfactory result. A particularly interesting finding was that unlike Muir's operators, Lee's did not tend to change to manual mode when the automatic system became unreliable. This was at first puzzling because of the very strong effect which Muir obtained and the very stable level of training which her operators had reached. Lee found on close inspection that the failure to replicate was only apparent. Many of his operators were already using manual control at the moment when the fault occurred, and hence it was impossible to detect a switch into manual mode. His later experiments, in which faults initially occurred either in manual mode or in automatic mode, but not in both, revealed that what was actually happening was that operators tended to shift away from the mode in which they were operating at the time that the fault was noticed. As a result Lee actually found in his first experiment that there was a tendency to switch *into* automatic mode when the plant became unreliable, but this was because, unlike Muir's operators, most were in manual control mode at the time the fault occurred.

These results suggested that there were more subjective intervening variables then just trust. In his later experiments Lee obtained ratings of self confidence in manual operations as well as trust in the automatic systems. He again was able to identify the variables which accounted for automatic control, and found that as we expected, it was the difference between trust and self confidence that was the driving force in deciding which mode to use.

He again developed ARMAV models, one of which is shown in Figure 3. In his experiments the operators were able to choose to control any of the three control subsystems in either automatic or manual mode, whereas in Muir's experiment only the feedstock pump could be manually controlled. Figure 3 shows the transfer function for the steam heater and steam pump.

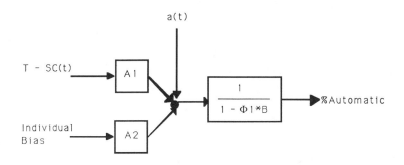

$$\%Automatic = \Phi_1(\%Automatic(t-1)) + \Phi_2(\%Automatic(t-2))$$
$$+ A_1((T - SC)(t)) + A_3(Individual\ Bias) + a(t)$$

FIGURE 3.   The transfer function and equations for allocation of function.

%(time in automatic mode) = $(F_1(\%automatic(t-1)) + F_2(\%automatic(t-2))$
$$+ A_1(T-SC(t)) + A_3(Individual\ Bias) + a(t))$$

where T is the rating of trust on trial (t); SC is the rating of self confidence on trial t; and Individual Bias is a factor reflecting the tendency of some operators inherently to prefer using one mode of control rather than the other.

The ARMAV models again accounted for over 70% and sometimes as much as 80% of the variance in the use of automatic control. The use of automatic control can be plotted against the T-SC term and results in a very beautiful "threshold curve" reminiscent of classical psychophysical functions and fitted closely by a logistic function (See Figure 4).

As an example of the phenomena which Lee was able to model, Figure 5 shows the history of a single operator over a series of trials in one of his later experiments (Lee, 1992; Lee & Moray, 1992).

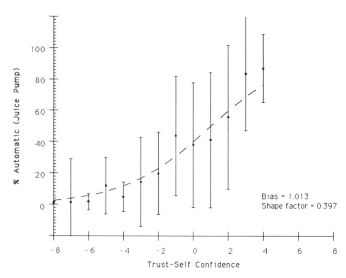

FIGURE 4.   The use of automation as a function of the difference between Trust and Self Confidence

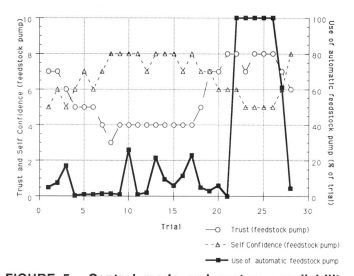

—○— Trust (feedstock pump)

- -△ - Self Confidence (feedstock pump)

—■— Use of automatic feedstock pump

FIGURE 5.   Control mode and system unreliability
Until Trial 16 the system is reliable. Trust is low and self confidence is high, and the operator is using manual control. After Trial 16 faults appear when the operator is in manual control. Self confidence declines, trust rises, and on Trial 21 the operator adopts 100% automation. On Trial 26 faults appear in the automated mode, but no longer in the manual mode. Trust falls, self confidence rises, and as they cross over the operator returns progressively to manual control.

CONCLUSIONS
FROM THE WORK OF MUIR AND LEE

Lee found a rich set of data concerning individual strategies of control, in the pattern of intervention over time, and in what appear to be reflections of the mental models of operators. The results on trust support the initial work of Muir, including increased monitoring of unreliable components. It is important to note that we have shown that trust is indeed a genuine causal variable. From Muir's results it was not quite certain whether plant unreliability caused trust to change, which in turn caused a change in the control mode, or whether the unreliability of the plant caused both trust to alter and the control mode to alter. The form of the regression equations and transfer functions found by Lee make it quite clear that the subjective variables are indeed a causal factor, and are not just an effect of unreliability. Unreliability changes productivity, trust, and self confidence, and those variables in turn change the mode of control. It is not sufficient to use merely productivity and the presence of a fault to predict operator performance. Subjective relationships to the machines must be included.

The practical importance of this work is in relation to the specification of a role for humans in the supervisory control of automated systems. First, it shows that it is possible to develop a quantitative basis for predicting when operators will intervene in the control of systems. From this it follows that we have a better starting point to discuss the extent to which systems design should be optimized only with respect to automatic control, or how much provision should be made for human intervention. The latter implies the need for displays and command languages which are optimized for human information processing. A further consequence of this work is that we must begin to consider how to include the question of social relations with machines in training. If trust and self-confidence play such an important role in determining the nature of the interaction between humans and machines, we need to design training programs which will support an appropriate calibration of the strength of these relationships and feelings. This suggests training scenarios which will make operators think in terms of whether intervention is appropriate, or whether a desire to intervene may simply be a result of a misperception of how reliable the system is.

We have found that the first experience of unreliability in a system which has been very reliable has a devastating effect on some operators. They initially assume that the error must be due to something they have done, especially if the control mode is predominately manual. Only when errors appear repeatedly do they accept the fact that the system is at fault. These dynamics of social interaction with the machines have never been taken into account in training. Finally, the work probably has applications of more generality. It is well known that people prefer "expert systems" which explain their intent and motivation. It is also well known that many such systems are abandoned once their designer departs, because people do not trust them. It appears from our work that there may be important research methodologies which can be brought to bear to understand this loss of trust, and thus lead to improved use of such expert systems, and it is therefore important to see how far our results can be generalized to other systems.

EXTENDING THE PARADIGM: THE DOMAIN OF DISCRETE MANUFACTURING

For this reason we have recently completed the first of a series of experiments using a simulated computer integrated manufacturing system (CIM) to investigate how operators decide to intervene to reschedule or otherwise tune a discrete system which is being monitored under supervisory control (Hiskes, 1994; Moray, Lee & Hiskes, 1994).

We have found changes in trust and in manual intervention with the appearance of unreliability in the CIM system that are very similar to those seen in the pasteurization plant. The psychology of decision making in discrete systems is a field much less well plowed than that of process control where there is a long history of modeling human intervention. (For work on continuous process control see Edwards & Lees, 1974; Crossman & Cooke, 1974; Bainbridge, 1981, 1992; Moray, Lootsteen & Pajak, 1986; Moray & Rotenberg, 1989. For an introduction to work on discrete manufacturing, see Sanderson, 1989; Sanderson & Moray, 1990.) There are many aspects of discrete systems which make it a difficult environment for the human operator. The nature of causality is different from that in process control, being "final" causality rather than "material" or "efficient" causality, purposeful rather than Newtonian. The subsystems of the plant are far less tightly coupled than is the case in continuous process control. Many states of the system are not readily observable - what feature of system performance is a sign now that the production run will be successfully completed in, say, 48 hours? Activity in different subsystems is asynchronous. The way in which faulty components make themselves apparent is quite different. All in all it is a fascinating new area for cognitive ergonomics, and one with very great practical implications for productivity and industrial efficiency.

Although for technical rather than conceptual reasons we have not been able to develop time series models for the discrete manufacturing case, the regression models are very similar, and include similar effects of faults, productivity, and the difference between trust and self confidence. Perhaps the most important result of this new work is that it proves that it is possible to generalize strong quantitative models relevant to the dynamic allocation of function from continuous to discrete complex industrial systems. This opens up the possibility of a widely applicable approach to supervisory control, one which we hope can lead to the fulfillment of the promise of Sheridan's original insights.

REFERENCES

Bainbridge, L. (1981). Mathematical equations or processing routines? In J. Rasmussen & W.B. Rouse (Eds.), *Human detection and diagnosis of system failures*, (pp. 259-286). New York: Plenum Press.

Bainbridge, L. (1992). Mental models in cognitive skill: the case of industrial process operation. In Y. Rogers, A. Rutherford, & P. Bibby (Eds.), *Models in the mind*. (pp. 119-143). New York: Academic Press.

Barber, B. (1983). *Logic and the limits of trust*. New Brunswick, NJ: Rutgers University Press.

Crossman, E.R., & Cooke, F.W. (1974). Manual control of slow response systems. In E. Edwards & F. Lees, (Eds.), *The human operator in process control*. (pp. 51-56). London: Taylor & Francis.

Edwards, E. & Lees, F. (1974). *The human operator in process control*. London: Taylor & Francis.

Hiskes, D. (1994). *Fault detection and human intervention in discrete manufacturing systems*. Unpublished doctoral dissertation, University of Illinois at Urbana-Champaign.

Huey, B.M. (1989). *The effect of function allocation schemes on operator performance in supervisory control systems*. Unpublished doctoral dissertation, George Mason University, Washington, D.C.

Lee, J.D. (1992). *Trust, self confidence, and operators' adaptation to automation*. Unpublished doctoral dissertation, University of Illinois at Urbana-Champaign.

Lee, J.D., & Moray, N. (1992). Trust and the allocation of function in human-machine systems. *Ergonomics, 35*, 1243-1270.

Lee, J.D., & Moray, N. (1994). Trust, self confidence and operators' adaptation to automation. *International Journal of Human-Computer Studies, 40*, 153-184.

Moray, N. (1981). The role of attention in the detection of errors and the diagnosis of failures in man-machine systems. In J. Rasmussen, & W. Rouse (Eds.), *Human detection and diagnosis of system failures* (pp. 185-199). New York: Plenum Press.

Moray, N., Lee, J. D., & Hiskes, D. (1994, April). *Why do people intervene in the control of automated systems?* Paper presented at the *First Automation and Technology Conference*. Washington, DC.

Moray, N., Lootsteen, P., & Pajak J. (1986). Acquisition of process control skills. *IEEE Transactions on Systems, Man and Cybernetics, SMC-16*, 497-504.

Moray, N., & Rotenberg, I. (1989). Fault management in process control: eyemovements and action. *Ergonomics, 32*, 1319-1342.

Muir, B.M. (1987). Trust between humans and machines, and the design of decision aides. *International Journal of Man-Machine Studies, 27*, 527-539.

Muir, B.M. (1989). *Operators' trust in and percentage of time spent using the automatic controllers in a supervisory process control task*. Unpublished doctoral dissertation, University of Toronto.

Muir. B.M. (in press). Trust in automation: Part 1 - Theoretical issues in the study of trust and human intervention in automated systems. *Ergonomics*.

Remple, J.K., Holmes, J.G., and Zanna, M.P. (1985). Trust in close relationships. *Journal of Personality and Social Psychology, 49,* 95-112.
Sanderson, P.M. (1989). The human planning and scheduling role in advanced manufacturing systems: an emerging human factors role. *Human Factors, 31,* 635-666.
Sanderson, P.M. (1991). Towards the model human scheduler. *International Journal of Human Factors in Manufacturing. 1,* 195-219.
Sanderson, P.M., & Moray, N. (1990). The human factors of scheduling behavior. In W. Karwowski and M. Rahimi (Eds.), *Ergonomics of hybrid automated systems II* (pp.399-406). Amsterdam: Elsevier.
Sheridan, T.B. (1976). Towards a general model of Supervisory Control. In T.B. Sheridan and G. Johannsen (Eds.), *Monitoring behavior and supervisory control* (pp. 271-282). New York: Plenum Press.
Sheridan, T.B. (1987). Supervisory control. In G. Salvendy, (Ed.). *Handbook of human factors.* (pp. 1243-1268). New York: Wiley.
Zuboff, S. (1988). *In the age of the smart machine.* New York: Basic Books.

ACKNOWLEDGMENTS

This work was supported in part by grants from the Canadian National Science and Engineering Research Council, and in part by a grant from the University of Illinois Research Board and the Beckman Bequest.

12

Handling Human Error

Antonio RIZZO
University of Siena
Donatella FERRANTE
University of Trieste
Sebastiano BAGNARA
University of Siena

Human-machine systems have become more and more risky and tightly coupled. Component failures can result in unacceptable disasters that not only affect workers and plants, but also neighbors and the environment. System Reliability Analysis has made noticeable progress in assessing technical component reliability, but the introduction of Human Reliability Analysis is a more of difficult task. This chapter attempts to define human error that should not necessarily be attributed to incompetence, but is considered a product of conflicts between the human and the physical or the social artifact. An overview of studies on human error commission, detection, and recovery is presented from which lessons are drawn and guidelines are provided for the design of operator support.

INTRODUCTION

Human interaction with objects and artifacts in both physical and social systems is frequently characterized by errors. However, "errors" are very often best attempts at accomplishing desired and sensible goals, and should not be necessarily attributed to incompetence (Lewis & Norman, 1986). People may not have any way of foreseeing the unintended and deleterious consequences of their decisions and actions, and only when negative modifications occur in the world, might they regret having taken a certain action or made a particular decision. The recent user-centered design approach of man-machine systems considers the error as the product of breakdowns in communication between the humans and the physical artifacts (e.g., Norman & Draper, 1986; Rasmussen, 1986; Shneiderman, 1992). These breakdowns, as claimed by Winograd and

Flores (1986), may play a fundamental role in the design process by revealing and creating space for problems and opportunities. Moreover, as these authors have observed, a structured analysis of the processes that cause breakdowns and of the processes that allow the handling of breakdowns should be useful to the designers. The inevitability of human error has led system designers to make a great effort to minimize the incidence of errors, to maximize their discovery, and to make easier their recovery or the repair of their consequences. However, despite the claims for user-centered systems, most of the available guidelines and design principles for error recovery are concerned with errors occurring at the syntactic level of the human-computer interaction, that is, errors concerning users' performances that violate rules in the grammar of the interaction. Guidelines and principles are not concerned with higher semantic and pragmatic levels of the interaction.

There are two main reasons for this. First, cognitive psychologists have historically considered perception and action two separate domains of study, and they have privileged the former. Actually, the distinction between perception and action is deceptive (see, e.g., Neisser, 1976; Arbib, 1989), since it has been shown that perception is involved in action selection, in action execution, and in the continuous evaluation of the results (Norman & Shallice, 1986). The study of human fallibility has also stressed the relationships between perception and action (see, e.g., Reason, 1990; Norman, 1988) to the point that human errors are conceived as breakdowns in the continuous action-perception loop. Second, within cognitive psychology there has been poor communication between researchers interested in perception and researchers interested in action. Indeed, ecological psychology advanced long ago the idea of perception as geared from action (Gibson, 1979). However, this idea did not play a visible role in research on cognitive processes for two main reasons. Gibsonians tended to consider their approach as alternative to that of cognitive psychology, and even recently they appear to stress the differences by downplaying the role of cognitive representations. In the ecological approach,, perception is still thought as a direct process that does not involve any high level process, such as inference (Turvey & Kugler, 1984). Also the relationships between experimental cognitive psychology and cognitive ergonomics have been very poor. The actual outcome of the scant communication among different fields of research and of the meagre cross-fertilization in the study of action and perception is that knowledge about cognitive processes of error handling that is not well established.

The main goal of the present chapter is to provide a cognitive analysis of error handling processes; an analysis of the processes by which negative outcome of human activity is made apparent, is related (properly or not) to previous activity, and is controlled by its consequences. The issues faced in this work are based on studies concerning errors conducted in laboratory (Rizzo, Bagnara, & Visciola, 1987; Rizzo, Ferrante, Stablum, & Bagnara, 1988), in industrial setting (Bagnara, Stablum, Rizzo, Fontana, & Ruo, 1987), and in everyday life (Rizzo, Ferrante, & Bagnara, 1992).

Special attention will be dedicated to the processes of mismatch emergence which are crucial in making the breakdowns apparent. Finally, we will attempt to provide guidelines to facilitate error detection in human-computer communication.

HUMAN ERROR

According to Reason, human error is a "generic term to encompass all those occasions in which a planned sequence of mental or physical activities fails to achieve its intended outcome, and when these failures cannot be attributed to the intervention of some change agency" (Reason, 1990; p. 9). By considering the behavioral output together with the knowledge activation processes involved and the level of cognitive control employed when an error occurs, human errors can be distinguished in the following categories (Reason, 1990):

i) Slip is characterized by a mismatch between intention and action: The intention is satisfactory, but the actions are not carried out as planned (Norman, 1981). A slip is mainly due to some kind of attentional failure in the low level of control of action, and normally occurs in routine situations characterized by automatic and over-practiced behavior;

ii) Lapse involves memory failures and does not necessarily manifest itself in overt behavior. A lapse may appear evident only to the person who experiences it. There are three main sub-classes: a) lapse of intention, which concerns the lost of intention that is currently under execution; b) Lapse of action, which refers to the failure to trigger the intended action at the proper moment; and c) Lapse of memory, where the intention is specified, but further information necessary to perform the action cannot be retrieved from memory, even though a deliberate attempt is made to do so (Sellen, 1990);

iii) Rule-based mistake usually consists of the wrong activation of well-known rules or procedures which have been consciously acquired. Rule-based mistakes depend on biases in the selection or in the quasi-automatic overriding by more familiar rules onto the appropriate ones, both in identifying the situation and in adopting the plan of action;

iv) Knowledge-based mistake occurs when a selected plan or even the intended goal turns out to be not wellfitted to the problem which is to be solved. Knowledge-based mistakes are attributed to the lack of completeness of the mental models used and/or a fault in causal thinking. People are not able to properly recognize the relation between different aspects of the problem or to achieve an adequate diagnosis of the problem. The context in which these errors occur is unfamiliar and requires diagnostic and planning behavior.

The distinction between the classes of error involved in this taxonomy is not clear cut. However, the taxonomy has been proven useful both in study of cognitive psychology and of cognitive ergonomics (van der Schaaf, Lucas, & Hale, 1991). In the present work it is instrumental to make evident the role of knowledge activation in error production.

ERROR HANDLING PROCESSES

Bagnara et al. (1987) singled out three main processes underlying the breakdowns in the action-perception loop: a) mismatch emergence, that is, the appearance of a discrepancy between feedback and active knowledge frame of reference, owned by the agent, which includes active expectations (e.g., the satisfaction conditions of a conscious intention) or implicit assumptions (e.g., embedded in the tacit knowledge); b) detection, that is, the awareness of what is wrong, which follows a causal assessment concerning the wrong outcome, the wrong action or both; c) recovery, that is, the overcome of the mismatch, where the goal is usually to reduce the mismatch or to get rid of it. Recovery is not necessarily based on a full understanding of the mismatch and of the error.

Sellen (1990) proposed another taxonomy of the main processes involved in breakdowns in the perception-action loop. These include the following: a) detection, that is knowing (either consciously or subconsciously) an error has occurred; b) identification, which refers to knowing what was done wrong and what should have been done; and c) correction, which refers to knowing how to undo the effects of the error and to achieve the desired state.

The crucial difference between the two taxonomies is about the role of mismatch. The following example (Rizzo, Ferrante, & Bagnara, 1992) shows that mismatch and detection processes do not necessarily overlap.

E1) I had to photocopy a paper from a journal. I set the machine in order to have the copy enlarged and double paged (side by side). Then I decided to duplicate the copy. I set back the size index to 100% and put the paper in the automatic feeder. The machine started to produce a copy plus an almost white sheet. At the beginning, I thought it was a dragging problem or that one of the originals was upside down. Then, the unexpected event was repeated over and over. I started to explore the machine, and noted the double page light on. The command was still on from the former setting.

In this case the mismatch emerged by the observation of an unexpected result, but the person did not assume that this outcome had been produced by his own wrong activity. Only when the identification of the source of the mismatch took place, did he detect his own error.

Considering Bagnara et al. (1987), Sellen (1990) and Rizzo et al. (1992) a new taxonomy of the processes underlying error handling can be put forward. It comprises four main processes: i) mismatch emergence (i.e., breakdown in the perception-action loop); ii) detection (i.e., awareness that an error occurred); iii) identification (i.e., knowledge of the source of the breakdown); iv) overcoming of the mismatch (i.e., strategies for either reducing the mismatch, to get rid of it, or to undo its cause).

So far, the proposed error detection processes have been based on the idea suggested by Norman (1984) that there can be essentially two ways to detect an error: either through "self monitoring," when the action is monitored and compared with expectations (if the action was not as planned, then the error would be detected), or through "deleterious outcome" (if the error causes some deleterious results, then it may be detected). Both modes rely upon 1) a feedback mechanism with some monitoring function that compares what is expected with what has occurred, and 2) the ability of the cognitive system to catch a discrepancy between expectations and occurrences (Norman, 1981). However, it is deceptive to assume that the knowledge frame of reference used to evaluate feedback collected along the action course remains stable and constant. Human knowledge is continuously activated and inhibited so the frame of reference is dynamic in nature. This dynamic characteristic of active knowledge and its role in the emergence of mismatches (which constitutes a central theme in this work) will be considered once the possible mismatches against a stable frame of reference have been described.

Mismatch

In what follows we present some examples of detected errors to show first the role played by different types of information, then the role of various reference systems against which the information is evaluated. The errors are selected because they represent proposed mechanisms and not because they represent dramatic and puzzling events that often occur in man-machine systems. However, we believe that the error sample can be useful to clarify the basic processes underlying the continuous supervision of human performance necessary for efficient interaction with the environment.

Mismatch and incoming information

The mismatch may be classified on the basis of the information that is matched against the frame of reference. From the analyses of the data of the previous studies, it has been possible to identify the following types of mismatch [1].

a) *Inner Feedback*. The information is available in the working memory and does not depend on feedback from either the action itself or more or less immediate consequences of it on the environment. It refers to the consequences of the wrong action on the cognitive system itself, as illustrated by the following examples.

E2) I had to meet a friend at a pub. Since she was late, I decided to leave before she arrived. Half an hour later, I was in my boyfriend's car and I felt lighter than before. I tried to understand why I felt so. I checked what I should have had with me. After a while I remembered I had left a big book in the pub.

E3) In LISP programming, the task was to extract the atom "PEAR" from the list "(APPLE GRAPES PEAR ORANGE"). The subject said: "I must do two REST and one FIRST." She began to write "(RES", then she stopped and said "No, the

---

[1] A similar taxonomy, though based on different principles, was proposed by Sellen (1990).

opposite... I am wrong because the LISP evaluate from the inside to the outside."

b) *Action Feedback*. Information comes from components of the action itself. This information is directly related to action execution not to its results. The latter can produce further evidence that an error occurred, but the person experiences the presence of a discrepancy even before knowing the results.

E4) I wanted to turn off the boiler. I had to act on a switch near to the light switch on the electric box. As I laid down my hand, I noted that it was in the wrong position, but I could not avoid turning on the light.

c) External or Outcome Feedback. The information does not come from the actions performed but from their consequences on the environment. The consequences can be related to the produced state of the world, detected soon after the action, to delayed effects or to delayed detection. In all three cases they concern states of the external world which do not fit with persons' active knowledge.

E5) I had hard day. In the evening, I had to dine out. So, I had to dress up. In the walk to the meeting, I felt an enduring pain at my ankle. Actually, I also was hobbling along a bit. I thought it was due to my old sick tendon. After dinner, I was on the sofa, I crossed my legs and I had a look at one shoe. After a while, I changed the position of crossing and I saw a different shoe. I looked at both feet... I had put two different shoes on, one heeled the other one not.

A special case of External Mismatch is that produced by an External Communication. In this case, the agent is informed by other people either about the specific wrong action or, more generally, about some undesired states of the world.

E6) A Plant Operator decided to inform the shift supervisor that Slab Yards OC3 1000 and GES 500 (having different characteristics) needed more slabs. In the inter-phone conversation the operator told of Yard OC3 1000 in a context that concerned the GES 500 and vice versa. The supervisor did not understand and asked why more slabs were needed. The unexpected request made the operator a little upset. He repeated the request with more details and stressed the need for more slabs, but this time asked for the slabs in the right context. The head of the shift at this point informed the operator about the former "spoonerism."

d) Forcing Function. The information comes from the environment and concerns constraints that prevent the performance of the intended action or the attainment of the desired state of the world. Sellen (1990) called this mismatch "Limiting Function." She observed that, in the engineering literature, a forcing function usually refers to the function which drives an action, while a limiting function is that which limits its progress. Even if we agree with Sellen's observation, we propose to stick with the old name proposed by Norman (1984), since it is already in use in the psychological literature.

E7) I wanted to set the property "Visible" of a field in HyperCard to "False." I modified the command on the message window only for the final part from "to 21, 35, 63, 85" to "to false." Then HyperCard presented a message "Invalid argument for command set." Looking back to my command in the message box, I read the full command "set rect of field X to false." As soon as I read the "rect" I understood what the error was.

e) Intention Uncertainty. The information concerns the feeling of being unsure about what to do next. There are two typical cases: One is related to the loss of activation of the ongoing intention (E8), the other to lack of adequate alternatives in adopting feasible intentions (E9).

E8) I was in the lab. I needed a document that was in the office. Along the way to the office, I met some friends. We started out chattering and joking. Anyway, I kept on moving. I reached the office. Then, I realized that I did not know what I was there for. I tried to remember. No way. I had to go back to the lab and ask my colleagues.

E9) An operator had to plan the daily production in the hot strip mill. This task was governed by constraints (e.g., to exploit to the utmost the hot strip mill, to make the most of the space in the Slab Stock Yard) and by rules (e.g., the sequence of slabs must respect the "grave" shape). In the computer system all the information on the slabs and on the condition of the plant were available under request. When the operator had already planned about 25% of the production, he stopped and said that he felt uneasy about what to do next. He suspected that the current plan was wrong. He re-decomposed the schedule and rearranged the slabs in a new order. The day after, the production was properly accomplished. Examining the former schedule it was observed that two slabs would not have been processed.

f) Standard Check Behavior. The information is actively searched with the aim to control its status in respect to the frame of reference. The number of checks depend on many factors: the personal characteristics, the risk associated with the task, the complexity of the environment, the level of accuracy needed, and so on.

E10) At a class, I was making notes. I wrote down some data presented by the teacher on experiments I'm really interested in. Five weeks later, I was at home studying on those notes. And, as I used to do when possible, I checked the data in my notes with those reported in the textbook. I realized I had mis-typed one figure and reversed others.

Mismatch and frame of reference

As anticipated, a mismatch may arise because the incoming information contrasts with the expected one or because the expectations are changed during the action course. In fact, to properly understand what happens during a mismatch, one should not assume that at time t_1 there is some active knowledge that forms the frame of reference against which at time t_2 some incoming information is evaluated. This view, which has heavily influenced the literature on error detection, implies a static representation of the knowledge or, at best, assumes that all the knowledge is always available and ready to be used.

Actually, the knowledge active in the working memory is continuously updated during the interaction with the environment. This updating process is shaped by two main sources: one internal an the other external. The internal source consists in knowledge that becomes active when its stronger competitors decay after they have been executed (e.g., Norman & Shallice, 1986, Umiltà, Nicoletti, Simion, Tagliabue, & Bagnara, 1992). The external source of updating arises from new information relative to the state of the world available after the interaction. The new information may either activate not still considered knowledge or produce a tuning up of the already activated knowledge. Therefore, this information, even if it does not violate the expectations, may provide the conditions for the activation of more appropriate knowledge.

There are situations where it is necessary to adopt a not quite appropriate knowledge to allow the proper one (but less used or less frequent in that context) to get space. The new one will define the "new" frame of reference against which outcome feedback, inner feedback, and forcing functions are matched. For the construction of this "new" frame of reference, both sources of updating can cooperate and are not mutually exclusive.

In the study on error in everyday life it has been possible to identify four possible classes of knowledge frames of reference. These include:

a) Stable knowledge frame of reference. The frame of reference active before the execution of the action remains about the same along the action execution. It includes the explicit expectations or implicit assumptions concerning the execution of the action and the modifications it is prone to bring about. It constitutes the usual frame of reference against which action and outcome feedback are matched.

E11) I did some computations with a calculator. I manipulated the data by following a formula kept in my mind. The final result did not seem correct to me. I remade the computation two more times and both results were the same, but different from the first. These latter results sounded right to me. Actually, I did not discover what the error was but only that I had made an error.

b) Frame of reference active after the adoption or execution of the intended actions. As already suggested, the emergence of mismatch have to be considered as constructive processes where the knowledge active in the working memory is continuously updated. For example, the incoming information can call by itself the knowledge on which to be evaluated. This position is close to that by Kahneman & Miller (1986), who maintain that a stimulus can be evaluated in respect to the norm that it evokes after the fact, rather than in relation to pre-established expectations. Moreover, after an action has been triggered, other schemata can gain the access to the working memory when their competitors decay.

E12) I had to make many Xeroxes in the shortest time. I prepared the sequence of articles. I put the sheets over the machine and collected the copies in order to rearrange them in "papers." I was Xeroxing a long paper when I noted that I had to reorder all the copies, because I was feeding from the first page on. Then, I realized that starting from the end of the paper would have spared time and work.

c) Distant frame of reference. The active frame of reference concerns a context distant either conceptually or in time or both from that in which the planning and the execution of the wrong intentions and actions took place. In this case the active knowledge is related to states of the world (usually provided through forcing function or external feedback) which may or may not have clear relationship with the error made.

E13) I decided to clean the luggage rack of my car. To ease the access to the hollow I removed the rear panel bus. Since in the panel there were the speakers of my stereo, I disconnected cables. The day after, I turned on my car stereo: the left speakers did not work. I thought it was a fault in the system. One week later, I was in the car talking with a friend about the possible causes of the left speakers' breakdown. I recalled that some days before I had my car in a garage to fix minor faults. The guys in the station could have forgotten to re-connect some electric cables. Then, suddenly, I remembered that I had put my hand on electric cables too....

d) Lack of meaning. This concerns the awareness that there is not a specific goal governing the ongoing activity. In the frame of reference there is no available schemata to fulfill people's constant need to give meaning to their activity.

E14) I intended to pick up the keys of the car. They are usually in a box at the entrance. Instead, I entered another room and searched in a drawer where I did not find any keys (but there were the documents about which I was talking before, but I did not pay attention to them). Then I found myself wondering what I was looking for and why I was there. I had to go back to my office to recall that I was leaving and so I needed the keys of my car.

As above reported, these examples of error detection were chosen with the idea of providing as simple as possible cases for circumstantial evidence of the proposed processes of mismatch. However, the process of error handling is very seldom characterized by only one mismatch. Many different types of mismatches can take place, relative to the very same event, by making reference to different types of knowledge, active in different moments. The process of matching usually continues until a stable frame of reference, which allows to restore smooth perception-action loops, is reached. In the above reported examples the specific type of mismatch was easily identifiable, but in many cases multiple and different mismatches can occur before a solution can be found. This is shown in the following example.

E15) I wanted to get money from an automatic teller. I put my card in and typed the personal code. I was waiting for the following message from the system when I got distracted by the traffic. In the while, the message on the screen changed from "Type the secret code" to "Push the operation button." I missed the change. I kept waiting for the new message. Of course, nothing happened, and I thought that I had mistyped the code. So, I typed it again, but I got a beep after each number. Then, I thought I had used a wrong secret code (that of my other, less used, card). When I was going to type the new code and to check it on the screen I finally noted the message.

This example illustrates a relatively simple case of multiple mismatches since the environment remained stable after the first mismatch. It is easy to figure out how much things can become complex when the environment changes.

After the Mismatch

We have already seen that the emergence of a mismatch does not directly imply that an error has occurred. Generally, with the increase in the complexity of the domain in which human performance transpires, it becomes necessary to distinguish in the occurrence of an error not only between the mismatch and the awareness, but also among detection, identification and recovery. Indeed only in a few cases the knowledge needed to understand what was wrongly done and how to undo the negative effects are available when a mismatch takes place.

What diagnosis behavior will be produced by the user depends on the information available after the mismatch. In particular it depends on: 1) the type of error; 2) the information involved in the mismatch; and 3) the active frame of reference.

Rizzo et al. (1988) have identified some patterns which describe different combinations of the main processes underlying error handling as a function of the three sources of information above reported.

As far as the present work is concerned we will just distinguish the situations in which there is co-occurrence among the different stages, from the situations in which they are separated, since the user needs further information to go from one stage to the next stage.

Detection

As we have seen before, in the literature there is no complete agreement on the definition of error detection. According to our definition, the term indicates the process through which people become aware that a self-produced error has occurred, but sometimes in the literature it includes the mismatch and/or the identification. This is mainly due to the frequent overlapping of these three stages in error handling.

The co-occurrence of mismatch and detection is typical of well-defined domains (e.g., computer programming, mathematical problem solving), where a mismatch is automatically considered the result of an error. For example, when the subjects in the LISP study (Rizzo et al., 1988) encountered a forcing function or received an unexpected outcome, they immediately assumed that they had made an error .

On the contrary, the detection temporally separated by the mismatch is usually found in relation to complex situations like some of those characterized in everyday life or industrial settings. Indeed, in these environments the emergence of a mismatch may occur due to system's malfunctions (industrial setting) or from conditions which come off independently from our actions.

Norman (1984, 1988) observed that before assuming a self-produced error it is necessary to eliminate alternative explanations. Conversely, such a caveat can give rise to the biased attitude of "explaining away errors," which is a crucial factor in facilitating major accidents.

The attitude to explaining away errors is made more evident when there is a distance between different frames of reference. That is, between the reference frame that guided the wrong action and the reference frame involved in the mismatch. In this case, as we have already pointed out, the active knowledge might not have a clear relationship with the error. A delayed detection usually takes place after an external mismatch. At difference, there is no indication of a privileged feedback in producing an automatic detection.

Therefore, the critical factors used to distinguish between situations in which mismatch and detection co-occurred from situations in which detection is delayed are: i) the general assumptions about the characteristics of the domains (i.e., open vs. close systems); and ii) the distance between the active frame of reference and the frame of reference in which the planning and the execution of the wrong action took place. Thus, all the necessary information to distinguish between these two situations concerns the frame of reference.

Identification

Only in some cases the emergence of mismatch makes automatically available the information necessary to identify what was wrongly done. The overlapping of mismatch, detection, and identification mainly happens when: i) the error is a slip (i.e. the intention is feasible and the agent can easily activate the knowledge to fulfill it); ii) the outcome of the action is readily available (generally when the mismatch is based on action or outcome feedback); iii) the frame of reference remains stable during the execution of the action.

When the error concerns the mis-activation of an intention (i.e., rule-based mistake) and/or the distance between frames of reference increases, error identification becomes more complex. The agent starts an activity of hypothesis testing, searching for evidence that can strengthen or weaken various possibilities. If the domain is well-defined, completely governed by dependencies and rules, the diagnosis behavior consists in finding which rule has been wrongly applied. A careful evaluation of outcomes obtained (either results or messages) and from the previous performed actions by backward chaining it is often sufficient to find the error. When the domain is not well-defined and a knowledge-based mistake occurs, knowledge triggered by the mismatch is distant from the knowledge necessary to identify the error. So the agent, finding him/herself uncertain, wavers between a backward and a forward analysis trying to advance a plausible hypothesis about when and what, if any, error has been made, and on how to recover from the undesired results.

As the psychological literature on thinking and decision making (e.g., Kahneman, Slovic, & Tversky, 1982) has pointed out, people's reasoning is biased in a systematic way. Most of these biases concern the ignoring of some kind of information and the focusing on only a small part of it (Legrenzi, Girotto, & Johnson-Laird, 1993). The more well documented bias, from which follows most of the studies on diagnosis is the confirmation bias (Wason, 1960). According to this bias, people sample information consistent with their current hypothesis rather that those that are inconsistent.

Unfortunately, until now most of these reasoning biases have been studied only in well-defined laboratory settings (see Hoc, Amalberti, & Boreham, chapter 2, this volume). It would be desirable to attain a greater communication between researchers interested in human error in real situations and cognitive psychologists, with the aim to prove which among these biases are held on and what new biases come out in real situations.

Recovery

When the system is "reversible," in many cases the identification of the error makes available the recovery path; even if, sometimes its execution may be quite time consuming. But if the system does not allow reversibility or if the agent, after an exploration about the discrepancy, realizes that he or she is unable to identify the causes, he tries to overcome the mismatch. He moves to a forward analysis trying to fulfill the goals to be reached through a repertoire of familiar actions in order to keep the system within an acceptable range. At the best, he directs his attention to the negative consequences and tries to eliminate or at least to reduce them. More often, he adopts a set of actions of repair/containment based on the symptoms noticed rather than looking for the identification of the source-event and its causes. These symptom-based actions are not derived from reasoning on the symptoms themselves (Brehmer, 1987), rather they are easily available and are familiar cognitive routines, which were proved to be effective in containment/repair of a system under failure.

It is interesting to underline that users, only if they appraise the situation as potentially manageable, try to understand the error that they had made. Otherwise they prefer to disregard the achieved results and focus their attention on alternative ways to reach their goal. Else, if they assess the goal as no more feasible, they try to adapt the goal to the current state.

GUIDELINES FOR HANDLING ERROR

Studies both in cognitive psychology and in cognitive ergonomics show that it is wrong to assume that, if a person is shown to possess a piece of knowledge in a circumstance, this knowledge should be available under all conditions in which it might be useful. Actually, the opposite effect is observable: Knowledge accessed in one context remains inert in another. "Thus, the fact that people possess relevant knowledge does not guarantee that this knowledge will be activated when needed. The critical factor is not whether the agent possesses domain knowledge but rather the more stringent criterion that relevant knowledge be accessible under the conditions in which the task is performed" (Woods, 1990, p. 253). Knowledge activation and its transformation are the crucial points which support the human error handling process. Indeed, on one side, most of the errors depend on the mis-activation, conscious or subconscious, of knowledge. On the other side, mismatches consist of conflicts or clashes of knowledge active in the working memory, and the identification of the breakdown is the possible resolution of the conflicts. But note that sometimes it is, or it seems, not possible to resolve the conflicts. However, other times the source identification of the breakdowns may be irrelevant, so the direct overcoming of the mismatch can be the best way for a smooth restarting of the activity.

Thus, the problem of error handling is, at least at a basic level, a problem of supporting the activation of relevant knowledge by modulating the conditions in which tasks are performed.

Lets consider how this could be done. We will provide a list of possible guidelines and for each of them we will identify the cases where they might apply. All the following guidelines are expressions of a general strategy aimed at augmenting the redundancy of objects, procedures, and feedback. Obviously, designing is a trade-off activity, so most of the following guidelines have to be weighed and balanced in respect to other guidelines that might point at different directions as, for examples, consistency, simplicity, reduction of information overload, and so on.

1) Make more perceptible the action. That is, design for human-computer interactions where actions with different goals are also different in their shape. This could have two advantages: i) it may reduce the possibilities of activating the execution of another action; ii) it would lead the components of the action itself to provide unambiguous information on the ongoing activity even before the knowledge of results (E3, E4, E6).

For example, in the Graphical User Interface (GUI) clicking outside the space dedicated to the active application produces a shift between applications. This switch is observable by the acknowledgment of the result but barely during the performance of the action, especially when the active application is distributed over more than one window. In safety critical application, actions that may produce dramatic and different outputs should be mediated by a well differentiated action pattern.

2) Use multi-sensory feedback. Users already exploit indirect feedback for evaluating the output of their action, like noise, vibration, time frequency of information updating, proprioceptive data. But most of the human skilled activities can be performed with a reduced amount of information flow from the environment, so, paradoxically, it is for these activities that we need an articulated, multimodal feedback to facilitate the early production of mismatch. The error E5 shows how proprioceptive and tactile information efficiently drive the action to dress a pair of shoes, but even if all the information needed for early evaluation of feedback is available, the subject does not experience a mismatch.

The use of an acoustic icon can be of special help for improving the redundancy of information provided for a given task. This solution has been explored in various interfaces (e.g., Gaver, Smith, & O'Shea, 1991). A less explored source of feedback for multi-sensory interaction is that to modify the button of the mouse from a simply input device to an input-output device. For example, the surface of the button could produce different tactile sensations as a function of the position of the pointing mark on the GUI.

3) Display message at high level but with specific content. When forcing functions are supported by a message this should provide information on what objects are involved and what values are improper for each object. For example, in the error E7, the message "Invalid argument for command set" should be completed with information on the "rect" item: "rect do not have false or true values" or "false is a value for x and y but not for rect." Note that all this information may easily be made available to the user. Recently, much effort has been put into improving the error messages provided by the system when it cannot interpret the commands given by the user. However, in these types of messages it is usually considered only the first information item that does not fit with the previous ones. If the aim is to help the user to activate alternative knowledge representations, information should be provided on possible and impossible states of all the items involved in the un-interpreted command.

4) Provide an activity log. People heavily depend on external memory aids. This is clearly shown in the example reported in error E8, E9, E14. Supporting HCI by means of an activity log that records time, action, and response for activities that do not leave a clear and permanent trace of their occurrence is a substantial tool for improving memory for actions and for intentions. There are mainly two ways to provide an activity log. One concerns the record of time, action, and system modifications by labels. The level at which user's action and system's response have to be classified (e.g., single action on objects or cluster of actions) might depend on the user's skill and/or on his evaluation of how fine he would track his session of interaction. In any case, the user should be in control of the level of action/response classification. Tools that provide activity logs are already available in labs where the software usability is tested. Versions of these tools with less programmable elements but with the same potentiality might easily be integrated into software dedicated to critical tasks. The other way for recording activity is sampling configurations of interaction in relation to given events. In this case, information is recorded not only for the objects that change in state but it also concerns all the information potentially available during a change of state. This more pictorial activity log may be instrumental for a long-lasting session with relatively few interactions occurring on complex graphical interfaces (e.g., in process control). Concerning the activity log it is interesting to note that users of command-line interface (e.g., VMS operating system), often when they have to use the e.mail system, prefer to move from terminals to PCs where it is running communication software that provide activity logs (e.g., NCSA™, VersaTerm™).

5) Allow comparisons. Outputs that could be related among them should be easily compared. People can perceive differences among states but may be unable to single out what the crucial differences are or what the causes are (e.g., E10). Furthermore, they may also mis-classify a given output as a new one or a different one. Misclassifications are especially challenging when they concern different outputs in time from the same process. Comparisons are particularly useful when activity is distributed over different tools that can manipulate the same object (e.g., process control). In any of these cases the comparison between outputs is a rich source of information for action evaluation and it has to be supported. The opportunity of frizzing a given output and comparing it with the one resulting from a repeated process would be of help in assessing differences.

6) Make result available to user evaluation as soon as possible and allow the user to have control on the format display. Feedback is crucial not only for allowing good execution of the desired actions but also for changing an idea about what action is to be performed or state of world pursued (E12, E13). To this aim, it is important that the user can manipulate the display of the results since it is not possible in advance to know which are the intentions of the user or his idiosyncratic way to evaluate outcomes (so far the tools developed for catching user's intentions have not produced sensible results, i.e., plan recognition). We suggest three possible ways by which result presentation can be improved: i) *Exploitation of layout.* Space is a formidable artifact that provides visibility, perceptual cues, and organizing structure (see Norman, 1993). ii) *Exaggeration of the differences.* Variations in the optical flow are adequate stimuli for our perceptual system, and variation in the proportion and relationship among objects are adequate stimuli for our categorical processes. Both can be used for producing salience in the system responses to the user. iii) *Stress on the aspects relevant to the just performed task.* As above reported only a subset of the information available is used for action control and result evaluation, so the information strictly related to the task should be privileged in result presentation.

The best strategy for coping with these principles is to provide the users with several possibilities for each of these aspects (layout management, differences exaggeration, and stress on the aspects relevant to the task) and allow them to manipulate the resulting presentation according to their needs and wishes. To avoid conflicts with guidelines that claim consistency and for avoiding collateral effects like focusing always on the same features of the output even when they are not any more relevant, it could be possible to contain the effects of the user's manipulation to the early presentation then return to the usual format.

7) Why the result? - Why the beep? The best way to support error identification after a mismatch is to give specific answers to the user (E11, E15). In some software package (e.g., Mathematica™) when the user asks the system to do something that does not make sense (to it), the system responds with a forcing function signaled by a Beep. At this point, the user can open a constrained dialogue session by calling the *Why the beep* command. As response, the system presents an error message where it provides information on the mismatch encountered by the system in interpreting the previous request of the user.

Further help is available to the user by pushing a Help button which would produce template examples of the correct commands that can be formulated with the key words used in the uninterpreted command. A similar strategy of presenting questions to the system could be adopted for each output of the system that could be inadequately evaluated by the user. For example, in relation to a given output of the system the user could ask *Why the result* and the system could respond by presenting the triggering conditions that would be present for producing that given output. It is important to note that these triggering conditions could be made available by the system with little memory load since they concern the last few steps of interaction or more permanent states that are still present after the result.

In concluding this session it is important to remind that all guidelines for system design have to be considered for their impact on specific and contextual situations of human-computer communication. Design is a trade-off activity where often no optimal solution exists.

CONCLUSION

In the last years, much has been done in human-computer interface design to ease the access to relevant knowledge. For example, the graphic-direct-manipulation interfaces allow access to knowledge through the more effective way of recognition rather than that of remembering, and they support a better control on intentions and actions by means of affordances. The massive use of metaphors in designing interfaces provides a successful application of the knowledge-activation issue. The approach of designing an interface that exploits the specific prior knowledge that users have of other domains represents a more effective tool for controlling the complexity of an interface than any other attempt to reduce the number of actions, procedures, and concepts that users must execute or remember.

However, such a change is of much but not conclusive use in coping with breakdowns. For example, the current available environmental cues can be misleading, and forcing functions apparently may leave no escape route. Desired states, even if feasible and sensible, might look hardly reachable to the agent, sometimes just for the role played by the adopted metaphor in driving action plans. This occurs since a metaphor, from one side makes ease to access knowledge, from the other side, constraints the way in which goals can be reached. Constraints can strongly arise from what designers think are the best ways to accomplish tasks and goals. In conformity, feedback, error messages, and help are provided according to the designer's decisions. However, computer tools offer a significant chance for substantially supporting the breakdowns that agents regularly encountered in everyday activities, in devising goals, and in carrying out actions and plans. It is our opinion that users should be provided with a richer variety of feedback, messages, and help and they should be allowed to manipulate these sources of information according to their wishes and needs. Following Winograd and Flores, a fundamental principle in the design of computer-based systems is that "computer tools can aid in the anticipation and correction of breakdowns that are not themselves computer breakdowns but are in the application domain" (1986; p. 166). This principle concerns the semantics and the pragmatics of the interaction; that is, the levels for which computer tools are devised.

According to the point of view presented in this paper the general principle of Winograd and Flores could be interpreted in the direction of making easy the activation of the knowledge relevant to cope with the variety of mismatches, which may occur in the most different situations. In fact, the present paper has shown that error handling qualitatively changes from one domain to another, not only with regard to the knowledge content to be used (which is rather obvious), but also for what concerns the feedback to be used, the relationships among the main cognitive processes underlying it, the reference systems used, and the types of errors.

Thus, a tool designed to support human error handling should sustain each cognitive process involved in this activity.

REFERENCES

Arbib, M. A. (1989). *The metaphorical brain 2*. New York: Wiley.

Bagnara, S., Stablum, F., Rizzo, A., Fontana, A., & Ruo, M. (1987, October). *Error detection and correction: A study on human-computer interaction in a hot strip mill production planning and control system.* Paper presented at the *First European Meeting on Cognitive Science Approaches to Process Control.* Marcoussis, France.

Brehmer, B. (1987). Models of diagnostic Judgements. In J. Rasmussen, K. Duncan, & J. Leplat (Eds.), *New Technology and Human Error* (pp. 87-95). Chichester: Wiley.

Gaver, W., Smith, R.B., & O'Shea, T. (1991). Effective sounds in complex systems: The ARKola simulation. *CHI 1991 Conference Proceedings* (pp. 85-90). New York: ACM Press.

Gibson, J. (1979). *The ecological approach to visual perception.* Boston: Houghton, Mifflin.

Kahneman, D., & Miller, D.T. (1986). Norm theory: Comparing reality to its alternatives. *Psychological Review, 93* , 136-153.

Kahneman, D., Slovic, P., & Tversky, A. (1982). *Judgment under uncertainty, heuristics and biases.* New York: Cambridge University Press.

Legrenzi, P., Girotto, V., Johnson-Laird, P. (in press). Focusing in reasoning and in decision making. *Cognition.*

Lewis, C., & Norman, D.A. (1986). Designing for error. In D.A. Norman & S.W. Draper (Eds.), *User centered system design.* (pp. 411-432). Hillsdale, NJ: Lawrence Erlbaum Associates.

Neisser, U. (1976). *Cognition and reality.* San Francisco: Freeman & Co.

Norman, D.A. (1981) Categorization of actions slips. *Psychology Review, 88,* 1-15

Norman, D.A. (1984) *Working papers on errors and error detection.* Unpublished manuscript.

Norman, D. A. (1988). *The psychology of everyday things.* New York: Basic Books.

Norman, D.A. (1993). *Things that make us smart: Tools.* Reading, MA: Addison Wesley.

Norman, D.A., & Draper, S.W. (Eds). (1986). *User Centered System Design: New Perspectives in Human Computer Interaction.* Hillsdale, NJ: Lawrence Erlbaum Associates.

Norman, D.A. & Shallice, T. (1986). Attention to action: Willed and automatic control of behavior. In R.J. Davidson, G.E., Schwartz, & D. Shapiro (Eds.), *Consciousness and Self Regulation: Advances in Research,* Vol. IV (pp. 1-18). New York: Plenum Press.

Rasmussen, J. (1986). *Information processing and human-machine interaction.* Amsterdam: North-Holland.

Reason, J. T. (1990). *Human error.* Cambridge, UK: Cambridge University Press.

Rizzo, A., Bagnara, S., & Visciola, M. (1987). Human error detection processes. *International Journal of Man-Machine Studies, 27,* 555-570.

Rizzo, A., Ferrante, D., & Bagnara, S. (1992). *Human action and error detection.* (Tech. Rep. No. 92MML1). Siena, Italy: Institute for Communication Science.

Rizzo A., Ferrante D., Stablum F., & Bagnara, S. (1988, September). *Causal analysis in HCI: When does it occur?* Paper presented at the *Fourth European Conference on Cognitive Ergonomics. ECCE4.* Cambridge, UK.

Sellen, A. (1990). *Mechanisms of human error and human error detection.* Unpublished doctoral dissertation, University of California, San Diego.

Shneiderman, B. (1992). *Design the user interface.* Reading, MA: Addison-Wesley.

Turvey, M.T., & Kugler, P.N. (1984). An ecological approach to perception and action. In H.T.A. Whiting (Ed.), *Human motor action: Bernestein reassessed* (pp. 373-412). Amsterdam: North-Holland.

Umiltà, C., Nicoletti, R., Simion, F., Tagliabue, M. E., & Bagnara, S. (1992). The cost of a strategy. *European Journal of Cognitive Psychology, 4,* 21-40.

Van der Schaaf, T. W., Lucas, D. A., & Hale, A. R. (1991). *Near miss reporting as a safety tool.* Oxford, UK: Butterworth-Heinemann.

Wason, P.C. (1960). On the failure to eliminate hypothesis in conceptual task. *Quartely Journal of Experimental Psychology, 12,* 128-140.

Winograd, T., & Flores F. (1986). *Understanding computer and cognition: A new foundation for design.* Norwood, NJ: Ablex.

Woods, D. D. (1990). Modeling and predicting human error. In J.I. Elkind, S.K. Card, J. Hochberg, & B.M. Huey (Eds), *Human performance models for computer-aided engineering* (pp. 248-274). San Diego, CA: Academic Press.

13

Man-Machine Cooperative Organizations: Formal and Pragmatic Implementation Methods

P. MILLOT, and R. MANDIAU
CNRS - University of Valenciennes

The present increase of decisional capabilities of Artificial Intelligence (AI) tools makes the problem of cooperation between humans and Intelligent Support Systems more and more actual in the high-level decision tasks for process supervision and control. This chapter tries to bring some elements for modeling and implementing cooperative organizations involving heterogeneous decision-makers: human and artificial. Distributed Artificial Intelligence approaches are first analyzed and illustrated through an example in the air traffic control domain (ATC). Then Human Engineering and Ergonomics approaches are described and analyzed in the same application domain. A comparison of both approaches is made through conceptual points of view and also through pragmatic criteria concerned by the implementation possibilities in concrete complex application domains such ATC.

INTRODUCTION

The present increase of decisional capabilities of Artificial Intelligence (AI) tools makes the problem of cooperation between humans and Intelligent Support Systems more crucial. This new kind of cooperative work at higher level decision-making tasks mandates reflection on how to model the organization of an heterogeneous team of decision-makers. For instance, the integration of decision support systems in a control room of a complex process creates a new situation in which human supervisors who already cooperate among themselves also have to cooperate with the support system. This situation should result in a cross-cooperation between men and machines (Bellorini et al., 1991). But this objective does not seem easily reached, not only for technical reasons linked with the present limitations of AI systems or for human reasons due, for instance, to their knowledge level on the process and on the AI system, but also for psychological reasons due, for instance, to the lack of operator's trust in the AI system (Moray, Hiskes, Lee, & Muir, chapter 11, this volume).

Therefore a new way of research seems to emerge for modeling these cooperative organizations. This chapter tries to bring some elements derived from Distributed Artificial Intelligence approaches (DAI) on one hand, and from on-site human engineering approaches in the field of man-machine cooperation. The first part discusses some characteristics of distributed decision making and illustrates this problem through the example of Air Traffic Control (ATC). The second part presents the solutions proposed by the DAI approaches. The last part deals with a more pragmatic solution in the ATC domain.

DISTRIBUTED DECISION-MAKING

The problem of distributed decision making has been investigated since the early eighties by the DAI community, with a view to modeling and implementing multi agent organizations. An agent is an autonomous artificial decision-maker (for instance an expert system) having its own source of knowledge, its own control mechanism (for instance an inference engine) and capabilities of communications with the other agents of the organization. The proposed organization models are often derived from the human society and can therefore be transposed to the heterogeneous organizations involving AI agents as well as human agents.

The cooperative process of decision making in a group of agents involves the interaction between multiple goals, each having different scope and nature as well as different heuristics. The distributed decision making in a cooperative work is a decomposition according to the nature of the problem. For instance we can give two forms of cooperation corresponding to two different hierarchical organizations:

- In the first organization the decision-makers are at the same level, and the tasks as well as the actions resulting from them can be distributed between them. This form of cooperation simply augments the information processing capacities of individual agents and thus enables a group to perform a task that would have been impossible to each of them individually within acceptable time. In this case, the agents have equivalent abilities. However, the principal problem consists in searching for a task allocation method between the participants for coordinating the problem solving.

- In the second organization, one decision-maker is responsible for all the tasks and if necessary he can call other agents. It integrates the contributions of multiple agents which are devoted to the operation of different specialized tasks. In this case, the abilities are different but complementary. However, it requires a great adaptivity so as to insure consistence between the cognitive level of agents.

Let us see the example of Air Traffic Control (ATC) in which these two kinds of organizations can be proposed. The ATC objectives consist in monitoring and controlling the traffic in such a way that aircrafts cross the air space with the maximum safety level.

In the present real organization, the ATC Centers monitor each aircraft and detect preventively the risks of conflicts (i.e., when two or more planes transgress the separation norms, which could result in a collision). When such a risk is detected the ATC controllers give to one of the pilots involved in the conflict, the order to modify his plane trajectory. This organization corresponds to the second one presented earlier in which the ATC controller is at the higher level of the hierarchy and the planes are the specialized agents.

In a more futuristic view of the ATC organization, some researchers have proposed a DAI approach in which each plane would be fitted with radar detection facilities and communications with the other planes and conflict solving support systems. In this organization the centralized ATC centers would no more be needed and the problem would be seen as a distributed decision-making between the planes (agents) involved in the conflict. This corresponds to the first organization described earlier in which the different agents must cooperate and coordinate themselves for solving the problem.

Through this example we can foresee the difficulties to be dealt with, in particular the work conducted collectively and directly may require the interaction of agents with multiple goals of different scope and nature. First, they can prefer different problem solving strategies or heuristics. Thus the cooperative decision making involves a continuous process of assessing the validity of the information produced by the others. Secondly, decisions are always generated within a specific conceptual framework, as answers to specific questions. Thus, a system supporting cooperative work involving decision-making should enhance the ability of cooperating agents to interrelate their partial and domain knowledge and facilitate the expression and communication of alternative perspectives on a given problem. The cooperation underlines different levels of problem. It thus addresses the organizational view.

We can now see two kinds of approaches and relevant problems for implementing a cooperative organization: the DAI approaches and the different kinds of formal solutions they propose, and a more pragmatic human engineering approach; these two kinds of approaches are both illustrated by the ATC problems.

DISTRIBUTED ARTIFICIAL INTELLIGENCE APPROACHES

In a multiagent environment, an organizational *structure* (Corkill, 1983) is the pattern of information and control relationships that exist between the agents, and the distribution of problem solving capabilities among the agents. In cooperative distributed problem solving, for example, a structure gives each agent a high-level view of how the group solves problems and the role that the agent plays within this structure. Generally, the structure must specify roles and relationships to meet these conditions: For.example, to ensure the problem coverage, the structure could assign roles to the agents according to their competences and knowledge for a given subproblem. The structure must then also indicate the connectivity information to the agents so that they can distribute subproblems to competent agents.

DAI approaches raise and study 2 kinds of problems to be solved for choosing and implementing the structure of the cooperative organization:
- the nature and modes of communications this structure needs,
- the degrees of cooperation this structure and these communication modes allow.

Furthermore, another concept does exist in DAI, linked with the flexibility of a structure, which allows a dynamic evolution of the organization from a structure to another one, according to the nature of the problem to be solved. These concepts will be illustrated trough the example of ATC.

Communication

In DAI the possible solutions to the communication problem range between those involving no communication to those involving high-level, sophisticated communication.

- *No communication:* Here the agent rationally infers the other agents' plans without communicating with them. To study this behavior, Genesereth & al. (1986) use a game-theory approach characterized by pay-off matrices that contain the agents' payoffs for each possible outcome of an interaction. Indeed, the agents must rely on sophisticated local reasoning compensating the lack of communication to decide appropriate actions and interactions.

- *Plan Passing:* In this approach, an agent A1 communicates its total plan to an agent A2, and A2 communicates its total plan to A1. Whichever plan arrives first is accepted (Rosenschein et al., 1985). While this method can achieve cooperative action, it leads to several problems. The total plan passing is difficult to achieve in a real world application because there is a great deal of uncertainty about the present state of the world, as well as its future. Consequently, for real life situations, total plans cannot be formulated in advance, and general strategies must be communicated to a recipient.

- *Information Exchanges through a Blackboard:* In AI, the blackboard model is most often used as a shared global memory (Nii, 1986) on which agents write messages, post partial results, and find information. It is usually partitioned into *levels* of abstraction of the problem, and agents working at a particular level of abstraction see a corresponding level of the blackboard within the adjacent levels. In this way, data that have been synthesized at any level can be communicated to the higher levels, while higher level goals can be filtered down to drive the expectations of lower level agents.

- *Message Passing:* Undoubtedly, the work of Hewitt and his colleagues (Kornfeld & Hewitt, 1981) on actor languages is an excellent representation of message passing application to DAI. In this work however, the agents have an extremely simple structure, and several works in DAI have used classical message passing with a protocol and a precise content (Cammarata et al., 1983).

- *High-Level Communication:* Research on natural language understanding and particularly research on intentions in communication (Cohen et al., 1990) is relevant to DAI research because both research areas must investigate reasoning about multiple agents with distinct and possibly contradictory intentional states such as beliefs and intentions. An agent must interpret messages from other agents, including what the messages imply about the agent's mental states, and must generate messages to change the mental states of other agents, taking into account its own potential actions and those of others.

Degree of Cooperation

The *Degree of cooperation* characterizes the amount of cooperation between agents that can range from fully cooperation (i.e., total cooperation) to antagonism. Fully cooperative agents which are able to resolve non-independent problems, often pay a price in high communications costs. These agents may change their goals to suit the needs of other agents in order to ensure cohesion and coordination. Conversely, the antagonistic systems may not cooperate at all and may even block each other's goals. Communication cost required by these systems is generally minimal. In the middle of the spectrum lie traditional systems that lack a clearly articulated set of goals. We can notice that most real systems are cooperative to some small degree.

- *hierarchical approach:* A total cooperation is done in the Cooperative Distributed Problem Solving studies (Durfee, 1989), where a loosely coupled network of agents can work together to solve problems that are beyond their individual capabilities. In this network, each agent is capable of resolving a complex problem and can work independently, but the problems faced by the agents cannot be completed without total cooperation. Here, total cooperation is necessary because no single agent has sufficient knowledge and resources to solve a problem, and different agents might have expertise for solving different subproblems of the given problem. Generally, agents cooperatively solve a problem 1) by using their local knowledge and resources needed for solving individually subproblems, and 2) by integrating these subproblem solutions into an overall solution.

- *autonomous approach:* The fully cooperative-to-antagonistic spectrum has been researched by Genesereth et al. (1986). They note that the situation of total cooperation, known as the *benevolent agent* assumption, is accepted by most DAI researchers but is not always true in the real world where agents may have conflicting goals. To study this type of interaction, Genesereth defines agents as entities operating under the constraints of various rationality axioms that restrict their choices in interactions. Each agent considers its own interest instead of the group one.

Dynamics

Given a distributed problem solving system, how does one define a control organization for it? In other words, how does one achieve coherent behavior and coordination between participant agents? This section deals with these two characteristics. In fact, a consistent and coordinated behavior creates dynamically a hierarchy. The goal develops a slave-master relationship.

In DAI, how agents should coordinate their distributed resources, which might be physical (such as communication capabilities) or informational (such as information about the problem decomposition), have a direct influence on the coordination. Clearly, agents must find an appropriate technique for working together harmoniously.

Generally, researchers in DAI use the *negotiation* process to coordinate a group of agents. Unfortunately, negotiation, like other human concepts, is difficult to define. Sycara (1989) for example, states that "the negotiation process involves identifying potential interactions either through communication or through reasoning about the current states and intentions of other agents in the system and modifying the intentions of these agents to avoid harmful interactions or create cooperative situations" (p. 120). Durfee (1989) defines the negotiation as "the process of improving agreement (reducing inconsistency and uncertainty) on common viewpoints or plans through the structured exchange of relevant information" (p. 64). Although these two descriptions of negotiation capture many of our intuitions about human negotiation, they are too vague to provide techniques for how to get agents to negotiate.

Smith's work on the Contract-Net (Smith, 1980) introduced a form of simple negotiation among cooperating agents by a protocol of task sharing. Precisely, an agent, who needs help, decomposes a large problem into subproblems, announces the subproblems to the group of agents, collects bids from agents, and awards the subproblem to the most suitable bidders. In fact, this protocol gives us the best negotiation process for dynamically decomposing problems because it is designed to support task allocation. It is also a way of providing dynamically opportunistic control for the coherence and the coordination.

Examples of DAI approaches in Air Traffic Control

The precedent characteristics highlight several difficulties: 1) the decomposition of the problem to be solved into sub-problems, and 2) the coordination of the different sub-problems assigned to agents especially in the cases of interconnected sub-problems. Let us see the problem of conflict avoidance in air traffic according to the multi-agent organization evoked previously: that is, each aircraft involved in the conflict is an agent and there is no ground air traffic control center which could constitute the higher level of the hierarchy.

When faced with such a problem it is necessary to define the problem solving strategy and the cooperative structure to be implemented for that purpose.

The problem solving strategy consists in that the agents adopt the problem as a goal and elaborate a plan to achieve it. Thus, the planning, that is, the choice of actions, is the main activity of the agents. Of course, each agent must have necessary knowledge which allows it to reason with other agents for sharing knowledge or sharing tasks. AI researchers consider the intelligent behavior like a choice of actions in terms of contribution to the satisfaction of the agent's goal.

This choice may be considered as deliberation among competing *desires* of planes. Notice also that the knowledge of each plane is not necessarily objective, and in this case, we call it *beliefs*. In fact, an agent structure includes a belief base, a desire base, and a reasoning mechanism. The role of the reasoning mechanism consists first in choosing *pertinent* goals and in producing *persistent* goals. These persistent goals express the way in which each agent is committed to its goal. Furthermore, the reasoning mechanism must also produce *intentions* to force the agent to act. Beliefs, commitments, and intentions, which constitutes the satisfaction of selected desire are so combined into a plan. These concepts are introduced by a formal theory which has been developed by Chaib Draa (1990).

For defining the cooperative structure to be implemented, Cammarata et al. (1983) have proposed four different structures. Three of the four structures embedded a task centralized policy for one agent: They differ in how to choose the agent that is the most appropriate for detecting the conflict, fixing a new flight plan, sending the new plan to the nearby aircrafts, and finally carrying out the new plan. The fourth structure is a task sharing policy. While in the centralized policy, a single negotiation determines the agent that is the most appropriate to avoid the conflict; in the task sharing policy, two rounds of negotiation are necessary: the first round determines the planner agent and the second one determines the plan executors. Therefore this task sharing policy is an extension of the centralized policy. Let us see it in further detail.

The negotiation is based on the exchange of two factors between the aircrafts involved in a potential conflict; one is the *knowledgeable factor* and the other one is the *constraint factor*:

- The *knowledgeable factor* is specific to each aircraft, and concerns the aircraft's beliefs about intentions of nearby aircrafts, and allows the planner-agent to be determined, since an aircraft having the best knowledgeable factor is able to elaborate a new plan to avoid the conflict, taking into account the intentions of nearby aircrafts. In fact, the most knowledgeable aircraft is the best one for fixing a new plan and evaluating its implications.

- The *constraint factor*, specific to each aircraft, is an aggregation of considerations such as the number of other nearby aircrafts, the fuel level and distance remaining, the emergency in the aircraft, that is, mechanical default. It allows an aircraft concerned by the conflict to determine the plan executor, since the lowest constrained aircraft has probably the most degrees of freedom for modifying its plan without any risk.

The sequence of tasks under this policy is depicted here. Let us consider the case where only two aircrafts, A1 and A2, are concerned by the conflict. We suppose that A1 is the most knowledgeable one and A2 is the least constrained one. In this case, when A1 (or A2) suspects a conflict, it sends its knowledgeable factor to A2 (or to A1) according to the "Inform Plan."

After the knowledgeable factor exchange, both aircrafts exchange their constraint factor in a similar fashion. At this time, they know who is the most knowledgeable and who is the least constrained. The aircraft A1 (the most knowledgeable) must follow a "Solving Plan." According to this plane, A1 fixes a new plan for A2, before sending it to A2. Parallely, A2 which is the least constrained, sends its actual flight plan to A1, and continues its routine activities while awaiting the new plan from A1. When it receives the new plan, it sends it to the nearby aircraft concerned by the same conflict and finally executes it to resolve the conflict.

Therefore implementing such a flexible task sharing policy raises several difficulties for modeling the organization in a formal way :
- to describe the agent actions and their effects in its environment,
- to represent beliefs,
- to take into account the agent intentions,
- to represent plans,
- to formulate communicative acts between the agents.

Solving these difficulties constitutes presently an important source of research in the AI field which also meet general difficulties for modeling high level processes of reasoning. Nevertheless it can bring about formal way for modeling cooperative structures involving not only artificial agents but also human decision-makers (see Benchekroun & Pavard, chapter 10, this volume).

For the present, a parallel way of thinking based on human engineering approaches can be followed for studying and implementing cooperative organizations. The next part deals with this approach.

HUMAN ENGINEERING APPROACHES

This approach first investigated relationships between one single human decision maker and one single AI support system, according to two possible structures called respectively "vertical" and "horizontal" cooperations (Millot, 1988). Let us see first these two structures separately and next, the multi-level cooperative organization which can be proposed. These concepts are deduced from studies in the realistic context of Air Traffic Control.

Man-machine cooperation principles

The vertical and horizontal cooperation principles are briefly recalled here.

In the *vertical cooperation,* the operator is responsible for all the process variables and if necessary he can call upon the decision support tool, which will supply him with advice (Figure 1). It is a simplified form of the hierarchized organization proposed in the first section of this chapter, in which the human operator is the decision-maker placed at the higher level of the hierarchy and the AI support system is an assistant. Therefore the human operator must be able to control the AI system by using its explanation and justification capabilities, that is, to solve what we called "decisional conflicts." For that purpose a justification graphical interface has been studied and integrated into the supervision system of a simulated power plant (Taborin & Millot, 1989).

Therefore, in this human engineering approach to vertical cooperation, we meet all the problems evoked in the DAI approach especially for the nature and modes of communications between both agents given that the structure and the degree of cooperation are already chosen. But the communication problem is particularly expressed in this heterogeneous mutli-agent organization, due to the presence of a human operator, which needs to take into account cognitive ergonomics concepts.

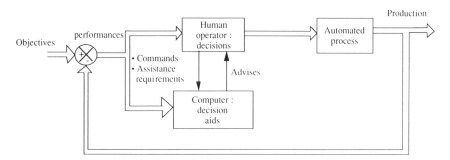

FIGURE 1. Man-machine vertical cooperation principle

In the *horizontal cooperation*, the AI decision tool outputs are directly connected to the process control system, Figure 2. Both agents, human, and AI tool are at the same hierarchical level, and the supervision tasks, as well as the actions resulting from them, can be dynamically distributed between them, according to performance and workload criteria. It is a form of horizontal organization proposed in the first section, but reduced to two agents, and which corresponds moreover to the task sharing policy proposed by Cammarata et al. (1983). But the main difference with Cammarata's organization concerns the control modes of the organization. Indeed in the DAI's approach each agent is a priori able to take in charge the coordination of the organization which needs high level cognitive capabilities, that is, planning capabilities, thus the whole tasks, that is high level planning tasks for coordination as well as tactical execution tasks, can be dynamically shared between the agents, according to the nature of the problem to be solved. While this idea appears very enticing, its implementation in real complex contexts raises many problems especially due to the present limitations of AI tools.

Therefore the organization we propose consists in reducing the dynamic allocation to the tactical level tasks, the coordination strategic tasks being fixed a priori. For that purpose a task allocation control is introduced at the higher level of the hierarchy (Figure 2). That needs the choice a priori of the actor responsible of the coordination, that is, the task allocation control, which can be:
.   a dedicated artificial decisional stage which needs capabilities for assessing human workload and performance; it is called an *implicit dynamic task allocation* (Millot & Kamoun, 1988),
.   the human operator himself who plays here a second role dealing with strategic and organizational tasks; it is called an *explicit dynamic task allocation* (Kamoun et al., 1989).

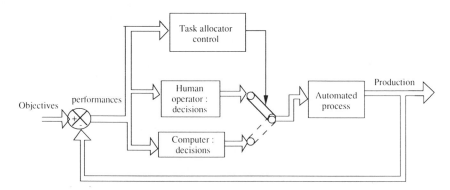

FIGURE 2. Man-machine horizontal cooperation principles

For extending these two principles we can foresee a *multi-level organization* in which the strategic level tasks could be performed by a second human operator and furthermore he could be supported by AI tools with prediction capabilities, for the tactical level tasks' allocation (Figure 3) (Vanderhaegen et al., 1992). This organization is then a combination of vertical and horizontal cooperations: a vertical cooperation at the strategic level and a horizontal one at the tactical level.

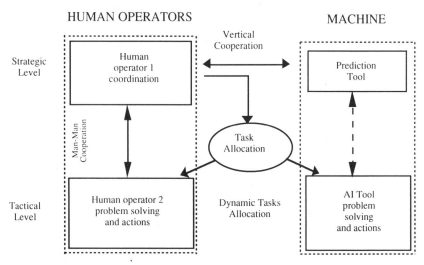

FIGURE 3. Multi-level Man-machine cooperation

The principles for explicit and implicit dynamic allocations have been implemented and evaluated in the air traffic control domain according to the real constraints and the already existing organization in this domain. The experiments and first results are briefly described below.

Horizontal cooperation study in air traffic control

The air traffic control objectives are globally the same as indicated in the first sections of this chapter. The major difference with the Cammarata's theoretical approach being the hierarchized overall organization in which the ATC Centers (the human controllers) are at the higher level of the hierarchy and the aircrafts (their pilots) must follow their orders. Then the flexible task sharing structure we deal with here concerns exclusively the organization of the ATC Center, but under the constraints imposed by the traffic, that is, the aircrafts. The ATC Center activities and organization are now described, followed by the dynamic allocation experiments at the tactical level of the ATC.

Air Traffic control center activities and organization

The air space is divided into geographical sectors that are managed by two controllers. The first one is a tactical controller, called "radar controller." Through a radar screen, he supervises the traffic and dialogues with the aircraft pilots. The supervision consists in detecting possible conflicts between planes that may transgress separation norms, and then in solving them. The dialogue with pilots consists in informing them about traffic and asking them to modify their flight level, cape, or speed in order to avoid a conflict.

The second one is a strategic controller, called "organic controller." First, he makes coordination between sectors in order to avoid unsolvable conflicts at the sectors' borders. Secondly, he anticipates the traffic density and regulates the radar controller workload. Third, he helps the radar controller in loaded traffic contexts, by taking charge of some tactical tasks.

In fact, these tasks are assumed according to the traffic density:
- For low traffic case, one controller manages the strategic and tactical tasks.
- For normal traffic case, there are two controllers: an organic one and a radar one.
- For loaded traffic case, the organic controller takes charge of some tactical tasks.
- For overloaded traffic case, there is an organic controller and two radar controllers.
- For saturated traffic case, the controlled sector is divided if it is possible.

At present, it seems difficult to reduce the main control tasks. For instance, the geographical sectors' size can't be reduced anymore, because both the input and output coordinations between sectors would increase and the conflict solving would be more difficult. So, we have implemented in a first step a dynamic task allocation at the tactical level.

The principle consists in inserting in the control and supervisory loop, a task allocation which shares control tasks between the radar controller and an expert system, called SAINTEX. This aims at regulating the human workload and at improving the performance and the reliability of the tactical controller-SAINTEX team.

Dynamic task allocation implementations at the tactical level

Both the implementation and tests of such a new organization of flexible task allocation cannot be made directly in a real control room without a sufficient validation in a simulated context. For these reasons, we have built a simplified but realistic experimental platform for air traffic control called SPECTRA (French acronym for Experimental System for the Air Traffic Control Tasks Allocation).

According to this principle, the two types of dynamic allocation managements have been integrated in SPECTRA structure (Figure 4). In the "explicit" task allocation the radar controller manages himself the task allocator through a dialogue interface. He is his own estimator of performance and workload, and he allocates tasks either to himself or to SAINTEX. The "implicit" task allocation is controlled by an automatic management system implemented on the calculator. This allocation depends on the capabilities of the two decision-makers. For SAINTEX, those abilities are functional ones: Only conflicts between two planes can be treated (solvable conflicts). For the human radar controller, these abilities are linked with his workload. At present, only the tasks demands are assessed. So, when these demands are too high and exceed a maximum level, the solvable conflicts are allocated to SAINTEX.

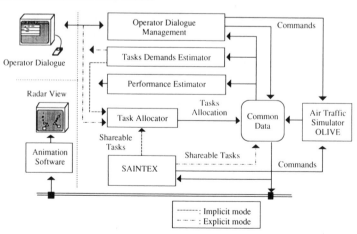

FIGURE 4. Explicit and implicit modes integrated into SPECTRA

Moreover, the performance estimator for the human controller-SAINTEX team is based on economic (comparison between the real and theoretical consumption) and security (the number of airmiss) criteria. This global performance criterion is not used in the control policy of the task allocator, but it is used to compare the results of the experiments.

The tasks demand estimator is a summation of the tasks demands to which the air traffic controllers are submitted. These functional demands are calculated in affecting a demand weight for each event that is appearing during the control tasks. Events are classified in two classes: one for the aircraft states and the second for the conflict states.

Experimental context and results (Debernard , Vanderhaegen, & Millot ,1992)

Nine qualified air traffic controllers and six novice controllers, who are Air Traffic engineers with great theoretical expertise but with a low level of practice, took part in a series of experiments. Each controller performed four experiments a training one, without assistance, in explicit mode, and in implicit mode using different scenarios in order to prevent learning effects. The scenarios involved a great number of planes and generated a lot of conflicts.

Three classes of parameters have been measured and recorded during each experiment:
- The first class concerns all the data needed to calculate the global performance.
- The second class consists of all the data needed to calculate the task demands.
- The last one concerns the subjective workload. One module was added to SPECTRA for that purpose. It concerns the workload estimation by the operator. The air traffic controller has to try to estimate his own workload, clicking with a mouse, on a small scale, graduated from 1 (lower load) to 10 (higher load). This board appears regularly every 5 minutes. It does not disturb the air traffic control because the operator answers when he wants to do. Those subjective workload estimations are used for validating the tasks demands calculation and improving the workload estimator.

In the final step of each experiment, two types of questionnaires have been submitted to the controller. The first class of questionnaires is the Task Load indeX (TLX) method (NASA, 1988) that permits calculation of a subjective global workload. The second class of questionnaires is a series of questions about general information, workload, comparisons between explicit and implicit modes that allowed us an oriented discussion with the controller.

Results have been analyzed for all the controllers who performed each simulated scenario seriously as in real control context. Conclusions are convincing:
- Our tasks demands calculation is validated.
- The dynamic allocation modes are real helps for loaded air traffic control.
- Globally, the implicit mode is more efficient than the explicit one.
- SPECTRA interface does not modify usual controllers strategies.

Synthesis

A lot of results can be deduced from these experiments and the analysis of the data is not yet over, especially concerning workload and performance assessment, but also concerning decisional strategies and operative modes used by the human controllers and the degree of cooperation they performed with SAINTEX in the explicit mode. Nevertheless it is possible to draw some conclusions about the explicit mode.

First, we have to notice that the human controller played a double role: a tactical role (solving conflicts for example) and a strategic role (anticipating possible conflicts and planning tasks in order to regulate his workload, for example). Therefore, he played the organic controller's role as well as the radar controller's role. That's why we plan to include another cooperation level on SPECTRA at the strategic level in order to implement and test the multi-level cooperative organization proposed in Figure 3. For that purpose a planning support system is studied.

Secondly, when studying the controllers' decisional strategies and operative modes, we first remarked differences in the degrees of cooperation performed with SAINTEX by the qualified controllers on the one hand and by the novice controllers on the other hand. In fact some qualified controllers did not really cooperate with SAINTEX and allocated very few air conflicts to it. Their answers to the questionnaires showed a very limited trust in SAINTEX. Further investigations will be pursued in order to know why and particularly if this behavior is due to a lack of knowledge about the capacities and structure of SAINTEX.

At the opposite end, novice controllers generally showed a high degree of cooperation with SAINTEX, and the performance of the teams they constituted with SAINTEX were similar to the teams involving qualified controllers.

These first qualitative statements must be confirmed by further analyses but it seems to confirm other results by Neville Moray et al. (chapter 11, this volume) on the importance of trust and self-confidence in human computer relationships.

Finally the choice of an organizational structure for Man-Machines cooperation is strongly dependent on the nature and the characteristics of the tasks to be shared between the different agents (either human or artificial) and needs a deep analysis of these tasks. This would result in a taxonomy of the tasks or subtasks according to different levels such as strategic and tactical. In our opinion, methodological and conceptual research is also needed in this way.

CONCLUSION

This chapter has proposed several approaches for designing cooperative organizations. Conceptual frameworks coming from the Distributed Artificial Intelligence community can be very helpful given the advanced reflection which has been made for identifying and analyzing the possible structures for these organizations and the constraints they raise: communication needs, degrees of cooperation needs. The organizations developed in parallel by the human engineering and ergonomics community who seems to deal more deeply with realistic on site application domains have also been described. Comparing these two kinds of approaches shows the important similarities of both approaches but also underlines some differences especially linked with implementation constraints. Nevertheless, it seems that some new ways of research could be born from these complementary points of view.

REFERENCES

Bellorini, A., Cacciabue, P.C., & Decortis, F. (1991, August). *Validation and development of a cognitive model by field experiments: Results and lesson learned*. Paper presented at the *Third European Conference Cognitive Approaches to Process Control.* Cardiff, UK.

Cammarata, S., McArthur, D., & Steeb, R. (1983, August). *Strategies of cooperation in distributed problem solving*. Paper presented at the *Eighth International Joint Conference on Artificial Intelligence,* Karlsruhe, Germany.

Chaib-Draa, B. (1990). *Contribution à la Résolution Distribuée de Problème: Une approche basée sur les états intentionnels* [Contribution to distributed problem-solving: an approach based on intentional states], Unpublished doctoral dissertation, Université de Valenciennes, France.

Cohen, P. R., & Levesque, H. J. (1990). Intention is choice with commitment. *Artificial Intelligence, 42,* 213-261.

Corkill, D.D., & Lesser, V.R. (1983, August). *The use of meta-level control for coordination in a distributed problem solving network*. Paper presented at the *Eighth International Joint Conference on Artificial Intelligence,* Karlsruhe, Germany.

Debernard, S., Vanderhaegen, F., & Millot, P. (1992, June). *An experimental dynamic tasks allocation between air traffic controller and A.I. system*. Paper presented at the *5th IFAC/IFIP/IFORS/IEA. Symposium on Analysis, Design and Evaluation of Man-Machine Systems.* MMS'92, The Hague, The Netherlands.

Durfee, E. H., Lesser, V. R., & Corkill, D. D. (1989). Trends in cooperative distributed problem solving. *IEEE Transaction on Knowledge and Data engineering, 1,* 63-83.

Genesereth, M. R., Ginsberg, M. L., & Rosenschein, J. S. (1986, October). *Cooperation without communication*. Paper presented at the *Fifth National Conference on Artificial Intelligence,* Philadelphia, PA.

Kamoun, A., Debernard, S., & Millot, P. (1989, October). *Comparison between two dynamic task allocations.* Paper presented at the *Second European meeting on Cognitive Science Approaches to Process Control,* Siena, Italy.

Kornfeld, W. A., & Hewitt, C. (1981). The Scientific community metaphor. *IEEE Transactions on Systems, Man and Cybernetics, 11,* 24-33.

Millot, P. (1988). *Supervision des procédés automatisés* [Supervisory control of automated processes]. Paris, Hermès.

Millot, P., & Kamoun, A. (1988, June). *An implicit method for dynamic allocation between man and computer in supervision posts of automated processes.* Paper presented at the *Third IFAC Congress on Analysis Design and Evaluation of Man Machine Systems,* Oulu, Finland.

NASA. (1988) version 1.0. *Booklet containing the theoretical background of the Task Load indeX NASA Ames research center.* T.L.X. Human Performance Group.

Nii, H. P. (1986). Blackboard systems: The blackboard model of problem solving and the evolution of blackboard architectures (part I). *AI Magazine, 7,* 38-53.

Rosenschein, J. S., & Genesereth, M. R. (1985, October). *Deals among rational agents.* Paper presented at the *Ninth International Joint Conference on Artificial Intelligence,* Washington, DC.

Schmidt, K. (1989, October). Modelling cooperative work in complex environments. Paper presented at the *Second European Meeting on Cognitive Sciences Approaches to Process Control,* Siena, Italy.

Smith, R. G. (1980). The contract-net protocol: High-level communication and control in a distributed problem solver. *IEEE Transactions on Computers, 29,* 1104-1113.

Sycara, K. R., (1989). Multiagent compromise via negotiation. In L. Gasser & M. N. Huhns (Eds), *Distributed Artificial Intelligence 2* (pp. 119-137). Los Altos, CA: Morgan Kaufmann Publishers.

Taborin, V., & Millot, P. (1989, June). *Cooperation between man and decision aid system in supervisory loop of continuous processes.* Paper presented at the *Eighth European Annual Conference on Decision making and Manual Control,* Copenhagen, Denmark.

Vanderhaegen, F., Crevits, I., Debernard, S., & Millot, P. (1992, August). *Multi-level cooperative organization in air traffic control.* Paper presented at the *Third International Conference on Human Aspects of Advanced Manufacturing and Hybrid Automation,* Gelsenkirchen, Germany.

14

The Art of Efficient Man-Machine Interaction: Improving the coupling between man and machine

Erik HOLLNAGEL
Human Reliability Associates

Efficient and safe man-machine interaction requires an efficient coupling between man and machine, in the sense that the machine performs and responds as the operator expects it to. Rather than force the user to adapt to the system, the system should be adapted to the user. This can be achieved either through design, during performance, or by management. Each of these cases are considered and evaluated against a common set of criteria.

THE NEED FOR ADAPTATION

There are many ways in which the current state of man-machine interaction can be characterized. On one side it is quite common to focus on how things can - and often do - go wrong, and lament on how miserable the situation of the human operator has become (e.g., Perrow, 1984). Although examples of accidents are many, this view may easily lead to a picture that is too gloomy. On the other side there are also people who see the state of man-machine interaction as being quite satisfactory, due not least to the technological developments. The only drawback is the continued presence of the operator as an unpredictable and uncontrollable source of disturbances, but the belief is that this will be only a temporary predicament. Yet even the most sanguine assessment cannot deny that there are a number of cases where things do go wrong and therefore, presumably, an even larger number of cases where they almost go wrong.

Human factors engineering and ergonomics arose as scientific disciplines because human adaptation alone was incapable of obtaining a satisfactory fit between unaided operators and machines. The notion of trying to improve the coupling between the work and the people involved is at least a century old (e.g., the Scientific Management movement, cf. Taylor, 1911) but human factors engineering did not start until the Forties. Since then the growth of the technology has accelerated and increased the gap between what people can do and what systems require. The general solution to reduce this gap is to enhance the functionality of the man-machine interaction by providing the operator with some kind of computerized support. But this solution may create more problems than it solves, unless an efficient coupling is obtained between the operator and the support. There is consequently ample reason to consider the ways in which this coupling between man and machine can be improved - not only as a theoretical exercise but also in terms of practical measures.

To be a little more precise, I will define efficient coupling to exist if the machine performs and responds as the operator expects it to - in terms of how it reacts to specific input (feedback to control actions) as well as in terms of the output it produces. This definition does not imply that the responsibility for the coupling rests completely with the machine. The operator's expectations are obviously shaped by the training, the design of the interface, and the dynamics of the interaction; the coupling may therefore also be achieved by operator conformance. Coupling should furthermore be considered for a representative range of tasks rather than for a small number of specific tasks.

THE USELESS AUTOMATON ANALOGY

In order to achieve a more efficient coupling between man and machine it is necessary to describe what the actual deficiencies are, such as they can be found in existing systems. This, in turn, requires that either part (man and machine) can be described in sufficient detail and with sufficient precision, and that the two descriptions either use the same semantics or can be translated into a common format or mode of representation.

Since the systematic study of MSS started from the need to solve practical, technological problems the basis for the description was the engineering view of men and machines. The technical and engineering fields had developed a powerful vocabulary to describe how machines worked and it was therefore natural to apply the same vocabulary to how people worked, that is, as a basis for modeling human performance (e.g., Stassen, 1986). I will refer to this as the *automaton analogy*.

The automaton analogy denotes how one can think of or describe a human being as an automaton or a machine. A particular case is the use of the information processing metaphor (Newell & Simon, 1972) - or even worse, assuming that a human being *is* an information processing system (as exemplified by Simon, 1972; Newell, 1990). But the automaton analogy has been used in practically all cases where explanations of human performance were sought, for example, by behaviorism or psychoanalytic theory (cf., e.g., Weizenbaum, 1976).

In the field of MMS studies the automaton analogy is, however, useless and even misleading. I will not argue that the automaton analogy is ineffectual as a basis for describing human performance *per se*; I simply take that for granted. (This point of view is certainly not always generally accepted and often not even explicitly stated, for instance, by the mainstream of American Cognitive Science; it is nevertheless a view which is fairly easy to support.) Instead I will go even further and argue that the automaton analogy is useless even for machines when the context is man-machine systems, that is, when the functioning of the machine must be seen together with the functioning of a human being.

In general, an automaton can be described by a set of inputs, outputs, internal states, and the corresponding state transitions; a classical example of this is the Turing machine. More formally, a finite automaton is a quintuple (e.g., Arbib, 1964; Lerner, 1975):

$$A = (I, O, S, ,)$$

where   I is the set of inputs,
O is the set of outputs
S is the set of internal states
: S x I → S is the next state function, and
: S x I → O is the next output function.

Assume, for instance, that the automaton is in a certain state S_j. From that state it can progress to a pre-defined set of other states $(S_k, ..., S_m)$ or produce a pre-defined output (O_j) only if it gets the correct input (I_j). If the system in question is a joint man-machine system then the input to the automaton must in most cases be provided by the user. Therefore, the user must reply or respond in a way that corresponds to the categories of input that the automaton can interpret. Any other response by the user will lead to one of two cases:

° The input may not be understood by the machine, that is., transition functions are not defined for the input. In this case the machine may either do nothing or move to a default state.

° The input may be misunderstood by the machine, for instance if the semantics or the syntax of the response have not been rigorously defined. In this case the machine may possibly malfunction, that is, be forced to a state which has not been anticipated. This happens in particular if the input was a physical control action or manipulation, for example, like switching something on or off, opening a valve, and so on.

If the machine therefore is to function properly the user must provide a response that falls within a pre-defined set of possible responses (the set of inputs). But the determination of the user's response is at least partly determined by the information that is available to him. The output from the machine constitutes an essential part of the input to the user and the output is partly determined by the previous input that is, what the user decided to do. The content and structure of the machine's output must therefore be such that it can be correctly understood by the user, that is, correctly interpreted or mapped onto one of the predefined answer options. In order to do that it is, however, necessary that the designer considers the user as a finite state automaton. We know from practice that people may interpret information in an infinite number of ways. We also realize that there is no way in which we can possibly account for this infinity of interpretations. Therefore we assume that the user only interprets the information in a limited number of specified ways - and as designers we of course take every precaution to prevent misinterpretations from happening. In other words, as designers we try to force the user to function as a finite automaton and we therefore think of the user in terms of a finite automaton. A good example of that is the graphical user interfaces, which basically serve to restrict the user's degrees of freedom.

This means that the starting point thinking of the machine as a finite automaton has forced us willy-nilly to think of the user as a finite automaton because there is no other conceptualization or model of the user that will fit the requirements of the design. Yet this is clearly unacceptable, no matter how sophisticated we assume the automaton to be (even if the number of states is exceedingly large and the state transitions are stochastic or multi-valued). It probably is the case that whatever analogy we use for one (machine, man) we will have to use for the other (man, machine) as well. Because we want to retain some distinct human elements in the description of the user we are forced by this argument to apply the same elements to the description of the machine. One proposal for an alternative description is the notion of a cognitive system as defined by Hollnagel and Woods (1983):

> A cognitive system produces intelligent action, that is, its behavior is goal oriented, based on symbol manipulation and uses knowledge of the world (heuristic knowledge) for guidance. Furthermore a cognitive system is adaptive and able to view a problem in more than one way. A cognitive system operates using knowledge about itself and the environment in the sense that it is able to plan and modify its actions on the basis of that knowledge. (Hollnagel and Woods, 1983, p. 589)

The idea of a cognitive system was based on extensive practical experience rather than on formal arguments. The empirical evidence gathered since then has corroborated this definition. In relation to the present discussion the important aspect is that of *adaptation*. Effective coupling between man and machine can be achieved if either adapt to the other. In order to achieve this it is therefore necessary that the language of description supports notions of adaptation and adaptivity. In the remaining part of this chapter I will consider the notion of adaptation and how it can be achieved in man-machine systems.

ADAPTATION

The problem of establishing efficient man-machine interaction can usefully be described in terms of control. The goal is to maintain system performance within a specified envelope, avoiding that critical functions go beyond (above or below) given limits. The purpose of system design is to make this control possible. The control is carried out by the system, by the operator, or by the two together. If the variety of the engineering (automatic) control system can be made large enough, it may handle the situation by itself. But if the requisite variety of the process exceeds that of the automatic control system, then the operator is needed. I shall assume that this is the case.

In order for the operator to work efficiently, that is, to serve as an efficient controller, he must have the necessary facilities to obtain information about the situation and to exercise judiciously control options. This requires that the designer is able to anticipate the possible situations and to invent means by which to deal with them. The tacit assumption of the design is that the operator can handle the situation if he has the means to provide the required control. Therefore, the designer must provide the operator with the proper facilities for getting the information needed *(retrieval)*, transforming it into a presentation form which is adequate for the problem at hand *(transformation)*, combining it on the presentation surface *(display)* so that it is well suited - or adapted - to the current needs, and effectuating the intended control actions *(control and feedback)*.

It is practically impossible to anticipate more than a limited set of situations, and it is therefore important that the operator is able to control how information is used. The actual interface must consequently be flexible enough to enable the operator to achieve his goals when unanticipated situations occur. The designer's job is to adapt the usage of the equipment to operator characteristics (human-factors design) and to the gross characteristics of the possible performance modes (event types). The design should provide the options for adaptation although it is, in fact, usually the operator who carries out the adaptation.

In order to achieve an efficient coupling between humans and machines (operators and systems) it is necessary that some kind of adaptation takes place. The experience to date indicates that the adaptation mostly has been made by the humans. It can be said, with some justification, that the reason why most systems function at all is that the human operator is able to adapt to the design. In other words, systems may sometimes work *despite* their design rather than *because* of it. Adaptation is an integral part of human life and something that comes natural to us. But the human ability to adapt may easily lead designers astray. The situation should preferably be changed to the opposite; the attitude should be that the machine must adapt to the human, rather than the other way around. In order to achieve this it is, however, necessary that one knows how to perform this adaptation. The rest of this chapter will discuss three different ways of doing this.

ADAPTATION THROUGH DESIGN

The basis for adaptation through design is the ability to predict the consequences of specific design decisions. If a designer wants to achieve a certain effect, he must be able to foresee what will happen if the system is used in specific ways under specific circumstances. Design is essentially decision making.

"...The choice of a design must be optimal among the available alternatives; the selection of a manifestation of the chosen design concept must be optimal among all permissible manifestations... Optimality must be established relative to a design criterion which represents the designer's compromise among possibly conflicting value judgments that include... his own." (Asimov, 1962, p. 5)

The fundamental art of design is to increase the constraints until only one solution or alternative is left. If the predominant design criteria relate only to technical or economic aspects of the system, then the outcome may easily be one that puts undue requirements on the operator's ability to adapt. (It is presumably Utopian to hope for a system that does not require some kind of adjustment - at least if it is made to be used by more than one individual.) It follows that the dominant design criteria should include some that address the man-machine interaction, thereby hopefully making it easier for the operator to adjust to the system.

In order to achieve this goal, in order to make correct predictions of what the design will accomplish, it is necessary to have sufficient knowledge about how the operator will respond. Such descriptions are commonly referred to as "user models" (although they properly speaking should be called "models of the user"). In some cases user models are used prescriptively as a basis for promoting a specific form of performance through the design: An example of that is the notion of ecological interface design (e.g., Rasmussen & Vicente, 1987). In other cases user models are applied more sparingly, as condensed descriptions of how one can expect a user to respond for a given set of circumstances (e.g., Smith et al., 1992)

In both cases the fundamental requirement is that an adequate model description of operator characteristics can be found and that sufficiently powerful design guidelines can be derived from this model. The latter might even be achieved by means of human factors guidelines alone - without an explicit model - provided the situation in itself can be sufficiently well predicted. Examples of that are very constrained working environments such as train driving, word processing, and the like. When models are used they are generally static, that is, verbal or graphical descriptions from which specific (expected) reactions to specific input conditions can be estimated or predicted. It may even be suggested that static adaptation is the noble goal of HCI as a scientific movement - although it is open to discussion whether that goal actually can be achieved.

The very complexity of system design has frequently made it evident that static models are inadequate. This seems to be the case at least for descriptive models; prescriptive or normative models usually simplify the situation so much that the limitations are less easy to see. The logical alternative is to use animated or dynamic models. Although this is significantly more difficult, it is nevertheless a worthwhile undertaking because it forces the designer to make everything explicit. A dynamic model of the user must describe in computational terms how a user will respond to a given development, whether that response is internal (as a "change of state") or external (as an action). This is tantamount to using dynamic models or simulations of the user. An example of this can be found in the System Response Generator project (Hollnagel et al., 1992). A more general discussion of uses of dynamic modeling or simulation is found in Cacciabue & Hollnagel (Chapter 4, this volume).

ADAPTATION DURING PERFORMANCE

Neither the best of models nor abundant resources available for system development may be enough to ensure sufficient adaptation through design. Firstly, because knowledge about the operator necessarily is incomplete, and secondly because it is impossible to predict all the conditions that may obtain Even in a completely deterministic world with complete information about the system and the user(s), the sheer number of possibilities may easily exhaust the resources that are available for design purposes. It is therefore customary to design the system with the most frequently occurring (or imagined) situations in mind, and leave the remaining problems to be solved in different ways, either to rely on human adaptation and ingenuity or to achieve some kind of adaptation during performance. The first of these solutions, while frequently applied, is clearly not desirable - and perhaps not even acceptable. To some extent this solution has been a necessary default because the other options have been limited. Until a few years ago adaptation during performance required technical solutions that were practically impossible to implement.

The notion of adaptive systems is well established in control theory. The nature of adaptive systems has been treated in detail in cybernetics, which also has contributed many concrete examples (e.g., Ashby, 1956). Adaptive control theory has, however, been concerned with improving the control of a process or a plant. The emphasis has therefore been on how the controller could adapt to changes or variations in the physical environment (input signals) rather than to changes in the operator.

If the purpose becomes one of facilitating the work of the operator or improving the coupling between man and machine, the adaptation must look towards the *interaction* rather than the process. The concept of an adaptive controller must therefore be extended to include the interaction between the operator and the process, and to cover an interaction policy in addition to a control policy. Extending the principle is a simple matter, but accomplishing it in practice is considerably harder. The main problems are that it is very difficult to identify a well-defined set of on-line performance measures for an operator; further, that it is equally difficult to specify a set of operational interaction policies which can be matched to the i⁻ ntified operator conditions; and finally, that it is (again) difficult to evaluate the effect of implementing a specific interaction policy.

The practical work on adaptive man-machine interaction was negligible until Artificial Intelligence started to apply inference techniques to plan recognition (e.g., Kautz & Allen, 1986). (It was quite characteristic that Artificial Intelligence (AI) saw this as an original invention and neglected to consider the substantial amount of work that had been done in adaptive control theory. Apparently the analogue and the digital worlds did not meet on this occasion.) Coupled with notable advances in the development and use of knowledge-based systems, it suddenly became possible to build convincing demonstrations of adaptive man-machine interfaces (e.g., Peddie and al., 1990; Hollnagel, 1992). Other applications are found in the field of Intelligent Tutoring Systems (ITS).

The option of achieving some kind of adaptation during performance is therefore a reality. Unfortunately, it does not make the designer's task any simpler. Unlike human adaptation, artificial adaptation must be designed in detail. Basically, the system must change its performance such that it matches the needs of the operator as far as they can be ascertained in a dynamic fashion - and AI techniques obviously set a limit for that. The use of AI technology, such as plan recognition and pattern identification, has partly overcome the need to define simple performance measurements. The limitations are nevertheless more or less the same, because the designer has to anticipate the possible situations. Unless plan recognition is supplemented by machine learning (and that is still a distant goal) the scope is obviously limited by the plans that are represented in the system. Similarly, the interaction policies must also be known in advance The designer therefore must consider not only, as before, the passive design of the interface but also the design of the active adaptive facilities. This increases the demands to, for example, modeling of the operator and maintaining an overview of the design. It may even, paradoxically, make the designer more dependent on his own support!

ADAPTATION THROUGH MANAGEMENT

The design of an efficient man-machine interaction, the development of effective operator support systems that not only work but also are used (!), does not occur in a vacuum. The context is the organization where the work takes place, hence also the way this organization is managed. Conversely, the way in which this management is carried out may in itself contribute to (or detract from) the efficiency of the man-machine interaction (Lucas, 1992; Wreathall & Reason, 1992).

Unlike the two previous ways of achieving adaptation, management cannot be designed in the same way. But management can serve to adapt the working environment to the specific task requirements (through interface designs, etc.). The efficient use of an interface or a support system depends not only on the systems in themselves but also on, for example, the procedures, the team structure, the communication links and command chains, and the atmosphere. The task is determined by a combination of the situation specific goals, the facilities for interaction and support (interfaces to the process), the local organization of work, and so on. Management can effectively counterbalance design oversights and compensate for structural or functional changes in the system that occur after the design has been completed. Management can also provide the short-term adaptations that may be needed until a part of the system can be redesigned. The design process in itself is usually rather lengthy and not easily started. Changes in the system, small and large, unfortunately do not wait patiently for a redesign to come about but appear randomly over time. The most effective way to compensate for them, and thereby maintain the efficient man-machine interaction, is through management.

Adaptation through management requires a continuous monitoring of effects, data collection, and analysis. It can be seen as adaptation by continuous redesign, hence working over and above what active adaptation may achieve. In other words, adaptation through design occurs at long intervals when the system is designed/redesigned. Adaptation during performance occurs continuously and rapidly but can only compensate for smaller deviations (and only for those that have been anticipated). Adaptation through management also occurs continuously, although with some delay. On the other hand, adaptation through management is able to cope with large deviations, even if they are completely unanticipated. Put differently, adaptation through management is the on-line use of human intelligence. The others are the use of off-line and "canned" intelligence, respectively.

DISCUSSION

One way to summarize the issues discussed above is to consider the three different ways of achieving adaptation against a common set of criteria. The criteria have all been mentioned in the preceding:

°   **Efficiency of adaptation.** This criterion refers to how efficient the adaptation is expected to be. It is closely related to how well it is possible to predict correctly the effects of the specific solution. Presumably, if an accurate prediction is possible, then the solution should be expected to be efficient - since it otherwise would not have been chosen. Conversely if the predictability is low one may expect that the solution is less efficient.

°   **Robustness.** This refers to how reliable and resistant the solution is, that is, how well it can withstand the deviations that may occur (working conditions, degraded information or noise, unexpected events, etc.).

°   **Delay in implementation.** The time from when a deviation or undesired condition is noted until something is done about it is the delay in implementation. Another view on that is how easy it is to implement the solution, not in terms of the resources and efforts that actually go into doing it but in terms of the difficulties that must be overcome before the implementation can be begun.

°   **Generality.** This concerns the general applicability of solutions, that is, whether solutions address a single issue or have a wider scope. Generality also refers to whether a solution is applicable to normal and contingency situations alike or only to one of these categories.

°   **Resources required.** The resources are those needed to implement the solution (to design and develop it) rather than the resources needed to use it.

°   **Applicability to safety critical tasks.** Safety critical tasks play a special role in man-machine systems. On the one hand they are the occasions where specific improvements of the man-machine interaction may be mostly needed; on the other hand they usually are subject to a number of restrictions from either management or regulatory bodies.

°   **Evaluation.** Evaluation is important in order to determine whether the coupling between man and machine works as expected and to gauge the efficiency of the adaptation. The evaluation can be considered with regard to how easy it is to accomplish (in terms of, e.g., money, manpower time) and in terms of whether suitable methods are available. A specific issue in evaluation is the need to separate the effects of the specific solutions from the effects of training in their use.

The result of applying these criteria to the three types of adaptation are shown in Table 1.

The classification provided earlier is only tentative. It does, however, serve to emphasize that there are no simple answers to how a more efficient man-machine interaction can be established, nor to which solutions are the best (or cheapest, or safest, etc.). As the discussion of adaptation through management pointed out, it is probably an over-simplification even to think of the three types of adaptation as distinct. It is more reasonable to assume that a proper solution will involve all three aspects. On way of indicating the coupling between the three types of adaptation is shown in Figure 1.

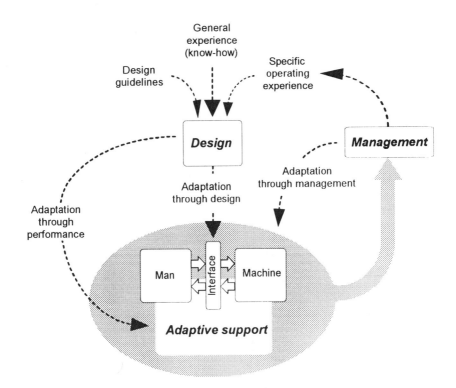

FIGURE 1. The coupling between the three types of adaptation

TABLE 1:
Evaluation of the three types of adaptation

	Adaptation through design	Adaptation during performance	Adaptation through management
Efficiency	High, but for a narrow, well-defined function. Solutions usually refer to well known aspects of performance.	Medium; highly dependent on the preceding analyses and requirement specifications.	Low, because predictability is low. On the other hand, there is wide scope for human adaptation to play a role and improve the result.
Robustness (reliability) of solution	Medium, but may range from low to high depending on the problem.	Medium; but very sensitive to the design basis.	Low, unless constant monitoring is implemented.
Delay in implemen-- tation	Long (months, years) - unless the consequences of waiting are very severe.	Very short (seconds, minutes).	Short (days, weeks).
Generality (applicabi- lity to normal & contin- gency situations)	Solutions are usually specific to one type of situation.	Solutions are generally focused at performance types.	Specific, but with a tendency to become general as time goes by (and if the solutions work).
Resource needs	Varies, but never really low. Interface design is becoming more and more costly.	Usually high, because the solutions are complex in many ways.	Usually low in direct costs (management by edict).
Applicabi- lity to safety critical tasks	Applicable, but requires approval or certification.	Doubtful, because the technology is considered unproved.	High, usually the default solution.
Evaluation	Possible, to the extent the solutions are specific.	Possible, to the extent the solutions are specific.	Difficult, both to find comparisons and to control conditions.

In scientific terms the coupling between man and machine is an issue where there are more questions than answers. We know something about basic human factors and basic ergonomics, but when we turn to a consideration of tasks where human cognition plays a major role, the lack of proven theories or methods is deplorable. Concerted efforts are increasing our knowledge bit by bit, but we are still far from having an adequate design basis. This is mainly because comprehensive theories for human action are few and far between. The situation is analogous to the state of human reliability analysis, as exposed by Dougherty (1990). There are many practitioners, and they all have their little flock of faithful followers. But when the methods are examined more closely they turn out to depend less on their own merits and more on the experience and know-how of those who use them. The same goes for design of efficient man-machine interaction when it goes beyond basic ergonomics. This does not imply that the current methods on the whole are ineffective. But it does mean that it may be difficult to generalize from them or to identify the common conceptual bases.

The coupling between man and machine is not simply a question of advancing human-computer interaction or of refining interface design. The essential coupling is to the process itself rather than to the support systems or the interface. It is a general experience that people who work with automated systems, such as flight management systems, often have great problems in understanding what the systems are doing (Wiener et at., 1991). In these cases the coupling to the underlying process is deficient and should therefore be improved. That can only be achieved if the interaction is considered in a larger context, rather than looked at in narrow terms of interface or support system design. Solutions that address specific problems tend, on the whole, to impair the coupling between man and machine rather than to improve it.

REFERENCES

Arbib, M. A. (1964). *Brains, machines and mathematics.* New York: McGraw-Hill.

Ashby, W. R. (1956). *An introduction to cybernetics.* London: Methuen & Co.

Asimov, M. (1962). *Introduction to design.* Englewood Cliffs, NJ: Prentice-Hall.

Dougherty, E. (1990). Human reliability analysis: Where shouldst thou turn? *Reliability Engineering and System Safety, 29,* 54-65.

Hollnagel, E. (1992). The design of fault tolerant systems: Prevention is better than cure. *Reliability Engineering and System Safety, 36,* 231-237.

Hollnagel, E., Cacciabue, P. C., & Rouhet, J.-C. (1992). *The use of an integrated system simulation for risk analysis and reliability assessment.* Paper presented at the *Seventh International Symposium on Loss Prevention,* Taormina, Italy.

Hollnagel, E., & Woods, D. D. (1983). Cognitive systems engineering: New wine in new bottles. *International Journal of Man-Machine Studies, 18,* 583-600.

Kautz, H. & Allen, J. (1986, Oct.). *Generalized plan recognition.* Paper presented at *AAAl-86,* Philadelphia, PA.

Lerner, A. Y. (1975). *Fundamentals of cybernetics.* London: Plenum.

Lucas, D. (1992). Understanding the human factor in disasters. *Interdisciplinary Science Reviews, 17,* 1185-1190.

Newell, A. (1990). *Unified theory of cognition.* Cambridge, MA: Harvard University Press.

Newell, A., & Simon, H. A. (1972). *Human problem solving.* Englewood Cliffs, NJ: Prentice-Hall.

Peddie, H., Filz, A. Y., Arnott, J. L., & Newell, A. F. (1990, September). *Extra-ordinary computer human operation (ECHO).* Paper presented at the *Second Joint GAF/RAF/USAF Workshop on Electronic Crew Teamwork,* Ingolstadt, Germany.

Perrow, C. (1984). *Normal accidents: Living with high-risk technologies.* New York: Basic Books.

Rasmussen, J., & Vicente, K. J. (1987). *Cognitive control of human activities and errors: Implications for ecological interface design* (Tech. Rep. No. Risø-M-2660). Roskilde, Denmark: Risø National Laboratory.

Simon, H. A. (1972). *The sciences of the artificial.* Cambridge, MA: The MIT Press.

Smith, W., Hill, B., Long, J., & Whitefield, A. (1992, March). *The planning and control of multiple task work: A study of secretarial office administration.* Paper presented at the *Second interdisciplinary Workshop on Mental Models,* Cambridge, UK.

Stassen, H. G. (1986). Decision demands and task requirements in work environments: What can be learned from human operator modeling? In E. Hollnagel, G. Mancini, & D. D. Woods (Eds.), *Intelligent decision support in process environments* (pp. 90-112). Berlin: Springer Verlag.

Taylor, F. W. (1911). *The principles of scientific management.* New York: Harper.

Weizenbaum, J. (1976). *Computer power and human reason: From judgment to calculation.* San Francisco: W. H. Freeman

Wiener, E. L., Chidester, T. R., Kanki, B. G., Palmer, E. A., Curry, R. E., & Gregorich, S. E. (1991). *The impact of cockpit automation on crew coordination and communication: I. Overview, LOFT evaluations, error severity, and questionnaire data.* (Tech. Rep. No. NCC2-581-177587). Moffet Field, CA: NASA, Ames Research Center.

Wreathall, J., & Reason, J. (1992). *Human errors and disasters.* Paper presented at the *Fifth IEEE Conference on Human Factors and Power Plants,* Monterey, CA.

15

"Human–like" System Certification and Evaluation

Guy BOY
European Institute of Cognitive Sciences and Engineering

This chapter presents a novel view of certification and evaluation in the specific case of "human–like" systems (HLS). Such systems are knowledge intensive. Thus, knowledge acquisition is a key issue to understanding, implementing, and evaluating related knowledge bases. Evaluation is incremental and situational. Experiences on the MESSAGE and HORSES projects have lead to the Situation Recognition Analytical Reasoning model that is proposed for use in knowledge acquisition and evaluation. This approach leads to the concept of Integrated Human–Machine Intelligence where HLS certification is viewed as an incremental process of operational knowledge acquisition.

INTRODUCTION

In this paper, we will take the view that mankind distinguishes itself from other species because it invents and builds tools to perform very sophisticated tasks. These tools are becoming so complex that people do not understand how they work anymore even if they use them routinely; for example, many people drive cars without knowing how a carburetor works. People need to trust these tools, therefore it follows that certification of these tools is an essential issue.

When can we declare that a tool is usable and safe for use? Certifying that a tool will be satisfactory in any situation for a (very) large group of users where it is intended to be used is a very serious enterprise. Usually, the difficulty is to define *criteria* or *norms* that will be socially acceptable to a wide range of domain experts and other people who will be connected to the use of the tool. Responsibility for the definition of such norms is taken by recognized national and international authorities. For instance, it is not unusual to see "well–known" norm labels on some home appliances. These labels warranty that the appliance will work under well–specified conditions. Such norms evolve with time. Furthermore, it is often difficult to test the tool against preexisting norms when the tool is fairly innovative. In reality, the norms are usually redefined with respect to the tool. An interesting question is: Would it make sense to anticipate evaluation criteria (norms) early on during design? Some answers are already available in the human-computer interaction (HCI) literature (Nielsen, 1993). They relate to user criteria such as learnability, efficiency, memorability, errors, and satisfaction. In any case, it is very difficult and often impossible to know if a tool is usable until we actually use it and access it.

Modern tools become more *knowledge* intensive in the sense that they include combined expertise of a few selected people. The more a tool improves by incremental additions of knowledge from an increasing number of users (usually domain experts), the more it is perceived as "intelligent." Completeness and consistency assessment are two major problems. However, the perceived complexity of the resulting envelope is the key factor to be grasped. The major difficulty comes from the fact that the perceived complexity is a function of the background of the user who performs the related task. Thus, the certification of resulting systems is extremely user specific. Certification is then necessarily incremental. Humans are evaluated through exams during their student and training periods, and throughout their lives humans continually evaluate themselves and are evaluated by others. Taking the viewpoint of Ford and Agnew (1992), expertise (i.e., knowledge) is socially situated, personally constructed, and "reality" relevant. This makes the process of validation of tools including expertise extremely difficult. Even if we take the computational view of model validation developed by Pylyshyn (1989), it is difficult to justify methods such as intermediate state evidence, complexity–equivalence, or cognitive penetrability when they are not situated (this makes them incremental). Indeed, users (even domain experts) usually have constructs different from those of the expert–designers.

The tools that we are studying here are complex (in structure and function) and difficult to understand for a non specialist. For instance, complex tools include modern airplanes, nuclear power plants, computers, electronic documentation, and so on. The evolution of such systems leads to the concept of *human–like systems*. It seems that tools evolve from physical to intellectual interactions. They tend to increase the distance between humans and the physical world. "Human–like" systems are electronic extensions of the capabilities of the user. They mediate between the mechanical parts of a system and share some of the intelligent functions with the user. Automated copilots, on–line "intelligent" user manuals, and "intelligent" notebooks are examples of such tools.

Turing's classic paper (Turing, 1950) raised an issue that lies at the heart of cognitive science: Can a machine[1] display the same kind of intelligence as does a human being? User–friendly systems such as current microcomputers allow humans to extend their cognitive capabilities. Such tools do not qualify as being intelligent in the human sense, but they permit "intelligent" interaction with users. In artificial intelligence (AI), intelligent behavior is defined in the following manner: faced with a *goal*, a set of *action principles* must be used to pass from an *initial situation* to a *final situation* which satisfies that *goal*. In accordance with this model, one of the goals of AI is to build "intelligent"

---

[1]We will consider machines as a subset of tools.

machines which interact with the environment (Boy, 1991a). A crucial question is: How is the AI of these tools perceived and understood by humans? In this perspective, the concept of an *agent* is essential. Agents can be both humans and machines. Modern work activities address a variety of issues concerning the distribution of tasks and responsibilities between human and machine agents. An initial model of interaction between human and machine agents was developed for the certification of modern commercial aircraft in the MESSAGE methodology (Boy & Tessier, 1985). Tools that were analyzed do not qualify as "intelligent" in the current AI sense. However, they include most of the latest advanced automation features, such as flight management tools for navigation control. Such features take over some very important cognitive tasks that were handled by humans in the past. These tasks have been replaced by new ones that are more information intensive, leading to new kinds of expertise.

Expertise is very difficult to elicit from experts (Feigenbaum & Barr, 1982; Leplat, 1985). What happens in the knowledge acquisition community is not so much the elicitation of an expert's preexisting knowledge, but rather the support of the expert's processes in overtly modeling the basis for his or her own skilled performance. Such a line of argument is reported by Gaines (1992), and strongly supported by Clancey (1990). In fact, "the shift from behaviorism to cognitive science has brought many changes in our methodologies, experimental techniques, and models of human activities" (Gaines, 1992, personal communication). Technology has followed the same track. Tools are less force intensive (sensory–motoric) and more information based. Furthermore, we will take the view that cognitive processes are not in agents but in the interaction between agents (Hegel, 1929). Providing an explanation for the fact that intelligence emerges from non intelligent components, Minsky (1985) defends the interactionist view of intelligence. The *interactionist* approach is very recent. It is based on the principle that knowledge is acquired and structured incrementally through interactions with other actors or *autonomous agents*. This approach is sociological (*versus* psychological). Interaction and auto organization are the key factors for the construction of general concepts. There are three main currents: automata networks (McCulloch & Pitts, 1943; Rosenblatt, 1958; von Neumann, 1966) and connectionism (McClelland et al., 1986; Rumelhart et al., 1986); and distributed AI (Hewitt, 1977; Lesser & Corkill, 1983; Minsky, 1985).

The problem of evaluating "human–like" systems also faces the general problem of measurement in psychology and cognitive science. Since we have adopted the view that intelligence is in the interactions, can we find measures that identify the quality of such interactions? Cognitive behaviors (like physical things) are perceived through their properties and attributes. Human factors measurements are usually grounded on *analogy* and *inference*. (1) Certification of a new tool may be accomplished by measuring *analogies* with an existing similar working tool already certified and explaining the differences. This approach is commonly used in aircraft cockpit certification. It does not allow drastic changes between the reference tool and the new tool. (2) Such abstract properties or attributes as intelligence are never directly measured but must be *inferred* from observable behavior; for instance, measuring temperature by feeling someone's forehead, or by reading a thermometer to infer fever. An important question is: Who defines or ratifies such measures? Who can qualify for being a certification authority?

Interaction between a human being and "human–like" systems assumes the definition of a structure and a function that allow this interaction. The structure allowing interaction is usually called the *user interface*, cockpit, control panel, and so on. The function takes the form of *procedures*, checklists, and so forth. There is always a tradeoff between structure and function. User–friendly interfaces better extend human cognitive capabilities, and thus augment intelligence of the interactions (Engelbart, 1963). For instance, hypertext systems are considered cognitive extensions of the associative memory of the user. Although, procedures are always used when safety is a key factor in routine control, the better the user interface is designed (e.g., insures the transparency of processes being controlled), the shorter and less strict the required procedures will be.

This paper proposes an approach to certification of "human–like" systems. It is based on the paradigm that agent models are essential in such assessment processes. The cockpit certification experience is taken as an example to show that highly interactive systems are necessary to incrementally store knowledge that will become useful at evaluation time. Furthermore, the concept of an agent is shown to be very useful in evaluation of cognitive human–machine interaction. The Situation Recognition/Analytical Reasoning (SRAR) model is useful for conceptualizing various types of agent behavior and interaction. In addition, the concept of Integrated Human–Machine Intelligence (IHMI) is useful for the validation of human–"human–like" system teams. The block representation has been developed to provide an appropriate language that supports contextual analysis of IHMI systems. In the balance of the chapter, we start a discussion of possible extensions of this view to certification problems in a variety of high–tech environments.

THE COCKPIT CERTIFICATION EXPERIENCE

A method has been developed to analyze and evaluate interactions between several agents including aircraft, flight crew, and air traffic control (Boy, 1983; Boy & Tessier, 1985), based on a system called MESSAGE (French acronym for "Model for Crew and Aircraft Sub–System Equipment Management"). MESSAGE is based on heuristics given by experts. In this sense, it is a knowledge–based system.

MESSAGE is a computerized analysis tool that provides the time–line of a mission, and the different evolution of indices representing different loads related to various agents. MESSAGE has been used to measure workload and performance indices, and to better understand information transfer and processing in crew–cockpit environments. Inputs are processing knowledge (in the form of rules) and data of missions to be analyzed. Outputs are crew performance and criticality (tolerance function), task demands (static functions), the perceptions of each agent versus time, and the simulated mission. The data of the mission to be analyzed includes continuous parameters recorded during a flight simulation and preprocessed, and discrete events from video and audio records. The simulated mission is a recognized (sometimes smaller) sequence of the previous input mission augmented by new messages generated by MESSAGE. The processing rules are acquired and modified incrementally, taking into account the relevance and accuracy of the simulated mission and the significance of the computed indices versus time. This knowledge acquisition and refinement process must be performed by domain experts.

MESSAGE is based on a five-level agent model (Boy, 1983): the human–vehicle interface for information acquisition, the coordination and management of emitting and receiving channels, the situation recognition, the strategic decision, and the plan execution processes. This model is an extension of the classical information processing model of Newell and Simon (1972). The MESSAGE agent model uses a *supervisor* which manages three types of processes called *channels*, that is, receiving, emitting, and cognitive. The function of the supervisor is analogous to that of the blackboard of Nii (1986). Each channel exchanges information with the supervisor. The concept of *automatic* and *controlled processes*, introduced and observed experimentally by Schneider and Shiffrin (1977a-b), was implemented at the level of the supervisor in the MESSAGE system (Tessier, 1984). This allows the generation and execution of tasks either in parallel (automatisms) or in sequence (controlled acts). The automatic processes or automatisms call upon a type of knowledge representation which we will describe as *situational representation*. The controlled processes may be defined by an *analytical representation*.

A "human–like" agent should be capable of anticipating the reactions of the environment as well as the consequences of its own actions. This anticipation will operate on the *messages* coming from either the environment (external inputs or observations) or the agent itself (internal inputs or inferred messages). A cockpit, for example, is a network of agents that relate to each other. The pilot interacts with a well–defined network of agents including his/her crew partners, air traffic control, and other airplanes. He/she knows complex relationships between these agents and constantly interprets from their behavior the overall behavior of the agent network. As a metaphor, the pilot is in a similar position to a manager dealing with his/her collaborators to carry out a job requiring a team effort. Usually, each crew member tries to get a vivid representation of the social field he/she is in. This notion of agent has been extended to various degrees of granularity that better describe the current situation. In this view, an agency (Minsky, 1986) is a vivid network of agents that can be human or machine channels (in the MESSAGE terminology). Through an analysis of audio and video recordings of the behavior of real airline flight crews performing in a high fidelity flight simulator, Hutchins and Klausen (1990) demonstrate that the expertise in this system resides not only in the knowledge and skills of the human actors, but in the organization of the tools in the work environment as well.

Because context changes all the time, one important issue brought up by the MESSAGE project is that the MESSAGE system is both a certification aid and a knowledge acquisition system. MESSAGE knowledge is case based and very context dependent. A new aircraft cannot be fully certified by using certification knowledge used for certification of other aircraft. New certification knowledge is being constructed during the certification process. MESSAGE brought up the first requirements for a knowledge representation (KR) that allows the capture of such contextual knowledge. In the next section, we develop the model that gives the foundations for such a KR.

THE SITUATION RECOGNITION ANALYTICAL REASONING MODEL

The term *situation* is used here to characterize the state of the environment with respect to an agent. In general, it refers to the state of the given world. A situation is described by a set of components which we will call *world facts*. For a generic world fact, at a given instant, it is possible to distinguish three types of situations (Boy, 1983). The *real situation* characterizes the true state of the world. It is often only partly available to the agent. The real situation is an attribute of the environment. It can be seen as the point of view of an external "objective" observer. The *situation perceived* by the agent characterizes an image of the world. It is the part of the world accessible to the agent. It is characterized by components which are incomplete, uncertain, and imprecise. A *situation pattern* is an element of the agent's long–term memory. It is composed of conditions, each of which applies to a finite set of world facts. It is the result of a long period of learning. Situation patterns can be seen as situated knowledge chunks. The situation *expected* by the agent at a given time, t, is the set of *situation patterns* included in the short–term memory of the agent. It is often called the focus of attention. At each time interval, the vigilance of the agent is characterized by the number and pertinence of the situation patterns present in short–term memory.

The *Situation recognition / analytical reasoning* (SRAR) model is an evolutionary model of the user (Figure 1). A chunk of knowledge is fired by the matching of a situation pattern with a perceived critical situation. This matching is either total or partial. After situation recognition, analytical reasoning is generally implemented. Let us describe SRAR in the fault identification domain. The Orbital Refueling System (ORS) is used in the space shuttle to refuel satellites and is controlled by the astronauts. A "human–like" system, called Human–ORS–Expert System (HORSES), was developed to perform interactive fault diagnosis (Boy, 1986). HORSES was tested in a series of experiments with users working in a simulated ORS environment. A malfunction generator runs concurrently and generates fault scenarios for the ORS at appropriate times in the simulations. The experiments produced data showing how users adapted to the task, and how their performance varied with different parameters. From these data, we developed the original SRAR model.

When a situation is recognized, it generally suggests how to solve an associated problem. We assume, and have experimentally confirmed in specific tasks such as fault identification (Boy, 1986, 1987a, 1987b), telerobotics (Boy & Mathé, 1989), and information retrieval (Boy, 1991b), that people use *chunks* of knowledge. It seems reasonable to envisage that situation patterns (i.e., situational knowledge) are *compiled* because they are the result of training. We have shown (Boy, 1987a, 1987b), in a particular case of fault diagnosis on a physical system, that the situational knowledge of an expert results mainly from the compilation, over time, of the analytical knowledge he relied on as a beginner. This situational knowledge is the essence of expertise. It corresponds to skill–based behavior in Rasmussen's terminology (1986). "Decompilation," that is, explanation of the intrinsic basic knowledge in each situation pattern, is a very difficult task, and is sometimes impossible. Such knowledge can be elicited only by an incremental observation process. Analytical knowledge can be decomposed into two types: procedures or know–how, and theoretical knowledge.

The chunks of knowledge are very different between beginners and experts. The situation patterns of beginners are simple, precise, and static, for example, "The pressure P_1 is less than 50 psia." Subsequent analytical reasoning is generally major and time–consuming. When a beginner uses an operation manual to make a diagnosis, his behavior is based on the *precompiled engineering logic* he has previously learned. In contrast, when he tries to solve the problem directly, the approach is very declarative and uses the first principles of the domain. Beginner subjects were observed to develop, with practice, a personal procedural logic (operator logic), either from the precompiled engineering logic or from a direct problem–solving approach. This process is called *knowledge compilation.* Conversely, the situation patterns of experts are sophisticated, fuzzy and dynamic, for example, "During fuel transfer, one of the fuel pressures is close to the isothermal limit and this pressure is decreasing."

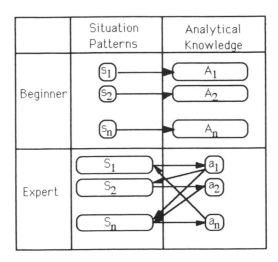

FIGURE 1. The situation recognition / analytical reasoning model.
Beginners have small, static, and crisp situation patterns associated with large analytical knowledge chunks. Experts have larger, dynamic, and fuzzy situation patterns associated with small analytical knowledge chunks. The number of beginner chunks is much smaller than the number of expert chunks.

This situation pattern includes many implicit variables defined in another *context*, for example, "during fuel transfer" means "in launch configuration, valves V_1 and V_2 closed, and V_3, V_4, V_7 open." Also, "a fuel pressure" is a more *general* statement than "the pressure P_1". The statement "isothermal limit" includes a *dynamic* mathematical model, that is, at each instant, actual values of fuel pressure are compared *fuzzily* ("close to") to a time–varying limit [P_{isoth} = f(Quantity, Time)]. Moreover, experts take this situation pattern into account only if "the pressure is decreasing," which is another dynamic and fuzzy pattern. It is obvious that experts have transferred part of analytical reasoning into situation patterns. This part seems to be concerned with dynamic aspects.

SRAR is interesting in the context of certification because it provides a framework for analyzing interface situation patterns from incremental situational testing and analytical knowledge (usually in the form of operational procedures).

INTEGRATED HUMAN–MACHINE INTELLIGENCE

This research effort has led to the concept of integrated human–machine intelligence (IHMI). The IHMI certification process can be seen as (Shalin & Boy, 1989): (1) parsing the operator's actions in order to understand what he/she is doing; (2) providing him/her with the appropriate level of information and proposing appropriate actions or procedures for him/her to execute. The IHMI model includes two loops: a short-term supervisory control loop and a long-term evaluation loop. A technical domain knowledge base includes descriptions of various objects relevant and necessary in the domain of expertise. The operational knowledge base includes available procedures necessary to handle various environmental situations that have already been encountered. The learning knowledge base includes necessary knowledge for upgrading *operational procedures*. If we assume that technical domain knowledge is a given, evaluation of an IHMI system (Boy & Gruber, 1990) is mainly concerned with operational knowledge. Such knowledge is very difficult both to construct and to validate. Its construction is necessarily incremental. A designer cannot imagine such knowledge in the first place. He/she can give guidelines for users to follow. However, the behavior of an IHMI system is discovered incrementally by operating it. An important question for the future is: Can we anticipate the behavior of such IHMI systems at design time? It seems that there is not yet enough knowledge to give general rules for this. We need to accumulate more research results and experience to get classes of behavior of IHMI systems.

Following this approach, we have started research on knowledge representation to analyze, design, and evaluate the functional part of IHMI systems. The type of knowledge that we are concerned with is composed of operational procedures. Since procedures are taken as the essential communication support between humans and "human–like" systems, we propose an appropriate knowledge representation (KR) which is tractable both for explaining human intelligence and implementing artificial intelligence. The KR currently in use was designed as a representation framework for operation manuals, procedures checklists, user guides (Boy, 1987b) and other on–line tools useful for controlling complex dynamic systems (Boy & Mathé, 1989). A body of procedures is thus represented by a network of *knowledge blocks*. Knowledge blocks are the basic representational structures for an alternative symbolic cognitive architecture.

The basic KR entity is a "knowledge block" (or "block" for short), which includes five characteristics: a *goal*, a *procedure*, *preconditions*, *abnormal conditions*, and a *context* (Boy & Caminel, 1989). Block components are its name, its hierarchical level, a list of preconditions, a list of actions, a list of goals with a list of associated blocks, a list of abnormal conditions (ACs) with their lists of associated blocks. Depending on its level of abstraction, a procedure may be represented by a single block, a hierarchy of blocks, or a network of blocks. These features have been extensively analyzed, implemented, and tested by Mathé (1990–1991). The block representation takes Pierce's view that "when we speak of truth and falsity, we refer to the possibility of proposition being refuted." (in Coplestone, 1985, p. 306). When a block is refuted, that is, it does not work in one situation called an abnormal situation, an appropriate abnormal condition (or exception) is added to the block. In a well–known paper on *How to make ideas clear*, Pierce asserts that "the essence of belief is the establishment of a habit, and different beliefs are distinguished by the different modes of action to which they give rise" . (in Coplestone, 1985, p. 306). Contextual and abnormal conditions of a block characterize positive and negative habits attached to the various actions of the block.

CONCLUSION

One of the primary jobs of a theory is to help us look for answers to questions in the right places. Even if there is no formal theory of certification of "human–like" systems, this chapter gives some directions which come from experience in real–world domains. Humans typically "tailor" their perception and action to the social field. This tailoring occurs at all levels of interaction: people say the "right" words at the "right" moment; they remember things from past experience; they try to preserve themselves from danger; they sometimes display a cumbersome sense of humor, and so on. Is there any artificial system to date that has such capabilities? The answer is no. As shown in this chapter, an important issue is the search for intelligence in the interaction, in contrast to intelligence in the individual system. Consequently, the concept of IHMI is essential.

Situational knowledge is difficult to elicit. However, it is crucial in the certification of "human–like" systems. We have developed the block representation to capture this situational knowledge. The resulting cognitive architecture differs from other attempts (e.g., Newell et al., 1989) in the way situational knowledge is incrementally built by block context reinforcement and considering abnormal situations as a model of imperfection. Indeed, actual procedures show that the same action may have various effects depending on the situation and the expected social field, giving rise to interactions with different content, structures, and syntactic forms. For example, giving a tutorial will give rise to a different interaction than providing an operational checklist. A procedure for an expert will be different than one for a layman. This concept of context is an essential feature to analyze, design and evaluate "human–like" systems. Indeed, when a machine is capable of "human–like" interaction, it is necessary to ensure that its language is appropriate for its intended social field. It is thus necessary for computational systems to be capable of appropriately tailoring their interactions. This is especially important as computer systems often need to communicate with an increasingly varied user community, across an ever more extensive range of situations. This emerging feature will complicate the certification process in the traditional sense. In particular, finding measures that provide good assessments of the resulting IHMI is a context–dependent knowledge acquisition process. Thus, it makes sense to anticipate evaluation criteria (norms) at the outset of design with the reservation that these criteria will be revised during the design cycle as more situational knowledge is acquired.

REFERENCES

Boy, G.A. (1983). The MESSAGE system: A first step towards a computer–assisted analysis of human–machine interactions. *Le Travail Humain, 46,* 58-65. (in French).

Boy, G.A. (1986, Jan.). *An expert system for fault diagnosis in orbital refueling operations.* Paper presented at the *AIAA 24th Aerospace Science Meeting,* Reno, Nevada.

Boy, G.A. (1987a, May). *Analytical representation and situational representation.* Paper presented at the *Seminar on Human Errors and Automation.*, ENAC, Toulouse. (in French).

Boy, G.A. (1987b). Operator assistant systems. *International Journal of Man–Machine Studies, 27,* 541-554.

Boy, G.A. (1991a). *Intelligent assistant systems.* London: Academic Press.

Boy, G.A. (1991b, December). *Indexing hypertext documents in context,* Paper presented at the *Hypertext'91 Conference,* San Antonio, Texas.

Boy, G.A., & Caminel, T. (1989, July). *Situation pattern acquisition improves the control of complex dynamic systems.* Paper presented at the *Third European Workshop on Knowledge Acquisition for Knowledge–Based Systems*, Paris, France.

Boy, G.A., & Gruber, T. (1990, March). *Intelligent assistant systems: support for integrated human–machine systems.* Paper presented at the *AAAI Spring Symposium on Knowledge–Based Human–Computer Communication,* Stanford, CA.

Boy, G.A., & Mathé, N. (1989, August). *Operator assistant systems: an experimental approach using a telerobotics application.* Paper presented at the *IJCAI Workshop on Integrated Human–Machine Intelligence in Aerospace Systems*, Detroit, Michigan, USA.

Boy, G.A. & Tessier, C. (1985, September). *Cockpit Analysis and Assessment by the MESSAGE Methodology.* Paper presented at the *Second IFAC/IFIP/IFORS/IEA Conference on Analysis, Design and Evaluation of Man–Machine Systems,* Varese, Italy.

Clancey, W.J. (1990). The frame of reference problem in the design of intelligent machines. In K. Van Lehn & A. Newell (Eds.), *Architectures for Intelligence: The 22nd Carnegie Symposium of Cognition* (pp. 103-107). Hillsdale, NJ: Lawrence Erlbaum Associates.

Copleston, F. (1985). *A history of philosophy.* Part IV. The Pragmatist Movement, Chapter XIV, The Philosophy of C.S. Pierce (pp. 304-329). New York: Doubleday.

Engelbart, D.C. (1963). *A conceptual framework for the augmentation of man's intellect.* Unpublished manuscript.

Feigenbaum, E.A., & Barr, A. (1982). *The handbook of artificial intelligence, Vols 1-2.* Los Altos, CA: Kaufmann.

Ford, K.M., & Agnew, N.M. (1992, March). *Expertise: Socially situated, personally constructed, and "reality" relevant.* Paper presented at the *AAAI 1992 Spring Symposium on the Cognitive Aspects of Knowledge Acquisition,* Stanford University, California.

Gaines, B.R. (1992, March). *The species as a cognitive agent.* Paper presented at the *AAAI 1992 Spring Symposium on the Cognitive Aspects of Knowledge Acquisition,* Stanford University, California.

Hegel, G.W.F. (1929). *Science of logic.* London: George Allen & Unwin.

Hewitt, C. (1977). Viewing control structures as patterns of message passing. *Artificial Intelligence, 8,* 115-121.

Hutchins, E., & Klausen, T. (1990). *Distributed cognition in an airline cockpit.* San Diego, CA: UCSD, Department of Cognitive Science.

Leplat, J. (1985, September). *The elicitation of expert knowledge.* Paper presented at the *NATO Workshop on Intelligent Decision Support in Process Environments,* Rome, Italy.

Lesser, V., & Corkill, D. (1983). The distributed vehicle monitoring testbed: a tool for investigating distributed solving networks. *AI Magazine, 4,* 25-29.

Mathé, N. (1990). *Assistance intelligente au contrôle de processus: Application à la télemanipulation spatiale* [Intelligent support to process control: application to spatial telemanipulating]. Unpublished doctoral dissertation, ENSAE, Toulouse, France.

Mathé, N. (1991). *Procedures management and maintenance* (Second ESA Grant Progress Report). NASA Ames Research Center, California.

McClelland, J.L., Rumelhart, D.E., & The PDP Research Group (1986). *Parallel Distributed Processing. Exploration in the Microstructure of Cognition. Volume 2 : Psychological and Biological Models.* Cambridge, MA: The MIT Press.

McCulloch, W., & Pitts, W. (1943). A logical calculus of the ideas imminent in nervous activity. *Bulletin of Mathematical Biophysics, 5,* 53-67.

Minsky, M. (1986). *The society of minds.* New York: Simon & Schuster.

Newell, A., & Simon, H.A. (1972). *Human problem solving.* Englewood Cliffs, NJ: Prentice Hall.

Newell, A., Rosenbloom, P.S., & Laird, J.E. (1989). Symbolic architectures of cognition. In M.I. Posner (Ed.), *Foundations of Cognitive Science*. Cambridge, MA: The MIT Press.

Nielsen, J. (1993). *Usability engineering*. London: Academic Press.

Nii, P. (1986). Blackboard systems. *AI Magazine, 7*, 38-53.

Pylyshyn, Z.W. (1989). Computing in Cognitive Science. In M.I. Posner (Ed.), *Foundations of Cognitive Science* (pp. 200-230). Cambridge, MA: The MIT Press.

Rasmussen, J. (1986). *Information pocessing and human–machine interaction: An approach to cognitive engineering*. Amsterdam: North Holland.

Rosenblatt, F. (1958). The perceptron: A probabilistic model for information storage and organization in the brain. *Psychological Review, 65*, 101-105.

Rumelhart, D.E., McClelland, J.L., & The PDP Research Group (1986). *Parallel distributed processing. Exploration in the microstructure of cognition. Volume 1: Foundations*. Cambridge, MA: The MIT Press.

Schneider, W., & Shiffrin, R.M. (1977a). Controlled and automatic human information processing: I. Detection, search, and attention. *Psychological Review, 84*, 1-66.

Schneider, W., & Shiffrin, R.M. (1977b). Controlled and automatic human information processing: II. Perceptual learning, automatic attending, and a general theory. *Psychological Review, 84*, 127-190.

Shalin, V.L. & Boy, G.A. (1989, August). *Integrated human-machine intelligence in aerospace systems*. Paper presented at the *IJCAI Workshop*, Detroit, MI.

Tessier, C. (1984). *MESSAGE: A human factors tool for fight management analysis*. Unpublished doctoral dissertation, ENSAE, Toulouse, France (in French).

Turing, A.M. (1950). Computing machinery and intelligence. *Mind, 5*, 433-460.

von Neumann, J. (1966). *The theory of self–reproducing automata*. Urbana, IL: University of Illinois Press.

ACKNOWLEDGMENTS

Claude Tessier, Nathalie Mathé, and I developed some of these ideas together when I worked in the Automation Department of ONERA/CERT. I also would like to acknowledge very rich interactions I had with my colleagues at the NASA Ames Research Center both in the Human Factors Research Division and the Information Science Division.

16

Planning Support
and the Intentionality
of Dynamic Environments

Morten LIND and Morten Norby LARSEN
Technical University of Denmark

When operators of complex plants are faced with a planning task, they find themselves in an environment designed with very specific purposes in mind. However, the support they receive, typically in the form of a prescribed procedure, does not reveal much of this knowledge to the operator. In this chapter we first discuss how existing procedures can be analyzed to capture some of the designer's intentions with the plant and the procedures. Then we will discuss how Multilevel Flow Modeling can be used to identify the means and ends of the plant, and lastly we will show how the two representations relate. The two representations are combined into a representation of tasks, which may serve as a basis for a planning support system for the operator or as a scheme to interpret the actions of the operator.

An agent involved in supervisory control of a dynamic environment diagnoses disturbances, makes decisions, and conceives plans of action within a context of purpose and intentions. In natural environments, for example, on the moon, the source of intentionality is the agent's own beliefs, objectives, and plans. In manmade environments, such as industrial plants, the intentions of the plant designers are another source. However, the aims and objectives of the supervisor and the plant designers are often implicit, and it is difficult to understand the meaning of actions (whether taken by operator or computer) by direct observation or from reading written operating procedures.

A human operator interacting with a control system that has some autonomy is faced with the same problems if he or she tries to understand actions taken or planned by the control system. The operator will thus need support from the system to understand the actions it has planned. This support must be rooted in a model that is able to express the intentions of the plant designer, and it should be given to the operator through an interface that expresses that aspect of the plant. The same intentions can be used by the computer system to generate plans that are congruent with the rest of the information given by the system, and hence the mental model developed by the operator.

In this chapter, we will address two issues in the discussions. The first is describing how to use knowledge of the intentions of the plant designer to synthesize plans. The other is describing how the same knowledge may be used in the interpretation of actions. In the design of human-machine interaction these two issues provide answers to the following questions:

- How can we apply knowledge about the intentional aspects of the environment in order to provide computer based planning support for supervisors?
- What do we need to know about the environment of the agent in order to recognize his/her behavior as being directed toward goals?

The first part of the chapter will give a discussion of intentionality of control actions, followed by an analysis of a start-up procedure, seen as an artifact. The analysis leads to an identification of the intentions behind the actions in the prescribed procedure.

The second part introduces the Multi Flow Modelling (MFM) system as a system that expresses the intentions behind the plant design, and a simple MFM model of a power plant is developed. In the last part, the intentions identified in the procedure are connected to the elements of the model, and it is discussed how this can be used to support the operator in performing a start-up of a plant.

ANALYZING THE INTENTIONALITY OF CONTROL ACTIONS

The intentionality of supervisors' actions originate from several sources which are difficult to separate. However, Simon's famous ant parable (Simon, 1981) can serve as a vehicle for an analysis. Simon tells us in his parable about an ant which is making its way across a wind and wave molded beach. By looking at the path of the ant's movements they seem irregular, but not completely random because it has an underlying sense of direction, of being aimed toward a goal. This leads Simon to the following hypothesis:

An ant, viewed as a behaving system, is quite simple. The apparent complexity of its behavior over time is largely a reflection of the complexity of the environment in which it finds itself.

The hypothesis Simon is proposing here is really about the fitness of the behavior of the ant to the constraints of its environment. If the ant is adapted to its environment, it will take advantage of or avoid its irregularities in its efforts to accomplish its goals. In other words, it is assumed that the ant has knowledge about the environment and that this knowledge is used with skill for diagnosing and evaluating the current environmental situation and for planning future actions.

Now, this hypothesis is obviously equally valid when analyzing actions of humans and other agents, such as computers. But more importantly, if we make the assumption that the agent is adapted to the environment we can understand the behavior of the agent in terms of the environmental constraints. Instead of trying to explain the complex psychological or physiological basis for the behavior of the agent, the problem will be transformed into an analysis of the environment. We only need to infer the goals and preferences of the agent from the overt behavior. The environment serves as a mold (Simon, 1981). If the assumption of adaptation is not valid, the analysis will be erroneous because the behavior of the agent then also will be determined by the psychological and physiological constraints of its own inner environment.

Simon's agent, the ant, is situated in a natural environment, the beach, and the understanding of its behavior only requires direct observation of the physical environment and some knowledge about the goals and preferences of the agent. These prerequisites for understanding behavior are however not sufficient for analyzing how human supervisors make plans and execute actions in industrial plants. The framework needs some expansion. We need to take into account the fact that the environment has been shaped by a plant designer according to his aims and purposes.

Due to the presence of a design agent, the supervising agent would not act as if the environment was natural, that is, without a preconceived plan or purpose. As we again assume that the supervisor is adapted to the environment, we must also assume that she/he/it is taking into account the artificial character of the environment and that this will affect behavior. An outside observer would in this case not be able to understand the agent's behavior from direct observation of the physical properties of the environment. The behavior can only be understood within the context of the objectives of plant operation and the purposes or functions of the plant equipment conceived by the designer. But these intentions are not directly observable. When the agent is acting in a natural environment, an observer only needs to know the goals and preferences of the agent and the physical characteristics of the environment in order to understand his behavior. If the environment is artificial, that is, manmade, the observer must also know the design intentions in order to understand the meaning of actions.

In the following we will concentrate on the analysis of the designer's intentions, that is, we will ignore the supervisor's own personal goals and objectives. In order to make our analysis valid, we therefore need to assume that behavior can be understood as being constrained by two *non conflicting* parts:
• The constraints on plant control actions resulting from plant design decisions and the control objectives and strategies intended by the plant designer.
• The constraints on operator's actions due to his own action preferences and objectives.
Assuming that these two types of constraints are non conflicting is a more precise way of characterizing the adaptation of the agent to the environment, as presumed in Simon's analysis.

The assumption of adaptation has consequences for the design of the interface between the agent and his environment, in particular for the provision of planning support in complex environments. As discussed later, the assumption above will in the context of design of planning support systems turn into a functional requirement for the interface. However, before we suspend the issue and introduce the planning problems in more detail, it may be useful with an elaboration of this adaptation assumption derived from Simon's ant fable.

According to the assumptions, the agent should comply with plant designer's control objectives and strategies (to the extent that they are given of course). This means that the agent's behavior could be considered as in agreement with the plant designer's intentions even when the agent is using plant resources not contemplated by the designer for the achievement of the design objectives. The evaluation of the fitness of the agent's behavior is in this case based on how well objectives have been met and not on what means has been used. If the designer has prescribed control strategies, that is, commended ways of using plant resources to achieve objectives, the agent would be considered as adapted to the environment if his own objectives and preferences provide tactical measures in compliance with the designers' strategies. In both cases we would say that the agent is acting within the envelope of plant design intentions.

We would characterize situations where the agent is not adapted to the environment as failures. In some situations the agent would not achieve the objectives prescribed by the plant designer. In other situations the agent is not following the strategies commended by the designer, for example, by implementing actions which may be dysfunctional to the environment.

ANALYSIS OF A START-UP PROCEDURE

In the preceding sections we argued that knowledge about plant design intentions is crucial for the planning of actions in artificial environments. We will in the following validate this claim by means of a detailed discussion of a concrete example of a start-up procedure for a power plant boiler. To show the relevance of knowledge about plant design intentions for planning, we will use such information to explain the reasons why steps of action are taken in the procedure. We will on this basis also show how the same aspects are also useful for the synthesis of plans.

The physical structure of the plant example considered is shown in Figure 1. and the procedure for start-up to be analyzed is shown in Figure 2. The procedure prescribes the sequence of actions and the conditions necessary for the initiation of these actions. The procedure shown is generic because it represents the steps typical for start-up of most drum boilers (West, 1972). Specific differences may occur for each individual boiler. The procedure shown in Figure 2 comprises the actions required to fill the boiler drum with water, to heat up the water until steam formation begins and the subsequent roll and synchronization of the turbine generator. Actions required to provide auxiliary services and to perform prestart checks are also included. But, as the latter types of actions are of minor importance for the analysis to be made, they will be ignored in the following. Figure 2 is a slightly reorganized presentation of the procedure given by West (op. cit.) where there is no explicit mention of the plant components or systems acted upon. This information is shown in the vertical axis of Figure 2.

At the present stage, operating procedures for industrial plants are often developed on an ad hoc basis by accumulation of practical experience. As a consequence, the correctness (i.e., whether the task is successfully accomplished or not) is only guaranteed in a pragmatic sense, by leading to the intended result when applied. A procedure contains no *explicit* information about the control tasks to be solved (i.e., goals to be met and the strategies applicable).

The *reasons* for the individual actions and the conditions for the implementation of the actions are therefore not stated. Given a procedure, this information can only be identified by an analysis of its historical development or from knowledge about the goals and functions of the controlled environment. The procedure or the plan itself is accordingly a necessary but not a sufficient source of information for the identification of control tasks. Such an identification can only be accomplished by a more fundamental understanding of the physical structure of the environment, design intentions and the decision criteria to be used in the selection between alternative courses of action.

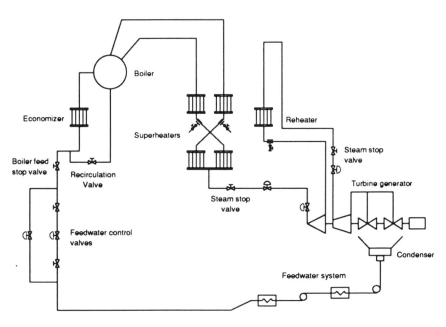

FIGURE 1. The power plant boiler.

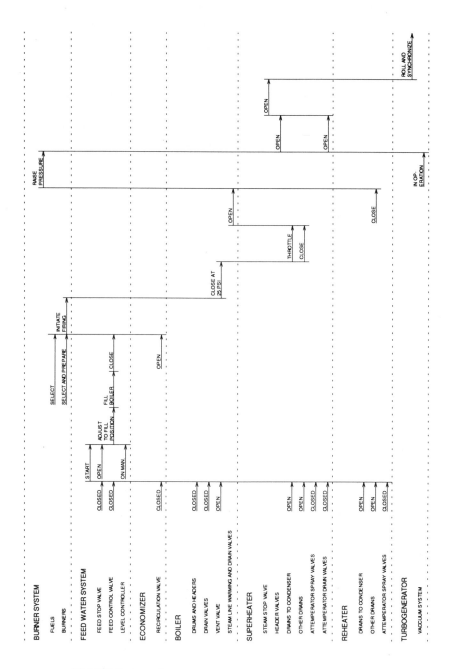

FIGURE 2. Generic start-up procedure for a
power plant boiler.

Uncovering Plant Design Intentions in the Start-Up

The procedure shown in Figure 2 is only describing the temporal ordering of control actions, that is, the durations of the different actions are ignored. The temporal ordering is a reflection of logical constraints between the different parts of the start-up. In order to uncover the nature of these constraints we will take advantage of the information presented along the vertical axis where we have listed different physical subsystems in the plant, that is, the boiler, the feed water system, the burner system, the economizer, the superheater and the reheater, and the turbine generator. For each subsystem we have also listed the components that are objects of the actions in the different phases of the start-up. These components are therefore objects that can be manipulated and they are all valves (with a few exceptions). The ordering of the systems along the vertical axis is not arbitrary and is in fact crucial for our recognition of plant design intentions. The ordering makes visible the patterns of action which lead to the increase of functional integration of the power plant during the start-up. This functional integration is intended by the plant designer.

The functional levels established during start-up are not directly observable properties of plant components or subsystems. The functions are more abstract relational entities representing intended patterns of interactions between the plant parts. If these plant functions are known we can classify the different actions according to the purpose they serve in the start-up. Each action is ultimately a means of reaching the overall goal of producing electricity by the turbine generator. The function of each action toward this end must be found by describing how the action contributes to the management of the means of production in the plant, that is, it must be related to a classification of the different types of plant resource management tasks involved in the start-up.

A Classification of Plant Resource Management Tasks

The classification of plant resource management tasks can be obtained by representing the plant in a so-called abstraction hierarchy based on a means-end and whole part concepts. Lind (1990) describes a modeling technique called Multilevel Flow Modelling (MFM) which is based on these concepts. MFM makes a distinction between goals, functions, and the physical levels in the description of plant processes. The levels of functions and the physical components represent means which can be instrumental in the achievement of plant safety, production, and economy goals. By using such a representational framework we obtain the following general task categories:
- Configuration management. This comprises the following two subordinate task types:
  Allocation of physical resources to functions. This is a planning task involving the choice between alternative physical implementations of a set of required plant functions. The task takes into account the interrelations

between the physical and the functional levels. When several alternatives exist for the physical realization of plant functions, a planning agent must make a choice on the basis of the performance required and the capabilities of the different physical alternatives. The planning of system start-up and shut down and change over involves the consideration of this type of allocation task. The planning may be performed as part of the design of the plant processes or could be made dynamically by an operator or by a computer. Such a planning takes into account the conditions for availability of the physical resources. A plant component may be taken out of service for repair or maintenance and may in a dynamic planning situation force the planner to look for other alternatives.

Coordination of physical parts into functions. The purpose of this type of task is to coordinate the selected physical parts to perform selected plant functions considering operational constraints and control objectives.

• Management of plant functions. This comprises the following two subordinate task types:

Allocation of function resources to goals. This is a planning task which comprises the use of overall control strategies for choosing between alternative plant functions for the achievement of a selected goal. This task involves an evaluation of alternatives with respect to capability.

Coordination of functions into high level functions. This is a control task including the coordination of plant functions in order to realize a given goal. The control task is designed on the basis of the functional resources identified in the function allocation task. Goals for the coordination tasks are often based on optimization criteria.

The task categories defined above can be further subdivided into subordinate categories. These subordinate categories would however only be applicable within restricted domains. In the power plant example above we can with advantage distinguish between tasks related to the management of mass and energy. These types of tasks are of particular interest here because we will show later how the intentional structure of the power plant can be represented in terms of the Multilevel Flow Modelling technique (MFM).

The Start-Up Procedure Reconsidered

We can now resume our analysis of the start-up procedure for the power plant boiler. The distinctions introduced above between different categories of resource management tasks can now be used to reveal patterns of intentionality in the sequences of actions in the start-up. The result of such an interpretation is shown in Figure 3. It is seen from Figure 3 that the start-up actions can be aggregated into a set of subordinate tasks dealing with configuration management (CM), material (mass or energy) management (MM) and function support (FS). The actions being parts of these activities acquire their meaning when classified according to their functional value in task achievement. In order to realize this let us consider some examples.

The meaning of the action 'close boiler feed control valve' ('stop feed water flow' in Figure 2) is to be a means for the management of the mass balances involved in filling up the boiler with water. Furthermore the meaning of the action "open economizer recirculation valve" is to be a means for managing the physical configuration of the economizer circuit, with the purpose of protecting it from boiling dry. We thus see that even though these two actions are similar (by being manipulations of valves) they have different purposes.

These different purposes can be revealed by classifying the start-up activities into tasks as shown in Figure 3.

It is also seen from Figure 3 that as the procedure is progressing, the plant develops into a functionally integrated system. The last material handling task (MM3) involves all plant parts as the change of the state on any plant component in principle would have a consequence (small or large) for the achievement of the goal for this task (the production of electric energy). A manipulation of the economizer recirculation valve discussed earlier could in this phase have the purpose of optimizing the energy economy of the plant. It is seen that changing the state of the recirculation valve could in this context have a distinctly different purpose (if the state was intentionally changed).

These informal interpretations of the actions in the procedure are based on knowledge about the purposes of the different phases of the start-up. In the following we will show how this knowledge can be formalized and used in a more systematic way for understanding control actions.

MULTILEVEL FLOW MODEL OF THE POWER PLANT BOILER

In order to demonstrate that the analysis of the start-up procedure in Figure 4 can be related to levels of means-end and part-whole abstractions of the power plant boiler, we will in the following describe an MFM model of the boiler. It will be indicated how the different phases of the start-up relate to different parts of the model. We will furthermore illustrate how the MFM model can be used for plan synthesis.

The MFM model of the power plant boiler is shown in Figure 4, where also the meaning of the symbols used are depicted. As Lind (1990) provides a detailed introduction, we will not describe the principles of MFM modeling here. We will, however, in the following explain the details of the model. When reading the explanation, the reader is encouraged to consult Figure 1. showing the physical layout of the plant. First, we will define the meaning of the goals G0,..., G10 and explain how they relate to the flow structures structure1, structure2 and structure3. Second, we will describe the flow structures.

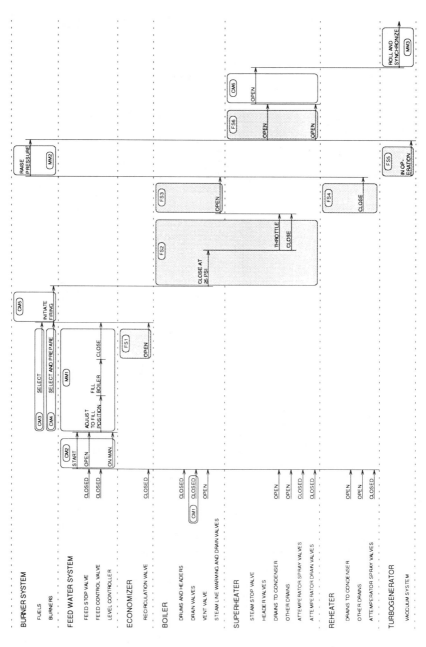

FIGURE 3. The start-up procedure with tasks indicated.

The Goals and the Related Flow Structures

The main goal of the power plant boiler is to provide an energy flow on the generator shaft. This goal is named G0 in the model, and the means to achieve it are the flow functions represented by structure1. This energy flow structure describes the functions provided by the burner, boiler, turbines, and generator. Structure2 describes the mass flow functions involved in the fuel combustion process, and structure3 describes the mass flow functions provided by the boiler, turbine, condenser, and the economizer.

Structure2 supports three goals named G1, G2 and G3. They are all related to provide and transport the energy at the first stages of structure1, the top-level energy flow. G1 is the goal of providing a proper ratio between the air and fuel flows (to ensure combustion). G2 is the goal of having a flame and G3 expresses that a flow of combustion gases is needed to carry the heat into the economizer. Related to G2 is G9, which is the goal of having a chemical reaction between the fuel and the oxygen. This goal is achieved by structure1, specifically by means of the energy transport Tr1 that again is supported by the goal G2. The two goals G2 and G9 thus support each other. In physical terms this means that when a flame is first established, it is self-supporting. This circularity in the MFM model illustrates the fact that abstraction levels in an MFM model often combine into cyclic networks of goal and means (i.e., they are not structured as trees). Such cycles are the source of start-up problems. In the specific case considered, the flame is needed to ensure transport of energy in the boiler and this transport is a necessary means to maintain the combustion processes, that is, the flame. We therefore need to start the combustion process by another means, which indeed is the purpose of the ignition system (not included in the model).

Structure3 is used for achieving five goals G4, G5, G6, G7, and G8 that all support the transport of energy from the boiler to the turbine. G4 expresses the need to maintain a sufficient level of water in the boiler and G5 is the goal of having a steam flow from the boiler to the turbine. The energy conversion in the turbine only works properly if the vacuum system is operating, and thus G6 expresses the need to having the vacuum system in operation. Cooling is of course needed, too, and G7 is the goal of having the cooling water at a proper flow, while G8 is the goal of having a feed water flow. One of the functions of structure3 is also conditioned by a goal. The function is Tr14, the mass transport that is provided by the steam piping from the boiler to the turbine. This flow is conditioned by the goal G10, which expresses the need to maintain a pressure in the boiler. This goal is therefore achieved by structure1. This part of the model also comprises a cyclic component.

Description of the Flow Structures

Resources provided in the plant for goal achievement are represented by the flow functions in structure1, structure2, and structure3. Below we will, without going into too much detail, describe all the flow functions and explain their physical realization.

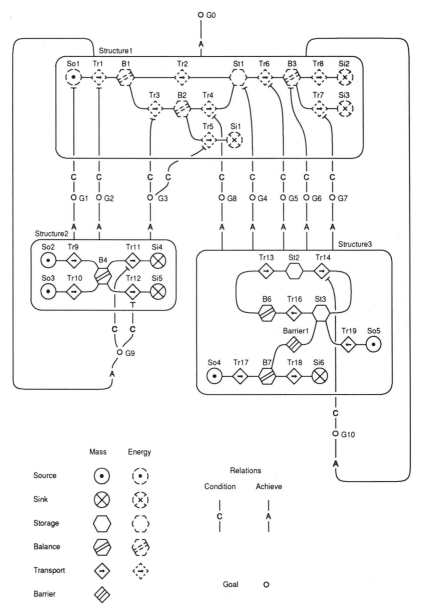

FIGURE 4.   The MFM model of the power plant boiler.

Structure1 consists of the following functions: The source So1 is the energy source provided by the combustion of fuel and air. This energy is transported by the transport function Tr1 into the balance function B1. Tr1 is realized by (is a function of) the flame, and is hence conditioned by the goal G2. B1 models the balance between the incoming energy flow (Tr1) and the flow of energy into the water in the boiler (Tr2) and the energy flow carried away by the exhaust gases (Tr3). The balance B2 models the energy balance in the economizer, where the heat from the exhaust gases is used to pre-heat the feed water, which provides an energy transport function, modeled by Tr4. The heat eventually carried away from the economizer and "lost" in the chimney is modeled by Tr5. This energy is absorbed by the atmosphere that has the function of a sink, modeled by Si1. The energy transported by Tr2 ends up in the energy storage St1 provided by the water in the boiler. From this energy storage a flow is led by a transport function (Tr6) into a balance (B3) provided by the turbine. From B3 the energy is transported by two flows, one representing the work done on the generator shaft (Tr8) and one representing the residual heat in the steam on the low-pressure side of the turbine (Tr7). These flows end in two energy sink functions. Si2 models the energy sink provided by the generator and Si3 models the heat sink provided by the environment through sea water or the atmosphere.

The functions of structure2 representing the mass flow functions involved in the management of the fuel and air flows in the burner and fuel supply system. The source function So2 models the oil or coal inventory, which, despite its limited nature, plays the role of an infinite source in view of day-to-day operations. Likewise, the source function So3 models the source of air (oxygen) provided by the atmosphere. From these sources two transport functions lead to the mass balance function provided by the combustion process. The transport Tr9 models the function of the fuel pumps and pipes and Tr10 models the function of the air blowers and B4 models the combustion mass balance. Tr11 models the outflow of CO_2 and Tr12 models the outflow of H_2O. Only these two exhaust gases are modeled, since they are the basic ones. The sink functions modeled by Si4 and Si5 are both realized by the atmosphere.

Structure3 comprises the functions that are involved in the management of the flows of water and steam around the boiler and the condenser. St2 is the mass storage function that is provided by the boiler, B6 models the mass balance provided by the economizer and St3 models the mass storage function provided by the condenser. The transport functions between the two storage functions are Tr13, which models the feed water system between the economizer and the boiler, and Tr16, which models the feed water system between the condenser and the economizer. Tr14 models the mass (steam) transport provided by the high-pressure steam piping, the re-heaters, the turbines and the vacuum system. Tr19 is transport into the condenser of feed water and So5 is its source. The network So4-Tr17-B7-Tr18-Si6 comprises the functions of the cooling water side of the condenser. The source (So4) and the sink (Si6) are both functions of the sea water or water in a cooling tower and the balance B7 is provided by the cold side of the condenser. The transports Tr17 and Tr18 are realized by the cooling water pumps and pipes. The barrier function Barrier1 is provided by the pipes in the heat exchanger of the condenser and has the purpose of separating the possibly polluted cooling water from the feed water involved in the energy production processes.

Using the Model For Planning Purposes

When the model thus developed is to be used for planning, the quite general nature of the knowledge discussed earlier needs some specialization. To provide deeper knowledge about the workings of the plant, more conditions must be associated with the functions of the model. In this paper, where the focus is on start-ups, the conditions are divided into three categories. It is possible that another focus (for instance on diagnosis) would require different categories. The three categories of condition used in this paper deal with the following aspects of a function:

- The structural support
- The materials being treated
- Fitness of the function to other functions

The structural support is either provided by equipment of the plant or by a lower level function that provide the means. In an MFM model this last possibility corresponds to functions that are not conditioned on a goal, and those that are, respectively.

The existence of a structural support ensures the *basic behavior* of the function, but the problem is that functions only exist in the context of the operation of the plant. This means that a function needs other functions surrounding it to provide the context, that is, the environment in which it makes sense to talk about it as a function.

Hence, the environment must on one hand provide the *material* (water or heat, for instance) that the function must treat. On the other hand it also induces limits on the states of the components themselves or the operation of them to ensure that the behavior is useful for the group of functions as a whole. The useful behavior is here considered to be the behavior of the function ensuring that other functions can cooperate with it, that is, where it *fits* them. Examples of this could be a minimum flow in a transport function or a minimum level in a storage function.

Fulfilling the material condition is done by the surrounding functions that then have the function of delivering material to the function in question. The fitness condition, on the other hand, must be met by tuning the state of the plant to ensure that the levels and the flows have correct values.

The conditions on the functions may therefore be expressed as states of the equipment or the process. A state of the equipment may be that a valve is open or closed, that a pump is turned on or that an entire sub system is in operation if it can be regarded as one unit. The state of the process is expressed in terms of pressure, temperature, concentration and so on for the materials being treated by the plant, and largely determines the fitness condition of the functions. It may for some functions be controlled directly, for instance by means of a pump or a control valve. These functions are active, whereas others, for which the behavior is determined by the operating of the surrounding systems or the plant in general, are passive functions.

As there is more than one condition for many functions, there is also the possibility that a function is only partly established if only some of the conditions are fulfilled. Some of these states may be meaningful, and as we concentrate on start-ups, we will focus on the intermediate steps before a function gets established. In this analysis only two main steps are recognized – the intermediate and the final. After the intermediate step a function is said to be *enabled* and after the final step it is said to be *established*.

An enabled function is a function that is ready to be integrated with the other functions, but it is not yet necessarily working, in the sense that it processes material. It thus means that it might be ready to receive a material, for instance. An example of this could be the boiler that is enabled as an energy storage when there is water in it, since it would be able to receive heat from the flame in a proper way. For a function to be established — the next step — the systems realizing it must be working as they are intended to, meaning that the material they are expected to process will be processed properly.

An established function is hence integrated with at least a necessary minimal number of surrounding functions, by which is referred to the functions that must be established (or enabled) around it for it to work.

INTERPRETATION OF THE START-UP PROCEDURE

We can now relate the MFM model in Figure 4 with the classification of tasks in the start-up procedure shown in Figure 3. Due to the relations between the flow structures given by the condition and achieve relations and the auxiliary conditions introduced above, we can directly recognize the overall structure of the procedure from the MFM model in Figure 4.

On a general level, we can see that functions of structure2 and structure3 must be established before the functions in structure1. Furthermore, the goals achieved by functions in structure2 and structure3 must be achieved before functions in structure1 are established. What we read directly from the overall structure of the MFM model corresponds in the procedure to the precedence of the tasks CM3, CM4, and MM1 to CM5 and MM2 and of the task CM6 to MM3.

The task MM1 corresponds to filing up the boiler with water. The associated plant resources and their interrelations are represented by the functions of structure3. The tasks CM3 and CM4 comprise the configuration of the fuel and burner system. The associated plant resources and their interrelations are represented by structure2. The task CM5 corresponds to a configuration of the energy flow, since a flow of energy into the boiler is established. The tasks MM2 and MM3 comprise the management of the heating up of the feed water, the production of steam and the conversion of steam energy to electricity in the turbine generator. These two tasks are separated by the task CM6, which comprises the configuration of the steam flow from the boiler to the turbines. MM2 and MM3 are both related to the plant resources in structure1, while CM6 is related to the plant resources in structure3, although this task has immediate consequences on the configuration of the energy flow, that is, the plant resources of structure1.

The function support tasks are less evident, but comprise configuration of the plant to ensure that the plant functions are also maintained when the operating point is changing. The task FS1 configures the equipment around the economizer to ensure that the water is kept at a satisfactory level all during the startup, ensuring that the proper mass balances are maintained. The purpose is to ensure that the economizer does not boil dry during the start-up, and hence to ensure the integrity of the equipment of the plant. The tasks FS2, FS3, and FS4 comprise configuring the equipment around the boiler and the steamline to maintain the ability of the boiler to receive the energy received from the burners, also at higher pressures and temperatures. The task FS5 comprises the configuration of the equipment around the low pressure turbine to ensure that the relation between the energy flows is satisfactory. The task FS6 comprises the configuration of the equipment around the superheater to ensure that it is able to handle the temperature of the steam.

Tying the Tasks to the Functions

Having identified both the nature of the tasks, as discussed above, and the functions of the plant as using the MFM model, the two analyses can be combined.

The Configuration Management tasks all correspond to tasks that more or less directly lead to a function being established. Using the terminology from above, most of these tasks establish the structural support for the function, which in turn leads to the establishment of the function.

Based on this principle, the Configuration Management tasks may be seen as establishing the following functions:

- CM1 enables the water storage function of the boiler, that is, St2 in the model.
- CM2 establishes the water transport function of the feed water system, that is, Tr16.
- CM3 establishes the fuel source function, that is, So2.
- CM4 enables the mass transport function of the burners, that is, Tr9.
- CM5 establishes the mass (fuel) and energy transport function corresponding to the burners, that is, Tr1.
- CM6 establishes the mass transport function from the boiler to the high pressure turbine, that is, Tr6.

All the functions being established above need other conditions to be fulfilled also, for instance, the task CM2 has as a pre condition that there is water present in the hotwell of the condenser.

The material handling tasks correspond to control tasks that serve to meet the fitness requirement for the function involved.

- MM1 ensures a level of water in the boiler that serves to fully establish the mass storage function of the boiler, that is, St2.
- MM2 is used for achieving the correct pressure in the boiler, hence establishing the boiler's energy storage function, that is, St1.
- MM3 brings the level of energy stored in the turbine generator to the prescribed level, thus ensuring that the energy balance function B3 is interacting correctly with the surrounding functions.

Two types of the Function Support tasks exist. One is the type of task that serves to ensure that the integrity of the equipment is kept, so that, for instance, material temperatures are not exceeded. The tasks of this kind are:

• FS3, which ensures that the steam line material is not exposed to excessive temperature gradients, that is, it ensures that the mass transport function Tr6 will be available also at higher temperatures.

The following tasks have the purpose of keeping a function enabled also when the operating conditions are changed:

• FS1, which ensures that the economizer does not boil dry, that is, that the mass balance function of the economizer (B6) is enabled also when the boiler is fired.

• FS2 and FS4 ensure that the boiler is able to receive energy also at higher pressures, which means that it keeps the energy storage function of the boiler (St1) enabled while the pressure is raised.

The task FS5 serves to ensure a proper distribution of the energy across the turbine, hence supporting the function of the turbine as an energy balance (B3).

The task FS6 serves to ensure the proper function of the superheater, both as a mass and as an energy transport function by removing excessive water. This is thus not a task that in itself establishes the function, but it is needed to ensure that the function is existing also at higher production rates.

It is important to emphasize that the procedure in Figure 2 (and Figure 3) and the MFM model are not equivalent representations of the power plant boiler. Actually, the MFM model represents plant control tasks, their interrelations, and the resources provided by the plant designer for their achievement. The MFM model is therefore not a plan representation but a basis for the synthesis of a plan and the procedure analyzed above comprises therefore only one set of actions out of many possible accomplishing the same purpose. MFM models can also be used for interpretation of plant states, that is, for diagnosis. The diagnostic aspects of MFM are described by Lind (1991).

THE USE OF MULTILEVEL FLOW MODELLING FOR PLANNING

MFM models represent only the plant goal-function structures, and rules of interpretation or reasoning about the model are therefore required in order to generate a plan. Below, we will describe how MFM models can be used for the synthesis of plans. The rules used for planning will actually reveal further intentional knowledge about the plant because they will express strategies for plant resource management.

The problem of synthesizing control task structures is basically a planning problem involving the composition of a sequence of actions that will lead to the system defined goal state. However, when modeling the plant in terms of MFM, we formulate the planning problem as being a problem of matching the goal to be achieved with the available plant means or resources. Accordingly, instead of formulating the planning problem in terms of actions on the plant we instead phrase it in terms of the plant resources available for control.

As MFM models describe goals and functions on different levels of abstraction, the generated plans will be composed of sequences of abstract actions (intentions). The intentions can be considered as goals as they cannot be directly implemented in terms of physically executable actions. A plan synthesized on the basis of an MFM model will accordingly represent a decomposition of an overall goal into a sequence of subgoals (abstract actions). Intentions can be implemented into physical actions if the plant control interface allows the operator to express abstract goals as commands (e.g., "establish mass transport TrXX").

When synthesizing a plan there will usually be many feasible solutions. To select a plan for execution it is accordingly necessary to use heuristics that express rules to follow based on experience. An important part of this knowledge is included in an MFM model in terms of the conditions which relate the different functional levels in the model. Conditions for existence of plant functions will always relate to operational constraints, that is, the conditions cannot be derived from the principles of physics but express conditions for proper function. This important difference between natural constraints and rules of rightness is discussed by Polyani (1962).

The conditions in MFM models represent heuristic information about operational experience. For start-up purposes the relevant operational experience is knowledge about what the sufficient conditions are for each function to exist. These conditions are expressed mainly by the MFM goals. And, as each goal may be achieved by one or more structures, meeting the goal induces the need of ensuring that the necessary functions of the underlying structure exist. The knowledge we can extract from this 'vertical' dimension of the MFM model is thus *which* lower level functions are needed to perform a desired (sub) task of establishing a function at a higher level. The functions at the lowest levels are not related to MFM goals but to the plant equipment and the process, in which case the knowledge that we can extract is which parts of the equipment to operate.

CONSTRUCTION OF THE TASK DESCRIPTIONS

Using the knowledge from the MFM models one can produce task descriptions that tell how to establish a function in the plant. The primary contents of these task descriptions are subgoals that correspond to the conditions of the three categories mentioned above.

The task descriptions are divided into two categories, reflecting that establishing a function is a task that must be done in several steps, and that for each step the functions get "more and more established." There are two types of tasks for the establishment of a function, corresponding to the two steps on the way to establishment of a function: enablement and establishment. The first is the enablement task and the other is the establishment task. The latter has the result of the former as a precondition. Further, there are also task descriptions for the achievement of an MFM goal.

The task descriptions consist of a list of subgoals consisting mainly of the three conditions (structural, material, and fitness) mentioned earlier. In the task descriptions mentioned below, three additional types will be used:

- *enablement precondition.* This is a type of precondition that is used for function establishment tasks to ensure that a function is enabled before it is established.
- *execution condition.* This is a type of condition that must be fulfilled all through the execution of the task. For a discussion of this, see (Hollnagel, 1993).
- *achievement subgoal.* This is a subgoal describing how an MFM goal element is achieved.

Examples of Task Descriptions

As an example of how the task descriptions are used in practice, the operation of the boiler can be used. The example will walk through the actions and the functions needed to fill the boiler with water, reach the boiling point and the pressure raised to a sufficient level. Some of the subgoals concerning purely passive functions are simplified to keep the example small. This is indicated for the subgoals in question. The task descriptions are listed in Table 1.

To achieve a goal of establishing the energy storage of the boiler, it must first be translated into the goal "St1 established." Using the task description above, this goal can be divided into three subgoals, "St1 enabled," "Heat from burner," and "Pressure within specified limits." These subgoals must be met in this order. Furthermore, the task leads to a subtask to ensure that St1 is kept enabled constantly.

The subgoal "St1 enabled" may be achieved by performing the subtask number two in the list above, which has itself only one subgoal, that G4 is achieved. To achieve G4, St2 must be established. This again gives rise to three subgoals. The first is that it is enabled. The second is that there is water to fill the boiler, and the third is that the level of water in the boiler is correct.

To enable the storage function, the last task mentioned above may be used, leading to the subgoal that the drain valves are closed. The subgoal of having feed water present to fill the boiler involves that Tr13, B6, and Tr16 must be established, leading to the demands that

1) the economizer recirculation valve be opened, as this is needed to establish B6, and
2) the feed water system be started, as this will establish Tr16.

TABLE 1
The task descriptions of the example

Description of task	Goals and conditions	
Establish St1	goal:	St1 established
	enablement precondition:	St1 enabled
	execution condition:	St1 enabled
	material condition:	Heat from the burners (more precisely: the energy flow through the boiler wall)
	fitness condition:	Pressure in boiler within specified limits.
Enable St1	goal:	St1 enabled
	structural condition:	G4 achieved.
Achieve G4	goal:	G4 achieved
	achievement subgoal:	St2 established.
Establish St2	goal:	St2 established
	enablement precondition:	St2 enabled
	material condition:	feed water (more precisely: water from the pipes between economizer and boiler)
	fitness condition:	level of water in boiler ok
Enable St2	goal:	St2 enabled
	structural condition:	boiler drain valves closed.

Once the feed water is available to the operator, the prescribed level of water in the boiler must be achieved. This task will fulfill the fitness condition of the mass storage function of the boiler, thus achieving the goal G4 and in turn also enabling the energy storage function of the water in the boiler. To establish this function, the heat transport must be established, which means that the burner system must be prepared and fired. As the last subtask of establishing the energy storage function of the boiler, the pressure must reach a prescribed value.

In Figure 5, the tasks are shown graphically, with labels showing the tasks from the chart in Figure 3 that may be used to establish a specific state. One label is "Always," as this is a state that can be considered to be reached at all times. The expansion of the task of providing heat from the burners is shown, and some intermediate functions are skipped in the branch of the task to provide feed water to the boiler.

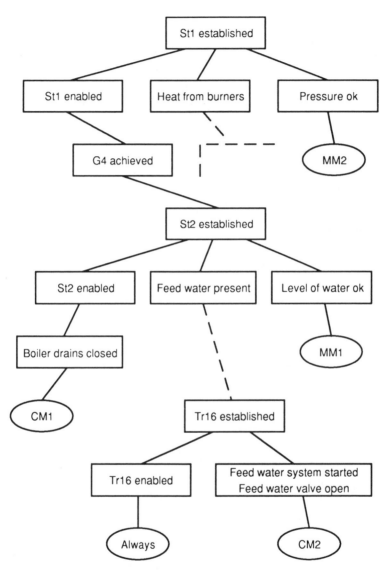

FIGURE 5. The goal structure as expanded by the task descriptions.

Interpretation of the Task Structure

The task structure has two interpretations. One is to specify a plan that will bring the system into the desired goal state. For this purpose the bottom level nodes of the structure provide a series of actions and if read from left to right, the order will comply with the requirements of the functions of the plant. Hence, from this little example it can be seen that the task CM1 must be carried out before CM2, which again must be carried out before MM1. This way to use the structure gives a simple plan in the form of a linear sequence of actions and the structure can accordingly serve as a basis for planning support of operators.

The other interpretation is to use the structure for understanding a sequence of actions by propagating information about actions carried out from the bottom upwards. In this way the immediate consequences of the actions can be seen, as well as the goals that may be achieved later on following the execution of the action. This interpretation will, however, be based on the knowledge that the overall context is a start-up. As an example of this, it may be seen that closing the boiler drain valves, in the context of a start-up, has the purpose of enabling the boiler as a mass (water) storage, which later will enable the energy storage. As all the tasks exist in the context of a start-up, the ultimate state that any action can lead to is that the plant is operating. Hence, it is the states in between the action and the final state that are interesting in this case. This interpretation of the task structure can be a basis for supervising the operator's actions.

PLANNING SUPPORT IN DYNAMIC ENVIRONMENTS

The discussions in the previous sections have demonstrated the relevance of plant design intentions for the planning of actions and for their interpretation. We have also shown that the MFM modeling technique can provide a basis for a formalized representation of design intentions and, by means of an example, that an MFM model can be used for the generation of plans. With this as a basis we will now address the human-machine interface design issues left unresolved in the beginning of the chapter.

We argued that agents acting in artificial environments necessarily would have knowledge about the design intentions in order to be adapted to the environment. However, in the analysis we did not make any assumptions about the nature of the interface between the agent and his environment. In other words, the adaptation was a feature of the total system agent-environment. From an overall systems design perspective, the required adaptation of the agent to the environment (and also the other way around for that matter) becomes a requirement to the design of the interface. But the complexity of the environment and the complexity of the planning task constrains the kinds of environment the agent can cope with without computer based support. The discussion of the planning task above and the MFM modeling demonstrates a representational problem. We will characterize this problem in some detail below.

The Problem of Representation

There is a representational problem because the agent is not able by direct inspection of the environment to infer the intentions of the plant designer from knowledge about the physical properties of the plant. This inference requires background knowledge about the functional requirements of the plant and about the designers' strategies. This means that it is difficult for the agent unaided to acquire the knowledge of the environment which is required to perform his tasks. This representational problem has a parallel in the understanding of natural language, where a representation of the underlying semantics of the situation is required in order to resolve ambiguities in the interpretation. Actually Schank's Conceptual Dependency for representation of natural language semantics (Schank & Abelson, 1977) is similar to MFM models, which represent semantic aspects of the artificial environment. Schank's work and the related work of Wilensky (1983) are discussed in Hoc, 1988, in relation to more general planning problems.

It should be noted that MFM models can be complex representations, even for systems which on the surface seem simple enough (see, e.g., the MFM model of a central heating system discussed in Lind (1990)). The semantics of the artificial environments will, in our experience with MFM modeling, turn out to be complex in most realistic cases. Their MFM representations will include several or many levels of abstraction and cyclic means-end structures.

Concluding Remarks

With this analysis of the planning tasks in artificial environments we may conclude that there is a need for computer based support in order to handle the representational problem.

We have not discussed how human operators actually perform in planning tasks. However, the findings of Suchman (1987) indicate that humans are very bad, or at least not optimal, planners. But supervisors interacting with an environment that has a complex intentional structure, a feature of most industrial plants, need to plan in order to stay tuned with the task environment. If Suchman's findings are correct, we therefore can conclude that supervisors interacting with such environments would need computer support, and that this support should reveal the intentional structure of the environment. There seems also to be scope for a human-computer cooperation, where the role of the computer is to resolve the complexity of the artificial environment, and where the operator is able to implement his own objectives and plans, as long as they are within the envelope of plant design intentions. Such a cooperation would require a combined use of the two interpretations of the task structures as described by Lind (1993) and Larsen (1993). The system would in this way take advantage of both the operator's expertise, that is his own strategies, and the knowledge and expertise of the plant designer.

REFERENCES

Hoc, J.M., (1988). *Cognitive Psychology of Planning*. London: Academic Press.

Hollnagel, E., (1993). *Human reliability analysis: Context and control*. London: Academic Press, .

Larsen, M. N. (1993) *Modelling start-up tasks using functional models* (Tech. Rep. No. 4937-92-08-ED ISP DK). Lyngby, Denmark: Technical University of Denmark..

Lind, M., (1990). *Representing goals and functions of complex systems* (Tech. Rep. No 90-D- 381). Lyngby, Denmark: Technical University of Denmark.

Lind, M., (1991, September). *On the modelling of diagnostic tasks*. Paper presented at the *Third Cognitive Science Approaches to Process Control conference*, Cardiff, UK.

Lind, M. (1993). *Interactive planning for integrated supervision and control in complex plant* (Tech. Rep. No. 4937-92-08-ED ISP DK). Ispra, Italy: CEC Joint Research Centre.

Polyani, M., (1962). *Personal knowledge*. London: Routledge & Kegan Paul.

Schank, R. & Abelson, R. (1977). *Scripts, plans, goals, and understanding*. Hillsdale, NJ: Lawrence Earlbaum Associates.

Simon, H.A. (1981). *The sciences of the artificial*. Cambridge, MA: MIT press.

Suchman, L.A. (1987). *Plans and situated actions*. Cambridge, UK: Cambridge University Press.

West, K.L. (1972, December). *Minimum recommended protection, interlocking and control for fossil fuel unit-connected steam station*. Paper presented at the *IEEE Winter Power Group Meeting*, New York.

Wilensky, R. (1983). *Planning and understanding*. London: Addison Wesley.

17

Expertise and Technology: "I Have a Feeling We Are Not in Kansas Anymore"

Erik HOLLNAGEL
Human Reliability Associates
Jean-Michel HOC
CNRS - University of Valenciennes
Pietro Carlo CACCIABUE
CEC Joint Research Centre, Ispra, Italy

It is a difficult and even daunting task to summarize this book. In it are fifteen chapters — sixteen if you include the introduction — which cover a wide range of topics and viewpoints. Each chapter has presented a perspective on expertise and technology, and although many of the chapters support and complement each other, none of them are redundant. We have tried to put them together in three main groups, but the fact remains that the book in a sense presents fifteen dimensions of expertise and technology. As if this was not enough, there is no guarantee that there may not be additional ones. We are thus faced with a set of problems that is more complex than we really would like it to be. As the fifteen contributions have made clear, we are not near the stage where a unified view on expertise and technology can be proposed. This is perhaps characteristic of the field itself: Expertise is not a one-dimensional phenomenon and cannot be given a single — or simple — description.

THE MULTIPLICITY OF EXPERTISE

That expertise is not a one-dimensional phenomenon means that it does not succumb to a binary classification, i.e., a person is not either an expert or a non-expert. Expertise comes in degrees and there is no absolute threshold beyond which a person becomes an expert; neither will a person remain an expert forever. The degree of expertise that a person has may vary with the state of mind and with the context. Expertise can be defined as the knowledge that a person can bring to bear on a situation. This knowledge is a function of two things, firstly the knowledge that the person in principle has, and secondly the subsets of knowledge that the person can actually make use of in the specific situation, i.e., the knowledge that the person can access, remember, or retrieve. We can also call these the *potential* competence and the *actual* competence.

This distinction is not trivial. The working conditions will often be counterproductive to the use of the potential competence, for instance if time is limited. Even though an operator may be capable of performing well, i.e., be a potential expert, time pressure may severely impair performance. This emphasizes the point that there are two kinds of expertise or knowledge. A person can be an expert in knowing *what* to do, i.e., having substantial knowledge about how a system works, what the fundamentals of a process are, how the system is composed, how it depends on other processes, etc. A person can also be an expert in knowing how to do things, for instance how to manage a difficult situation, how to perform a diagnosis when the symptoms are unrecognizable, etc. The expertise that a person can use in a situation is determined by the extent of "knowing what" and of "knowing how." In particular, technology may influence how easy it is to comprehend a situation and how easy it is to apply the appropriate knowledge. In many cases technology exerts a negative influence which makes it more difficult for the operator to understand the situation. The essence of expertise is, however, the ability to see what is relevant and then to be able to get that knowledge — from memory or from other sources.

The point is sometimes made that cognition is situated, which means that it depends on the context. This point may be worth making when the background is knowledge engineering and knowledge representation, as these techniques have developed in the field of expert systems. Here the aim has been the isolation of knowledge and expertise, and the efforts have been directed at finding that which can be described separately from being in the situation. Yet if the basis has been the study of the expertise that people have in their daily work, i.e., the study of praxis seen as the unification of theory and practice, then it is trivial to say that cognition and expertise depends on the context. In fact, it will be preposterous to say that expertise can be context independent. Expertise is the bright elusive butterfly of knowing how to cope with the vagaries of the real world. If expertise could be formalized then, almost by definition, we would no longer need operators. We could implement the expertise in an information processing artifact and be done with that. Expertise, however, resides in people, not in machines.

MENTAL MODELS AND TRAINING

Expertise is frequently discussed in terms of the operator's mental model of the domain or of the system. By this we mean that people who are familiar with a task or an application have learned something that is essential to make performance more efficient. This knowledge, and in particular the knowledge about the internal functioning of the system, is commonly referred to as the mental model. In particular, it is a common finding that a higher degree of expertise will enable the operator to remain in control in a larger number of situations and to perform with the use of less effort. We say that performance is efficient because the expert has an adequate mental model of the domain. (Note, however, that this almost amounts to a definition of what a mental model is. If the idea of a mental model is not defined independently of the observable performance characteristics, then there is a potential circularity in the arguments.) According to this logic it should therefore be possible to improve performance by making sure that the operator has the proper mental model from the beginning, i.e., that the operator is provided with the mental model rather than having to build it up in a slowly and elaborate way.

There are several ways in which we can try to ensure that the operator has the appropriate knowledge to perform efficiently in a task. The three main avenues are system design, training, and selection. Unless operators already have the requisite expertise, by having been carefully selected from a larger population, then the mental model is usually provided through training and instruction. Training confronts the operator with the knowledge needed to control a system. But what should the basis for training and instruction be? In other words, how can we know what the correct mental model is? Should training be based on design knowledge or on operational knowledge?

It is indeed tempting to base training on design knowledge. System designers may be able clearly to say that to use the system well — or to use it at all — the operator must know "how to do X, how to avoid Y, and how to diagnose Z." To employ the functionality of the system operators must have a certain competence, and that can be provided through training. A possible danger of this view is that training can be used as a compensation for design deficiencies, or as an easy way to adapt the system to changed operating conditions. Another concern is that the designer's mental model may fail to match reality.

This can happen in two different ways. The first is that designers may not fully take into account the actual working conditions that operators have to cope with. The working conditions are not only the exchange of information across the man-machine interface but also the way in which work is embedded in a larger context — consisting of the technical and administrative organization, of colleagues and authorities, of resources and demands to the production, of the local and global environment. The second is that designers may have too simple a view of human cognition — despite being humans themselves. The metaphor of the human as an information processing system has been extremely successful, to the extent that the disadvantages has begun to outweigh the advantages. It cannot be emphasized strongly enough that the human mind is not an information processing machine, and that it is misleading to describe human cognition as simple information processing. The human operator does not just react to events; the operator acts in a context which is shaped by the all the information available — from the mind, from the process, and from the environment.

Although design knowledge is a useful input for training, it cannot be the sole source. Training must also take into account operational experience and empirical data. It is useful to formalize the basis for training by means of e.g. a task analysis. If the system has not yet been built, the task analysis should consider the design basis, similar systems — e.g. older versions without the new design - or data from experimental situations that reproduce the essential features of the design. If the system exists, it is, of course, essential that the operational experience is fully considered.

The mental model can be shaped through training, but only partly so. A more pervasive influence comes from the actual system design. While training is an isolated and often irregular experience, the influence from system design is present at every moment. It is therefore of little use to teach operators to do one thing if reality forces them to do something else. (The reason for that can be design deficiencies, maintenance, modifications, etc.) It is through actual experience that expertise gradually is built - and the expertise may be how to make the system work despite the design! Feedback from operational experience is therefore essential to determine what the operators ought to know and what their mental models actually are. Yet such feedback will also show that there is no single mental model for a task. Although there obviously are significant commonalties — because the nominal working conditions are the same — there will also be vast differences between the mental models that individual operators develop. Mental models have at least as many dimensions as expertise — which is another way of saying that the notion of a single and common mental model as the basis for training is a deceptive simplification. Operators can therefore not be "designed" through training.

SYSTEM DESIGN, AUTOMATION, AND HUMAN ADAPTATION

The design of an interactive system is based on encapsulated expertise and the results express the consequences of that expertise. Scientists and developers try to formulate the necessary expertise in a concise way, to enable system designers to make the right decisions. An important issue is the distribution of roles and responsibilities between the operators and the technology. One version of that is the level of automation, i.e., how much of the system functionality should be automated, how much should be left for the operators to do, and under what conditions the transition from automation to manual operation should be made.

When a system provides support for the operators — as diagnostic support, as planning support, as procedural support, or as automation in general — it is important that the operators can understand *why* a specific recommendation is given and *how* the support or the automation functions. Despite steady technological advances operators are still required to intervene in the control of automated systems, for instance to cope with emergencies or to improve the productivity of discrete manufacturing processes. To do that appropriately should not require that the operators must monitor the functioning of the support system or the automation, since that would mean the addition of yet another task. The operator should not have to become an expert of the support system as well as of the process. The understanding can be achieved if the expertise, on which the support system is based, is apparent from the way in which the system works. Automation and support systems must not be impenetrable black boxes, since that would leave the operator guessing *when* an intervention would be appropriate and what should be done. Experimental investigations have shown that intervention is governed to a large extent by the operators' trust in the efficacy of the automated systems and their confidence in their own abilities as manual controllers. This can obviously be enhanced by making the system easier to understand.

One of the main concerns throughout this book has been adaptation, as a crucial aspect of dynamic environment supervision and control. It is a primary concern of system design to reduce variability in order to insure adequate product quality, system safety, and — not to forget — lower production costs. The design specifies how the system — the automation together with the humans — should operate and respond under given conditions. It follows that the functionality of the system will only be appropriate if the actual conditions match the expected conditions. In other words, the intentional structure of the system is only valid within the boundaries of a synthetic world where the unexpected does not happen. The real world, unfortunately, has a deplorable tendency to go beyond these artificial imposed boundaries; and if the conditions are unfavorable the result may be a major accident.

In order to improve these situations it is necessary to recognize the natural limitations of a deterministic design. The obvious solution is to make use of the flexibility of the operator, since that cannot be bound by design specifications. It is the expertise of the human operator that makes it possible to adapt the performance of the joint system, in real time, to unexpected events and disturbances. Every working day, across the whole spectrum of human enterprise, a large number of near-misses are prevented from turning into accidents only because human operators intervene. The system should therefore be designed so that human adaptation is enhanced. This will ensure that the joint system has the requisite variety to maintain control in an unpredictable environment.

Several chapters of this book has focused on a major aim of human-machine cooperation: the operator's supervision of the joint system. Cooperation should, however, be understood as a symmetric concept — technology and automation should help the humans to perform their tasks and humans should be able to improve and facilitate the performance of the technological parts of the system. Although the cooperation nominally is between humans and technology, it can also be seen as a cooperation between humans — except that one of the participants is represented by the implemented design. The machine's capabilities for adaptation have been explicitly provided by designers. It is thus a kind of vicarious cooperation, which makes it all the more important that designers fully understands the situations they help create.

ERRONEOUS ACTIONS

Understanding the system is important in another sense because it may reduce the occurrence of erroneous actions. Although erroneous actions are inevitable, they are now usually seen as the result of a mismatch or a discrepancy between the actual and assumed modes of system functioning rather than as a result of inherent weaknesses of human cognition. Increased expertise will consequently lead to a change in the occurrence of erroneous actions because the discrepancies will be different — and hopefully fewer. Yet even operators with a high degree of expertise will every now and then do things that lead to an undesired result, either because the situation is unfamiliar or because they rely too much on their routine and experience. It is, in practice as well as in principle, impossible completely to eliminate erroneous actions. Fortunately, erroneous actions are important sources of information about the nature of the operators' expertise, and in particular about how well their mental models comply with the stipulated requirements to competence. As such the study of erroneous actions is vital for both system design, training, and learning.

Every adaptive system needs to fail now and then in order to be able to adapt. Without failures — in a wide sense of the word — there will never be any difference between expected and actual outcomes, hence no opportunity to improve performance. Erroneous actions are therefore essential for the operator to learn about the world and the actions. (Note, by the way, that an action is classified as erroneous only in hindsight.) Put differently, if all actions lead to success, i.e., if there never are any unwanted consequences, then there is no reason to change the actions, hence no need to learn. But if actions sometimes do not lead to the desired consequences, i.e., if there are failures, then it is necessary for the operator to determine why the failure occurred and adapt or change the behavior accordingly. This means changing the basis for the behavior, e.g. the knowledge, the assumptions (models), the ways of reasoning and deciding, etc. It is therefore important that the system provides the operator with adequate feedback. Dangerous consequences of erroneous actions should naturally be prevented, but without removing the feedback necessary for adaptation. This was emphasized by Reason (1988, p. 7) who noted that "system designers have unwittingly created a work situation in which many of the normally adaptive characteristics of human cognition are transformed into dangerous liabilities."

Human performance is complex. Simon (1969, p. 25) offered the hypothesis that the apparent complexity of human behavior was a reflection of the complexity of the environment, rather than of the complexity of human cognition (or of human information processing). In other words, we are forced to complex behavior because we do not understand the complexity of the systems we have to deal with. There are several problems with this hypothesis. Firstly, the complexity of the environment is relative to the degree of expertise, i.e., the complexity is subjective rather than objective. One could rightly argue that a high degree of expertise amounts to a high level of complexity of cognition and of knowledge. Secondly, if the hypothesis was correct then we should be able to produce simple performance just by making the environment less complex. Since simple performance presumably is both more efficient and less riddled by erroneous actions, many of the problems we struggle with could be solved in a simple stroke. One may wonder why no one has done it yet.

One reason for that might be that the underlying premise is wrong. In other words, the complexity of human performance is not just a result of the complexity of the environment (which, after all, to a large extent is man-made). It is also a result of the complexity of human cognition. As several of the studies in this book have shown, human cognition is not a simple or single process that goes on during a given time interval. A diagnosis, for instance, may involve many separate activities that take place in parallel so that, in a sense, there is no single process of diagnosis. Even if we analytically go to a higher level of abstraction and refer to diagnosis as a concerted effort or function, or even if diagnosis could go on sequentially and unperturbed from start to end, then that diagnosis would itself be embedded in other activities and in other tasks. This goes to show two essential things about human expertise: (1) actions and performance are always continuous, i.e., they do not abruptly start and stop; and (2) actions and performance — and therefore also cognition — are always part of a context.

WHY MUST WE BE EXPERTS?

Why does technology require that we are experts? If the answer is that we must be experts to cope with the complexity that technology carries with it, then why are technological systems so complex?

The complexity of technological systems can be reduced by decomposition or by isolating specific aspects of the functionality. Yet even if individual systems, or parts of systems, can be made simple — thereby improving usability and reducing the need for expertise — the technology we use is coupled. Systems, sub-systems and components are interdependent, and when the parts of the system have to work together it becomes necessary at some stage and at some level to aggregate the decomposed system. This aggregation will inevitably require expertise, but if this expertise is concentrated on the design level the system becomes brittle.

High usability at one point in the system will therefore require high complexity in other parts. Complexity can only be reduced so long as the actual operating conditions comply with the design assumptions. When something goes wrong, the full complexity of the system strikes back — and pity the user who is not an expert. A good example of that is in the field of automation. A highly automated system, for instance a flight management system, can be simpler to use and easier to learn, but the operator is needed in whenever automation fails — in which situation the system no longer is so simple. In other words, although the operator's expertise is not required when everything works well and smoothly, it is definitely required when things begin to break down. The need for expertise is only curtailed as long as the system stays within the narrow limits of normal operation. This sharpens the distinction between normal and abnormal states, but also makes the transition from automatic to manual functions more abrupt, which in turn makes the situation more difficult for the operator. From the view of cognitive systems engineering it would be more sensible to have a gradual transition from normal to abnormal situations. Expertise can only develop through experience in a relatively stable environment, and if an operator is deprived of that experience it will be difficult to become an expert. Vicarious experience provided through training can only be a partial substitute for the real thing. Attempts of codifying the experience and encapsulating it in operator support systems (such as expert systems and the like) are bound to aggravate the situation, because these solutions remove the operator even further from the process. Embedding the operator in additional layers of technology and complexity increases the needs for expertise without giving it a natural opportunity to grow. Therefore, as long as complexity cannot be removed through radical changes to system design, operational expertise will be needed.

THE YELLOW BRICK ROAD

When we talk about expertise and technology, we are definitely not in Kansas anymore. We have been uprooted by a hurricane called "technology and complexity", and find ourselves in a strange country that perhaps is Oz, but perhaps is not. We should recognize the possibility that there may not be a benign wizard at the end of the yellow brick road who can bring us back to the state of innocence. There may not even be a yellow brick road. We therefore need considerable courage, brains, and heart to find our way through the complexity we have been thrown into. This book has hopefully provided a good description of where we stand, and also of what some of the possible routes are. *Bon Voyage!*

REFERENCES

Reason, J. (1988). Cognitive aids in process environments: prostheses or tools? In E. Hollnagel, G. Mancini, & D.D. Woods (Eds.), *Cognitive engineering in complex dynamic worlds* (pp. 7-14). London: Academic Press.

Simon, H. A. (1969). The sciences of the artificial. Cambridge, MA.: The MIT Press.

SUBJECT INDEX